Great Central Railway's London Extension

E.

Great Central Railway's London Extension

ROBERT ROBOTHAM

Ian Allan
PUBLISHING

First published 1999

ISBN 0 7110 2618 1

Published by Ian Allan Publishing

an imprint of Ian Allan Publishing Ltd, Terminal House, Station Approach, Shepperton, Surrey TW17 8AS.
Printed by Ian Allan Printing Ltd, Riverdene Business Park, Hersham, Surrey KT12 4RG.

Code: 9905/A3

Front cover:
'B1' No 61036 *Ralph Assheton* enters Nottingham Victoria with a York-Bournemouth service in June 1956. *A. G. Cramp/ Colour-Rail (BRE1036)*

Back cover, top:
'V2' No 60831 stops at Lutterworth with a down Nottingham service in July 1959. *G. H. Hunt/Colour-Rail (BRE1356)*

Back cover, bottom:
'9F' No 92091 near Loughborough Central with an up 'Runner' in March 1965. *N. S. Ingram/Colour-Rail (BRE1367)*

Contents

Half title page:
The '9Fs' soon dominated the 'Runners' and here is an excellent photograph of a typical train for Woodford heading towards Barnston Tunnel, situated between East Leake and Loughborough Central. Annesley '9F' No 92072 is seen at 14.42 on 20 June 1964. The 'Runners' would load up to 50 loaded wagons, with up to 60 empties on their return journey. *Tom Boustead*

Title page:
The 'A3s' followed the 'B17s' on main line passenger services before World War 2, but were transferred back to the GN line on its outbreak. They returned after the Armistice and a brief interlude when the new Thompson 'B1s' were introduced. The 'Master Cutler' was a regular 'A3' turn and No 60054 *Prince of Wales* makes an almost triumphant departure from Nottingham as it runs past Queen's Walk Sidings with the up train on 2 March 1949. *J. F. Henton*

The 'Bournemouth' is seen on its journey north racing through Charwelton, where demolition of the station and its associated buildings is taking place. Initially hauled by Type 3 Class 37s these were later replaced by Brush Type 4s and No D1769, with headcode 1N83 for the northern working of the train, is in charge. The train is formed of Eastern Region stock on this occasion which was on 2 October 1965. Charwelton's once busy ironstone sidings and branch have also been lifted as part of the general run down. *Mike Mensing*

Introduction

This book paints a portrait of the London Extension of the Great Central Railway that ran from Annesley North Junction in Nottinghamshire to London Marylebone. The Great Central was a most innovative railway that developed a strong business in its hinterland between Liverpool and the East Coast and was a major player in the development of ports and shipping as well as railways. Ever keen to expand, Sir Edward Watkin, a member of the board, persuaded them that a link through the industrial Midlands to London and a tunnel under the English Channel to link to the Continent was the way forward. There could also be strategic links with other railways on the journey south. The line would be built to be able to take Continental rolling stock and there would be no level crossings while the ruling gradient would be 1 in 176 and curves minimised as much as possible. And so this great pioneering link was built, but the Channel Tunnel was not and the line had to suffice with a terminus station in London at Marylebone, and develop strategic links with other railways.

Not surprisingly, other railways, notably the Midland and the London & North Western, were not pleased with the opening of this new, intruding line. To survive, the Great Central ran fast flyer trains to attempt to capture the business market and was a pioneer in the introduction of high quality cross-country services and long-distance leisure travel. Indeed, the GC was the first railway company to employ an advertising agency, Dean & Dawson, to promote its services. Long-distance, cross-country, goods services carrying perishables, general merchandise and fish were introduced, along with trains of coal and ore, and the fastest timetabled regular freight service in the country was run day in day out between Annesley and Woodford Halse. These trains were driven in a typical GC style, whether freight or passenger, fast start-to-stop timings meant vigorous accelerations and screeching 'GC' stops. The line was only double track, but operated to a very high standard — even in bad weather the railway ran fast services while its competitors' trains seemed to slow to a crawl.

But by the end of the 1950s and into the early 1960s the railways were being pressurised by the rapid expansion of road traffic, car ownership, motorway building and long-distance fast lorries. It did not help that the GC penetrated the then British Railways London Midland Region, as it was an ex-Eastern Region route 'competing' with their lines to St Pancras and Euston. It was always useful as a diversionary route, and especially so when the former LNWR West Coast main line was being electrified in the 1960s, but traffic was deliberately routed away by the LMR and passenger services reduced from restaurant Car

Below:
GC Atlantic, No 192, arrives at Marylebone with the 1.13pm express from Sheffield in 1924. The locomotive is carrying early LNER livery and the cab road on the right is covered by a series of classic enamel advertisements. So handsome were the Atlantics, they were nicknamed 'Jersey Lillies' after Lilly Langtree.
F. R. Hebron/Rail Archive Stephenson

expresses to a semi-fast service with badly timed or non-existent 'connections' not especially timed to meet the needs of any particular passenger. A similar attempt of 'closure by stealth' was tried with the Settle to Carlisle route some years later, but fortunately failed. Due to this rundown, closure became inevitable, interest in rail issues in 1966 not being as great as it is today. The line just slipped away as a through route on the night of 3 and 4 September 1966 — only the Marylebone to Aylesbury DMU service surviving, as well as a rump service that the Transport Minister insisted was retained, from Rugby to Nottingham. Even this latter service was withdrawn by 1969 as the disinterested LMR did nothing to encourage or develop traffic.

At least closure allowed one good thing. A preserved main line steam railway, the new Great Central is being developed at Loughborough and from the year 2000 will operate a section of double track with an eight-mile run from Loughborough to just south of Belgrave & Birstall station — now being rebuilt and called Leicester North. Even more exciting is the development and reopening of the route north of Loughborough — to the new Heritage Centre at Ruddington, near Nottingham. The Great Central Nottingham is currently purchasing the line from Loughborough to Rushcliffe Halt and will maintain it to the standards required for freight trains to access the gypsum sidings there. Track is already owned north of Rushcliffe to Ruddington with the associated link to the Heritage Centre — the old MOD depot. What an exciting prospect this will eventually be with 17 miles of main line steam!

This book covers every GC London Extension station and notable structure and examines the train services that ran on the line. I have attempted to compress 67 years of history into a relatively small space, including line track plans, sections from public and working timetables and illustrating the story with a selection of photographs. I have also included some reminiscences from Clive Boardman, a fireman who was based at Woodford Halse in the 1950s and whose experiences provide a first-hand account of what it was like to work trains on the line, and I am most grateful to him.

I hope that this book allows the reader a glimpse of the spirit and style of the line — talk to the railwaymen that ran it; as you will encounter no one else like them. Spare a thought too for those who were made redundant *en masse* when the line closed, and another for the folly of the closure decision which would not have been made today. The GC, had it survived just 10 more years, would have most probably lived on and now be carrying Class 92-hauled Channel Tunnel freight services to and from the North. Nottingham would have a station situated in the heart of the city connected to a suburban network. The movement of population out of towns and the development of commuting would see Brackley and Woodford doing great business as Parkway-type stations with fast trains to London. Cross-country services would have a far faster journey and pass through Nottingham direct. These would connect to InterCity services that would most probably run via the GW/GC joint line into Marylebone or Paddington stations.

Let us learn for the future and realise that the decision to close the Great Central's London Extension in 1966 was a huge mistake that, with hindsight, should never have happened. In the end it was a combination of railway politics, a line being transferred to a hostile region that had old scores to settle, and the short-sightedness of a government which did not see the route's potential as a Channel Tunnel link, realised only 20 years later.

Over the last few years interest has increased enormously in the GC London Extension. This interest can be developed through reading books on the line, by becoming a member of the Main Line Steam Trust, the supporting body of today's Great Central Railway based at Loughborough, and by visiting the railway. Also, the Great Central Northern Development Association, based at the Nottingham Heritage Centre at Ruddington is pushing the reopening of the line south to Loughborough to achieve the dream of a 17-mile preserved double-track main line.

Colin Walker's *Main Line Lament* is for me the most evocative book produced on the GC, with excellent subsequent volumes, *Great Central Twilight* and *Great Central Twilight Finale*. David Jackson and Owen Russell's *The Great Central in LNER Days* Volumes 1 and 2 are excellent and entertaining reading, as is George Dow's famous trilogy, *Great Central*. Another must for all GC enthusiasts is Mac Hawkins' *Great Central Then and Now*, albeit the 'now' photographs are just appalling in showing how some parts of the route have been completely obliterated. As always, many thanks are due to all the photographers who so generously make their work available, and in particular to Brian Stephenson, who has devoted considerable time to helping me in my quest for some very high quality photographs.

It is also worth mentioning that the track plans in this book are not to scale, but allow the reader to see the layout with the accompanying photographs.

Robert Robotham
Sherborne, 1999

Below:
The London Extension was always a heavy carrier of freight. Express fish trains ran regularly on the line from Hull and Grimsby to the South. 'K3' 2-6-0s made an impact on these trains as older GC types were phased out — not to the pleasure of many of the locomotive crews, but at least they were not Midland engines! 'K3' No 61800 rolls through the impressive station of Nottingham Victoria on 4 June 1949 with a 'Fish' from New Clee to Swindon. Note a 'real' GC engine — 'J11' No 64324 of Langwith Junction depot in the up bay platform. Woodford fireman, Clive Boardman, tells the story of working one of the fish services in Chapter 6. *T. G. Hepburn/Rail Archive Stephenson*

1. The London Extension from 1899 — 'Forward'

On 15 March 1899 passenger services began on a new line that ran from Manchester and South Yorkshire through the East Midlands to London. This line was the London Extension of the Great Central Railway, whose forebear had been the Manchester, Sheffield & Lincolnshire Railway, a railway that had struggled financially but had nevertheless become a powerful force in the area in which it ran and carried the confident motto 'Forward' on its new coat of arms.

This was mainly due to the relationships that it had with its larger neighbours — with whom it shared most of its traffic and against whom it competed on many of its key routes. The desire to open a line to London or at least gain access to the capital dated back to 1873 when the MS&LR worked with the Midland Railway to examine the building of lines to join their systems, which would have allowed running powers from Rushden, Northamptonshire, to London. The mastermind of expansion was one of the so-called railway barons of the latter part of the 19th century, Sir Edward Watkin, who was a member of the board of the MS&L as well as that of the Metropolitan and the South Eastern railways, and the Channel Tunnel Company. Watkin's grand plan was to link his four companies together and secure rail access to the Continent. This new main line would be able to take Continental rolling stock direct from Europe to Manchester, through London and the Midlands, and Parliamentary Powers were granted in 1889. In 1891, the Manchester, Sheffield & Lincolnshire Railway London Extension Bill was rejected. Not surprisingly, those railways with existing routes to London complained bitterly and lobbied hard to get the bill stopped. So an amended version was resubmitted (supported by many of the towns and cities that it would pass through) in 1892 for a line that would run from Annesley, in Nottinghamshire, to Quainton Road, in Buckinghamshire, which was already served by the Metropolitan Railway from Baker Street. Parliamentary procedures again caused a

Below:
The Great Central London Extension was famous for its fast freight services that ran between Annesley yard and Woodford Halse. They were known as 'Windcutters' and 'Runners' and were introduced as such by the LNER in 1947. They were supplemented by other fast express freights which ran from the North Eastern Region to the Western and the London area, as well as the local pick-up services. Nottingham had a large goods yard for general merchandise traffic generated from the city, situated at Queen's Walk, just to the north of Trent Bridge (which can be seen in the background). Annesley '9F' No 92043 races past the sidings at 2.30pm on 18 August 1958 with a down 'Runner' from Woodford to Annesley. *Tom Boustead*

delay, this time the Dissolution which delayed Royal Assent until 28 March 1893. In 1897 the MS&L renamed itself very grandly, the Great Central Railway, a title that had been used before by a scheme that failed when turned down by Parliament, and by the Lincolnshire, Derbyshire & East Coast Railway in their bill of 1891 — a company the MS&L later took over.

With the expected heavy Continental traffic that the line was planned to generate, the ruling gradient was kept to 1 in 176 and there were no level crossings. Most of the stations on the double-track main line were built with island platforms and in some cases, enough land was acquired for an expected quadrupling of the route as traffic grew. The Metropolitan route south of Quainton Road was not so suitable and had sharp curves at Aylesbury, Rickmansworth and Harrow, together with a suburban train service that in the main ran stopping services, as well as Pullmans to Verney Junction, and local goods services. This did not fit in with the Great Central's new flyers and express suburban trains and the relationship between the two companies deteriorated, not least because Watkin was no longer Chairman of the Metropolitan. Disputes raged over bad pathing causing delays to the expresses. The Metropolitan signalmen were instructed to give their own trains priority. An argument over the carriage of coal traffic also saw legal action being resorted to by the two companies. In the end, a separate double-track was built from Harrow to Canfield Place to try to minimise congestion, followed by a later agreement with the Great Western Railway. This led to the construction of joint lines that allowed a diversion of GC trains via Princes Risborough and Northolt as well as giving valuable links between the two systems. The Great Central had built the line itself from Canfield Place to Marylebone and optimistically planned a pair of two-track tunnels, which widened to three at Lord's Tunnel, two of which were a headshunt for the goods yard plus another single-track headshunt for the carriage sidings at Marylebone. In the event one tunnel was only ever used from Canfield Place to Marylebone — being sufficient for both express and suburban services. A bridge took the double track across the London & North Western's line to Euston in a short break between St John's Wood and Hampstead tunnel with a ruling gradient of 1 in 100.

There was much opposition as the line passed by Lord's Cricket Ground and the Artists' Colony, which would necessitate the demolition of many houses, for which the GC had to pay compensation to chimney sweeps for loss of business. The areas around Marylebone were also a 'red light' district which caused much embarrassment for the Company's agents as they went about their business. The Middlesex Cricket Club was calmed by the fact that the construction of the line would not affect the cricket season, it being specially carried out between 31 August 1896 and 8 May 1897. In fact the club was given a larger area of land than that lost once construction had finished, as a compensatory gesture.

It is a common misconception that the GC had the best route in terms of gradients on its way to London. The LNWR's line was kept to 1 in 330 in the first 200 miles with only Camden Bank out of London Euston being steeper, at 1 in 70. The Great Northern main line was no steeper than 1 in 178 between Doncaster and London, with the Midland being steeper — 1 in 120 around Sharnbrook, but mostly 1 in 176 to 1 in 200. GC line trains were faced with a sharp climb of 1 in 95 from Marylebone up to Kilburn, a 1 in 91 to 101 climb through Harrow and then six miles at 1 in 105 following a severe slack at Rickmansworth due to an extremely sharp curve through the station. By Amersham, a height of 620ft had been reached above that of Marylebone station, at Dutchlands, high in the Chiltern Hills. At the other end of the climb was Aylesbury and its speed restriction (later improved) before the switchback 1 in 176 of the extension proper began from Quainton Road, the line before Quainton being the Metropolitan's and not designed for the high speed flyers that the GC was to run. The next section of steep grades came after Nottingham in the coalfields with a 1 in 130/132 for 10 miles up to Kirkby South Junction, levelling off for a short section around Bulwell Common. Another climb, at 1 in 100, followed from Staveley to Springwood Tunnel up to Pilsley. This stretch of line was also plagued with speed restrictions due to mining subsidence which meant that trains had to make swift accelerations with sharp braking to keep time. By Annesley, trains had climbed 1,885ft from leaving Marylebone, and by Sheffield this was 2,100ft.

At the end of construction the line exceeded the £8 million budget. The route had been laid out in fine style with high embankments and deep cuttings to keep to the ruling gradient. All the structures were built to a very high standard with top quality engineers' blue brick, for here was a line that was going to last for a very long time and be an important link between Britain and Europe. The line strode across the River Great Ouse at Brackley on a magnificent viaduct and passed through the 3,000yd Catesby Tunnel before it crossed the LNWR at Rugby on a viaduct and lattice girder bridge, which allowed GC trains to pass through at 70mph plus, while the LNWR's had to slow to a crawl to thread through many points and curves. To quote John Betjeman's poem *Great Central Railway Sheffield Victoria to Banbury*: 'Above the fields of Leicestershire on arches we were borne'; indeed that city was approached by viaducts and girder bridge structures that were magnificent in their construction as well as their style.

Nottingham was approached by a superb bridge over the River Trent followed by another blue brick viaduct and girder bridge which took the line over the rival Midland Railway into Nottingham Victoria station. Unlike the Midland station, Victoria was in the centre of the city. The line north of Nottingham had another blue brick viaduct at

Right:
Excursion traffic was common on the Great Central, usually as services from the Midlands and South Yorkshire to the coast and London. However, a significant number of enthusiast's specials also used the line and one such train is seen here at the site of Woodford South Junction where the direct spur off the GC, disused from September 1899, branched off to the west to join the Stratford & Midland Junction route. The RCTS 'Grafton' railtour had worked in from Towcester and had crossed over the S&MJ bridge, seen behind the train, before reversing down from Byfield and Woodford West Junction to Woodford station. 'Black 5' No 45091 is in charge as the train makes off for Calvert on 9 August 1959. *Mike Mensing*

Bulwell and connected with many cross-country routes, mainly in conjunction with the Great Northern Railway. How marvellous those departures were from Nottingham Victoria, usually with just one locomotive on the front (unlike the Midland's two even in BR days) of a Great Central line express, probably an 'A3' Pacific, in apple green or even BR Blue livery with a train of varnished teak coaches in tow, storming out of the city over the Midland's station causing everyone to look up and marvel. How annoying it must have been for the competing Midland Region lines at Nottingham and Rugby to see this and the subsequent traffic that the Great Central line attracted by its fast departures with rousing starts, smart point-to-point timings, 'GC' stops that involved putting on the brake at the last moment, engine changes that took 3min, a passenger service intertwined with a very intensive freight service, and all on a double track.

Four passengers travelled on the first train from Marylebone which left at 5.15am on 15 March 1899. Fourteen travelled on the 9.15am and 34 on the 1.15pm. Fifteen first class passengers were recorded on the 5.15pm. This may not have been too bad a start, but despite fast timings the extension did not initially produce a large amount of passenger traffic. Despite a steeply graded route, the GC express timings were extremely impressive, albeit with short trains. Trains were all-corridor with buffet facilities at the least. Marylebone to Sheffield by the GC took 170min for 167 miles — faster than the Midland and the GN — and served major cities such as Nottingham and Leicester en route. (More about the GC passenger services can be found in the following chapters.) The GC could certainly claim to have assembled one of the most innovative management teams in railway history. In 1899, the Chairman was Alexander Henderson, and in 1902 Sam Fay was appointed General Manager. He gradually set about building up traffic as he had done previously on the Midland & South West Junction Railway. John Robinson had taken over from Harry Pollitt as Chief Mechanical Engineer and A. F. Bound was the innovative Signalling Engineer. Joseph Rostern was Superintendent of the Line, with W. G. P. Maclure as Locomotive Running Superintendent.

The expresses that had previously run as Marylebone to Manchester services were diversified to serve Bradford, Halifax and Huddersfield. Co-operation with other systems, notably the Great Western, allowed the rapid expansion of cross-country services, including Stratford-upon-Avon. The famous 'Sheffield Special' to Marylebone was also introduced. The London Extension was fed by freight traffic from the MS&L hinterland that also saw rapid expansion and development, such as the construction of the new docks at Immingham, where Sam Fay was knighted in 1912. It was intended that this would rival the North Eastern and the Hull & Barnsley railways at Hull, thus giving the Great Central a more direct hold on traffic to and from the Continent and Scandinavia. Marshalling yards were constructed at Wath to cope with a rapid increase in coal traffic, and the GC/GW joint line was constructed to allow a link between the two systems and give GC line trains a less congested run to the capital. The Grouping saw Alexander Henderson become Deputy Chairman of the London & North Eastern Railway. Even under the LNER development continued, with a fish dock being constructed at Grimsby, and the expansion of steel and iron sidings at Frodingham. Mottram yard was opened in 1935 and as early as 1924 it was proposed that the line from Sheffield to Manchester via Woodhead should be electrified. Economic downturn in the late 1920s and 1930 severely affected the GC line's traffic but the London Extension benefited from these developments in the North and benefited from the fact that the LNER used it as a penetrating route through to the West for both freight and passenger services. Large amounts of mineral traffic were sent to the Great Western via Woodford and Banbury, and the transfer freights that ran from Annesley yard in Nottinghamshire and Woodford were supplemented by a variety of fast fitted freight services that carried perishable traffic.

The new fish dock produced fish trains; indeed some fish traffic was carried on the back of some through passenger coaches. However, the LNER soon transferred most of the London fish traffic to the GN line, leaving only cross-country services via Woodford. It was with these fast through services that the GC excelled and in any case, although the

GC did run a general merchandise service with the local stations all having small goods yards with cattle pens, this was in decline due to the growth in road transport. The main line passenger service remained similar to that of the GC era, with an extra train from Marylebone to Sheffield at 4.55pm in 1929, which was extended to Manchester in 1930. Even this train, known locally as 'Promptitude' did not make sufficient impact on the Manchester market and it was cut back to Sheffield by 1938. However, on the South Yorkshire and East Midlands axis, the London Extension's services were always a thorn in the side of the Midland, not least because they were more reliable and north of Aylesbury ran very fast — speeds in the 90s were not uncommon.

Passenger services did see a growth in leisure travel (known in the 1920s and 1930s as excursion travel) as more people had time and money to spend going to watch sport and take holidays. The Great Central had stations close to Wembley Stadium, Old Trafford, Leeds Road Huddersfield and Hillsborough grounds. The LNER also used the GC route to relieve overcrowding on the GN main line south of York and cheap overnight services began to run from Marylebone to Newcastle. These were revived by British Railways after the war, running as far as Glasgow and Edinburgh under the name 'Starlight Specials'. Cruises were run from Immingham and special trains ran from Marylebone to the port, known as 'Orient Line Specials'. Motive power was still dominated by ex-GC types — indeed some of these found themselves working on the Great Northern main line. The GC's Locomotive Running Superintendent, W. G. P. Maclure, continued into LNER days and exerted considerable influence. GC types were always considered to be superior to the GN's by GC line enginemen but 'A1' class Pacifics, along with others, were tried on the London Extension. In 1931, two 'B17' class 4-6-0s, Nos 2816 *Fallodon* and 2834 *Hinchingbrooke* were allocated to Gorton depot and, unlike some of Doncaster's other productions, were more successful. They supplemented work by GN interlopers, notably the 'K3' 2-6-0s, and they initially worked to Banbury on a fish service before heading back with the Penzance to Aberdeen service. Having proved themselves, three 'B17s' were sent to Neasden depot at the end of 1934 and more followed, these being of the second batch and named after football clubs.

The on-going development of passenger services brought about a demand for even stronger motive power and 'A3' Pacifics were trialled on the GC before introduction in September 1938 when arrangements had been made to strengthen and extend the turntables at Marylebone and Leicester. The 'A3s' were joined by 'V2s' primarily on cross-country workings, but the outbreak of war saw a return to more traditional GC types. Passenger services were recast for the war years with additional cross-country services, but it was mainly in freight that the GC began to be developed as a prime route, allowing the LNER access into Midland territory and a route to the West that avoided London. Woodford Halse's yards were expanded early in the war with two new up and down yards. Cross-country freights were numerous but in 1947 the LNER introduced the Annesley to Woodford fast freight service, which led to a million wagons per year in the 1950s being exchanged between the two yards. These trains, known as 'Modified Class F' freights, were worked by Annesley crews on an out-and-home basis and, in some cases, were timetabled to get two return trips per day from the locomotive. Crews were given an incentive to achieve right-time departures — if a locomotive was late off depot its train was cancelled. The introduction of the BR Standard '9F' 2-10-0s to the service was a hallmark of the Great Central's postwar era. If nothing else, the GC was a major freight carrier, with the Annesley 'Runners', various cross-country freight services, such as the York to Bristol, and the fish trains. Steel trains were also introduced, running from the North East to South Wales carrying products for finishing. These trains left the GC at Woodford and took the S&MJ route to the West via Stratford-upon-Avon and Broom Junction to South Wales.

Overnight mails, the 'Newspaper' from Marylebone to Sheffield, diverted sleeping car trains to Manchester and Glasgow, 'Starlight Specials' and car sleepers were all GC main line turns and the postwar express passenger services were revived by the return of the 'A3s', replacing the 'B1s' which were finding it hard to keep to the timetable. The following'V2s' were considered even better than the 'A3s', their smaller driving wheels giving faster, more rousing starts — as were required on the GC — than was possible with the larger-wheeled Pacifics. Wartime speed restrictions were gradually removed, and although times were longer than on the competing Midland routes, GC expresses were more reliable and had a large 'following'. Two named trains, the 'Master Cutler' and the 'South Yorkshireman', were introduced and the expresses were added to by a local and semi-fast service with all-year-round cross-country connections that were added to in summer by overnight holiday expresses and more excursions. It was therefore surprising to those who watched, travelled and worked on the line to learn that there were no plans afoot to modernise the route. The 'Midland Pullman' sets were considered at one time but it was decided to transfer most of the express passenger traffic to other lines and concentrate on the Extension as a mover of cross-country freight. Due to the vast increase in competition that had come in the shape of the lorry, bus and private car, the railways were also evaluating their future. The 'Development of the Major Trunk Routes' — a strategy considered in the 1950s and early 1960s — did not suggest that the GC was to be a part of the future and even before Beeching, the GC was being considered a candidate for closure by the more radical railway managers, who were based, ironically, in the former Great Central Hotel at 222 Marylebone Road. Then, on 1 February 1958, a major change was announced that was to spell the end for the Great Central . The line was to be transferred to the management of the London Midland Region — the very managers and routes it had competed against in an almost 'cock-a-snook' fashion for the last 57 years. Despite the large volumes of traffic carried in 1958 the expresses were already under pressure. Loadings were not as high they might have been and in this era of the private car, when there were few traffic jams, local services were also in decline, as was the carriage of general merchandise freight to local goods yards. The LMR wasted no time.

From 2 January 1960, the expresses were withdrawn and replaced by three semi-fast services that did not connect particularly well with locals, especially north of Nottingham. The local trains were withdrawn from March 1963 and most of the local stations were closed. By 1963 only 5,000 passengers a week were using the trains between Aylesbury and Rugby, with 10,000 per week between Nottingham and Rugby. Only Marylebone, Aylesbury, Leicester and Nottingham took more than £25,000 per week. However, overnight services were very active with traffic diverted from the West Coast main line which was then being electrified, and mail and newspaper services, which were far more akin to the line's former LNER and Eastern Region days. In addition, the freight services from Annesley to Woodford all still ran up until 1965. However, rationalisation and service withdrawal were taking place at an alarming rate that would not be tolerated today and it was obvious that a deliberate rundown with closure in mind was happening. The exceptions were the London suburban services to Aylesbury, where the Met service was extended out to Amersham, but other cross-country locals running through Nottingham from Grantham to Derby were centralised on to Midland lines or withdrawn totally, and all daytime cross-country services —bar the famous Bournemouth to York — were withdrawn from 1964/5. Proposals were even made to extend the Metropolitan Line to Aylesbury, close Marylebone station and run the service to Baker Street. Joint line trains would run via High Wycombe going to Paddington. Only the semi-fasts remained and from 1963 some carried four coaches only and one diagram was for a non-corridor Marylebone DMU set.

The Midland's replacement motive power for the 'A3s' and 'V2s' were run-down 'Black 5s' and worn-out but famous 'Royal Scots' and 'Britannias', the first batch of the latter being replaced by others with high capacity tenders to cope with the long out-and-back turns required once all the line's motive power depots had been closed. The infrastructure was also run down — especially following the withdrawal of the freight service — and intermediate signalboxes were closed leaving long block sections. A few brief words can hardly describe all this — I trust the pages that follow will illustrate this to the reader in greater detail, but the contrast between the optimism of the opening of the London Extension on 15 March 1899 and the note of resignation on the weekend that the last through trains ran — on 3 and 4 September 1966 — cannot have been greater. After only 67 years, how many of those that stood on the platform at Marylebone for the opening ceremony would have thought such an end would come so soon?

2. The Route in Detail

Annesley North Junction to Nottingham Victoria

Annesley

The London Extension of the Great Central commenced at Annesley North Junction, just to the south of Annesley Tunnel and the entrance to Annesley yard and locomotive depot.

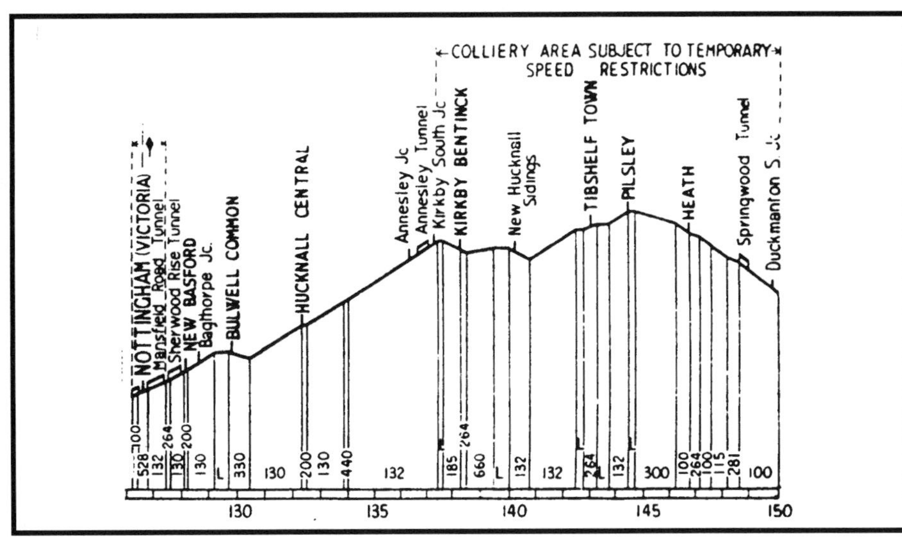

Below and Overleaf:
Annesley 'DIDO' Working timetable — 26 September 1949

RAILWAY WORKMEN'S TRAINS (Worked by Push and Pull Unit)

BULWELL COMMON TO NEWSTEAD AND ANNESLEY

DOWN **WEEKDAYS**

No.	2000	2000	2002	2002		2006	2006	2008	2008		2010	2010	2014	2016
	MX am	MO am	MX am	MO am		MX am	MO am	MO am	MX am		MX am	MO am	am	am
Bulwell Common	12 30	12 32	1 39	1 40	..	2 25	2 35	3 40	3 40	..	4 33	4 40	5 30	6 40
Hucknall Central		12 38		1 46			2 41	3 46				4 46	5 36	6 46
Hucknall Town	12 36	..	1 45	..	..	2 31	..	..	3 46	..	4 39	..	..	..
Newstead	12 47		1 56			2 42			3 57		4 50			
Annesley South Jct. Halt		12 45		1 53	..		2 48	3 53		..		4 53	5 43	..
Hollinwell and Annesley		12 47		1 55			2 50	3 55				4 55	5 45	
Annesley Sidings	..		..		..	..			..	..	..			6 55

No.		2020	2022	2026	2028		2032	2034	2036	2038		2042	2042	2046	2048
		J am	am	am	am		am	PM	PM	PM		SX PM	SO PM	PM	J PM
Bulwell Common	..	7 28	8 45	9 40	10 38	..	11 45	12 35	1 35	2 45	..	3 40	3 48	5 5	5 38
Hucknall Central									1 41					5 12	
Hucknall Town	..	7 34	8 51	9 46	10 44	..	11 51	12 41	..	2 51	..	3 46	3 54	..	5 44
Newstead		7 45	9 2	9 57	10 55		12 2	12 52		3 2		3 57	4 5		5 55
Annesley South Jct. Halt	..					..			1 48		..			..	
Hollinwell and Annesley									1 50						
Annesley Sidings	..	..	..	..	..	..	..	..		..	..	..	..	5 21	..

J.—Steam train.

DOWN **WEEKDAYS**

No.	2050		2052	2056		2060	2062	2066	2066						
	J PM		J SO PM	PM		PM	PM	SO PM	SX PM						
Bulwell Common	7† 0	..	..	7 47	..	9 33	10 35	11 28	11 30	..	..	..	..	..	..
Hucknall Central						9 39		11 34							
Hucknall Town	..	..	..	7 53	..	..	10 41	..	11 36	..	..	..	..	..	..
Newstead	7†12		7†20	8 4			10 52		11 47						
Annesley South Jct. Halt		..	..		..	9 46		11 41		..	..	..	..	..	..
Hollinwell and Annesley						9 48		11 43							
Annesley Sidings	..	..	7†25	..	..		..	..	..	..	..	..	..	..	..

DOWN **SUNDAYS**

No.			2000	2002	2006	2008		2010	2014	2020	2024		2066	
			am	am	am	am		am	am	am	am		PM	
Bulwell Common	..	..	12 42	1 40	2 35	3 40	..	4 37	5 30	7 30	*8†40*	..	11 46	..
Hucknall Central			12 48	1 46	2 41	3 46		4 43	5 36	7 36	..	..	11 52	
Hucknall Town	..	..	..	..	..	..	..	..	..	..	..	..	..	..
Newstead														
Annesley South Jct. Halt	..	..	12 55	1 53	2 48	3 53	..	4 50	5 43	7 43	..	..	11 59	..
Hollinwell and Annesley			12 57	1 55	2 50	3 55		4 52	5 45		*8†55*		12 1	
Annesley Sidings	..	..					..			7 45	..	..		..

J.—Steam train.

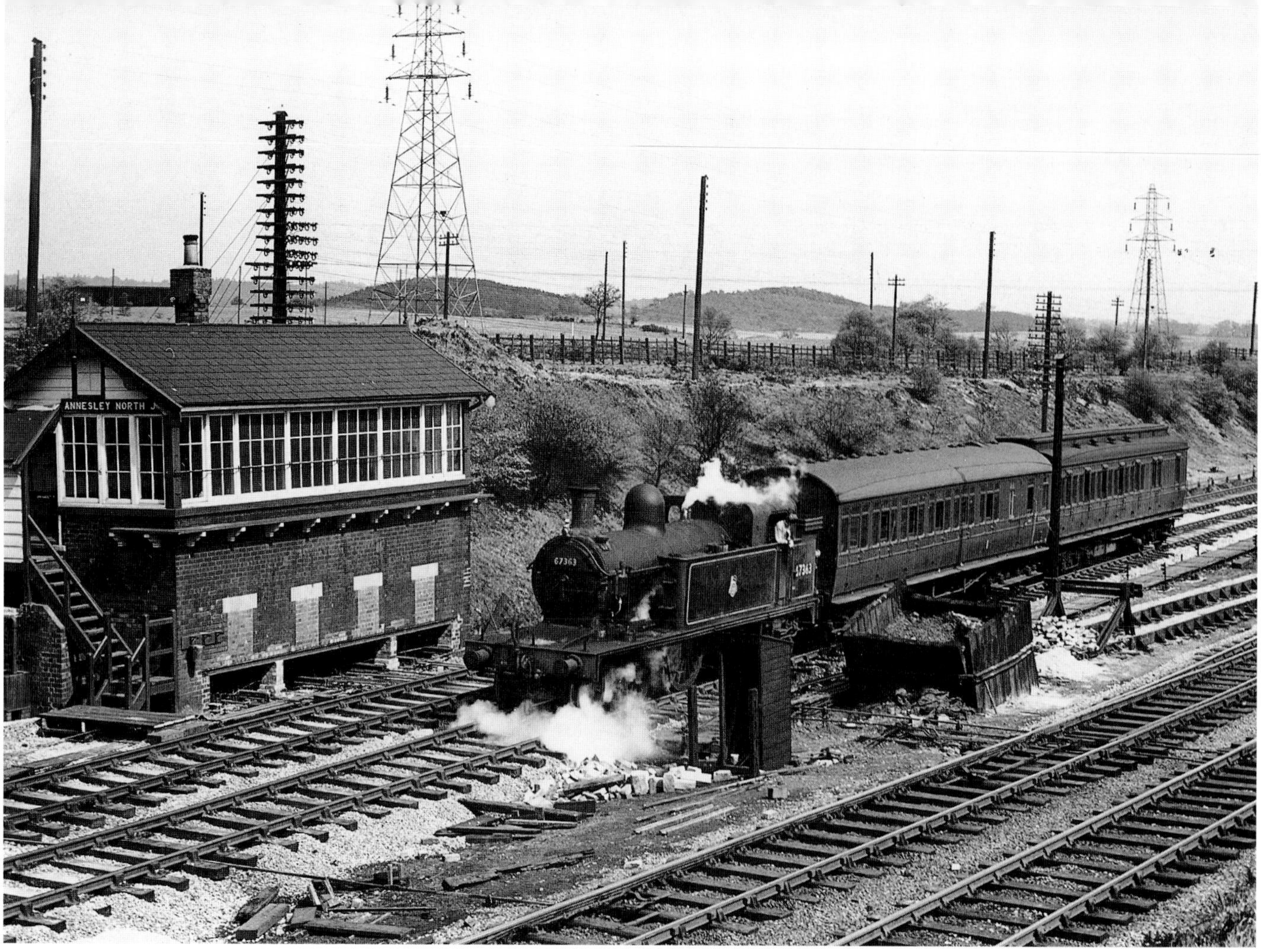

Above:
The famous Annesley 'DIDO' is seen at Annesley North Junction signalbox, hauled by GN Class C12 4-4-2 tank No 67363. This train was run for railway workers and picked up from stations in the surrounding area. It was known as the 'DIDO' because it ran day in, day out and usually consisted of the oldest coaches and locomotives available with some exceptions. The train is on the down GC main line, the tracks in the foreground being the Great Northern Leen Valley line to Leen Valley Junction on the GN Derby to Grantham line that passed to the north of Nottingham. The entrance into the large marshalling yards, a collection and distribution point for wagons travelling from and to the Nottinghamshire and South Yorkshire coalfields, can just be seen branching off the Leen Valley line. Other freight traffic passed through Annesley and in 1947 the LNER introduced the now famous Annesley to Woodford fast freight services known as 'Runners' or 'Windcutters', hauled initially by Robinson's 'O4' class 2-8-0 freight engines and later by BR Standard '9F' 2-10-0s. These trains survived until June 1965, by which time passenger services had been significantly run down. Their withdrawal, together with the withdrawal of through fitted freight workings, was to deprive the line of its major source of revenue. *J. Cupit/Ian Allan Library*

RAILWAY WORKMEN'S TRAINS (Worked by Push and Pull Unit)

ANNESLEY AND NEWSTEAD TO BULWELL

UP — **WEEKDAYS**

No.	2001	2001	2003	2003	2007	2007	2011	2011	2015	2015	2017	2017
	MO am	MX am	MX am	MO am	MX am	MO am	MO am	MX am	MO am	MX am	MO am	MX am
Annesley Sidings	..	..	..	..	..	..	..	..	..	..	..	..
Hollinwell and Annesley	12 7	..	..	1 5	..	2 5	3 0	..	4 8	..	5 0	..
Annesley South Jct. Halt	12 9	..	..	1 7	..	2 7	3 2	..	4 10	..	5 2	..
Newstead	..	12 7	1 3	..	1 58	..	..	3 10	..	4 10	..	5 10
Hucknall Town	..	12 15	1 11	..	2 6	..	..	3 18	..	4 18	..	5 18
Hucknall Central	12 15	..	..	1 13	..	2 13	3 8	..	4 16	..	5 8	..
Bulwell Common	12 20	12 21	1 17	1 18	2 12	2 18	3 13	3 24	4 21	4 24	5 13	5 26

No.	2021	2023	2023	2025	2029	2031	2033	2037	2039	2041	2045	2045
	am	J MO am	J MX am	am	am	am	am	PM	PM	PM	SX PM	SO PM
Annesley Sidings	..	6 50	..	..	..	..	..	..	..	..	..	..
Hollinwell and Annesley	6 10	..	..	..	..	..	..	..	..	2 16	..	..
Annesley South Jct. Halt	6 12	..	..	..	..	..	..	..	..	2 18	..	..
Newstead	..	..	6 50	8 17	9 15	10 10	11 5	12 10	1 7	..	3 18	3 20
Hucknall Town	..	..	6 58	8 25	9 23	10 18	11 13	12 18	1 15	..	3 26	3 28
Hucknall Central	6 18	6 58	..	..	..	..	..	..	..	2 24	..	..
Bulwell Common	6 23	7 3	7 4	8 32	9 29	10 24	11 19	12 24	1 21	2 29	3 32	3 35

J.—Steam train.

UP — **WEEKDAYS**

No.	2047	2049	2049	2051	2055	2059	2061	2063
	PM	J PM FSO	J PM FSX	J PM	PM	PM	PM	PM
Annesley Sidings	..	5 10	5 15	..	..	..	..	..
Hollinwell and Annesley	..	..	..	..	..	..	10 15	..
Annesley South Jct. Halt	..	..	..	..	..	..	10 17	..
Newstead	4 40	..	..	6 10	7 15	9 8	..	11 7
Hucknall Town	4 48	..	..	6 18	7 23	9 16	..	11 17
Hucknall Central	..	5 18	5 23	..	..	..	10 23	..
Bulwell Common	4 54	5 23	5 28	6 24	7 29	9 22	10 28	11 23

UP — **SUNDAYS**

No.	2001	2005	2007	2011	2015	2017	2021	2025	2063
	am	am	am	am	am	am	am	am	PM
Annesley Sidings	..	..	..	..	..	..	..	..	..
Hollinwell and Annesley	12 10	1 25	2 10	3 10	4 5	5 9	6 15	8 15	11 0
Annesley South Jct. Halt	12 12	1 27	2 12	3 12	4 7	5 11	6 17	8 17	11 2
Newstead	..	..	..	..	..	..	..	..	..
Hucknall Town	..	..	..	..	..	..	..	..	..
Hucknall Central	12 18	1 33	2 18	3 18	4 13	5 17	6 23	8 23	11 8
Bulwell Common	12 23	1 38	2 23	3 23	4 18	5 22	6 28	8 28	11 13

J.—Steam train.

ANNESLEY YARD

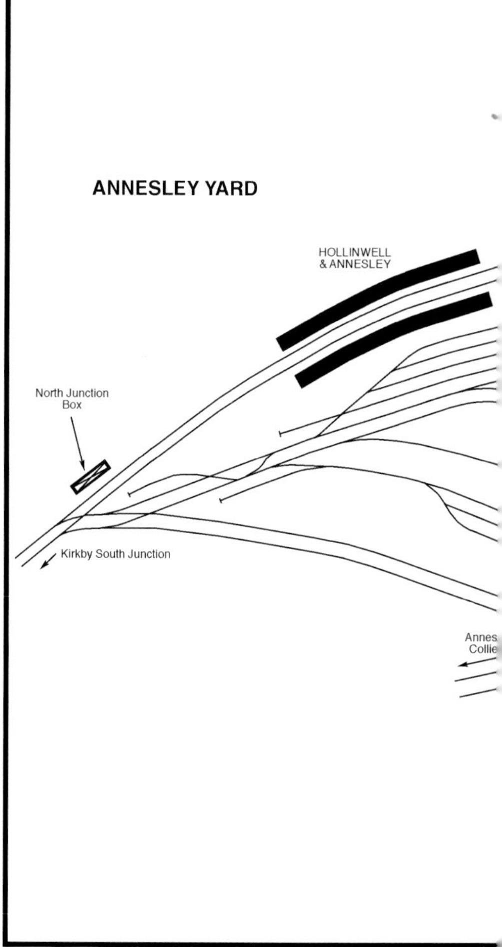

Above:
The station itself at Hollin Well & Annesley was a simple two-platform affair and was probably more use to railwaymen than to any potential passenger traffic. Two coal trains can be seen: Class O4/8 No 63683 enters the yard with a fully loaded train that would most likely have been formed into a southbound 'Runner' for Woodford while another 'O4/3', No 63835, hauls away a train of empties back to a colliery on 16 July 1955. The Midland route through the area can be seen in the background — which passed through Newstead Colliery situated between the GN/GC line and the Midland. There was another station on the GC at Annesley — Annesley South Halt — which was used by railwaymen to gain access to the locomotive depot. This can be seen next to Annesley South Junction on the track plan. (Annesley depot is covered in the motive power depot section — Chapter 7.) *H. B. Priestley*

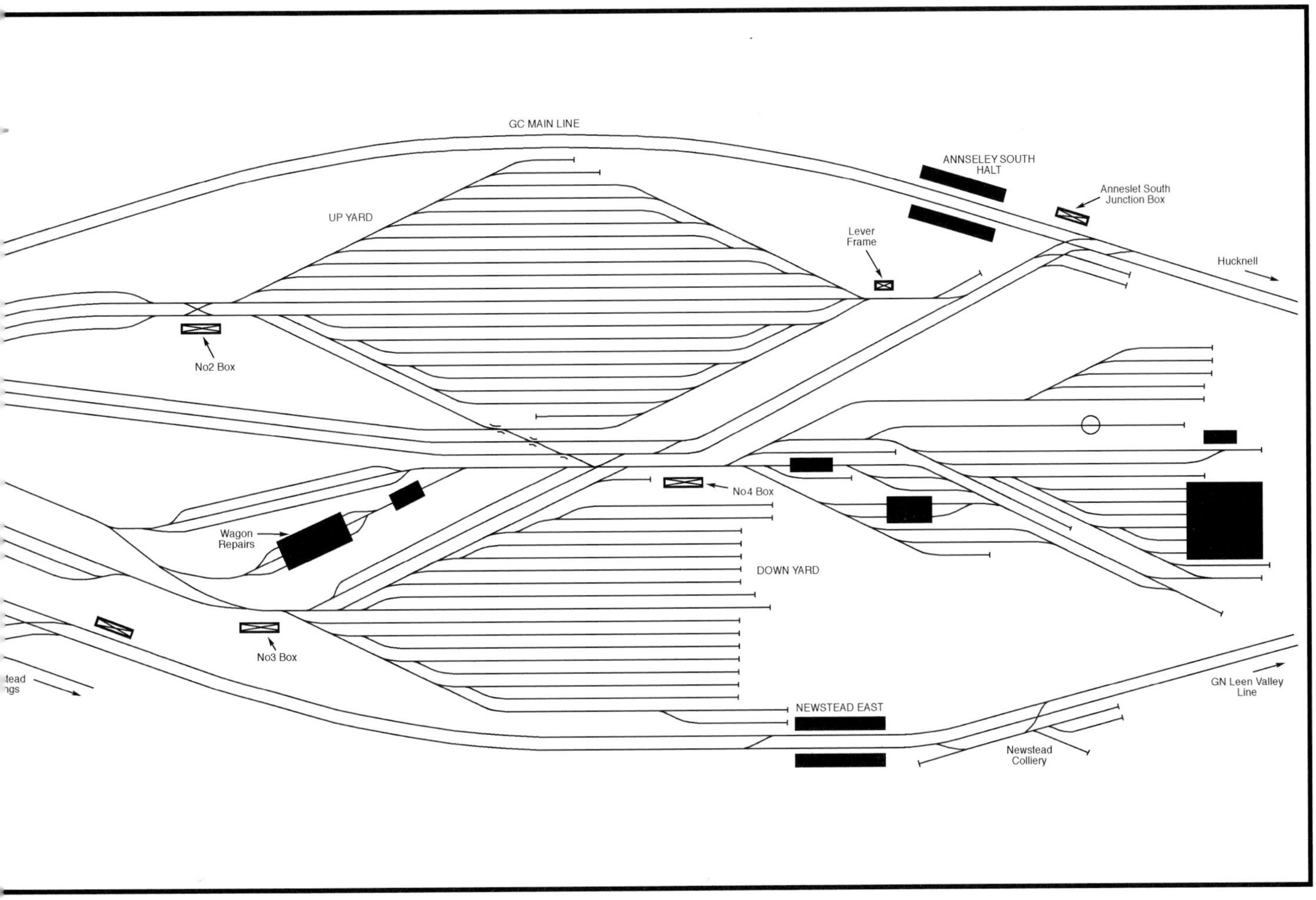

GC MAIN LINE
ANNSELEY SOUTH HALT
Anneslet South Junction Box
UP YARD
Lever Frame
Hucknell
No2 Box
No4 Box
Wagon Repairs
DOWN YARD
No3 Box
tead ngs
NEWSTEAD EAST
Newstead Colliery
GN Leen Valley Line

Left:
Looking back from the footbridge on the small station at Hollin Well and Annesley, the entrance to the yards can be seen as well as 'K2' 2-6-0, No 61754, of 38A Colwick shed, arriving on the 10.10am 'Ord' from Sheffield Victoria to Nottingham Victoria on 16 July 1955. The Leen Valley route runs off the extreme left, the yard entrance, which led to a large fan of sidings totalling over 17 miles of track, are the roads in the centre. In the background, the south portal of Annesley Tunnel can just be seen — all this today is just raised fields and the tunnel cutting has been filled in. *H. B. Priestley*

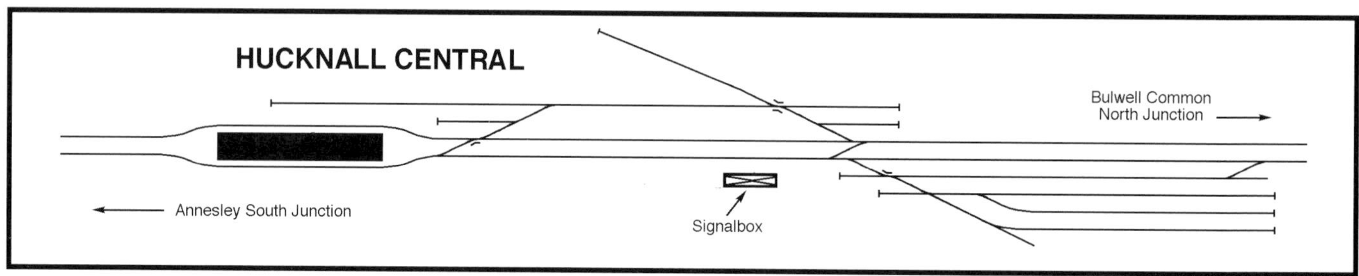

Hucknall Central

From Annesley South Junction the line descended through 1 in 132 to 1 in 130 and levelled off for Hucknall Central station.

Below:
One of the famous GC 'Director' class 4-4-0 locomotives, classified by the LNER as 'D11/1' No 62670 *Marne* of Sheffield Darnall calls at Hucknall Central with a mixed bag of stock on a local 'Ord', the 6.36pm Nottingham Victoria to Sheffield Victoria on 21 June 1957. Pigeons are being carried along the platform for loading and the small goods yard can be seen in the background. Hucknall Central was the first island platform station on the London Extension. It was closed on 4 March 1963 when all local services between Aylesbury and Rugby and north of Nottingham were withdrawn.
T. G. Hepburn/Rail Archive Stephenson

Bulwell Common

A two-mile descent from Hucknall Central to Bulwell at 1 in 130 switchbacked up to Bulwell Common after passing over the impressive 25-arch Bulwell Viaduct.

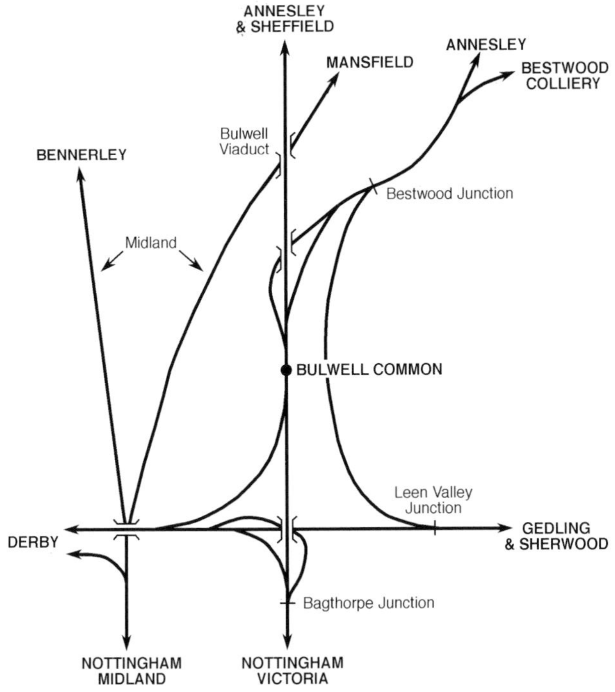

ANNESLEY & SHEFFIELD
MANSFIELD
ANNESLEY
BESTWOOD COLLIERY
Bulwell Viaduct
BENNERLEY
Bestwood Junction
Midland
BULWELL COMMON
Leen Valley Junction
DERBY
GEDLING & SHERWOOD
Bagthorpe Junction
NOTTINGHAM MIDLAND
NOTTINGHAM VICTORIA

Left:
General track plan of railways in the Bulwell area.

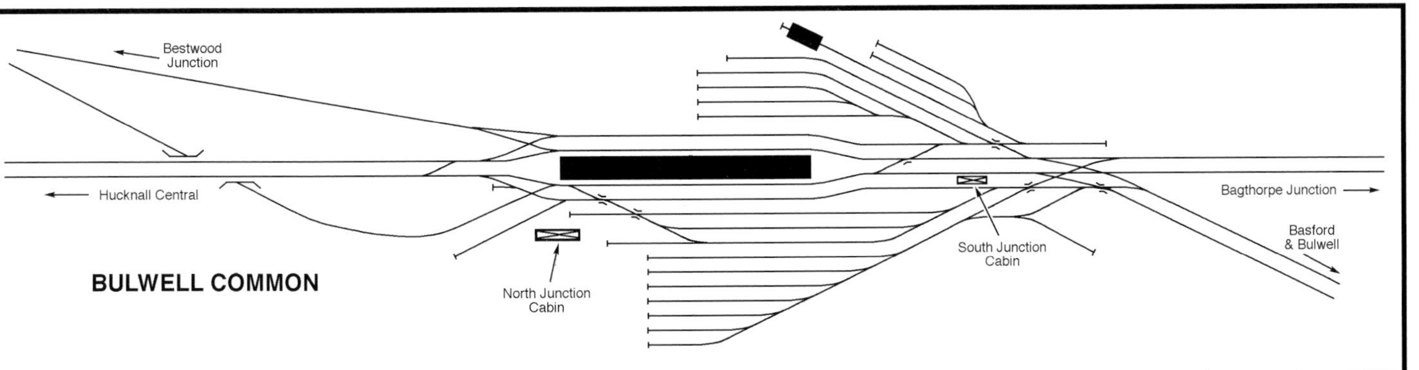

Bottom:
The southern connection to the GN's Leen Valley line can be seen forking off to the left, the line then becoming single and burrowing under the GC. A point on the GC up main was the link to the other track to the Leen Valley route as shown on the track plan. This route carried yet more coal traffic as well as local passenger services into Nottingham Victoria. ' 9F' No 92073 passes Bulwell North Junction and is about to run through the station with a fast freight for Woodford in September 1958. *T. G. Hepburn/Rail Archive Stephenson*

Left:
Further south, another Annesley to Woodford freight passes through Bulwell Common with 'Austerity' '2F' No 90040 of Woodford Halse in charge on 27 July 1963. Woodford's 'Austerities' did make trips to Annesley on 'Runners', but more usually it was an Annesley locomotive that would have worked a train out and back. Woodford's 'Austerities' ran south to the London area with long transfer freights. Behind the train, the South box can be seen with the line leading off to a fan of sidings which were used to store coaches and in the foreground on the left is the double-track line that connected to the GN Derby Friargate to Gedling and Grantham route.
T. G. Hepburn/Rail Archive Stephenson

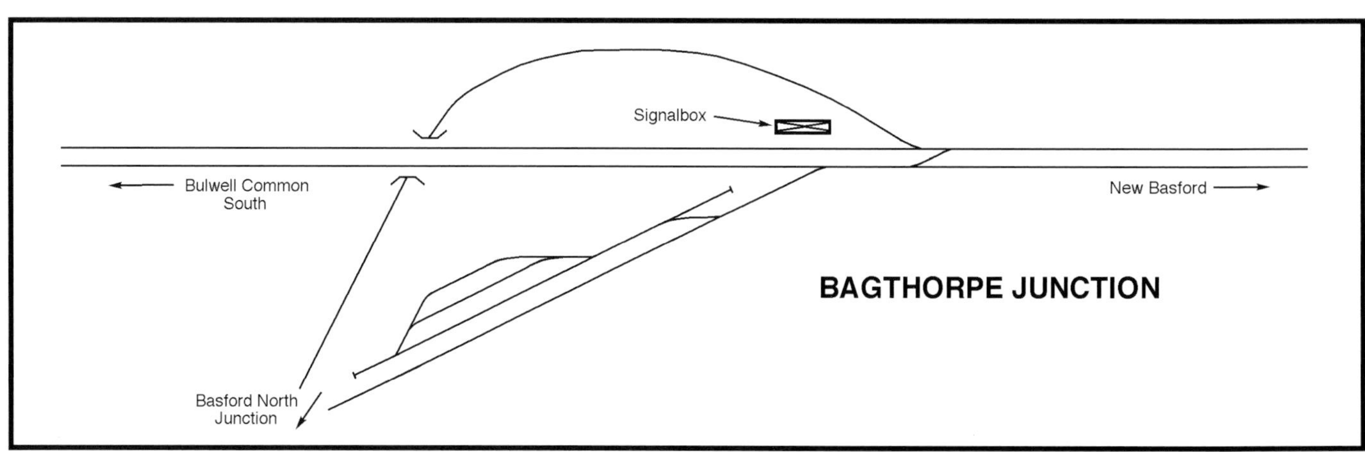

Bagthorpe Junction

The Derby to Gedling line was connected into the GC main line to allow access to Nottingham Victoria from where, via Weekday Cross Junction, the Grantham line could be reached again via Netherfield. At Bagthorpe Junction the up GN line joined the up GC main line by means of a fly-under, the down line running in from the west.

Left:
GC 'Director' class No 5504 *Jutland* of Neasden depot, in LNER black livery, heads the 2.20pm express from Manchester to Marylebone past Bagthorpe Junction on 9 August 1932. The 'Directors' and GC Atlantics, together with the larger Robinson 4-6-0s, were the standard motive power for these expresses — but the newer 'B17s' were about to enter service on the line and displace some of the traditional GC types from their express duties. *T. G. Hepburn/ Rail Archive Stephenson*

New Basford

Still on the descent to Nottingham came the next station, New Basford. It had a small goods yard and is today the site of a new housing estate.

Above:
'9F' No 92067 of Annesley on a 'Runner' for Woodford races through New Basford and approaches Sherwood Rise Tunnel at 1.9pm on 29 September 1962. The standard GC island platform of the station can be seen in the background together with the carriage sheds for stock used on passenger services from Nottingham Victoria. *Tom Boustead*

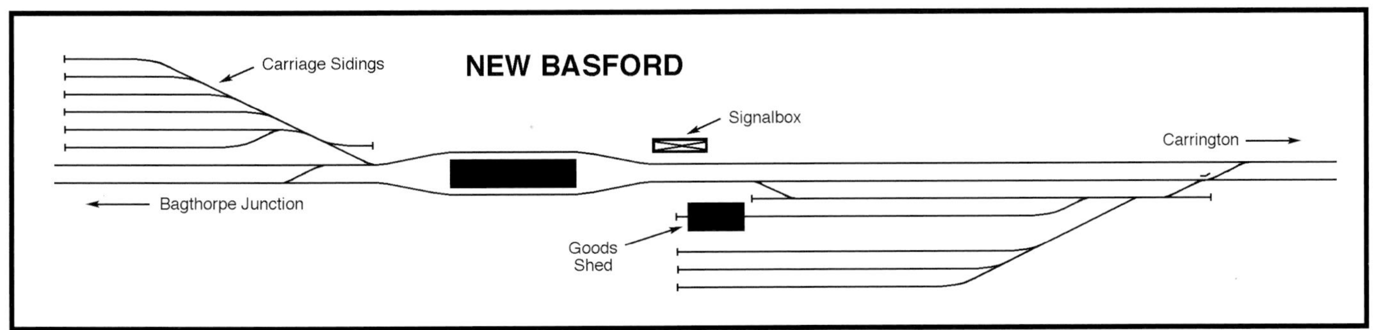

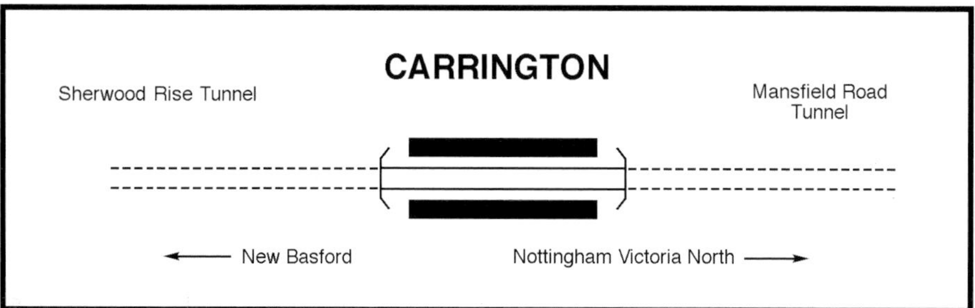

Above:
Carrington, seen in semi-demolished condition at 1.32pm on 19 September 1964 as 'Austerity' 2-8-0 No 90002 heads a train of iron ore empties past the platforms. The demolished footbridge abutments can also be seen. *Tom Boustead*

Carrington

At the southern end of the 662yd Sherwood Rise Tunnel was the small station of Carrington, built as two platforms due to the lack of space between the tunnel entrance and the next tunnel at Mansfield Road. There was also a signalbox which was burnt down on 8 December 1966. Carrington was an extra block post between New Basford and Nottingham Victoria North. It was closed as early as 1929 by the LNER, a victim of competition from local bus services.

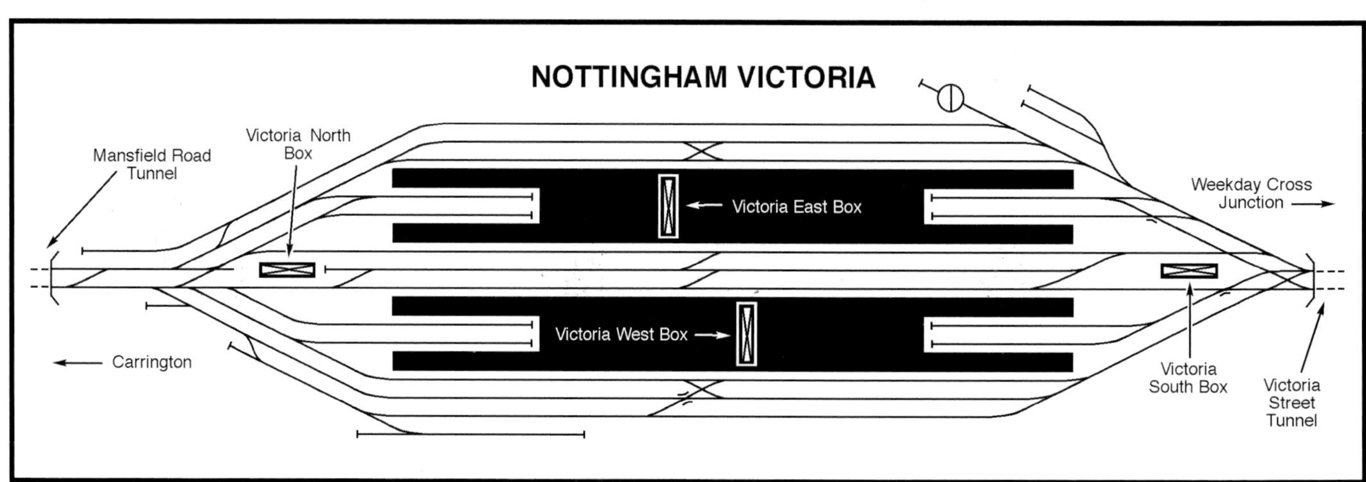

Above:
'Director' 'D10' No 5434 *The Earl of Kerry* arrives at Nottingham Victoria with the 2.20pm Manchester to Marylebone in 1931. It is passing the impressive North signalbox, which like South box, was not a standard GC or GN design. It was worked by one GC and two GN staff, while the South box had the same arrangement in reverse to keep both companies happy! The train has just pulled out of the southern end of Mansfield Road Tunnel and is about to draw alongside the up island platform. *T. G. Hepburn/ Rail Archive Stephenson*

Right:
At the southern end of the station the lines passed under Parliament Street and into Victoria Street Tunnel. The South box is clearly visible as is the approach to the down island platform. Class D11/1 4-4-0 No 5508 *Prince of Wales* departs from Nottingham Victoria with the 12.15pm Sunday service from Manchester Central (with connections from the Cheshire Lines) to London Marylebone on 7 May 1939. Despite the arrival of the new 'B17s', GC types were still very much in charge of express services, and preferred by the locomotive crews! Who would have guessed that in only another 30 years the demolition men would be moving in? *T. G. Hepburn/Rail Archive Stephenson*

Nottingham Victoria

Nottingham Victoria was opened on 24 May 1900, which was over a year after main line services from Marylebone to Manchester had started. These had called temporarily at Arkwright Street until the 'Vic' had opened. Many houses in the area had to be demolished during construction and over 500,000cu yd of sandstone excavated, leaving a large cavern into which the station, a joint venture between the GC and GN, was built. The people who were displaced by the construction of the railway were rehoused in a new development in the Meadows area of Nottingham near Arkwright Street and the building of the aptly named Watkin Street near to Woodborough Road. The original proposal to call the station Nottingham Central, as it was indeed so placed, was vetoed by the Great Northern and it was eventually agreed that the name Victoria should be used and the station would open on The Queen's birthday. As well as the GC express and local services, the GN ran four fast trains per day from here to London King's Cross and introduced services to Derby and Stafford. It also transferred all services that had terminated at London Road Low Level to Victoria.

Nottingham Victoria to Leicester Central

Left:
An overview of Nottingham Victoria from the south end of the station shows the cavernous nature — almost cathedral-like — of 'the Vic' that was its main feature. The famous clock tower, which still stands today, fronted the main entrance of the station onto Mansfield Road and can be seen in the top left of the photograph. Bay platforms for local services are visible to the left of the locomotive and a DMU from Grantham stands in one of the down bay platforms. The day that this photograph was taken, 3 September 1966, was the last occasion of through passenger workings and 'Black 5' No 44872 gets under way from the 'Vic' with the last 08.15 semi-fast train for Marylebone, strengthened from its usual four coaches to eight.
Tom Boustead

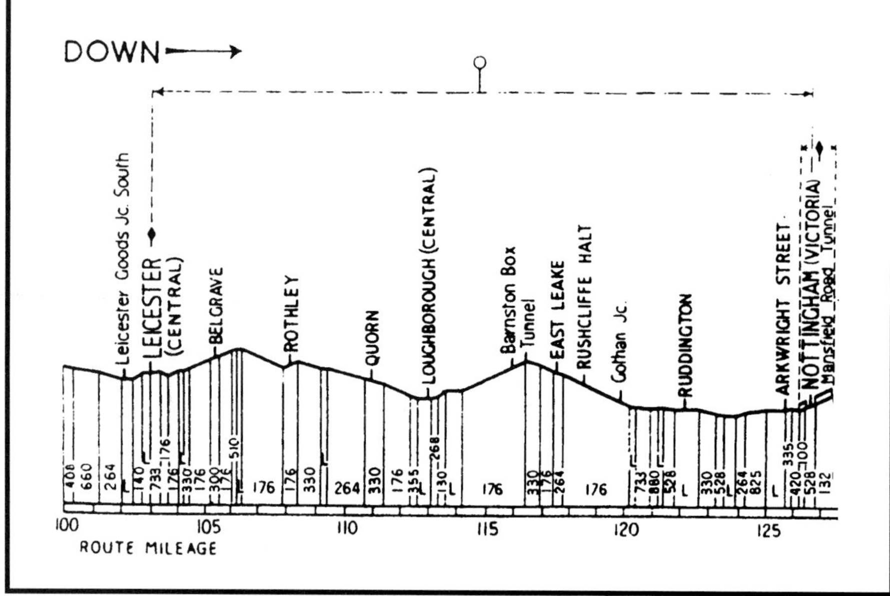

Weekday Cross Junction

On the other side of Victoria Street Tunnel was Weekday Cross Junction, where the GN line to Grantham forked off to the east and travelled through London Road High Level and on to Netherfield. GC main line trains ran out over a long blue brick viaduct that passed over the Midland station by means of a 170ft girder bridge. Weekday Cross signalbox was situated between the GN and GC lines on the viaduct.

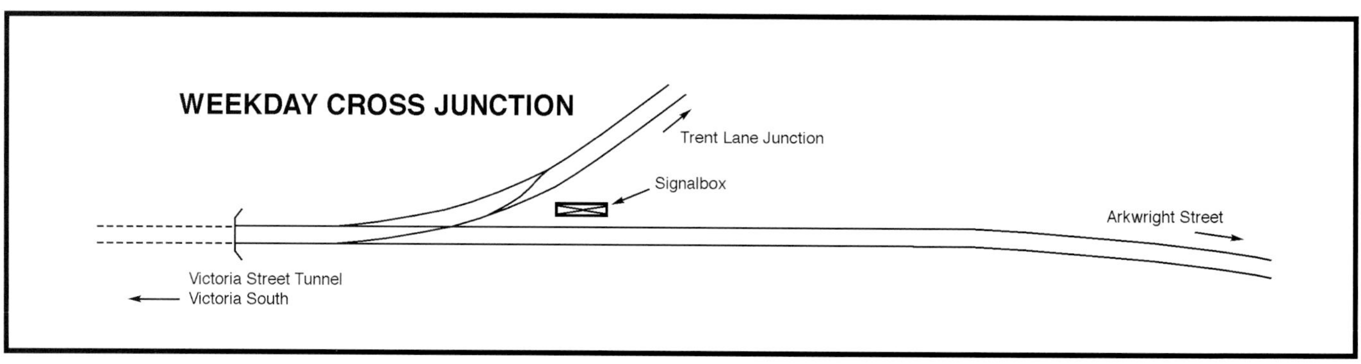

Right:
After the withdrawal of the semi-fast services to Marylebone and cross-country services in September 1966, a DMU service was retained, running from Nottingham Victoria to Rugby Central only. The service lasted until 5 May 1969, but Nottingham Victoria closed in September 1967 after the last remaining local service to Grantham was re-routed into Nottingham Midland. A DMU for Rugby passes Weekday Cross Junction on the last day of services into Victoria on 2 September 1967 with one such working, which would call at East Leake, Loughborough, Leicester, Ashby Magna, Lutterworth and Rugby.
T. G. Hepburn/Rail Archive Stephenson

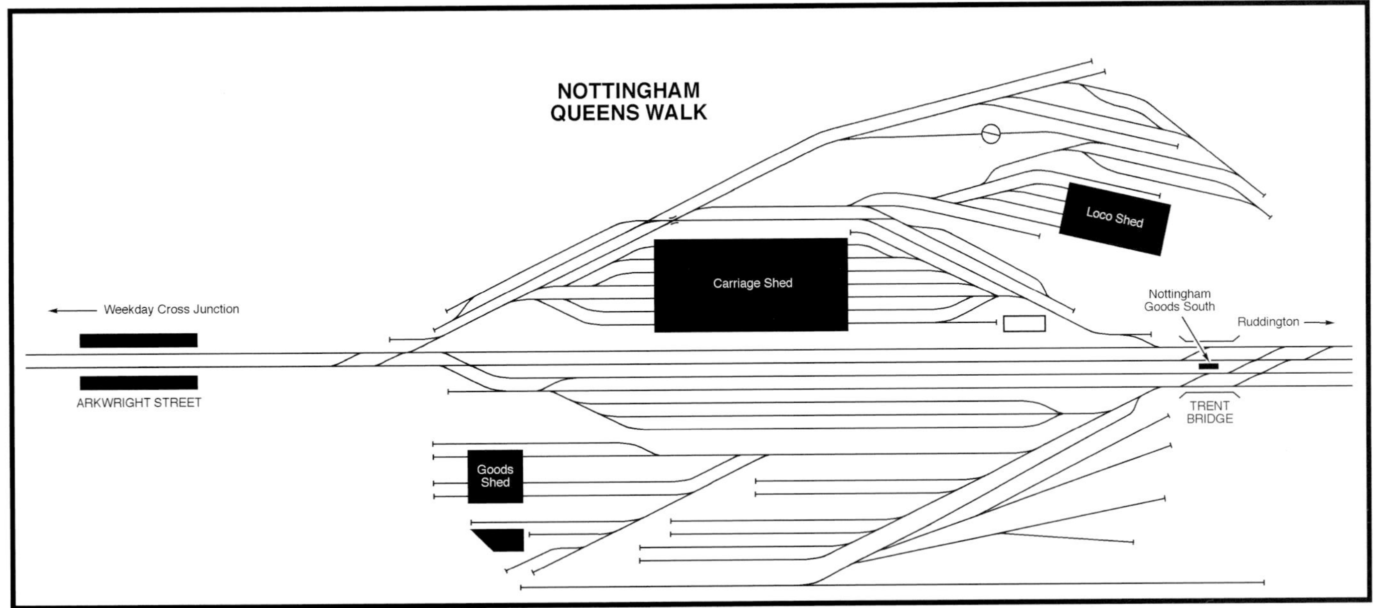

Nottingham Arkwright Street

Once over the Midland line the GC, still on its blue brick viaduct, passed through the Meadows area of Nottingham and its goods yard at Queen's Walk, where there was also a locomotive depot, known as Arkwright Street shed. The shed was not used from 1909 onwards and most crews and locomotives were transferred to Annesley, mainly due to the higher water rates charged to the railway by Nottingham City Council. Queen's Walk Sidings were situated either side of the main line as it ran towards the River Trent and Nottingham Goods South.

Above:
GCR 4-6-0 No 6164 *Earl Beatty* passes Arkwright Street with the Cleethorpes to Leicester through train one day in 1928. The train has fish vans on the tail which duplicated a complete train that would be running independently. Arkwright Street was close to Nottingham's three famous sports grounds: Notts County at Meadow Lane; Nottingham Forest at the City Ground; and Nottinghamshire County Cricket Club at Trent Bridge. It was also the station where the famous 'Newspaper' train stopped to set down Nottingham's newspapers every night as they were whisked down from Marylebone leaving there at 2.32am and arriving at Arkwright Street before 5am. The station was fitted with spiral metal shoots at the north end of the platforms to speed the unloading process. It was hastily reopened in September 1967 to be the terminus of the DMU Nottingham to Rugby services after Nottingham Victoria closed. *T. G. Hepburn/Rail Archive Stephenson*

Nottingham Goods South

The GC crossed the River Trent on two double-track girder bridges and the two goods lines departed from the main lines at Nottingham Goods South. The box was situated just over the girder bridge on a blue brick viaduct, now demolished.

Left:
'K3s' were not normal power for GC line expresses but were used if needs demanded it. Here, Woodford's No 1870 gets away from Nottingham in fine style with the 3.41pm departure from Victoria, which conveyed through coaches from Manchester to Leicester on 16 August 1947.
T. G. Hepburn/Rail Archive Stephenson

Ruddington

After a relatively level run from Nottingham through Wilford, past Wilford Brick Sidings, where there was a signalbox, Ruddington was reached. Another GC island platform and a small goods yard for local traffic was supplemented by a connection to a Ministry of Defence depot which generated large amounts of business for the line.

Above:
'Royal Scot' class locomotives were transferred to the line in the 1960s and were common performers on semi-fasts, the many overnight trains and even goods services. In fact, Annesley used them for any job that was going and here, No 46165 *The Ranger 12th London Regiment* shunts wagons off the MoD branch which can be seen leaving the main line in the foreground. Happily, this is the site where the Great Central Nottingham is restoring the line for the run south to Loughborough. A new terminus is being constructed at the Nottingham Heritage Centre on the site of the old MoD depot and at this site there will be loops to allow trains to reverse in and out of the depot. The photographer is standing on Fifty Steps Bridge and thankfully this sort of scene will be visible from here again. The way the main line was laid out for high speed running is evident in this view taken on 14 September 1964. *T. G. Hepburn/Rail Archive Stephenson*

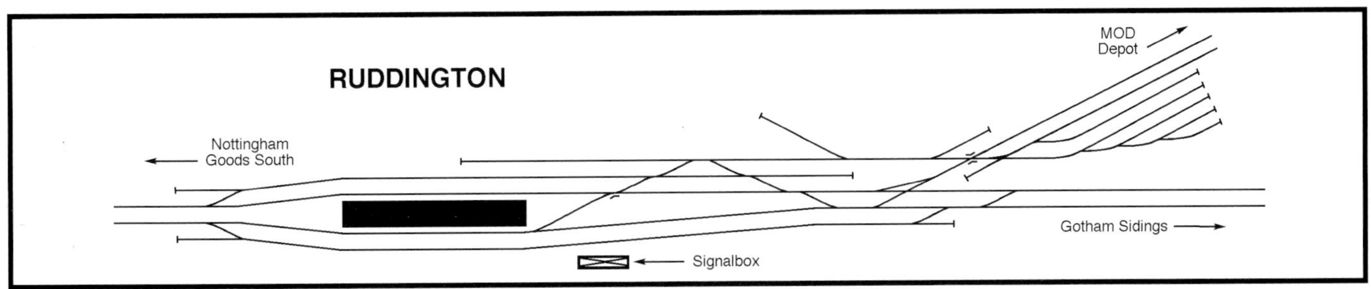

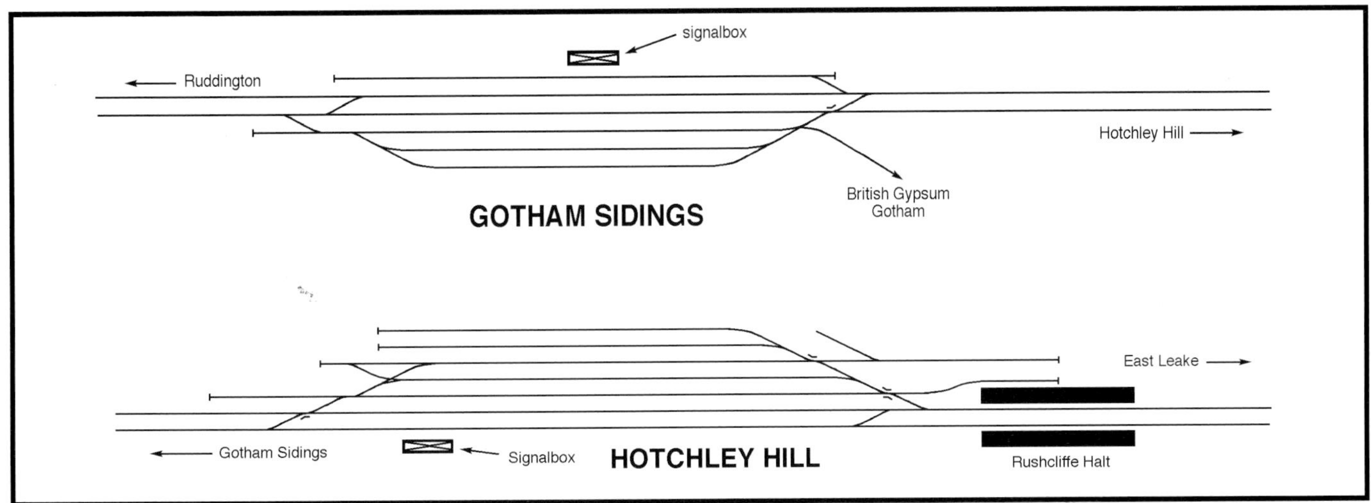

Gotham Sidings and Hotchley Hill/Rushcliffe Halt

From Ruddington the line runs virtually level over Gotham Moor to Gotham Sidings where the short spur to the gypsum factory branched off west. From Gotham Moor, the line climbed at 1 in 176 through Hotchley Hill and East Leake to Barnston Tunnel. At Hotchley Hill is a British Gypsum plant with a rail connection and sidings. This has now been re-opened by GC Nottingham so once again freight trains run on this section. In fact, track is down all the way from Loughborough to Ruddington and has been upgraded for freight traffic and preserved trains from the Nottingham Heritage Centre.

Below:
Passing the 1940s-built signalbox and approaching the two simple concrete platforms at Rushcliffe Halt is 'Britannia' No 70036 *Boadicea* with one of the GC line's famous fish trains from Grimsby to the West. After the replacement of traditional GC types on these trains, 'K3s' from Woodford or Immingham tended to work them. However, 'Britannias' allocated to Immingham became common performers on these services as the 'K3s' were withdrawn. The gypsum sidings (now re-opened) can be seen on the right of the train. The date is 7 June 1963. *T. G. Hepburn/Rail Archive Stephenson*

Above:
'9F' No 92068 heads a southbound 'Runner' into the deep cutting south of the station at 15.25 on 10 July 1964. The 'Runners' had less than a year to go, being withdrawn in June 1965. The spoil from the cutting was used to build the embankment that ran up to River Soar Viaduct just north of Loughborough. The goods shed can be seen behind the train where there was a small yard for local general merchandise traffic and coal. *Tom Boustead*

East Leake

East Leake, despite being only a local station, survived the 1963 closures and was open right to the end of passenger services to 5 May 1969. A traditional island platform, it had a goods yard and the platform remains with track by it to this day, patiently awaiting the reintroduction of passenger services.

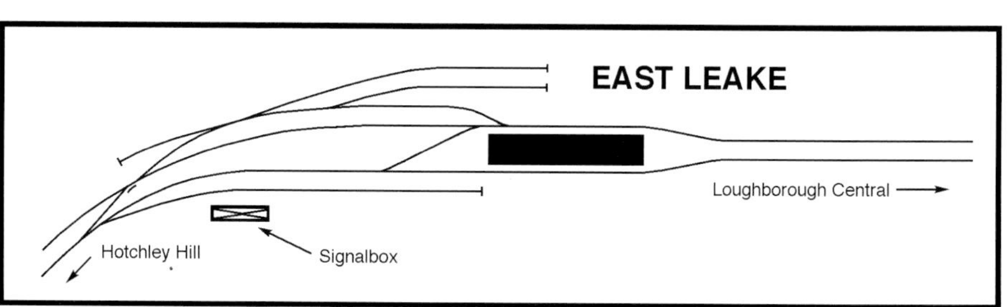

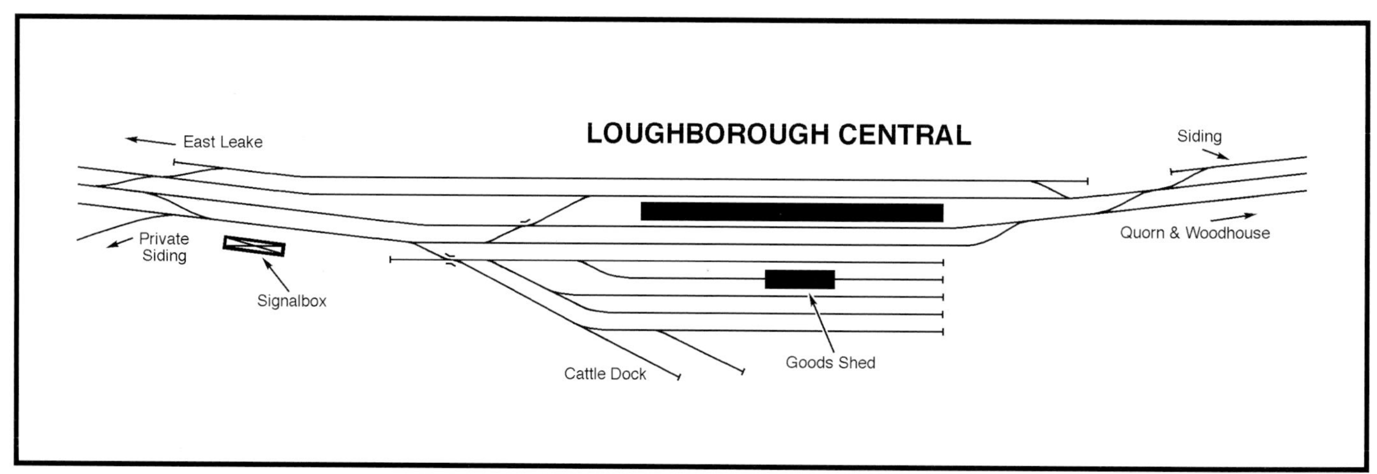

Loughborough Central

A descent of 1 in 176 through Barnston Tunnel, over River Soar Viaduct and the Midland line at Loughborough bridge 328, was usually made at high speed as most trains completed the Nottingham to Leicester stretch in less than even time. The Brush locomotive works were passed to the western side of the line just before the Midland bridge and before Loughborough Central was reached. A larger island platform with more comprehensive waiting rooms and facilities was provided here, together with a large goods shed and yard. Happily, the station is completely restored and running steam and diesel trains today.

Above:
Loughborough Central is seen in July 1965 with the 08.38 semi-fast service from Marylebone to Nottingham. The goods yard to the right had been lifted by this date but there were still passing loops. Most of the signalboxes had been closed, although Loughborough Central was still open. This train and its return working, the 12.25 from Nottingham to Marylebone, was a DMU diagram at this time so the fireman travelled as 'second man' and can be seen on the left, looking quite bored in this instance! *Andrew Muckley*

Below:
Using the speed that it has gained on the 1 in 176 descent from Barnston to good effect, '9F' No 92108 races through Loughborough Central with an oil train for Abbey Lane sidings in Leicester. Oil was sent to Leicester from Fawley in Hampshire as well as from the North East, and was the last freight traffic to use the Great Central — the final booked working from Leicester to Fawley running on 11 June 1965, hauled by '9F' No 92032. *Tom Boustead*

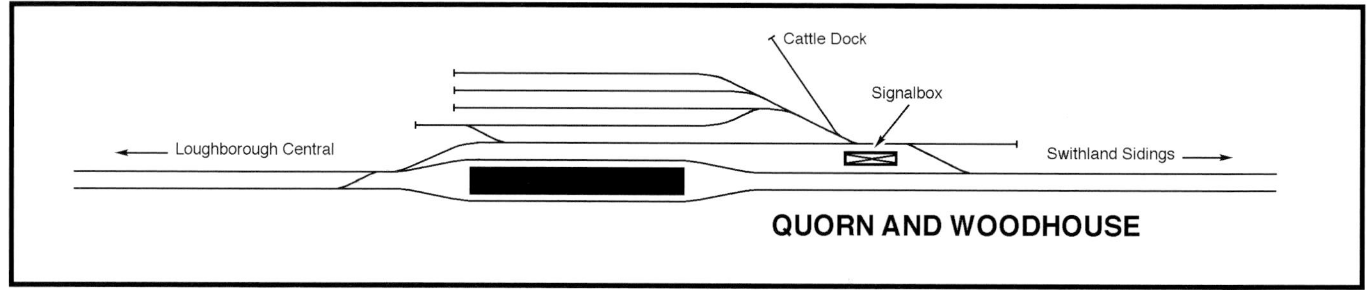

Quorn & Woodhouse

From Loughborough Central the line climbs at 1 in 176 through Quorn and Woodhouse which had a large goods yard used to good effect in World War 2 when many troops began their journey for the D-day invasion from here.

Below:
On 1 September 1966, only three days before the withdrawal of the through semi-fasts, 'Black 5' No 45493 races through Quorn & Woodhouse with the 14.38 from Marylebone to Nottingham. The lifted goods yard can be seen on the left and the signalbox was sited on the down side, roughly behind the last carriage of the train. This station was closed on 4 March 1963, together with most of the other local stations. It is good news indeed that trains are once again running on double track through here. *Tom Boustead*

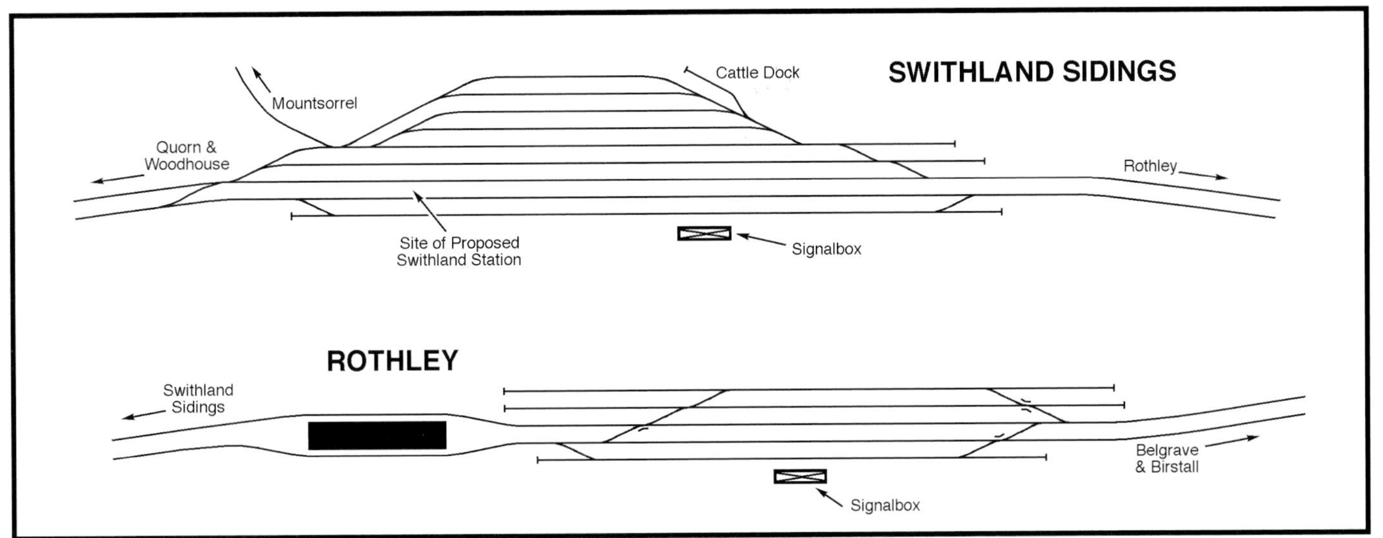

Swithland Sidings and Rothley

The shallow 1 in 264/330 climb dropped towards Rothley from Swithland Sidings, which were situated approximately 2½ miles from Quorn. After passing over Swithland Reservoir, the sidings were laid for storage of wagons on the mineral branch to Mountsorrel. At Swithland the up and down main lines part and run either side of an imaginary GC island platform — at one time it had been thought that a small station would be provided here, but it was not to be.

Below:
Class B3 4-6-0 No 1166 *Earl Haig* passes Rothley with the 3.20pm from Marylebone to Manchester in 1922. The length of the expresses had increased since the early 'Flyer' days of three or four coaches necessitating the development of larger locomotives such as the 'B3s'. The small yard at Rothley can be seen complete with coal and other wagons and Rothley signal cabin is also shown perched on stilts on the side of the embankment that carries the line over Rothley Brook. *Real Photographs/Ian Allan Library*

Belgrave & Birstall

Belgrave & Birstall station, another GC island platform, was situated on the 1 in 176 descent into Leicester and is now the southern terminus of the preserved Great Central Railway. It had no goods yard, but it did have a signalbox and a handy path for photographers right by the side of the line! As with other local stations, it was closed on 4 March 1963.

Left:
Class K3 2-6-0 No 61975 heads an up mixed freight containing petrol for Leicester Abbey Lane through Belgrave & Birstall on 24 April 1957. Here, the station still has its original wooden nameboards but these were later replaced by BR-style boards. *G. D. King*

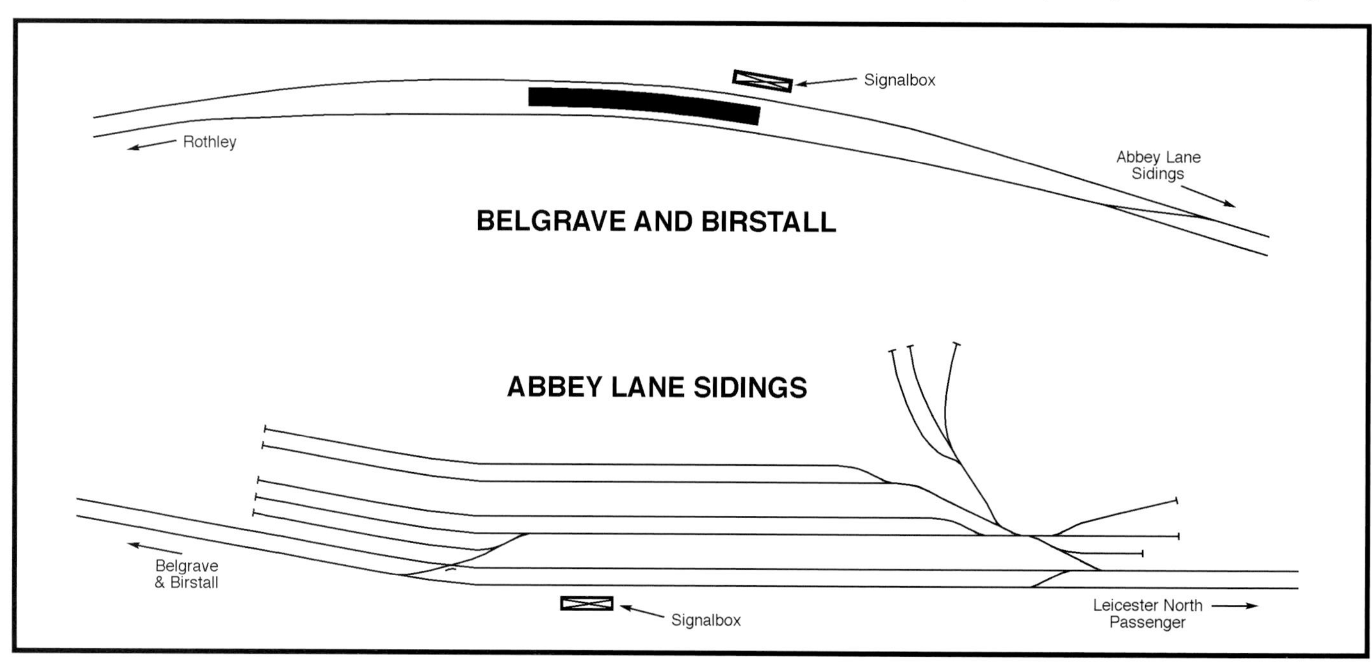

Leicester, Abbey Lane Sidings

The line continued the descent through the northern outskirts of Leicester to another long blue brick viaduct on which it strode into the city of Leicester. Before it ran onto the viaduct the line passed Abbey Lane where there were sidings for petrol, oil trains and other goods traffic.

Left:
The petrol sidings can be seen to the left of Great Western 'Hall' class 4-6-0 No 6911 *Holker Hall* as it climbs out of Leicester with one of the many cross-country services that still ran on the GC in 1964, this being a Poole to Bradford train on 8 August that year. *H. A. Gamble*

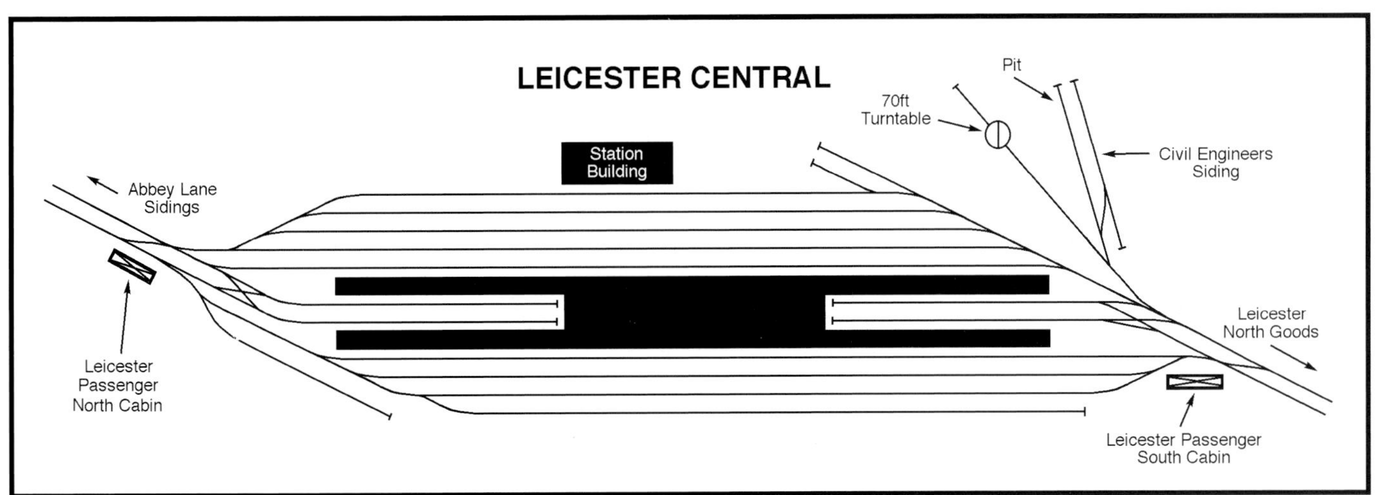

Leicester Central

Once over the 35-chain-long blue brick viaduct with girder spans over the River Soar and the Grand Union Canal, the final bridge (a skew girder type that was wider at the southern end than it was at the north to cope with the tracks fanning out for Leicester Central station) crossed over Northgate Street in Leicester. The station was a large island platform 1,300ft long with double-track bays at either end. Major facilities were provided on the platform, but the main station buildings were accessed by means of a subway and are still situated to the eastern side of the site. A small locomotive servicing depot and a 70ft turntable were provided on the eastern side of the station.

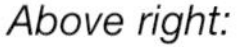

Above right:
GC 'Directors' were still very much in service in the late 1950s and early 1960s. A regular turn was an evening Sheffield to Leicester local and its return working, nicknamed the 'Spitfire' due to its quick turnaround at Leicester. No 62667 *Somme* runs off Northgate Street bridge and past Leicester Passenger North signalbox on 29 July 1959. The two lines in the foreground lead to the northern bay platforms and the down main line can be seen joining by the signalbox.
Barry Hilton

Right:
A view from the large island platform shows the locomotive servicing point on the right-hand side of the train, complete with a 'K3' 2-6-0 as BR Standard Class 5 No 73066 leaves Leicester Central with the up 'South Yorkshireman', the 10.00 Bradford to Marylebone on 2 January 1966. This was no ordinary departure; for this was the last day of express working on the London Extension. Famous Leicester crew, Driver Albert Durrington and Fireman Ron Cassie, are on the footplate and the train is running 36min late. On the Monday a service of semi-fasts started — it was the first stage in the LMR's plan to close the Great Central.
Barry Hilton

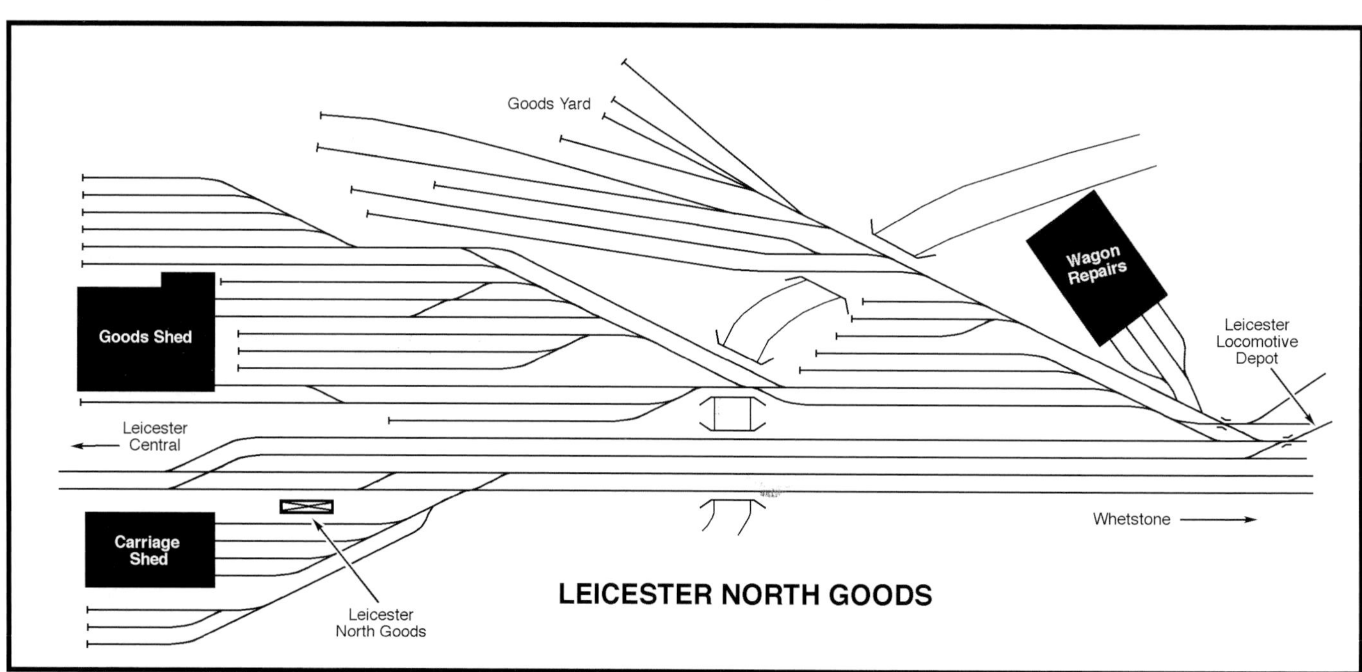

Leicester North and South Goods

The line continued from Leicester Central on another bridge over Welles Street, a blue brick viaduct, and out over a series of girder bridges and viaducts crossing Braunston Gate, the River Soar and the Grand Union Canal. Then came Leicester North Goods box where the line was quadrupled once more and on the down side was the carriage shed and sidings. On the up side was the extensive goods yard with a large goods shed and fan of sidings that bordered Western Boulevard. Then came bridge 378 where, just on the southern side came the wagon repair shops, followed by the well-known Leicester locomotive depot that provided the motive power for the expresses.

After Leicester South Goods the formation reduced to the two main lines and crossed under the Midland line from Knighton to Burton upon Trent via Coalville. After closure, a spur was built up from the GC formation to this line to allow Berry's scrapyard, situated in the former GC goods shed and yard, to receive rolling stock and locomotives for cutting up.

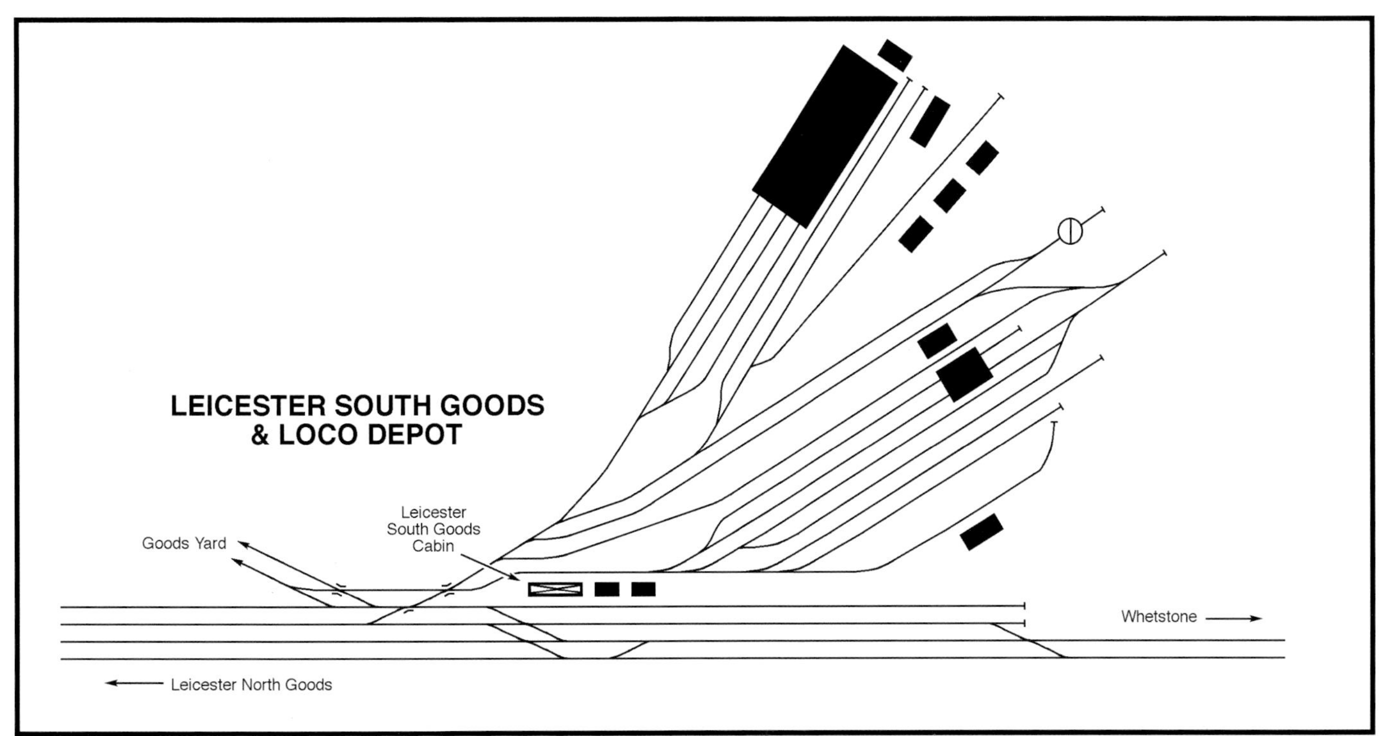

Left:
Heading south from Leicester Central, 'Black 5' No 45299 works the 18.15 Nottingham to Rugby local service and was photographed from bridge 378 on 7 August 1965. Goods services had been withdrawn two months earlier when the Annesley 'Runners' had been taken out of service, and the sidings to the goods shed that can be seen on the right look rusty. Leicester North Goods box is visible to the rear of the train on the down side and just behind that was the carriage shed. *H. A. Gamble*

Right:
Looking back towards Leicester South Goods box, which can be seen just to the right of the rear carriages of the train, the goods yards can be seen stretching into the distance to the east of the main lines and beyond bridge 378 in the background. There, the main goods shed was located, later to become the home of Vic Berry's scrapyard. The locomotive depot was also situated to this side, the access spur being located just by the signalbox. The fine repeater bracket signal guards the entrance to the yards and the other pair of lines are the down goods arrival and a shunting neck. 'Director' class No 2664 *Princess Mary* gets away from Leicester with an 'Ord' for Marylebone in early LNER days. This was the spot where engines were really opened up for a typically vigorous GC-style departure, much to the displeasure of the owners of the terraced houses to the left of the train — their washing was regularly blackened with soot! *S. Newton*

Leicester South Goods to Aylesbury

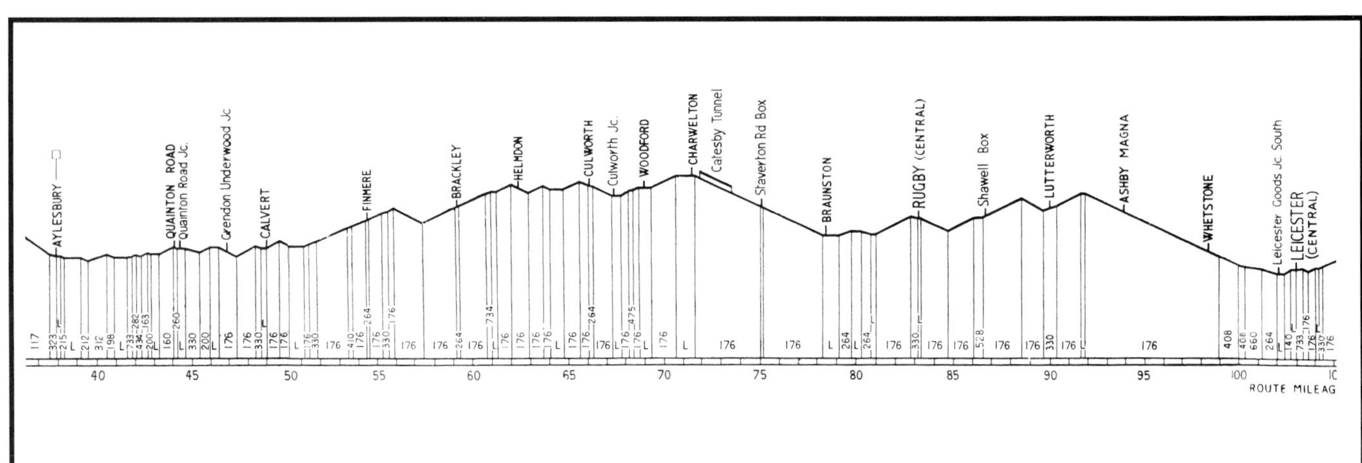

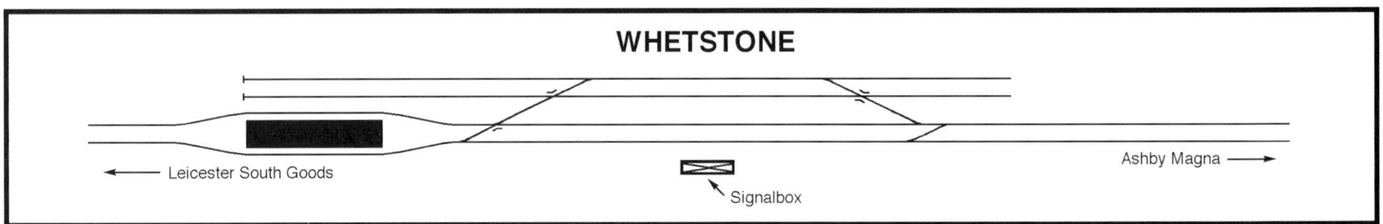

Whetstone

On leaving Leicester South Goods, the line climbed gently to approximately a mile south of Whetstone where the 7-mile 1 in 176 Ashby Bank started. It ran through Aylestone fields and then on a blue brick viaduct and girder bridge over the Midland line from Wigston Junction to Birmingham. Whetstone was situated on an embankment just after the bridge and was another classic island platform with steps down to the road at the north end.

Below:
The GC local trains were either long-distance stoppers or short locals and were all withdrawn from March 1963, along with the closure of most of the stations they served. They were known to the staff as 'Ords' and here the 12 noon from Leicester Central to Woodford calls at Whetstone on 25 March 1961. 'B1s' were common on all types of GC passenger services and No 61186 was based at Woodford Halse. The original GC gas lamps are still on the platform and a train of bogie bolsters are recessed in the sidings on the up side. There was also a cement siding at Whetstone which saw trains of Presflow wagons being loaded there. *Mike Mitchell*

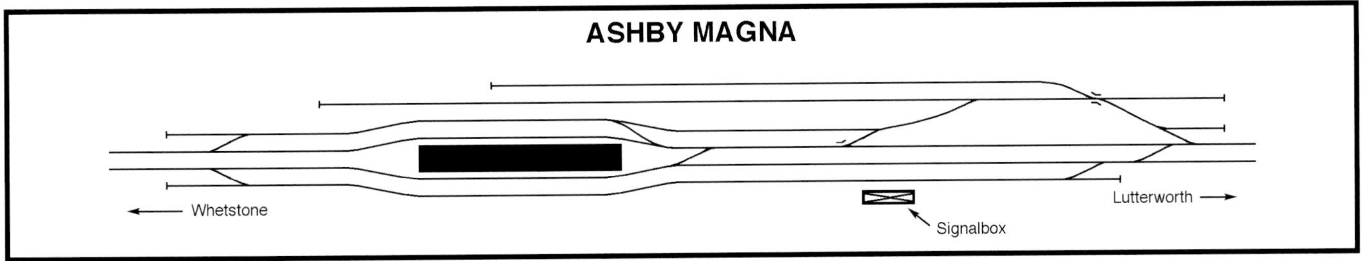

Ashby Magna

Roughly three-quarters of the way up Ashby Bank came Ashby Magna station. To the southern end of the station was Ashby Tunnel — also known as Dunton Bassett Tunnel — situated at the end of another long cutting. A small goods yard was provided on the up side and recess sidings for trains to be 'put inside' to allow faster workings to pass.

Below:
The layout of the station is well shown as 'V2' 2-6-2 No 60924 of New England shed storms up Ashby Bank through the station on 25 July 1959. The train is one of the many summer through services that ran to and from a variety of holiday destinations via the GC main line. The scene was transformed just a few years later as the M1 motorway was built on the up side of the GC main line between Ashby Magna and Lutterworth. Gone would be the peace and quiet, previously disturbed only by the 'Runners' pounding up Ashby Bank. The field on the right of the photograph disappeared under the motorway, and a journey along this section today allows the traveller to see the formation of the GC running alongside. *Barry Hilton*

Lutterworth

Lutterworth was situated at the bottom of the 1 in 176 dip, the line dropping from the summit of Ashby Bank before rising again before the descent through Shawell to Rugby. Lutterworth was another island platform with a goods yard on the down side and with recess sidings.

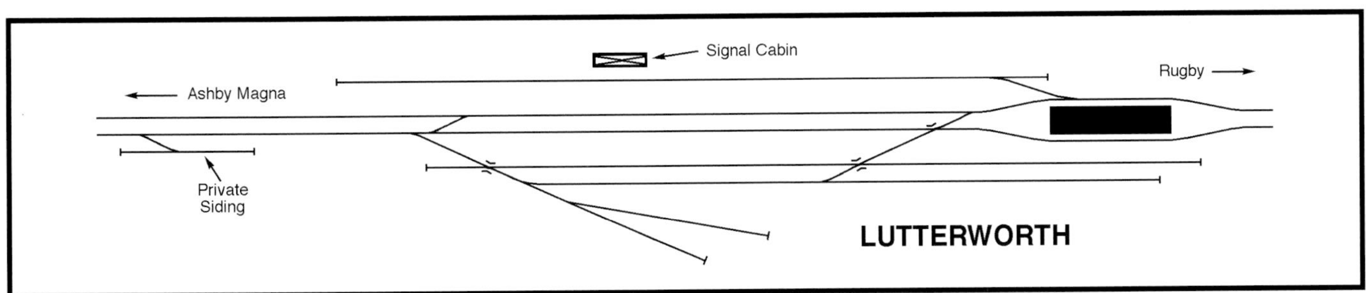

Above:
A close-up of the station buildings at Lutterworth shows the lavatory block furthest from the camera, the waiting room and Ladies next with canopy, and the brick and glass structure covering the steps leading down to the road below that provided access to the public. The original GC oil lamp has been partly replaced by a rather strange electric affair and the LMR sign has been added. The date is March 1966 and only three months are left for the Nottingham to Marylebone service. However, Lutterworth stayed open as part of the Nottingham to Rugby DMU service and did not close until 5 May 1969. Only the main lines remain here, all the sidings and loops having been lifted the previous year together with the closure of the signalbox on 20 June 1965 following the demise of the Annesley 'Runners' which meant that less track capacity was required. The photographer is facing north and the remains of the goods yard can be seen on the left. The climb of the line up to the summit of Ashby Bank is evident. *Andrew Muckley*

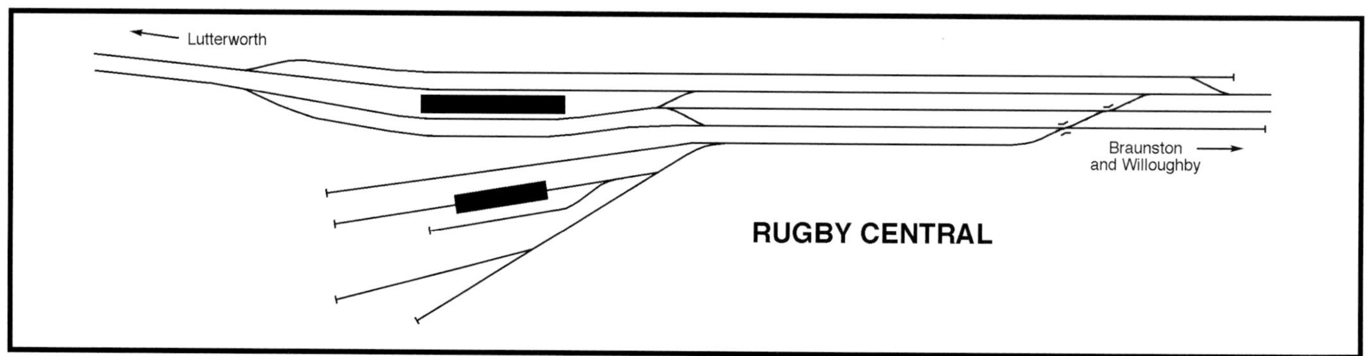

Rugby Central

From Lutterworth, the line climbed for a mile at 1 in 176 before dropping to Rugby Central through Shawell. Shawell cabin was situated on the up side near the bridge that carried the line over the A5 road. The box was closed on 10 May 1959 — a victim of the introduction of intermediate block signalling. It was burned down by vandals shortly after closure. From there, there was once a signal cabin at Newton, where there was a ballast siding, but this had closed as early as 1900 when it was removed and taken to Aylestone where it increased line capacity between Leicester South Goods and Whetstone. It was closed again in 1925, another victim of intermediate block working. Once over the viaduct across the Oxford Canal the LNWR main line was crossed by means of the Birdcage Bridge. Just after the Birdcage was Rugby Cattle Sidings cabin — a standard GC design for the adjacent cattle sidings that never really generated significant business and had declined with the reduction in livestock traffic. The cabin was closed after war was declared in 1939, but was still capable of functioning as it was used as a control point for a temporary facing crossover that was used for single-line working from Shawell when the decking on the Birdcage was renewed in 1950. Rugby Central was situated at the end of a deep cutting and the station was a large island platform with the booking hall situated in Hillmorton Road, above the main line. A small goods yard was provided on the down side and there were loops for recessing and turning back local trains from Leicester. It was much smaller than the LNWR station and almost inconspicuous — John Betjeman was right in his poem 'Great Central Railway Sheffield Victoria to Banbury' as he wrote, 'And quite where Rugby Central is does only Rugby know'. Rugby lasted until the end of the DMU service being the southern terminus from Nottingham, that was withdrawn from May 1969. The main line south of here was closed on 4 September 1966. The week after closure stop blocks were installed and the lifting of the main line to the South began.

Above:
The station platform is hidden behind the train, but a good view of the station buildings in Hillmorton Road is provided, together with Rugby's signalbox which was closed on 4 May 1969. Behind the box is the goods yard and the two loops either side of the up and down main lines can be seen. Before the '9F' era began on the Annesley 'Runners', 'O1' 2-8-0 No 63879 passes through with a goods for Woodford on 13 May 1950. *H. Weston*

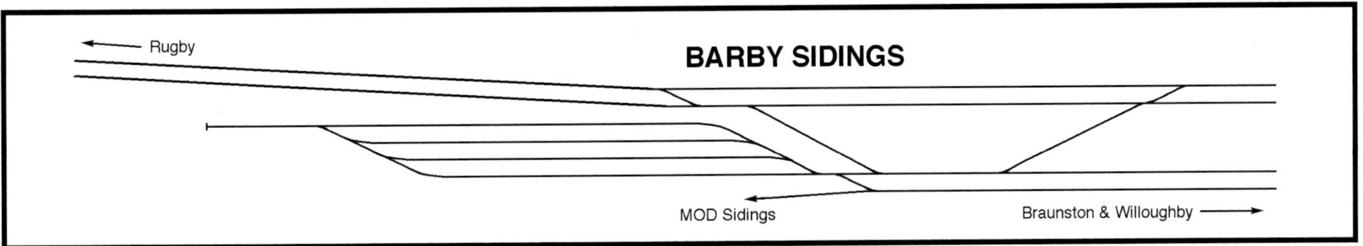

Barby Sidings

Barby Sidings were constructed during World War 2 in 1943 and laid to the west of the main line. They were used for military traffic and had their own locomotive, an austerity USA tank engine. The sidings had a small ground frame housed in a brick cabin, similar to that at Calvert North Junction. It was rumoured that the USA tank occasionally travelled to Rugby on Saturdays — a cheap way of taking service personnel for a day out! However, the locomotive would not operate the track circuits for the approach-lit signals at Barby, and the practice was discouraged. After the war, 'J94' 0-6-0STs worked in the sidings. They were run down from 1953 and eventually the box was closed on 29 September 1955. Barby Sidings' trailing crossover was the scene of a tragic accident in August 1955 when an express running 'wrong line' due to engineering work took the crossover at an excessive speed causing a derailment where the locomotive fell down the embankment, killing the driver.

Braunston & Willoughby

Braunston & Willoughby station was situated between the two villages and was a standard island platform with sidings, mainly on the down side for agricultural traffic. It was never well used and was closed as early as 29 September 1958, along with Culworth. It was renamed Braunston & Willoughby in 1904, having previously just been Willoughby.

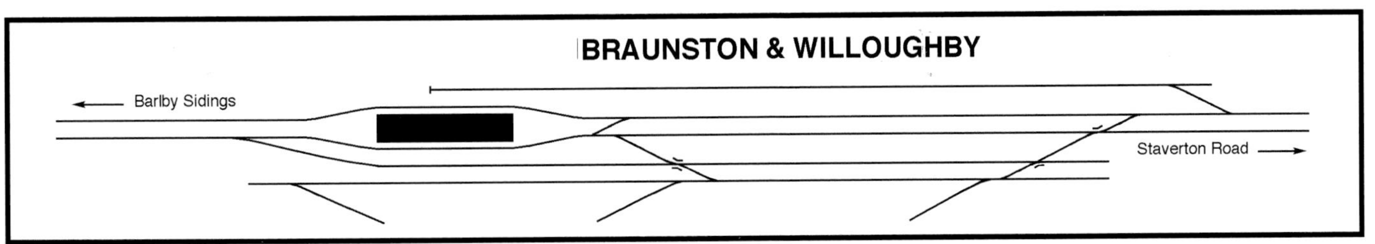

92012

Left:
Braunston & Willoughby station looks in dilapidated condition, but still has the main nameboard and gas lamps despite having been closed for nearly two years. Sidings, mainly for agricultural traffic, can be seen in the foreground and there was a long recess siding on the up side. The signalbox was also situated on the up side and closed on 13 June 1965 along with others such as Staverton Road when the freight services ceased. This left much longer block sections and reduced the line capacity considerably, thus making the GC even less attractive as a main line route. 'V2' No 60863 heads the 5.20pm Leicester to Woodford 'Ord', complete with ex-LMS coaches, on 26 August 1961. *Mike Mitchell*

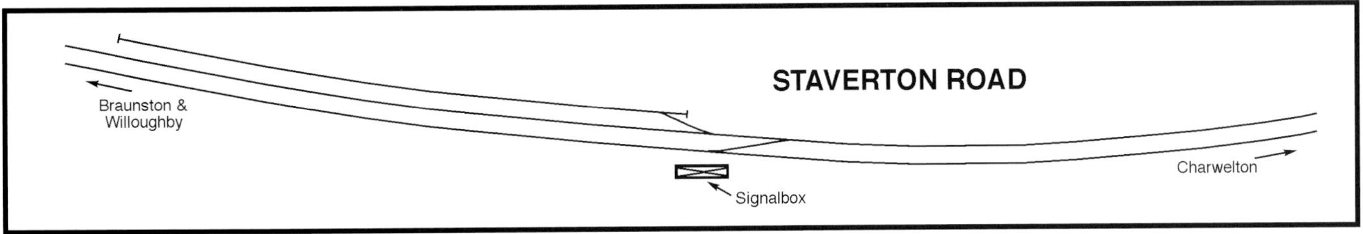

Staverton Road

Staverton Road was an intermediate block post situated midway on the 1 in 176 climb from Braunston & Willoughby to Charwelton. It had an up siding only, for the use of recessing climbing goods trains to allow faster passenger workings to pass if the goods could not make it through Catesby Tunnel to the loops at Charwelton in time.

Charwelton

Once through Catesby Tunnel, the small station of Charwelton marked a level section of the route — important because just to the south of the station were Charwelton water troughs which were installed in 1903 to allow non-stop running from Marylebone to Sheffield. The station was the standard island platform with access from the road over bridge for foot passengers. Loops were provided on both the up and down main lines but there were also a number of tracks that served as storage and reception sidings for a branch to a small ironstone quarry. A small industrial locomotive would pull the wagons to Charwelton sidings, where a main line locomotive would take them to Woodford yard for onward shipment.

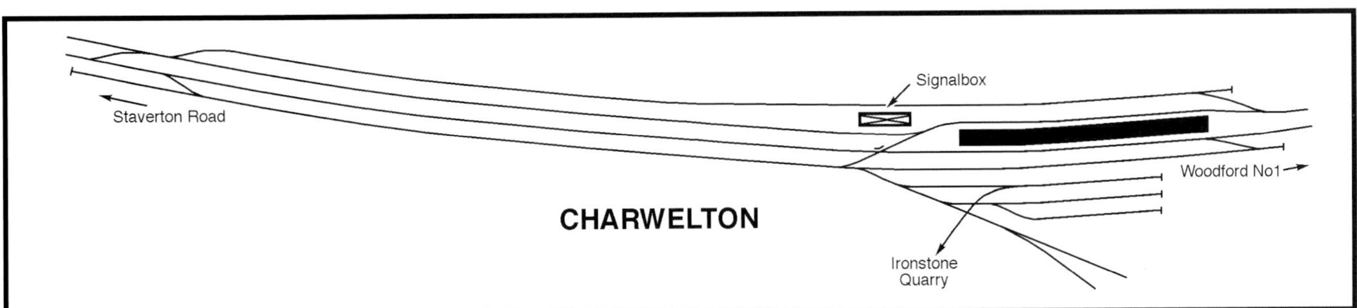

Below left:
The rural location of Staverton Road cabin is well illustrated — it was actually supported on stilts like those at Rothley and Whetstone — as '9F' No 92012 of Annesley depot slogs up the 1 in 176 to Catesby Tunnel and Charwelton with an up 'Runner' on 27 May 1961. *Mike Mitchell*

Right:
The ironstone sidings are clearly in evidence as 'B1' No 61186, with 'British Railways' still on the tender, gets away from Charwelton with an 'Ord' from Marylebone to Leicester on 29 July 1950. The branch to the quarry is the line sharply curving away over the diamond crossings. The train length was quite common for a stopping service and is made up of a variety of ex-LNER coaches, one of which has already been painted out of its brown livery into 'blood and custard'. *L. Hanson*

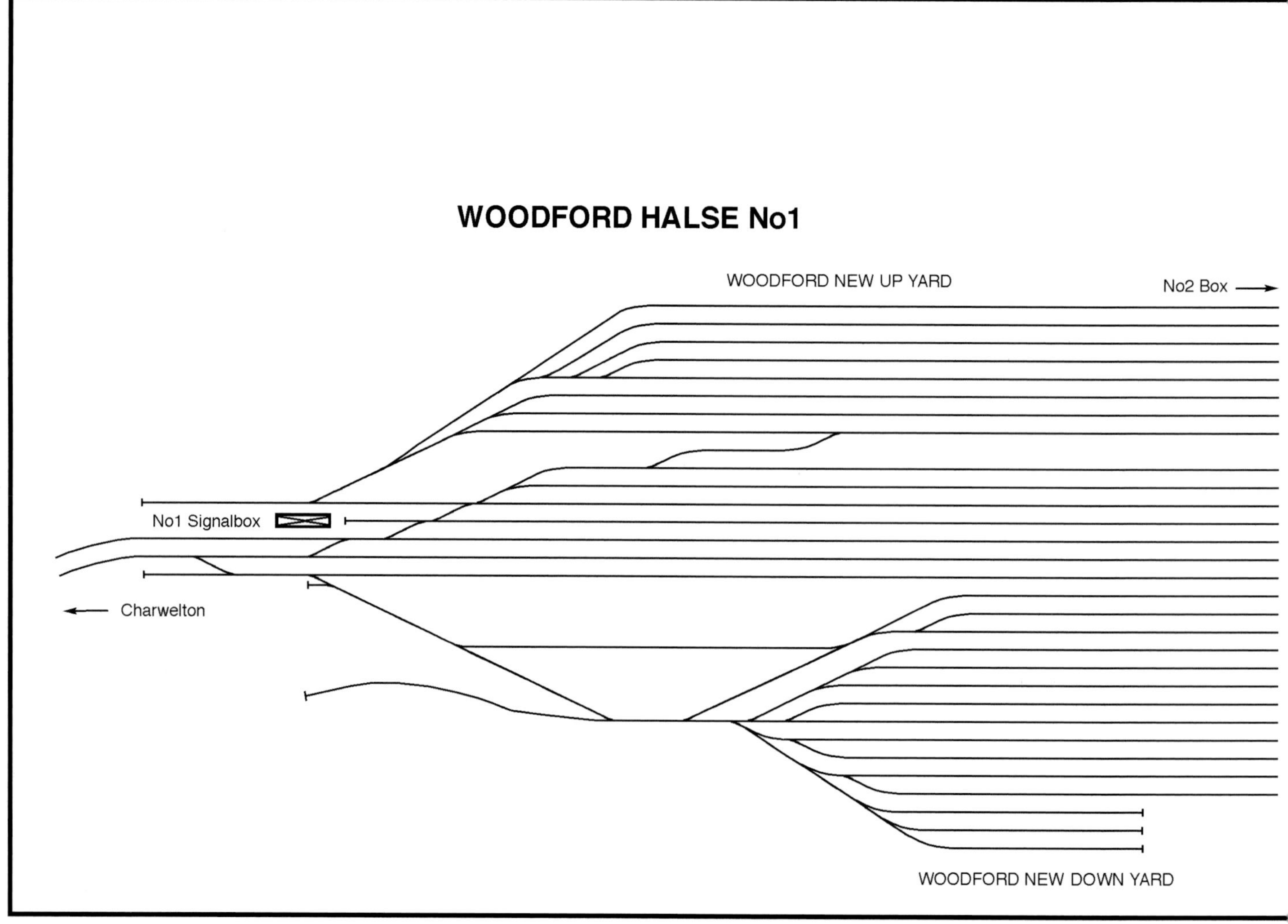

Woodford Halse

Woodford Halse was a unique railway community which, until the arrival of the Great Central, was a small, typical Northamptonshire village. Originally the GC was planned to run straight through the area on its way to London, but the desire to develop cross-country freight and passenger services saw the opening of a most important link to Banbury from the remote Culworth Junction, two miles south of Woodford. This line was opened on 1 June 1900 for freight traffic, and large marshalling yards were constructed on the up and down sides (using the spoil excavated from Catesby Tunnel) which allowed wagons to be exchanged as they ran down from the North to GWR destinations. Just south of the station another spur connected the GC to the Stratford & Midland Junction Railway that ran from Towcester to Stratford-upon-Avon, via Fenny Compton on the GW main line from Paddington to Birkenhead.

Woodford also had a large engine shed complete with a turntable used to turn locomotives which was later replaced by a triangle. Gorton-style terraced housing was constructed to cope with the influx of railway workers as well as an accommodation building for railwaymen on lodging turns and those who were temporarily transferred in from other depots. This was known as the 'Barracks'. The station was small by comparison, being a standard island platform with access from the road below by means of a stairway. The Banbury branch local platform was situated on the down side loop and was initially timber-built. Even after it was rebuilt in concrete it was still called the 'wooden platform'.

There was a small goods yard for local traffic situated on the up side. In 1941, two more yards — known as the New Yards — were built to the north of the existing ones. This was for the heavy growth of wartime traffic. Heavy traffic continued after the war and over one million wagons per year were regularly handled as they arrived and departed by the famous Annesley 'Runners' and were transferred to freights for the Western Region via Banbury and for London via the main line. The S&MJ line also generated much traffic — and was upgraded in the 1950s to carry steel from the North East to South Wales and vice versa, going on from Stratford to Broom Junction and Ashchurch and later down via Toddington and Cheltenham.

Freight was the life-blood of the GC, so the gradual rundown of the freight service and its withdrawal in June 1965 saw the closure of the yards and shed, train crews then having to book on at the station. For the last year the area took on an air of general dereliction, as the yards and sidings were gradually lifted and buildings demolished. Of all places on the GC, Woodford was virtually entirely dependent on the railway. It was not at all surprising that there was considerable bitterness around for a long time following the deliberate transfer of traffic away to other routes and the rundown of passenger services.

Right:
In April 1961, a BR Standard Mogul, No 76039, from Neasden shed, has worked into Woodford from the London area with a train of wagons for the North. It has now crossed to the up side and is taking a train for the South out of Woodford New Up Yard past the locomotive shed, situated behind the train, and has crossed to the up goods line. The Old Up Yard is in the distance and the photographer is standing by Woodford No 2 box which was situated on the down side. *G. C. Farnell*

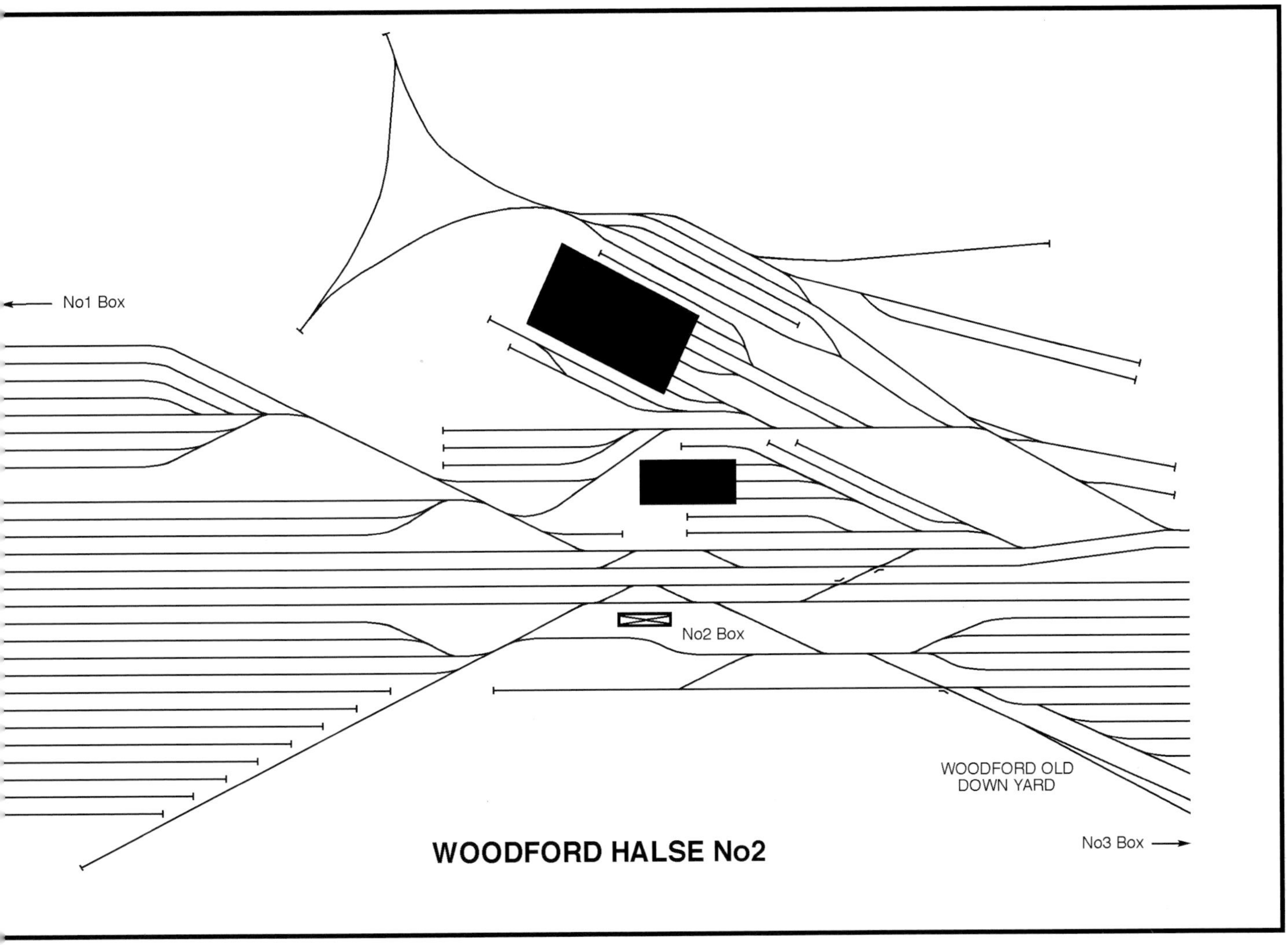

← No1 Box

No2 Box

WOODFORD OLD DOWN YARD

No3 Box →

WOODFORD HALSE No2

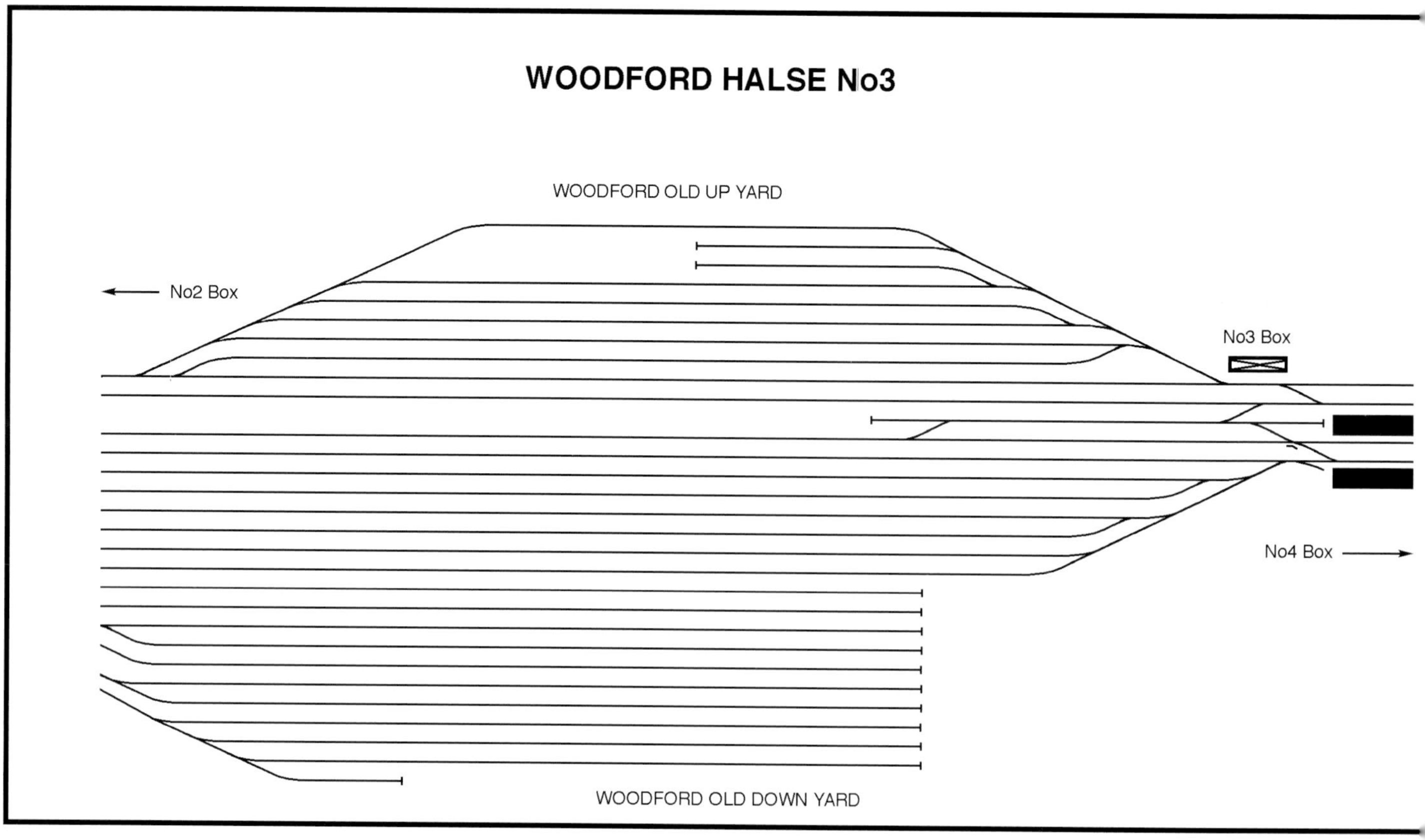

WOODFORD HALSE No3

WOODFORD OLD UP YARD

No2 Box

No3 Box

No4 Box

WOODFORD OLD DOWN YARD

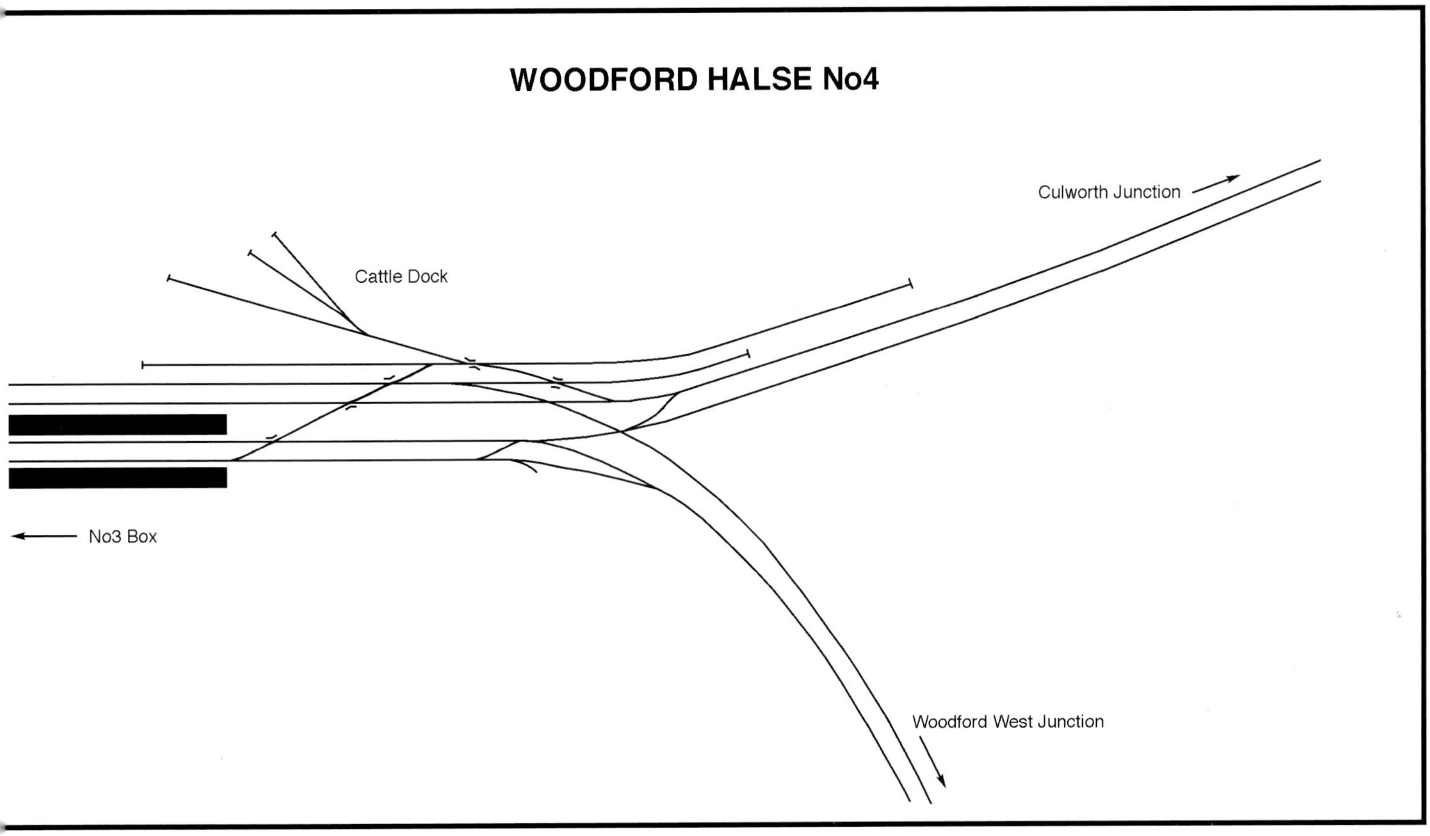

WOODFORD HALSE No4

Culworth Junction

Cattle Dock

No3 Box

Woodford West Junction

Left:
Looking into the entrance to the Old Up Yard on a murky day in April 1961, station pilot, 'L1' No 67789 indulges in some shunting. Woodford No 3 cabin can be seen behind the locomotive which is standing on the up goods loop with the 'dolly' of the setting back signal into the sidings to the left. The GC-style Gorton houses can be seen through the gloom on the right. *G. C. Farnell*

Above:
From the down side of the platform, an 'Austerity' 2-8-0 is seen entering the Old Down Yard with an arrival from the London area. Wagons can be seen in the yard already formed up into trains for one of the northbound 'Runners'. The 'Austerities' were common on this sort of job, but Western engines would also work in from Banbury and, on occasions, a Southern locomotive would arrive. Some fast fitted trains such as the York to Bristol and the fish trains would still call at Woodford for a crew or locomotive change and be put inside one of the yards or goods loops without having to be shunted, unless some wagons required detachment. The date is April 1961.
G. C. Farnell

Looking back to Woodford station from a large blue brick road bridge that still stands to this day, a Woodford 'Austerity' leaves the up goods loop for the South and strikes off towards Culworth Junction with a general goods for West London. The S&MJ line can be clearly seen coming in from the West by Woodford No 4 signal cabin. The 'wooden' platform is now concrete. The train would pass under this bridge, sometimes referred to as 'Marble Arch' by train crews (although some dispute this and say that was a bridge on the Banbury branch), and then enter a deep cutting where it ran under another bridge that carried the S&MJ to Towcester. Just beyond that point was Woodford South Junction, which originally allowed GC trains direct access to Stratford-upon-Avon. The direct service lasted only from August to September in 1899 when the through carriages were re-routed and reversed via the station. No 90095 was viewed in September 1961 when little thought was given to what was to happen just five years later. *G. C. Farnell*

Right:
Looking from the wooden 'Banbury Motor' platform, a general view of the main island platform could be seen. The station island platform had an overall canopy and a buffet for cross-country travellers who had to change trains. A footbridge connected the island platform to the Banbury platform. Trains formed up into 'Runners' and arrival wagons can be seen in the Old Down Yard and the tender of a GWR locomotive is standing on the up goods loop can be seen in this 1951 scene. *Real Photographs/ Ian Allan Library*

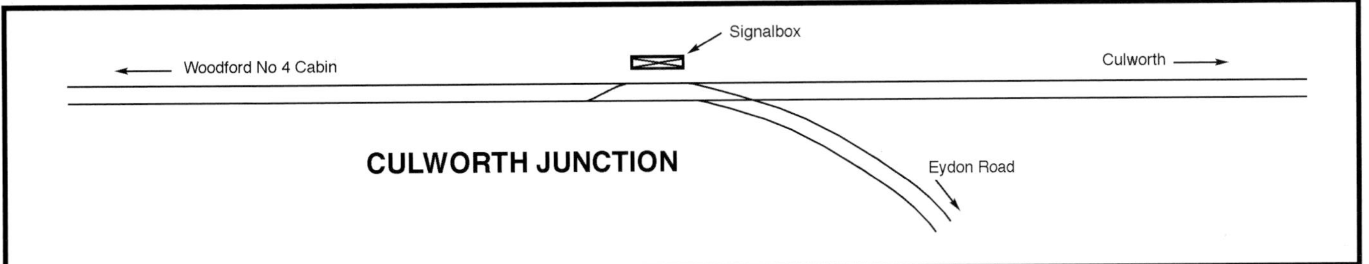

Culworth Junction

Culworth Junction was situated on a level section in a 1 in 176 dip some two miles south of Woodford. It was a most important location; much of the GC's main traffic flowed through here to and from the Great Western at Banbury. In fact, it was considered at one time that the route would be closed south of Culworth, the Banbury link becoming the main line as the GC's main artery was a freight and passenger link from the North East to the South West.

Right:
A view of the junction and signal cabin, complete with lineside hut, sees a special RCTS working approaching behind 'West Country' Pacific No 34002 *Salisbury* on 13 August 1966. The Banbury line can be seen branching off to the right. *J. Scrace*

Left:
One year later the demolition men wasted no time in getting rid of the cabin in a most barbarous fashion, merely burning it down. (I leave the reader to make their own comments on this as mine are unprintable!) *J. Sketchley*

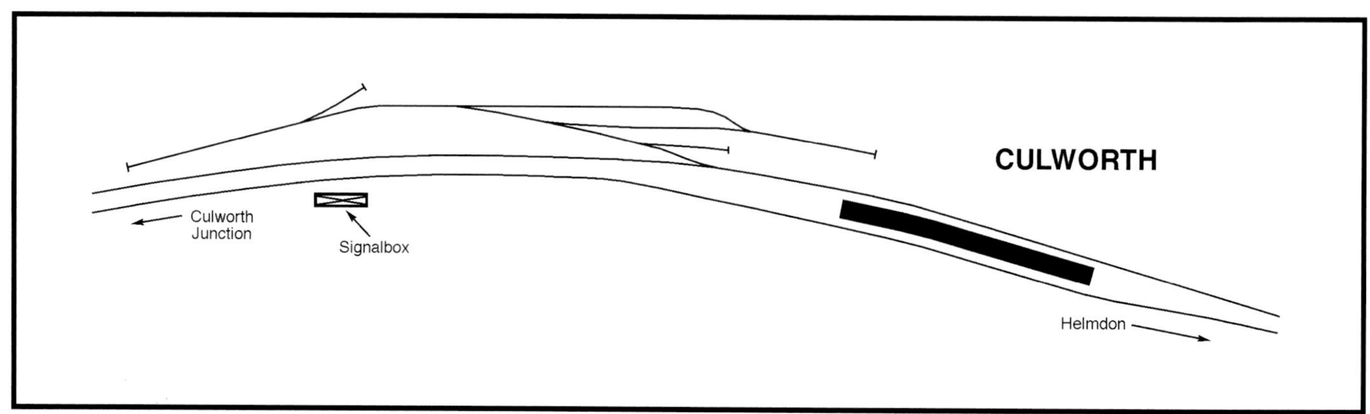

Culworth

Culworth was situated a mile and a quarter on from Culworth Junction as the line switchbacked at 1 in 176 from there towards Brackley. Culworth station was a classic GC design and served the villages of Culworth and Moreton Pinkney. It had a small goods yard that would have generated and received a small amount of general merchandise and coal. It closed earlier than most of the local stations, on 29 September 1958.

Left:
This classic view of Culworth was taken by Ivo Peters and illustrates the station and its small goods yard as 'Austerity' No 90299 passes with a southbound train of house coal for the London area. Although the date is 4 June 1963, the station is still fully intact. What a lovely subject for the modeller Culworth could be. *Ivo Peters*

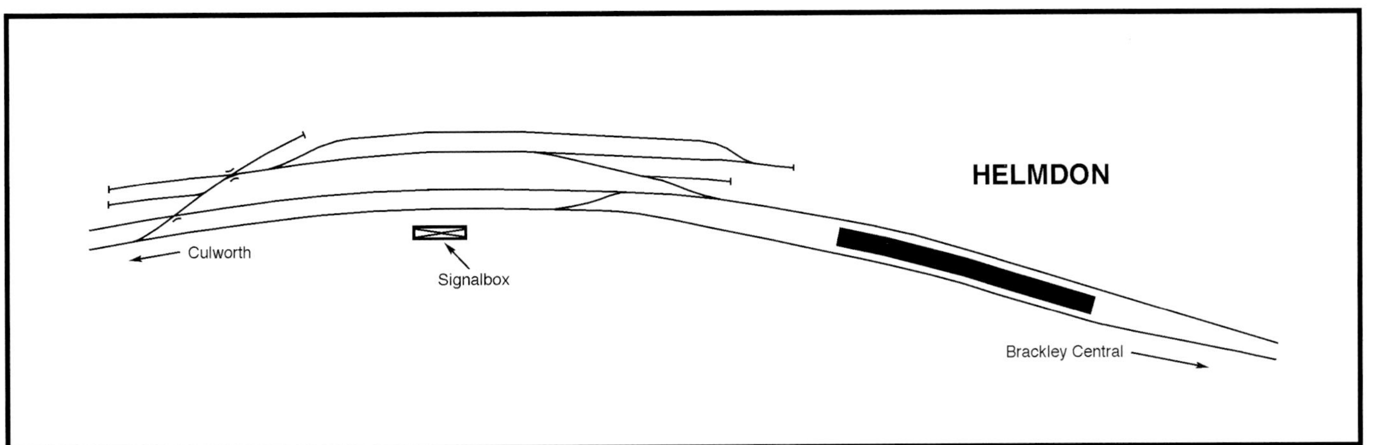

Helmdon

Almost the same as Culworth, Helmdon was roughly five miles further south. However, it survived until 4 March 1964, general goods traffic ceasing on 2 November of the same year.

Right:
Helmdon was beautifully decorated with flowerbeds and other plants tended by the staff. These are evident as 'B1' No 61138 on a long-distance 'Ord' — the 1.5pm Marylebone to Woodford — calls at Helmdon on 11 June 1962. The small goods yard can be seen behind the train on the right-hand side of the scene opposite the signal cabin. *Mike Mitchell*

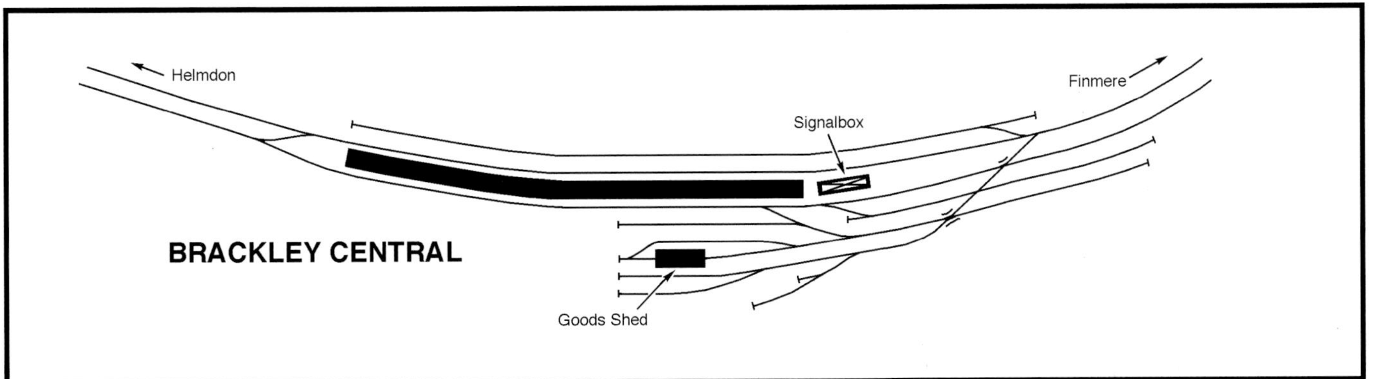

Brackley Central

Brackley Central was similar in size to Rugby Central but its station buildings were situated to one side on a separate approach road as the authorities were concerned about traffic congestion on the bridge that carried the main road from Oxford to Northampton over the railway. Thus a unique footbridge was built which provided access to the station buildings. Brackley had a recess siding on the up side with the goods yard on the down side and just beyond was the famous Brackley Viaduct over the River Great Ouse. The signal cabin was located between the running lines so as to give a better view of the whole station — situated on a curve on a 1 in 176 gradient.

Left:
A general view of Brackley Central on 13 August 1959, looking south, sees a Woodford 'Austerity' climbing towards the station with a goods train for Woodford Halse from the London area. The goods yard and shed can be seen on the right and the signal cabin is visible by the locomotive. In the background the viaduct can be just made out together with bridge 528 that carried the Brackley to Buckingham Road over the GC. *H. B. Priestley*

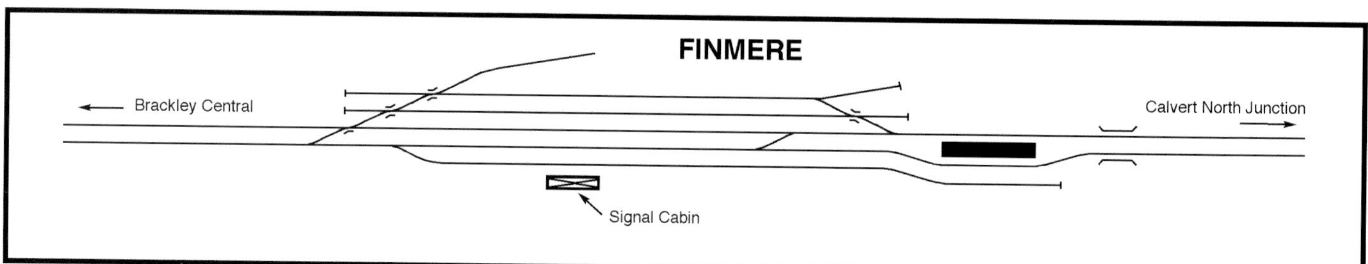

Above:
This 1963 photograph shows Finmere in its last days of operation as it was closed on 4 March. The small goods yard is seen on the up side as we look towards London and the line descends at 1 in 176 towards Calvert North Junction some five miles distant.
Lens of Sutton

Finmere

Despite being over a mile from the village of Finmere, the station enjoyed a main line service from Marylebone in GC and LNER days — and even a slip coach was detached there at one time. This was because Finmere was near to Buckingham and was originally referred to as Finmere for Buckingham in the timetable. It generated some traffic to the town but was also near to Stowe School and saw schools traffic at term times. During World War 2, several airfields and camps were built or expanded in the area and the GC provided a fast link to the joys of London for those in the services when on leave.

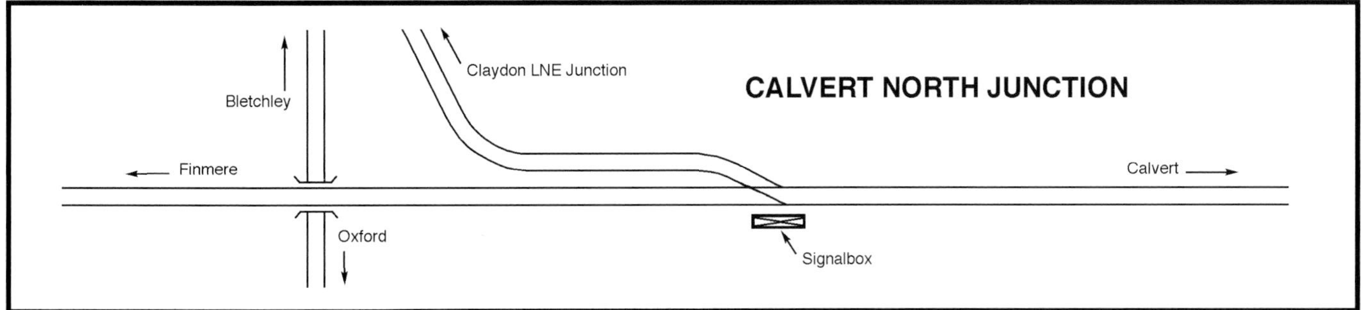

Calvert North Junction

The Oxford to Bletchley line was linked to the GC main line just after the London Extension had passed over it. The link was built in 1940 and the LNWR signalbox was called Claydon LNE Junction. The GC signalbox was a simple brick-built affair not in the normal style, but a wartime austerity measure. It gave the railways added flexibility should bombing cause disruption elsewhere, but was used for freight workings to and from the brickworks and for diversions, especially some of the night-time sleepers diverted to Marylebone during the West Coast main line electrification. For a time, one of the fish trains reversed down from the GC here and accessed the Western Region via Bicester London Road and Oxford. The box was closed 10 December 1967, but track is still extant here to allow rubbish trains access to landfill sites in the old clay pits, the northernmost point that track still exists from Marylebone.

Right:
An unusual sight on the GC as the 'Midland Pullman' approaches Calvert North Junction on 2 May 1964 forming a Preston to Wembley Hill special for the Cup Final at Wembley. The train is travelling up the spur from Claydon LNE Junction on the Oxford to Bletchley line having run down the former LNWR main line via that route. This is the furthest north that GC metals from Marylebone remain to this day. Will they ever carry passengers again as part of a route from Aylesbury to Milton Keynes? The small signalbox is evident to the right of the junction and the GC main line's approach to Calvert's island platform can be seen. *Brian Stephenson*

Right:
Grimy 'B1' No 61152 slows for a signal check at Calvert with a Rugby League Cup Final special returning from Wembley to Wigan on 8 May 1959. The station buildings are standard London Extension type, with the addition of a bicycle shed. The goods yard can be seen on the up side and a train of wagons for the London Brick Company are stabled in the down siding. The signalbox could also work the points and signals for Calvert North Junction if that box was not manned. *Mike Mitchell*

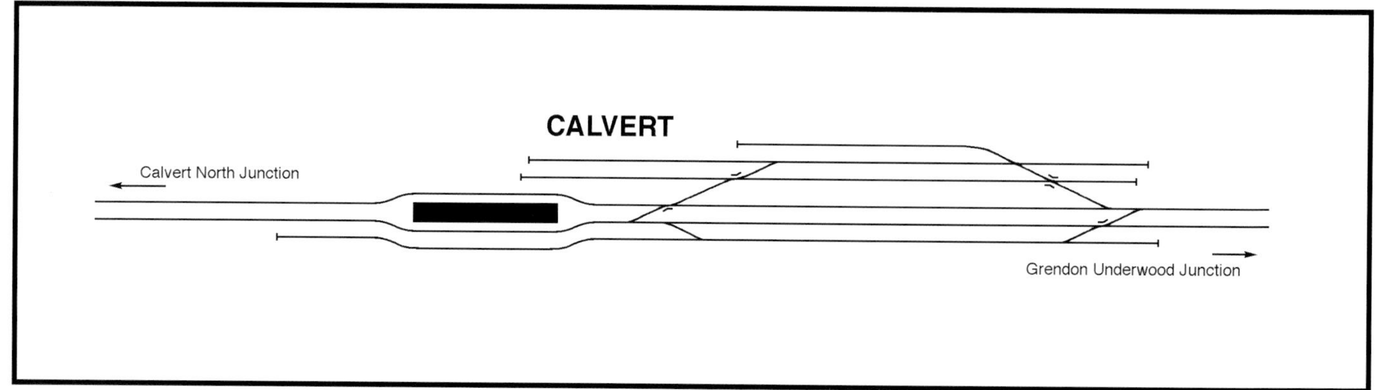

Calvert

Calvert station was named after the local landowner, Sir Harry Calvert, who changed his name to Verney after he inherited the Verney estates. (Another station, Verney Junction, was also named after him!) At Calvert there was a brickworks and associated sidings. This was the last island platform station to be built on the London Extension and was another casualty of the March 1963 closures.

Below:
The line to Ashendon from Grendon Underwood Junction is under construction as the signalman poses in front of his brand-new signal cabin in 1905. The contractors are still working as there is a gate across the track and the down line has yet to be laid. However, the down starting signal has been installed and the point in the foreground will be the down connection to the Ashendon line.
S. W. Newton

Grendon Underwood Junction

Still on GC tracks the next place of significance was Grendon Underwood Junction. It connected the GC to the Great Western at Ashendon Junction and allowed an access to London via High Wycombe and Northolt Junction. This permitted the GC to re-route some trains away from its joint line with the Metropolitan that began at Quainton Road Junction and had been the source of many delays as GC expresses got stuck behind slow-moving Metropolitan suburban services. The link from Grendon Underwood to Ashendon opened for freight traffic in November 1905, with passenger services commencing in April 1906.

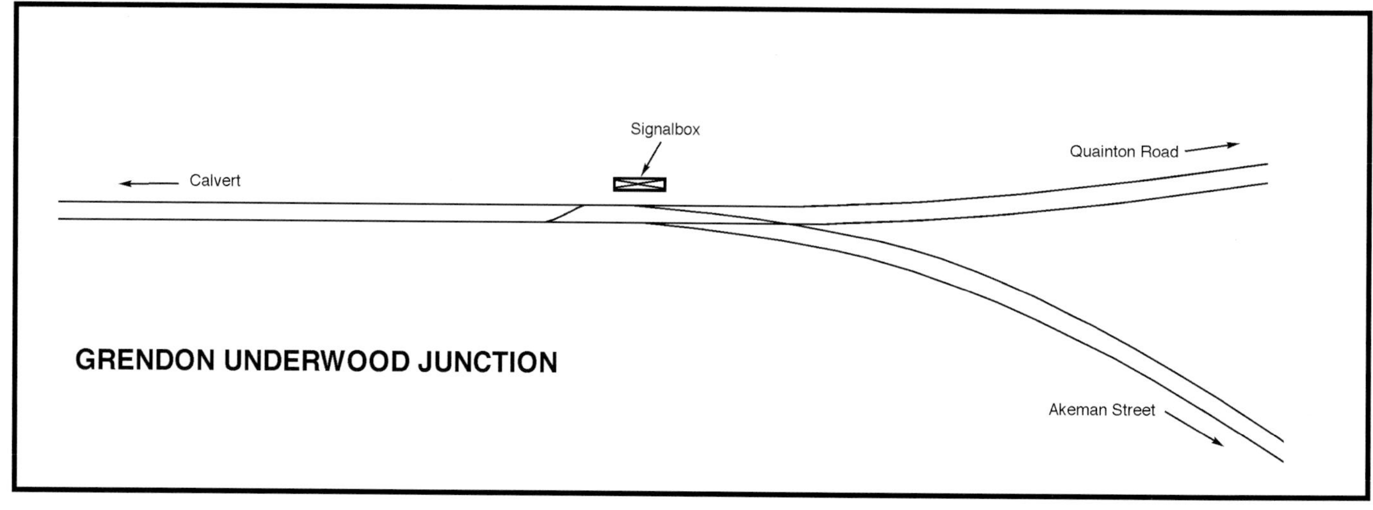

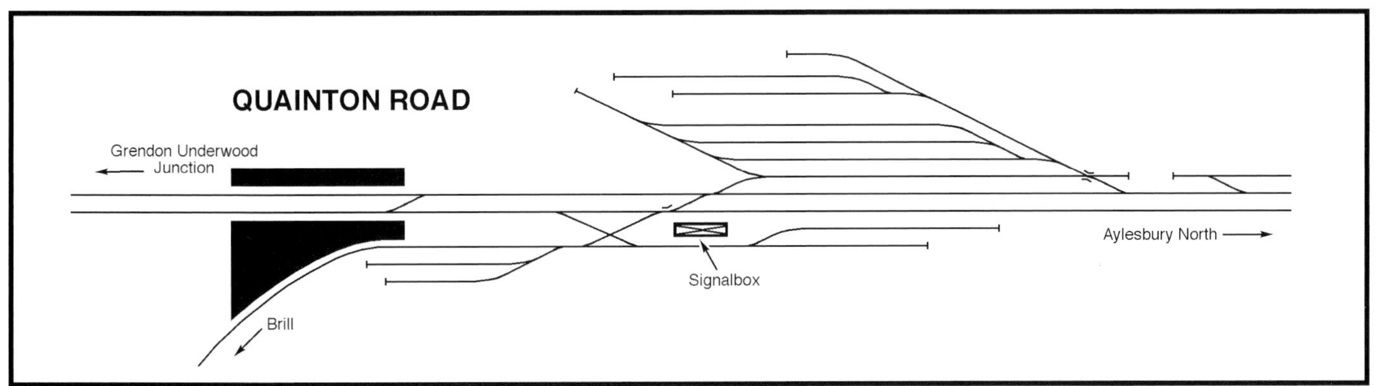

Quainton Road

The Metropolitan Railway ran out as far as Verney Junction on the LNWR Oxford to Bletchley line through Quainton Road where there was also a junction to the hamlet of Brill. The Brill Tramway was opened in 1871 and closed in 1935, Quainton Road, opened as early as 1868 by the Aylesbury & Buckingham Railway, later absorbed by the Metropolitan. The London Extension joined onto the Met at a junction just north of the station, called Quainton Road Junction, where the Met line ran to Verney Junction and from there shared track for most of the way to London. It was not a happy situation due to the GC's fast expresses and comfortable London suburban trains being delayed on the intensively worked Met. line and thus the GC was prompted to build the Ashendon line.

Above:
Quainton Road was a Metropolitan station and was a two-platform affair with a small goods yard. The Metropolitan signalbox can be seen on the down side as can the Brill platform which still had track in 1959. This pattern of station was common on the route to London, except at Aylesbury which was of a more Great Central style. Today the station is preserved along with a collection of locomotives and rolling stock as the Buckinghamshire Railway Centre.
Mike Mitchell

The GW/GC Joint Line — Grendon Underwood Junction via High Wycombe to Neasden South and the Woodford Halse to Banbury Link

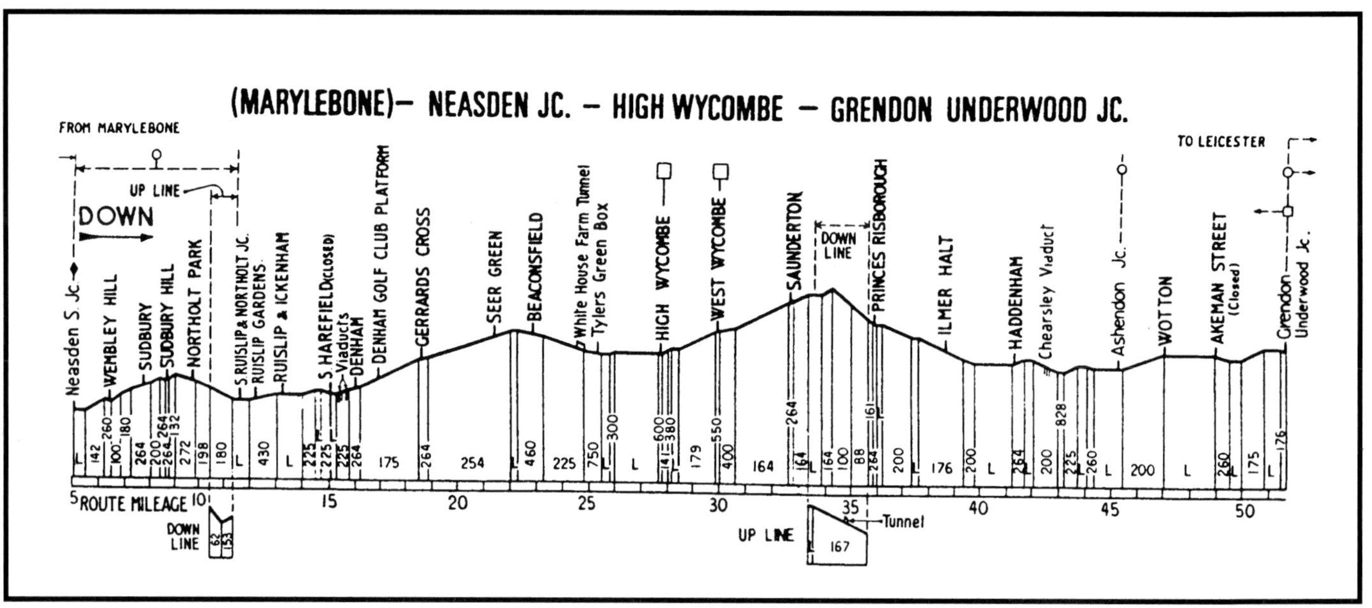

Above:
'London Midlandisation' was clearly in evidence in this photograph taken on 22 August 1959. The LMR had taken over ownership of the route in February 1958 and the 'Master Cutler' had been transferred by the Eastern Region to London King's Cross as a new Pullman service. The GC expresses survived for another 23 months and the 6.18pm from Marylebone to Sheffield — formerly the 'Master Cutler' — continued to run unnamed and with a variety of motive power; in this case, 'Black 5' No 44691. The fertiliser sidings are behind the photographer and the cabin, which closed on 9 December 1967, was still in excellent condition. *Mike Mitchell*

The GW/GC Joint Line

The need for an alternative route to London that avoided the slow trains that delayed the Great Central's on the Met and GC joint line via Aylesbury prompted the Great Western and Great Central to build a new railway. The Great Western was also looking for a new line to bypass Oxford and it seemed logical that a joint approach would prove to be a sensible solution. The route was indeed 4½ miles longer than the Aylesbury line, but was quicker and more easily graded and aligned. Mileposts were measured from Northolt to Ashendon. The Neasden to Northolt section was opened for goods traffic on 20 November 1905, along with the rest of the route through High Wycombe to Ashendon Junction and on to Grendon Underwood Junction, north of Quainton Road. Passenger services followed from March and April 1906.

The line between High Wycombe and Princes Risborough was single track and was taken over on 1 August 1899. This was doubled and re-aligned, together with the construction of a goods yard at High Wycombe and the rebuilding of the stations at West Wycombe and Saunderton. Princes Risborough was completely rebuilt too and a new station was provided at Haddenham. Ashendon was the northern boundary between the two lines and from where the Great Western would extend to Aynho and Banbury to complete the 'Bicester Cut Off'. The line was classic Great Central in construction, consisting of high embankments, deep cuttings and blue brick structures and retaining walls. However, the signalling from Northolt to Ashendon was all GW lower quadrant with GW-style boxes and all the station buildings on this section were also GW pattern. Only the Neasden to Northolt section, Akeman Street and Grendon Underwood Junction were GC structures. From Northolt Junction four tracks were in place to West Ruislip crossing the Metropolitan's Uxbridge line to the south of the station. This was followed by a blue brick viaduct over the Grand Union Canal and then another over the River Colne. Next came Denham station, situated on an embankment and then another viaduct over the River Misbourne (and now the M25 motorway!) before Denham Golf Club Halt and then Gerrards Cross, situated in a deep cutting which required considerable excavation. Beaconsfield followed and then the line proceeded on high embankment through the Chilterns to White House Farm Tunnel. Situated on the side of a hill, the new station at High Wycombe was the junction for Maidenhead and had a retaining wall of one and a quarter million blue bricks. From there the line was doubled through Saunderton to Princes Risborough. From a mile past Saunderton the up and down lines parted and the up line passed through a short tunnel on a grade of 1 in 167, joining again just south of the station throat. This was done to relieve up services from having to climb gradients of up to 1 in 88 as they left the station.

Princes Risborough was the junction for lines to Aylesbury, Watlington and Oxford via Thame. From Princes Risborough the line ran into the Vale of Aylesbury and across Chearsley Viaduct over the River Thame. Then came Haddenham and Ashendon Junction where the Aynho line to Banbury left, the GC forking right under the up GW main and on through Wotton and Akeman Street to Grendon Underwood Junction and the North. Staff wore 'GW & GC JC' on their uniforms. Freight traffic began on 20 November 1905, with passenger services commencing on 2 April 1906. The line from Ashendon to Aynho was completed for freight on 4 April 1910, passenger services following on 1 July. The line was jointly administered between the LNER and the Great Western, but in BR days it was firmly in Western Region territory until regional boundary changes put it into the London Midland Region.

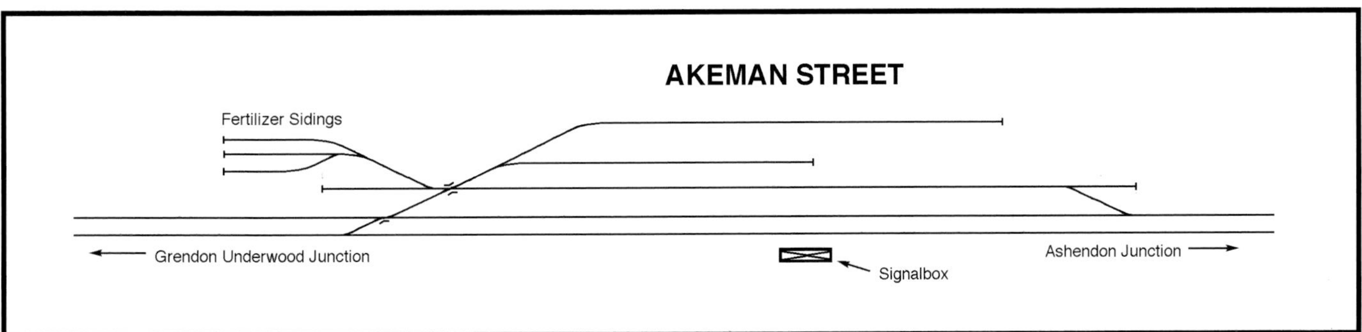

Akeman Street

Two and a half miles from Grendon Underwood Junction came Akeman Street, which at one time had a small halt for local passengers. The line was situated in the Vale of Aylesbury which had a very rural farming population and there were no large towns other than Aylesbury itself, and Princes Risborough on the joint line. Akeman Street was a block post between Grendon Underwood Junction and Ashendon Junction and was laid out with agricultural sidings — the main traffic being fertiliser.

Ashendon Junction

The line from Grendon Underwood joined the GW Birkenhead main line at the remote Ashendon Junction, and was designed for high speed running. The up GW main was carried over the GC on a girder bridge and the GC burrowed underneath. Just before the junction was another small halt at Wotton which was open from November 1905 until 7 December 1953. Amazingly, Wotton had two stations: one on the GC and the other on the Brill Tramway from Quainton Road.

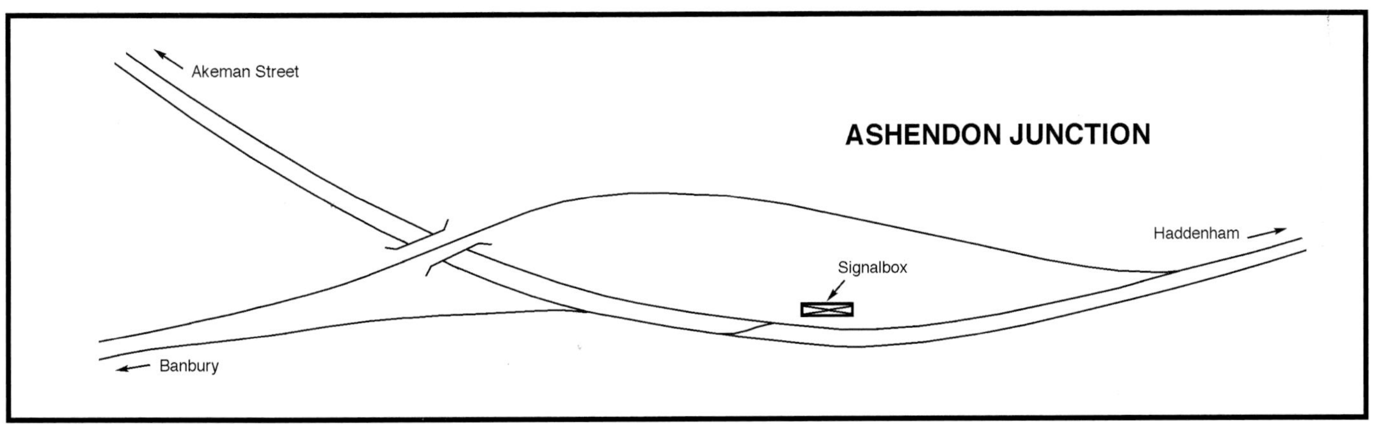

Left:
'V2' No 60863 — one of Leicester's finest — passes beneath the flyover on the up GW main line as it rounds the curve to approach Ashendon Junction with an excursion for Wembley from the North on 27 August 1955. Behind the photographer is the GW up main line and the signalbox is situated on the up side just south of the junction. Ashendon was at the bottom of a dip from Wotton and after a relatively level stretch through Haddenham, a climb up into the Chilterns began. *Stanley Creer*

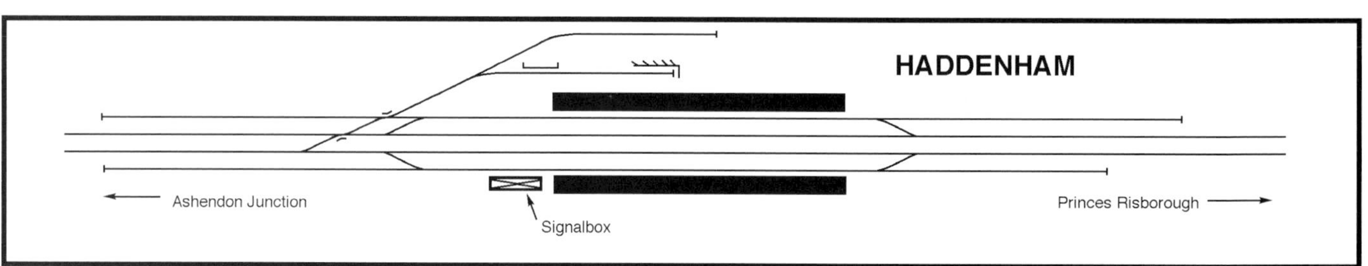

Haddenham

Roughly five miles from Ashendon came Haddenham — a typical Bicester cut-off GW station with platforms situated on the passing loops.

Below:
'A3' Pacific No 60050 *Persimmon* passes the Thame road bridge near Haddenham station in May 1949. The locomotive looks rather grubby as it runs light to the South. This scene is typical of the bridge structures and deep cuttings that the joint line had — and still has to this day. No 60050 carries 'King's Cross' on its bufferbeam and looks to be still carrying LNER apple green livery with 'British Railways' on the tender. *H. K. Harman/Rail Archive Stephenson*

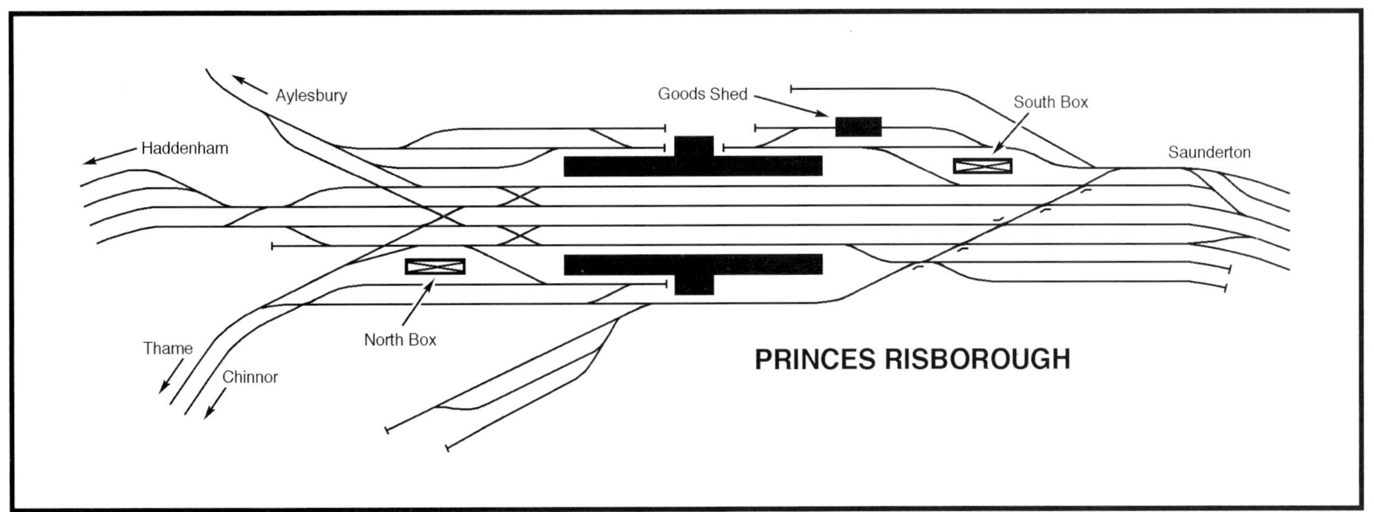

Princes Risborough

Princes Risborough was an important junction with branches coming in from Chinnor, Oxford and Aylesbury. It was situated on the climb into the Chilterns and GC down trains would pass through at high speed. A marvellous recording exists — made by Peter Handford and called *Trains in the Night* — of a diverted GC newspaper train passing through Princes Risborough with 'V2' No 60831 in charge. It will give the listener some idea as to the spirit of the GC as the train passes through at high speed and can be heard for many minutes crossing the Vale of Aylesbury before whistling up for Ashendon Junction.

Right:
A scene from the down island platform at Princes Risborough sees '5400' class No 5420 of Banbury shed with a stopper from High Wycombe to Banbury in August 1960. The fast lines are visible to the right of the train and a suburban train for Paddington is waiting to leave. *G. C. Farnell*

Right:
At the southern end of Princes Risborough, the South box evident on the right of the photograph, a Woodford 'Austerity', No 90137, waits in the up loop, having passed through the up platform, with a general merchandise train for Neasden yards in July 1957. Pannier tank No 4680 (85B, Gloucester) indulges in some shunting in the up sidings. Behind the train the station footbridge can be seen linking the up side platform, which had a bay for the Aylesbury service, to the down island platform. Just to the south of this point, the up and down lines parted for 2½ miles to allow up trains an easier climb through the Chilterns on their way to Saunderton. *G. C. Farnell*

Above:
'9F' No 92092 passes Princes Risborough North with a mixed goods train for the London area from Woodford Halse on 26 September 1964. Usually a Woodford locomotive would have undertaken this work, but No 92092, an Annesley engine, must have been made available to cover a failure — it was not common practice to take an Annesley locomotive south of Woodford. The points leading to the Chinnor and Oxford lines can be seen just beyond the signalbox.
Brian Stephenson

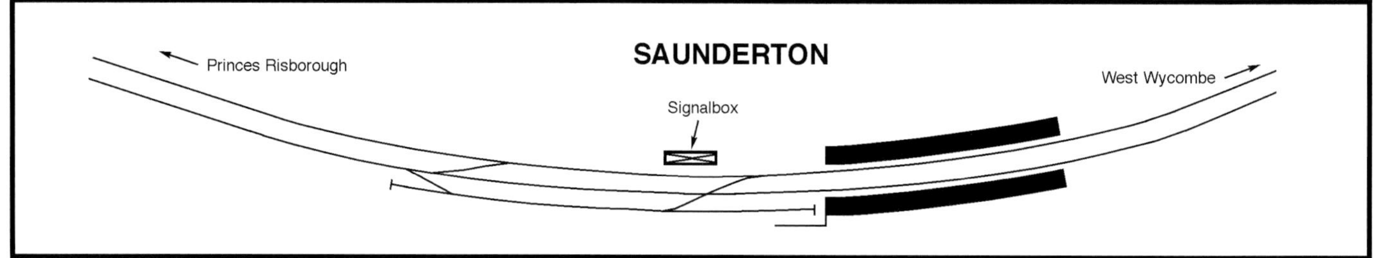

Saunderton

Saunderton is a simple two-platform station with GW-style buildings, as had all other stations on the joint line. The station is situated on the long descent to High Wycombe. On 10 March 1913, Saunderton was nearly destroyed by a fire, allegedly started by suffragettes.

Left:
Looking towards Princes Risborough, a good view of the station can be seen from the footbridge. The signalbox, of Great Western design, as were all those on the joint line, is on the up side, the small goods loop on the down. A '9400' class pannier tank storms the 1 in 164 climb through the station on its way to Princes Risborough in July 1961.
C. R. L. Coles/Rail Archive Stephenson

Right:
'2884' class No 3837 passes down the grade through West Wycombe towards High Wycombe with a train from the West Midlands to London. The '28XXs' often worked through to Woodford Halse via the Banbury line and were a common site on the GC main line as far as Woodford. West Wycombe station can be seen in the background, along with the signalbox, but the goods yard has been lifted. Behind the station, on the side of the hill, is West Wycombe church which was quite a tourist attraction in Victorian times. The date is 26 September 1964. *Brian Stephenson*

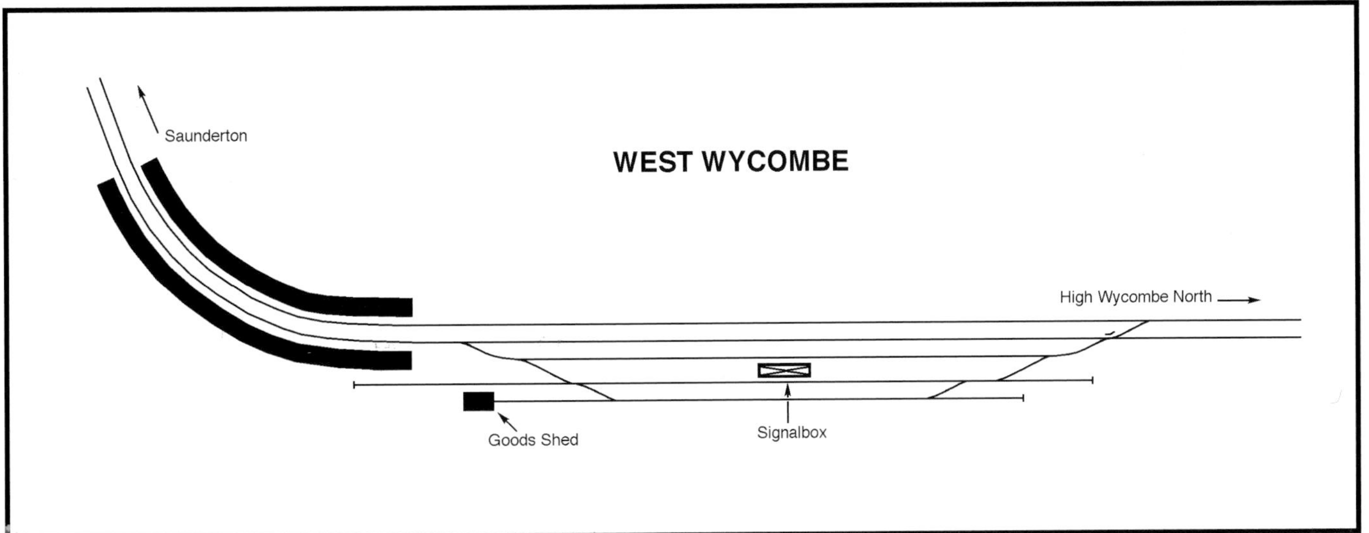

West Wycombe

The small station of West Wycombe was situated on a curve roughly two miles from High Wycombe station. It had a signalbox and a small goods yard and was on the descent from Saunderton to High Wycombe.

High Wycombe North

High Wycombe station is approached on a long reverse curve and the main goods yard was situated to the north of the station at High Wycombe North.

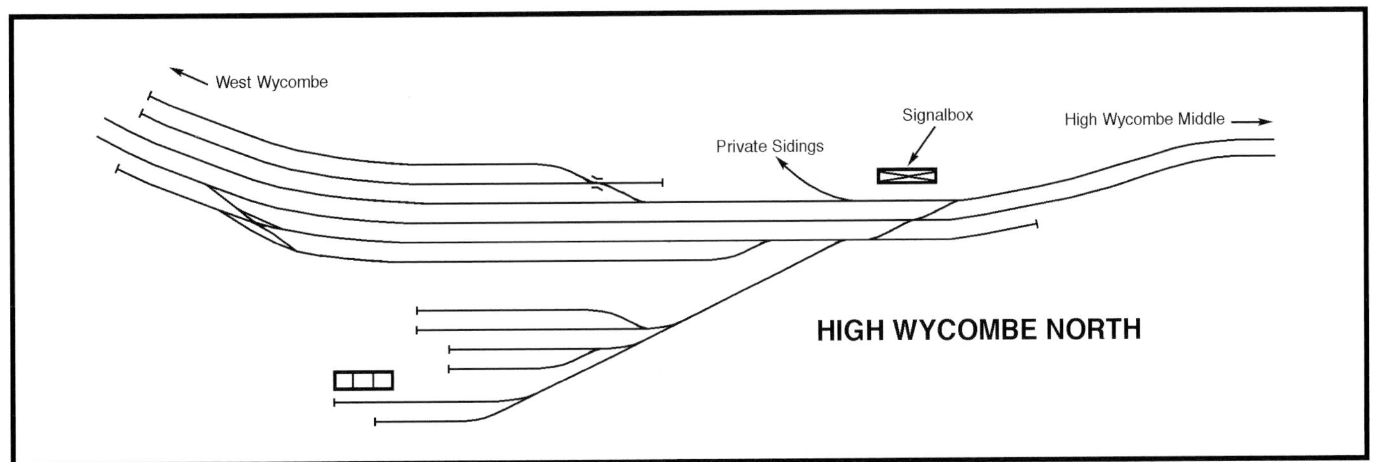

Above:
The goods yards are evident to the right of the train, complete with mobile cranes. Prairie tank No 6142 makes a brisk start from High Wycombe and passes the North goods yards with the 3.46pm High Wycombe to Aylesbury on 15 May 1962.
H. K. Harman/Rail Archive Stephenson

High Wycombe

High Wycombe station is approached via the reverse curve from High Wycombe North before the loops for the platforms are reached. It was controlled by High Wycombe South signalbox and was at the junction for the line to Bourne End and Maidenhead. The platforms are situated on two long loops either side of now-lifted through roads and linked by means of a subway. A bay platform was provided on the down side for turning back trains to London and for the since-closed Maidenhead service, which often ran through Princes Risborough to Aylesbury to provide connections to the GC service.

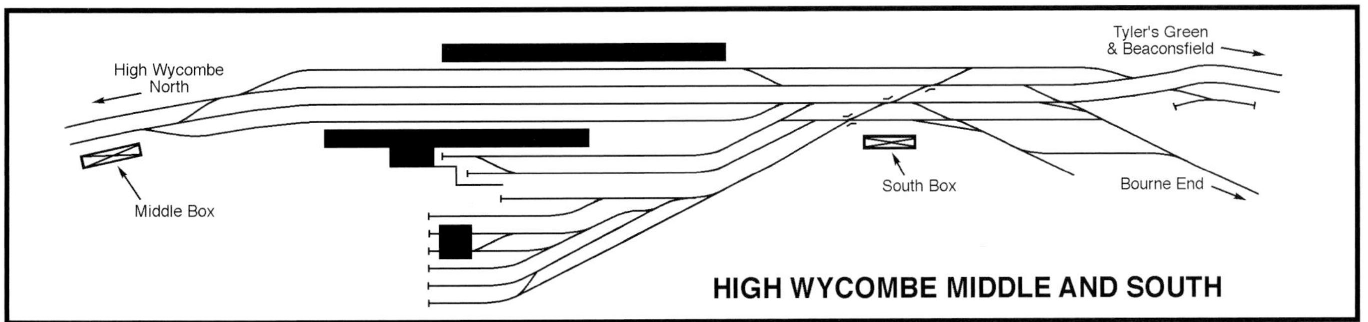

Below left:
'B1' No 61167 of Mexborough/Wath passes High Wycombe with a Mexborough to Marylebone excursion on 11 March 1961. The large retaining wall, a notable feature of High Wycombe station, for it was cut into the side of the Chiltern Hills at this point, is evident as are the banner repeaters for the signals in the cutting just to the north of the station platforms. These through roads were lifted as part of the 'Chiltern Line' route modernisation that was carried out in the 1980s.
H. K. Harman/Rail Archive Stephenson

Right:
After running out of the station area the branch to Bourne End dropped away from the main line running down across the valley to the south east. Just beyond the junction on 28 July 1963, 'Patriot' No 45534 *E. Tootal Broadhurst* of Crewe North, sets off from High Wycombe with the overnight 9.25pm from Glasgow Central (having left on the 27th) to Kensington Olympia which had been diverted into Marylebone. It is travelling 'wrong line' after setting back to run to Beaconsfield due to PW work on the down main line.
H. K. Harman/Rail Archive Stephenson

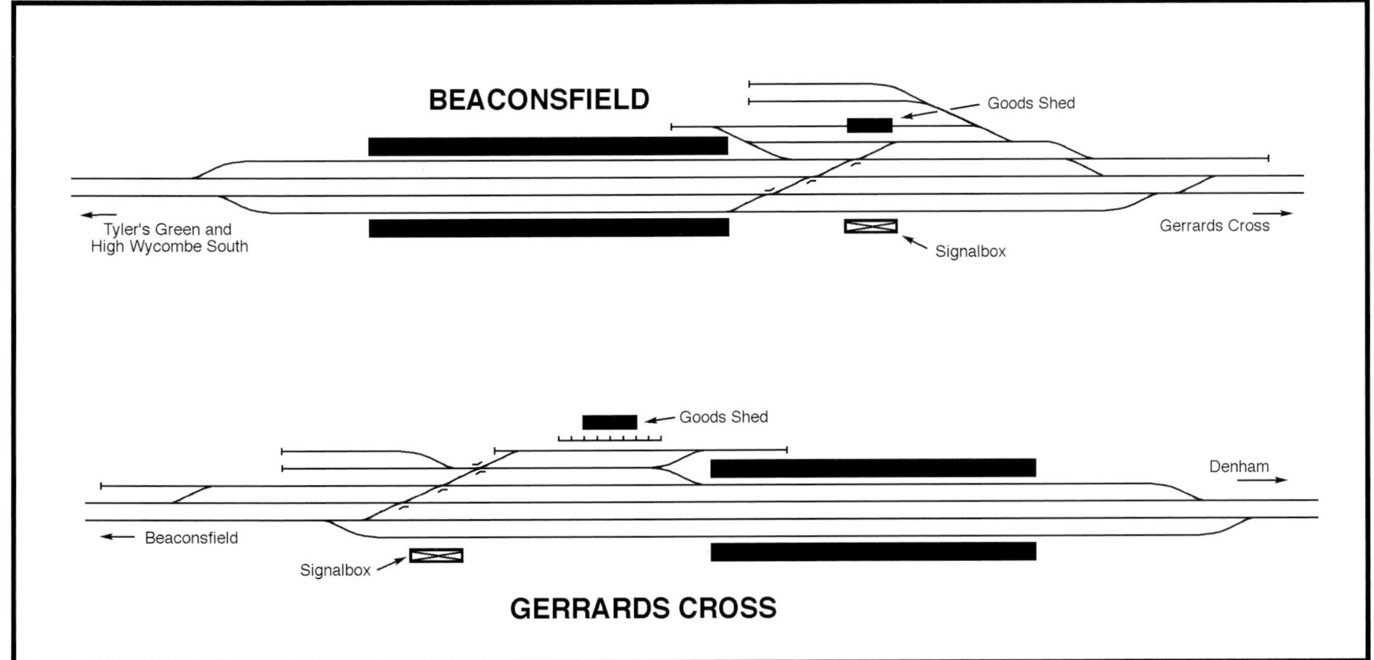

Gerrards Cross and Beaconsfield

From High Wycombe the line runs virtually level, high in the Chilterns to White House Farm Tunnel passing the block post of Tyler's Green.

From the tunnel a 1 in 225 climb to Beaconsfield begins. Beaconsfield is roughly similar in layout and situation to Gerrards Cross. Both stations are located in deep cuttings with, until the modernisation scheme in the 1980s, passing loops and small goods depots for general merchandise traffic. From Beaconsfield, the line drops down though Seer Green & Jordans Halt to Gerrards Cross.

Above:
'L1' tanks were common on the Marylebone suburban services, replacing the 'A5' GC types and were in turn replaced by Stanier and Fairburn 2-6-4Ts under the London Midland Region. They in turn were replaced by DMUs, but on 27 July 1957, 'L1s' from Neasden were still very much in charge. No 67767 arrives at Gerrards Cross with the 5.33pm to Marylebone. The box can be seen on the down side in the distance and the small goods yard is evident just behind the train. The brick building in the foreground is the goods office.
K. L. Cook/Rail Archive Stephenson

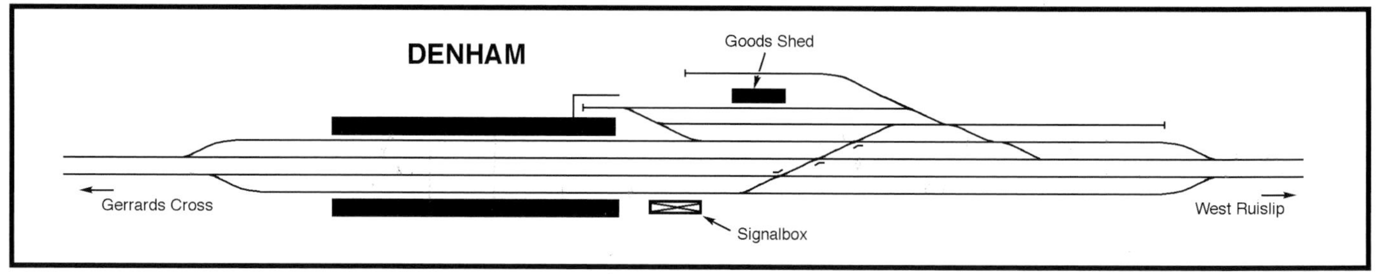

Denham

On the descent from Gerrards Cross to Denham, Denham Golf Club Halt was passed. Denham was a small station, with passing loops and a small goods yard and also served the nearby village of Harefield.

Left:
A wet day at Denham station on 9 February 1957 sees the 12.20pm 'Footex' from Whitton to High Wycombe passing Denham on the now-removed centre roads. A Southern Region BR Standard '5', No 73118 of Nine Elms, is the motive power and the train is made up of Southern stock. The small goods yard can be seen to the left of the train. The signalbox was situated on the down platform and the station buildings, which still survive, are typical Great Western design. *Neil Sprinks*

Above:
Before the extension of the Central Line, 'A5' tank No 5046 pulls into the loop at West Ruislip on a suburban train for Marylebone in 1934. Here began a four-track section that ran up to Northolt Junction, where the GC branched off for Neasden and Marylebone. The loop in the photograph was extended with a point leading off to the depot at West Ruislip, following the advent of the Central Line. It still provides a connection between the two networks for Underground trains to travel to contractors for refurbishment and repairs.
H. Gordon Tidey/Rail Archive Stephenson

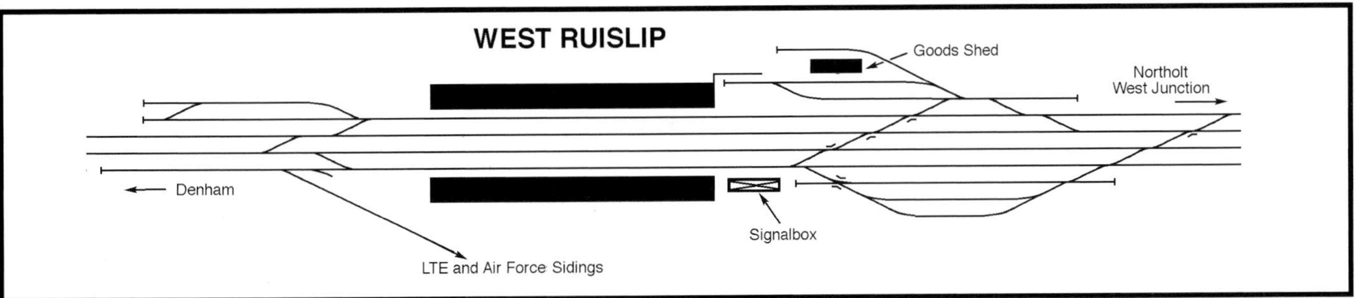

West Ruislip

Once past Denham came Denham East where a short branch, opened on 1 May 1907, ran to Uxbridge. Then came the blue brick viaducts over the Lido where so many famous films were made. The Central Line was eventually extended out to West Ruislip, opening in 1948, which involved the construction of a new depot.

Northolt West Junction-South Ruislip-Northolt East Junction

From West Ruislip, the four-track section continued through South Ruislip to Northolt East Junction.

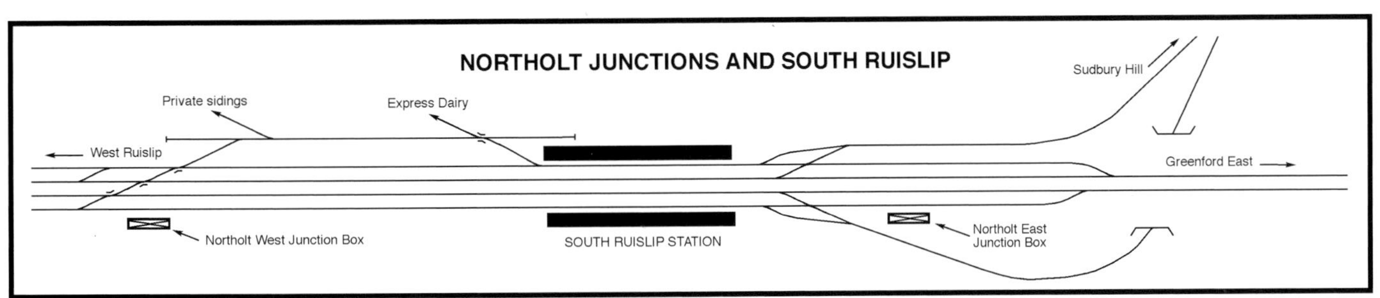

Left:
In 1948 an up Great Central line train for Marylebone is seen approaching the station at South Ruislip behind 'A5' tank (GC Class 45) No 9824. GWR pannier tank No 5799 is seen shunting one of the private sidings at South Ruislip. Northolt West Junction box was situated on the down side, virtually opposite to the end of the last carriage and in the distance, framed by the signal gantry, West Ruislip signalbox can just be seen, which stood at the end of the down platform of the station. *C. R. L. Coles/Ian Allan Library*

Centre left:
From the station at South Ruislip, on 7 July 1954, the down 'Master Cutler', which had left Marylebone at 6.15pm, crosses onto the down main line having passed Northolt East Junction box, just visible behind the train. The train will have passed under the GW main line as the down line from Neasden South burrows under the line to Paddington. It was here that the 'Master Cutler' used to get delayed behind a GW 'King' on the 6.15pm Paddington to Wolverhampton — the cause of much colourful comment from the crew! The Neasden 'B1' will put up a credible performance, (it must have replaced an 'A3' or a 'V2'), and the crew will no doubt 'flail it along' on its run to Leicester. The 'Cutler' headboard shows the coats of arms of Sheffield and London and is in ER blue. South Ruislip station has GW-style buildings while the more modern Central Line station can just be seen on the right.
Neil Sprinks

Below:
With the centre roads for through running still in situ, a Marylebone DMU set that forms the 12.46 Marylebone to High Wycombe calls additionally at Sudbury Hill on 15 March 1972. These units dominated the London end of the GC for nearly 30 years, having replaced the steam suburban service in the early 1960s, even venturing as far as Nottingham Victoria on one diagram, the 08.38 from Marylebone and its return working at 12.25 from Nottingham.
G. S. Cocks

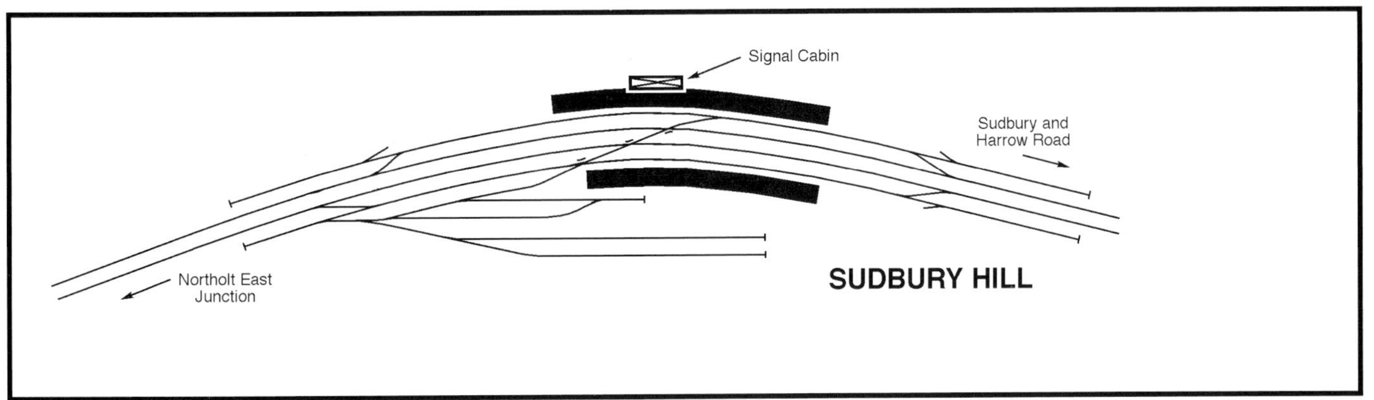

Sudbury Hill

From Northolt, the GC was back on its own tracks and passed through the small station of Northolt Park. Next came the more substantial station of Sudbury Hill where the signalbox was situated on the up side platform and there was a small goods yard.

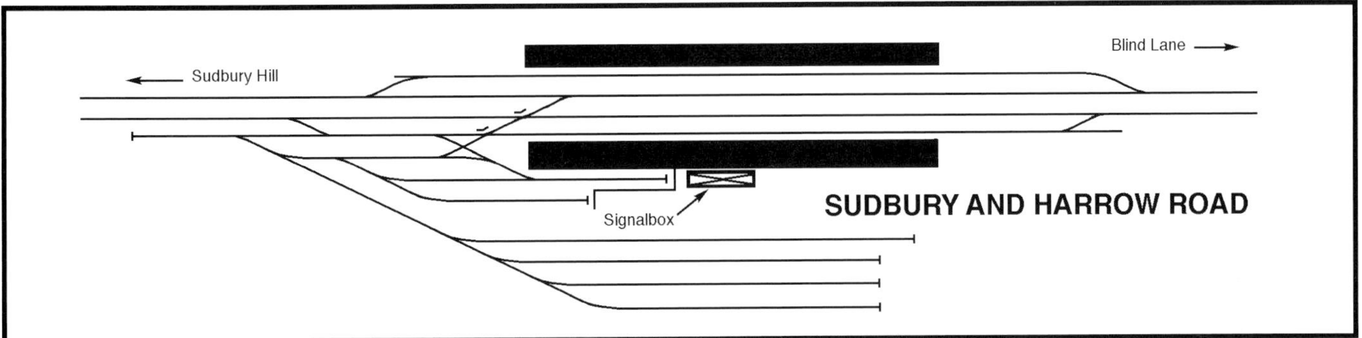

Sudbury & Harrow Road

The next station was Sudbury & Harrow Road, only a mile on from Sudbury Hill and virtually identical in terms of layout. It was here that the Great Central tested the Brown Mackenzie automatic electric signalling apparatus and equipped a locomotive with collector gear and signal repeater indicators.

Below:
A contrast in motive power to the last photograph and which shows Sudbury & Harrow Road station. The signalbox can be seen on the down platform on which side were also located the goods sidings. Expresses used the centre roads through all the joint line stations and a Marylebone to Immingham boat train passes through with GC 'B3' No 6167 in charge in 1937. *C. R. L Coles/Rail Archive Stephenson*

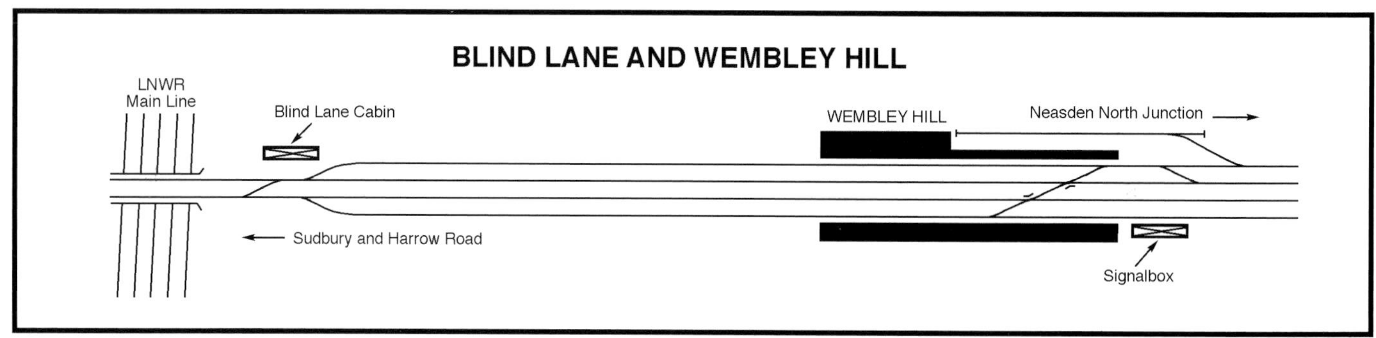

Wembley Hill

From Sudbury & Harrow Road the line crossed over the LNWR main line on a girder bridge and then quadrupled at Blind Lane (the signal cabin now being at Rothley on the Great Central preserved section). Next came Wembley Hill, now known as Wembley Complex, where a station was sited for both the local area and Wembley Stadium, and where many GC line special trains started from or terminated.

Below:
On 13 May 1953 the 6.15pm 'Master Cutler' with 'A3' No 60108 *Gay Crusader* in charge storms through Wembley Hill on its way to Sheffield. Note the GC signals and signalbox and the four-track formation which extended from Neasden to Blind Lane. *Neil Sprinks*

Neasden North and South Junctions

From Wembley Hill the four-track section spawned goods sidings both on the up and down sides where wagons were interchanged with other lines. The famous Wembley Stadium loop also branched off here and was used for turning locomotives as well as trains. At Neasden South (the box now residing at the Nottingham Heritage Centre at Ruddington) the connection was made to the GC/Met line from Aylesbury and the journey via the joint line was complete.

Above:
'Schools' class locomotives and, for that matter, many other types of locomotive were common sites at the southern end on the London Extension as they accessed Wembley Stadium or Wembley Hill with special excursion trains. No 30938 *St Olave's* from Stewart's Lane shed takes the western-most entrance to the Stadium station loop in April 1959, complete with a train of Southern stock. The four-track main line is to the right, beyond which was the North signalbox and down sidings. At Neasden the Great Central's London locomotive depot was also situated, along with connections to the West London line. *C. R. L. Coles/Rail Archive Stephenson*

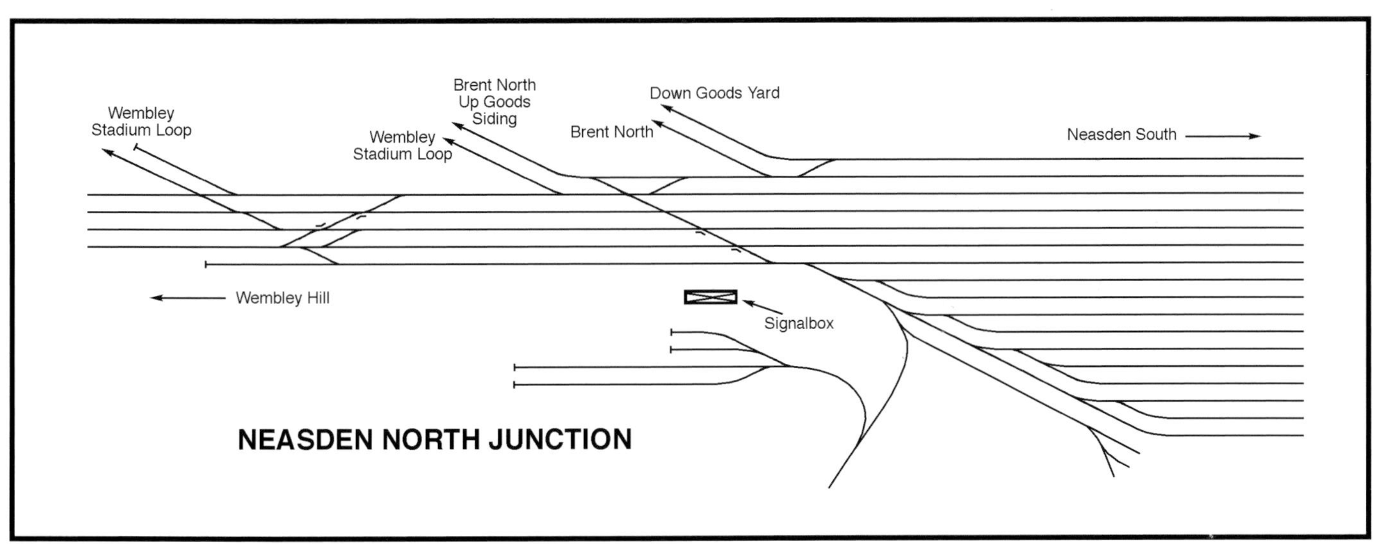

Banbury to Woodford Halse

The Banbury 'Branch'

One of the most important features of the London Extension was the 8¾ mile link to Banbury Junction from Culworth Junction. It provided the GC with an important link to the Great Western for both freight and long-distance cross-country passenger trains which Sam Fay was eager to exploit. Goods services began to operate on 1 June 1900 and use of the Aylesbury route to the Great Western at Princes Risborough ceased for through traffic. The Great Western commenced through services for passengers on 13 August 1900 running from Oxford to Leicester, later calling additionally at Banbury. The GC commenced services in late 1900 with a local service from Woodford to Banbury that connected to trains at either end. But although throughout the life of the London Extension the Banbury branch was regularly used by passenger trains, it was equally if not more important as a freight carrier linking the yards at Woodford with the Great Western. It is a sobering thought that over one million wagons per year were exchanged at Woodford in the 1950s, the majority traversing the Banbury line. Where has all this traffic gone today one wonders? The line also had two halts — at Chalcombe Road, opened on 17 April 1911, and at Eydon Road, opened on 1 October 1913. A feature of the line was deep cuttings with large blue brick viaducts carrying lanes over the railway. Many of these are still in situ today, but gone are the reception yards at Banbury, together with Banbury Junction. However, Banbury's 'modern' station still has one bay with track on the down side for the 'Banbury Motor' and the up side Woodford platform is still there, but trackless.

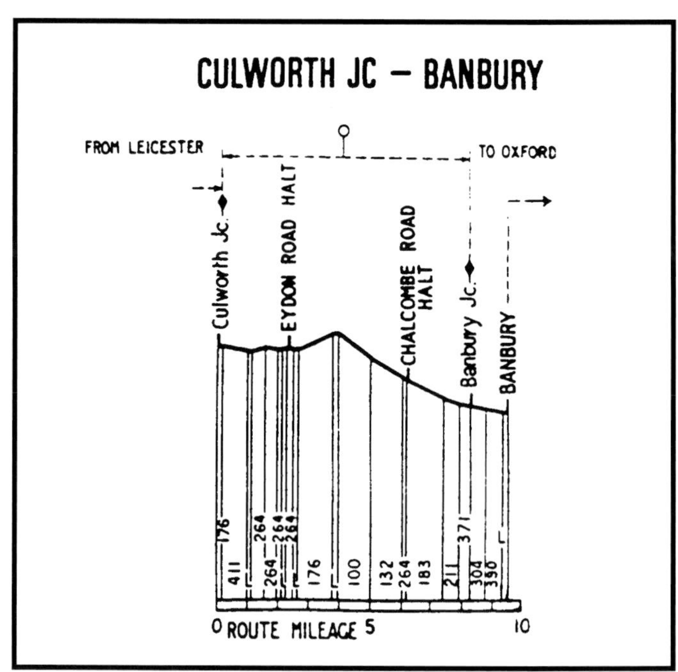

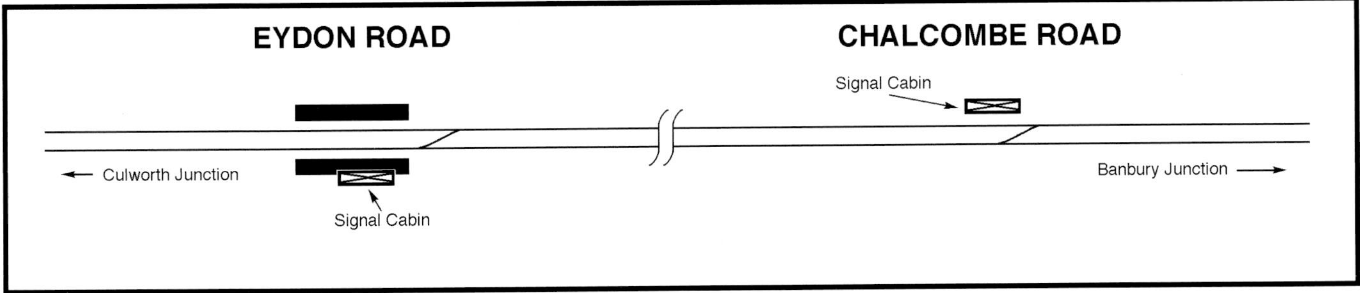

Left:
The signalman seems to be relaxing in a rather comfortable wooden chair as the 12.30pm 'Banbury Motor' arrives at Eydon Road on 6 May 1953. The train is three corridor coaches plus 'J11' No 64369. The 'Banbury Motor' had been worked as a motor train service — hence the name — but after that short-lived era was replaced by a conventional locomotive and coaches. The 'Motor' was withdrawn from 1963 when replaced by buses as the only other services were long-distance cross-country passenger trains that ran at inconvenient times for the local traveller. Eydon Road and Chalcombe Road were most useful as block posts on this line which was busy with many transfer freights and cross-country passenger services, especially during the summer months. *Neil Sprinks*

Eydon Road and Chalcombe Road

From Culworth Junction, the first halt was Eydon Road, situated some 2¼ miles away. It was a simple two-platform station as was the next halt at Chalcombe Road. The line climbed at 1 in 176 through Eydon Road and thence descended to Banbury Junction (after passing Chalcombe Road Halt on the way), 8¼ miles from Culworth Junction.

Banbury General

Banbury General station was situated south of new yards built on the up side for traffic to arrive on the GW from the GC, the lines joining at Banbury Junction. Banbury General had bay platforms at the north end for trains to and from Woodford and main line cross-country trains changed locomotives in the station roads, the relief engine usually being stabled in a bay platform. Banbury station was rebuilt in the 1950s, still with facilities for GC line trains including a down bay platform. Banbury depot was also used to stable GC line locomotives in 1965 after Annesley and Willesden had closed. This involved long-distance light engine running which made the GC even less economic to its unfriendly masters.

Above:
In this August 1956 view of Banbury, taken from the north end, 'V2' No 60863 waits with a 'Motor' for Woodford Halse as station pilot 'Hall' class No 6906 *Chicheley Hall* shunts a goods train on the up main line. It was in these centre roads that GC line expresses would change locomotives as necessary. Banbury Merton Street, terminus of the LNWR branch from Buckingham, was situated behind the GW goods yard to the left of the photograph.
Real Photographs/Ian Allan Library

Aylesbury to London Marylebone

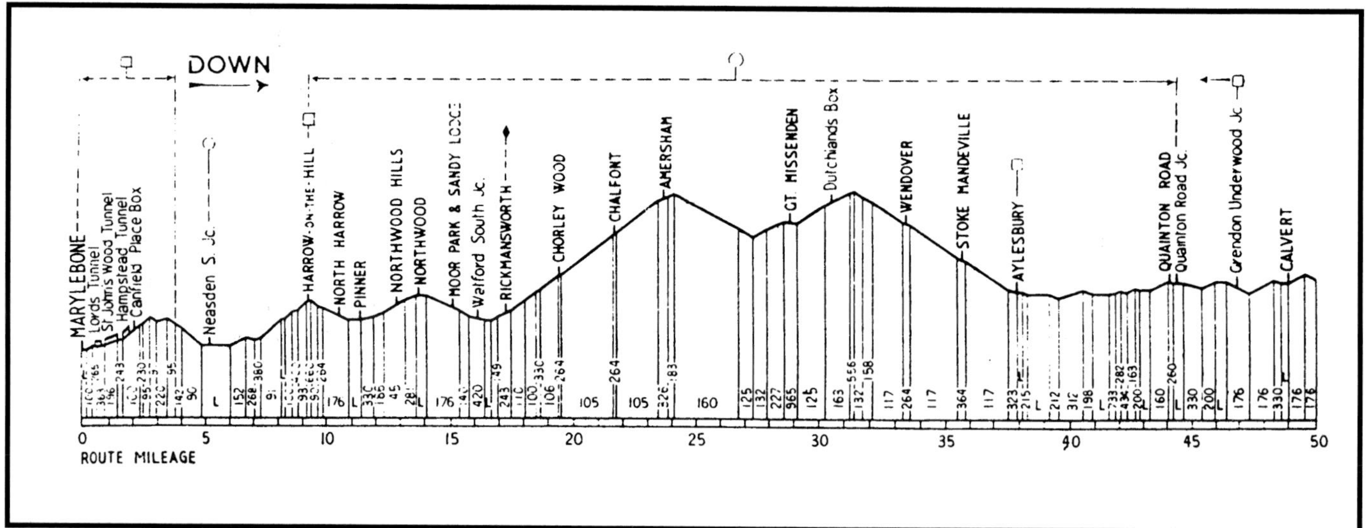

Aylesbury

From Quainton Road Junction and station the line passed through the Vale of Aylesbury on a virtually level course through a small halt at Waddesdon, a two-platform structure built to serve the village. The Aylesbury & Buckingham Railway from Verney Junction met with the Metropolitan at Quainton Road Junction, complete with the branch to Brill. From the start, the relationship between the Met and the GC had never been good. By the end of 1901, Pollitt was no longer the GC's General Manager and Bell was no longer Chairman of the Metropolitan and it was time to put past disputes behind the two partners. The original Met and GC act of 1899 had caused a dispute of over £1 million to arise — mainly in the allocation of passenger receipts and running costs. However, this was settled in 1904 and the Met was assured of revenue; it then allowed GC trains to call at local stations to Aylesbury via Amersham — until then they had only been allowed to run a suburban service via High Wycombe. A new act in 1905 confirmed the situation and the suburban service began a year later. The Metropolitan and Great Central Joint Committee were responsible for its administration and included lines out to Verney Junction and Brill. Aylesbury station was joint line property and was situated on a sharp curve south of the main station. In 1907 this was improved, together with a new GC signalbox at Aylesbury South. The station acquired GC style station buildings which have survived the Total Route Modernisation of the 1980s. The goods yard was to the north of the station on the down side and there was a small locomotive shed, an outbase of Neasden, on the down side by the down island platform where trains terminated on the GW branch from Princes Risborough — a one-time link for freight to the Great Western before the Banbury to Woodford line had opened.

Above right:
Looking north towards the goods yard on the right, as 'B1' No 61156 approaches Aylesbury with the up 'South Yorkshireman', the 10am Bradford to Marylebone in 1950. The locomotive still carries 'British Railways' on the tender and the 11-coach train is all Thompson stock except for the Gresley catering kitchen and dining car in the centre of the formation. The North box can be seen next to the sixth coach. *C. R. L. Coles/Rail Archive Stephenson*

Right:
GC services were rarely double-headed as it was considered uneconomic and light engine movements also wasted track capacity space. So double-heading was reserved for especially heavy services or excursions; pilot locomotives were generally attached to a service train for their balancing working again, saving a path. Other double heading was caused by failures although it is unclear if that has happened in this case. An up 'Ord' with a 'B1' piloted by 'Black 5' No 44862, which was working back to the London area and then back to Rugby Midland shed, waits to leave Aylesbury in August 1960. The up bay can be seen to the right with parcels vans in one of the sidings, the photographer standing on the down platform. A GW auto train with a Class 1400 0-4-2T at the head can just be seen on the left in the platform, with a train for Princes Risborough. *G. C. Farnell*

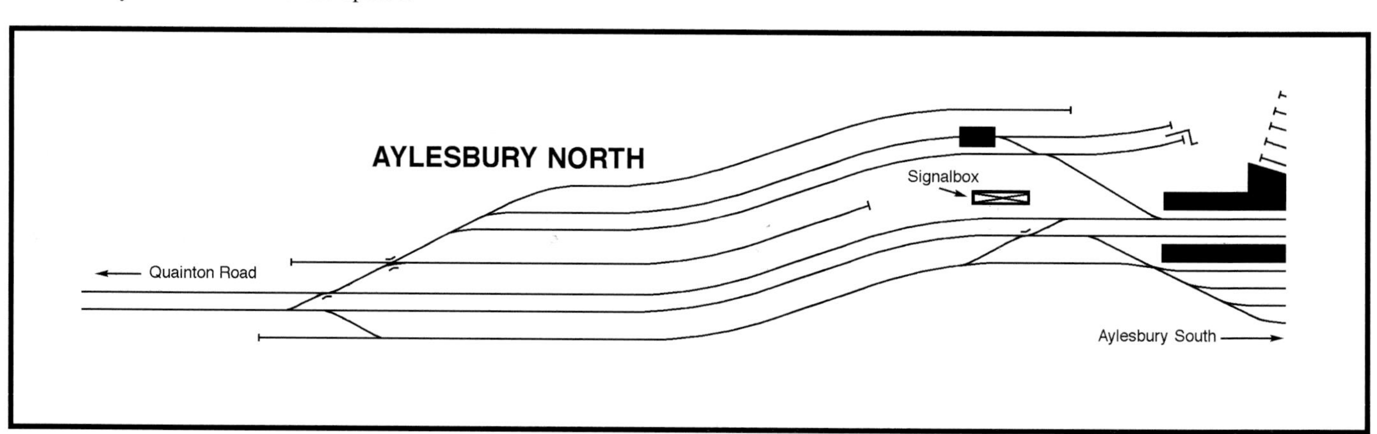

61156

44862

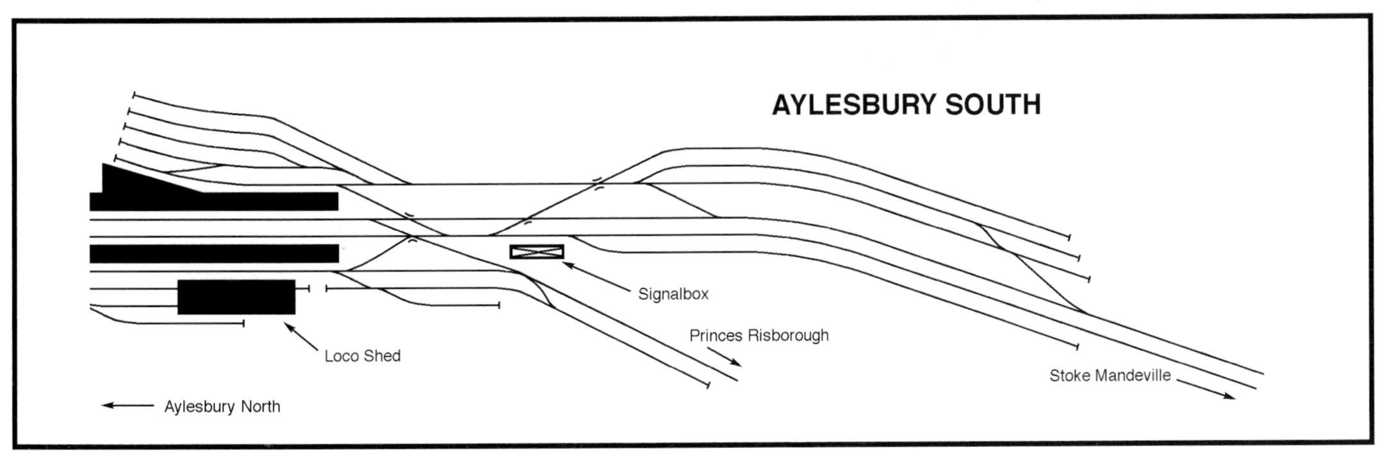
AYLESBURY SOUTH
Signalbox
Loco Shed
Princes Risborough
Stoke Mandeville
Aylesbury North

Above:
The GC signalbox at Aylesbury South can just be seen as the 10am Bradford to Marylebone 'South Yorkshireman' gets away from Aylesbury with 'A3' Pacific No 60049 *Galtee More* in charge on 16 August 1952. This view of the train sees many more Gresley coaches in the formation and some Gresley suburban coaches are also stabled in the sidings adjacent to the Princes Risborough branch on the left. The signal posts are of GC origin but have been fitted with BR signal arms, while the Princes Risborough branch post is a newer structure. *Neil Sprinks*

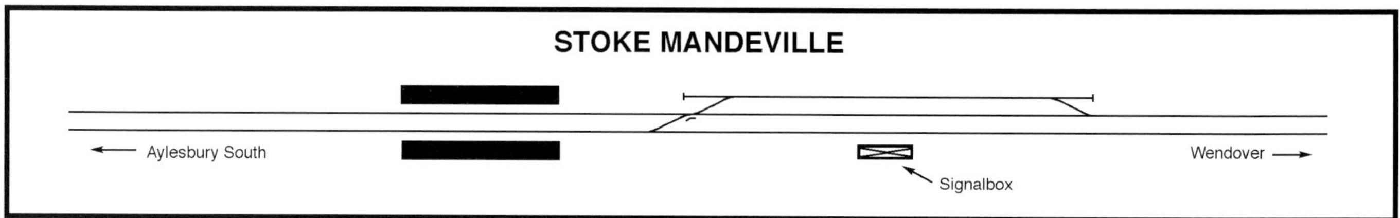

Stoke Mandeville

Immediately after leaving Aylesbury a stiff climb of seven miles followed into the Chilterns. No longer subject to the 1 in 176 ruling gradient, this section was as steep as 1 in 117. The first station was at Stoke Mandeville and from here onwards all stations were of Metropolitan design, with Met signalboxes.

Left:
With the Met signalbox clearly evident (but with LNER nameboard) on the down side, there is another view of the up 'South Yorkshireman', this time at Stoke Mandeville. 'V2' No 60831 from Leicester heads the train on 22 April 1953. The station is behind the train and has two platforms, the GC island variety having finished at Calvert. There was an up siding for freight which can be seen to the right of the locomotive. *Neil Sprinks*

Right:
'B1' No 61179 climbs through Wendover with a relief train to the 10.25am Manchester to Marylebone on Good Friday, 11 April 1952. Relief trains often preceded the expresses, especially on public holidays and on summer Saturdays. *Neil Sprinks*

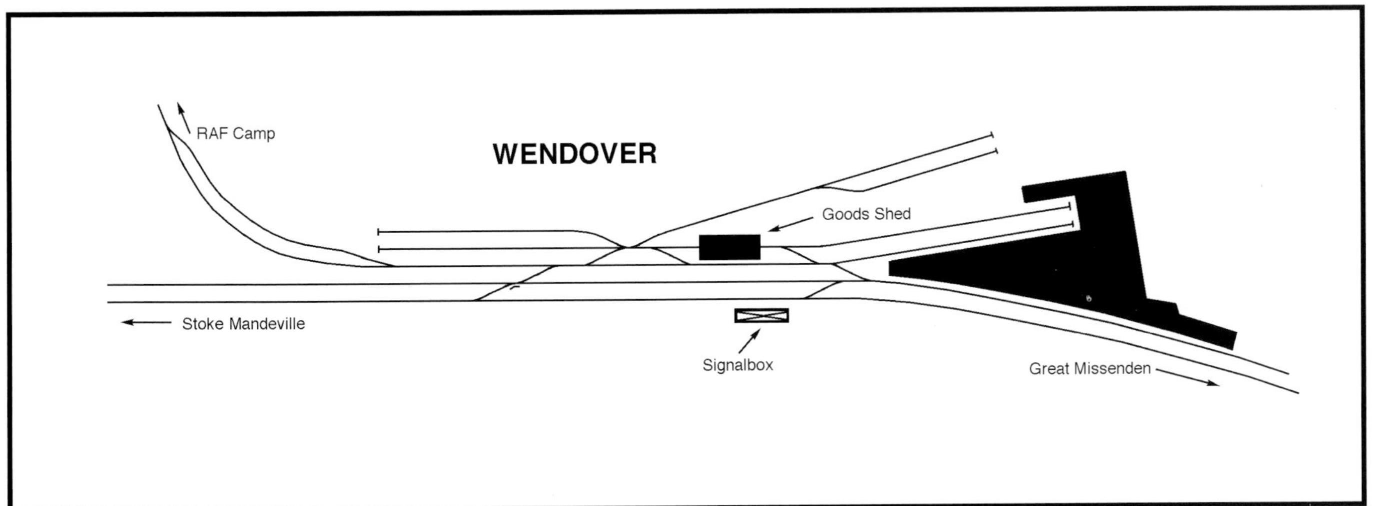

Wendover

Still on the 1 in 117 grade, the next station is Wendover. Wendover was similar to Stoke Mandeville but had much more extensive sidings as a short branch from RAF Halton joined here on the up side, just north of the station. Wendover also had a goods shed and a goods loading bay as well as a small yard.

Great Missenden

Great Missenden is approximately 4½ miles from Wendover. At Milepost 28½ the GC took over maintenance of the line from the Metropolitan, which was responsible as far as Harrow-on-the-Hill. The summit of the climb from Aylesbury is passed just before Dutchlands where there was a signalbox. From there a descent towards Great Missenden begins before a short switchback through the station leads to another 1 in 160 climb to Amersham.

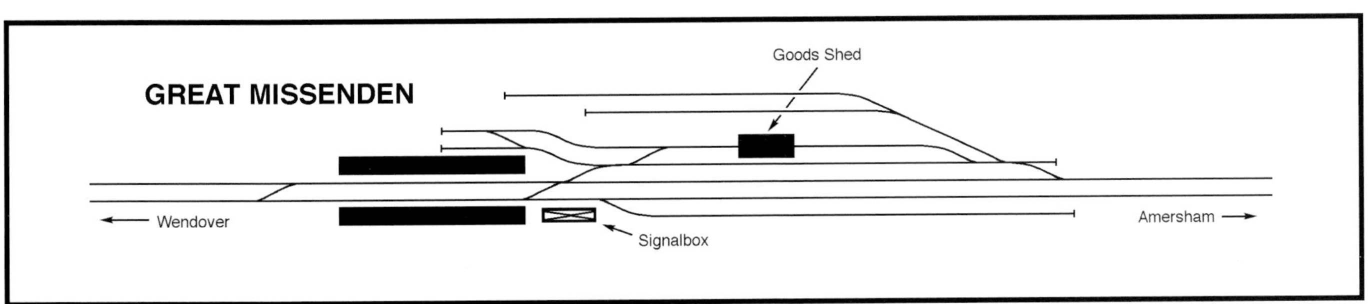

Left:
In June 1957 a northbound 'Ord' from Marylebone to Woodford waits to leave Great Missenden. The slight descent and rise in grade can be clearly seen in the track formation as 'B1' No 61299 simmers at the head of the train. The goods yard was on the up southern side of the station which had its own goods shed. *G. C. Farnell*

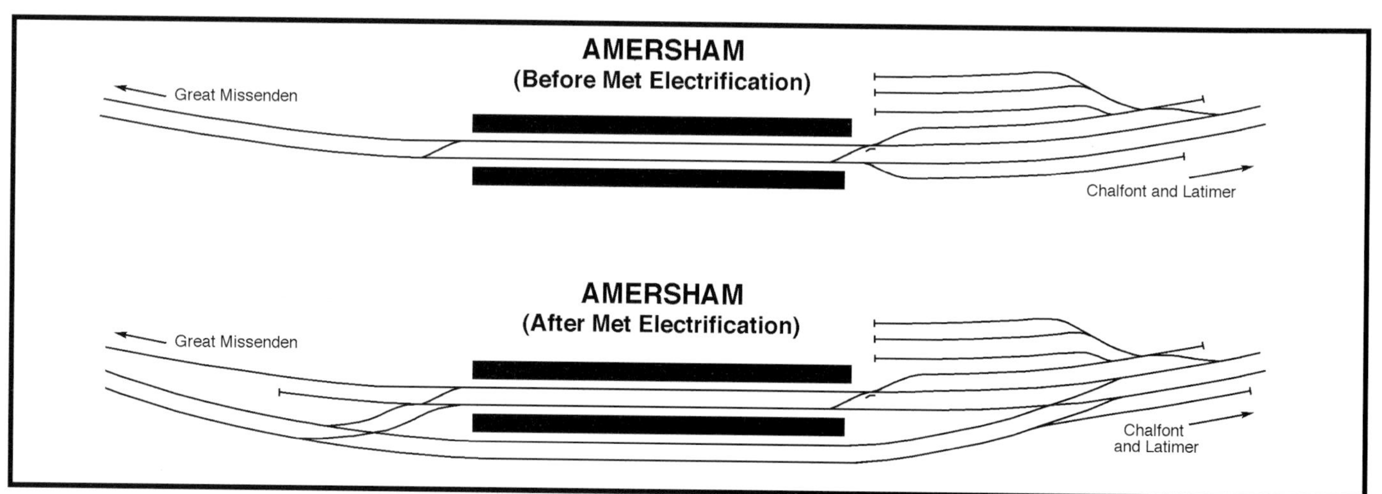

Amersham

Just beyond the summit of the climb from Great Missenden comes Amersham, the end of the 'Juice' from Baker Street, although this was only extended in 1964 from Rickmansworth. Originally, Amersham was another Met two-platform station with a goods yard on the up side.

Below:
This 1965 photograph shows the extent of the changes that have taken place on the down side. 'Black 5' No 45450 runs through with the 08.15 Nottingham to Marylebone on the old up main line; the new down main and island platform can be seen to the left. Beyond the station there are new turn-back headshunts for the 'Tube' trains. The date is 3 April 1965. *Brian Stephenson*

Right:
Leicester 'A3' No 60107 *Royal Lancer*, in blue livery, races through Chalfont and Latimer with the 8.25am from Manchester London Road to Marylebone on 15 March 1952. The branch train for Chesham can be seen in the bay and there are coal wagons in the goods yard. The signalbox is of Met design, as are the signals. *Neil Sprinks*

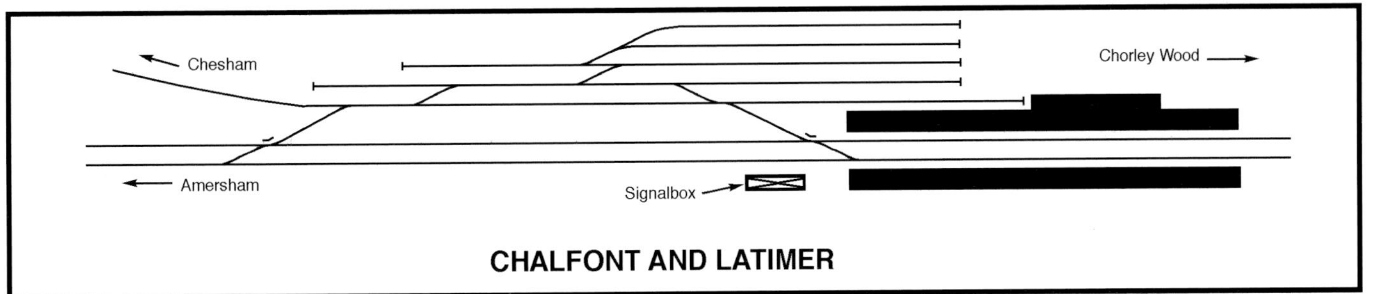

Chalfont & Latimer

Chalfont & Latimer was the junction for the branch to Chesham. As well as a bay platform for the Chesham trains there was also a small goods yard. Chalfont & Latimer is situated on the 1 in 105 descent to Rickmansworth.

Chesham

The Met branch to Chesham terminated at a small station with an interesting layout and goods yard. It is still open, but much reduced in size, and is now worked on a 'one-engine in-steam' basis from Chalfont & Latimer. The line was electrified in 1964 when the Met extended to Amersham from Rickmansworth.

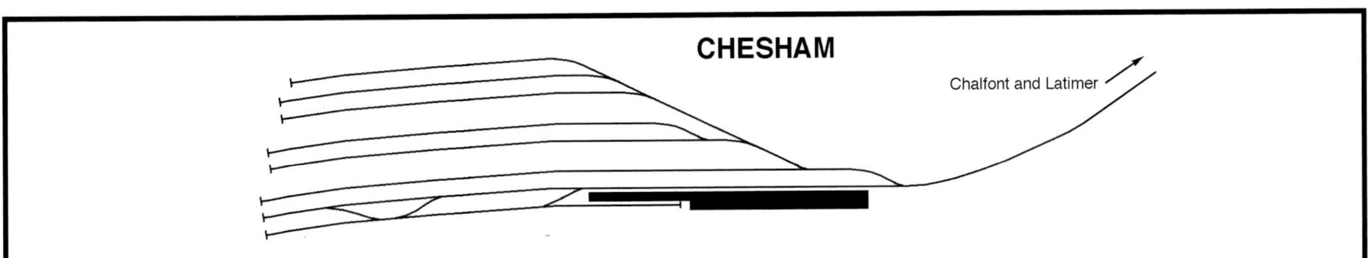

Right:
On Christmas Day 1953 (when the railways still provided a service, in this case a Sunday service) GC 'C13' tank No 67418 waits to leave with the 12.14pm to Chalfont and Latimer. The train is formed of ex-Metropolitan Railway electric stock converted for use as a push-pull set. The 'C13' would be allocated to Neasden, but was outbased at Chesham for a week. The 'C13s' were replaced by ex-LMS/BR 2-6-2 'Mickey Mouse' tanks in the late 1950s. *Neil Sprinks*

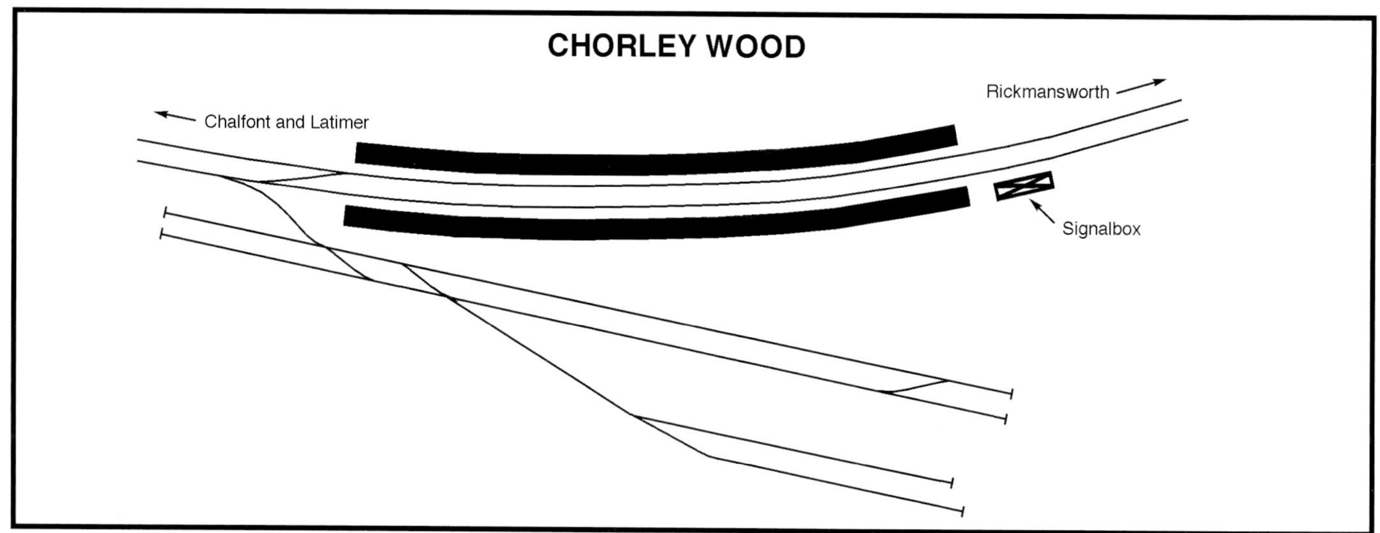

Chorley Wood

On the descent to Rickmansworth came the Met suburban station of Chorley Wood with its small yard. GC expresses were usually in full cry at this point as they descended the 1 in 105 to Amersham

Rickmansworth

Rickmansworth was situated at the bottom of the 1 in 100 from Amersham on a tight curve that was always a bottleneck in the running of GC line expresses. This meant a permanent speed restriction and, for northbound trains, a stiff climb into the Chilterns. It was the terminus of the Metropolitan electric service from Baker Street and locomotives were changed here for steam; initially the Met 'H' types, followed by GC 'A5s', LNER 'L1s' and Stanier, Fairburn and BR Standard tanks. Locomotive sidings were situated north of the station for this procedure.

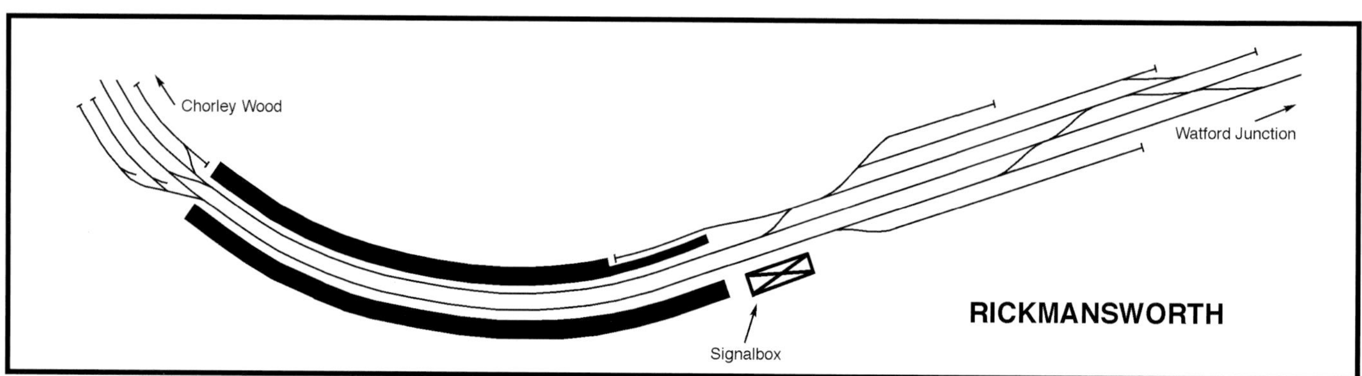

Left:
On Sunday, 9 September 1951, the 3.30pm Marylebone to Manchester with 'V2' No 60966 at the head prepares to assault the climb to Amersham as it passes through Rickmansworth. The Met signalbox is seen behind the locomotive, and the up bay platform is visible on the left. The electric locomotives would run back through the station and wait to take over from steam locomotives for the journey to Baker Street. The Met signals for this procedure can be clearly seen, together with numerous dolly signals for shunting movements. *Neil Sprinks*

Moor Park/ Sandy Lodge

Sandy Lodge, later 'Moor Park' was situated just beyond the triangular junction for Watford, where the GC originally ran a service to and from Marylebone for a short time. This was on the section that was quadrupled in the early 1960s when Moor Park was completely rebuilt with two island platforms.

Right:
On 4 March 1961, 'B1' No 61116 passes through Moor Park with the return empty newspaper vans that had gone down earlier that morning as the 'Newspaper'. This train left Nottingham at around 10.15am daily. It was later retimed to run about an hour later and was a feature of the London Extension until the last day of operation, leaving Nottingham at 11.25am. *Frank Hornby*

Above:
Approaching Harrow-on-the-Hill before the 1960s widening scheme had added a further two tracks to this scene, 'B17' No 2834 *Hinchingbrooke* arrives with an up 'Ord' from Woodford in 1936. The fly-under, added in 1936, can be seen beyond the train with the north signalbox and goods yard in the background.
C. R. L. Coles/Rail Archive Stephenson

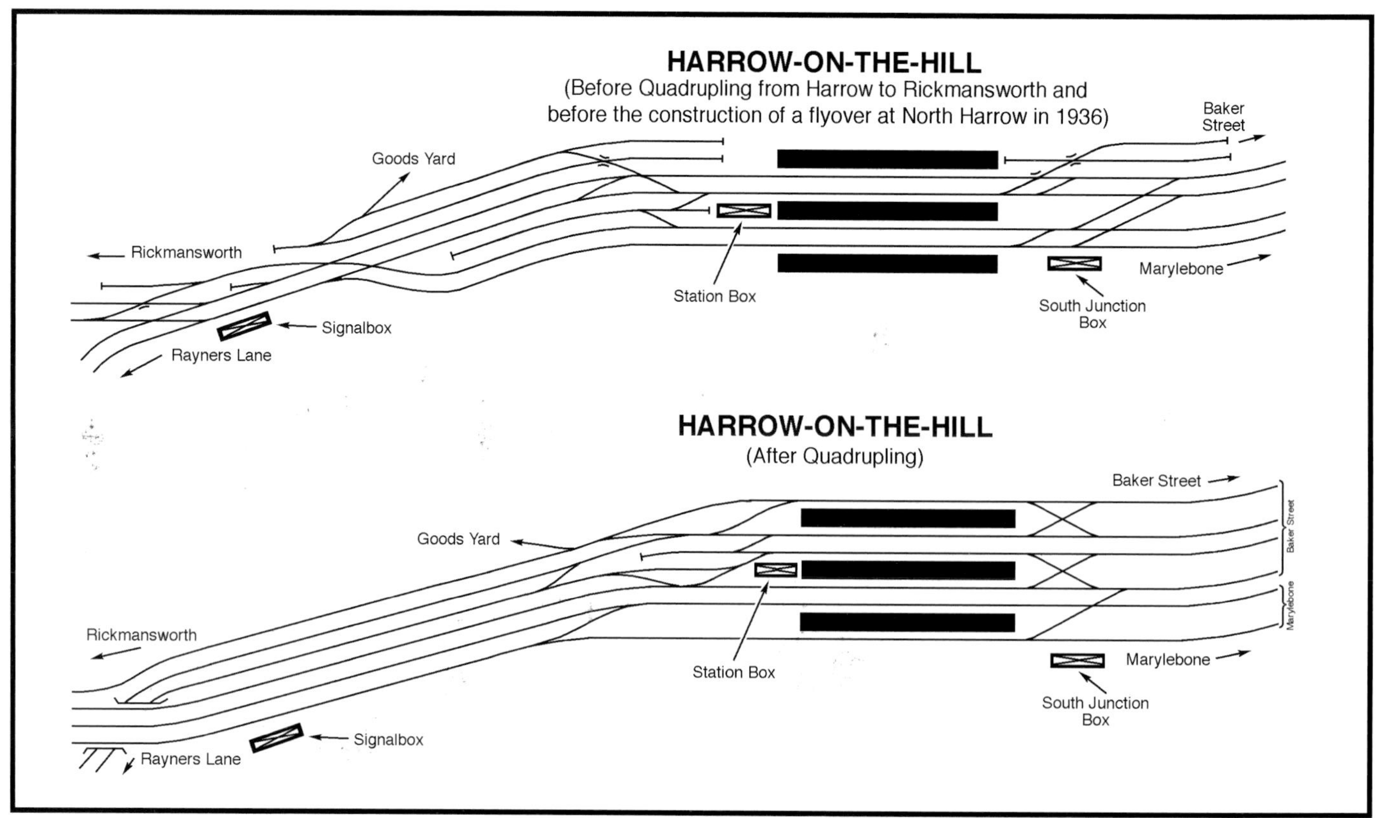

Harrow-on-the-Hill

Harrow-on-the-Hill is situated on an 'S' curve and is also the junction of the line to Rayners Lane and Uxbridge. The Uxbridge line was electrified and brought into operation on 1 January 1905. The line was quadrupled to the north in the 1960s and the layout changed. However, a fly-under junction for the Uxbridge branch was opened in the 1930s which gave greater capacity on the main line as the line to Harrow North was no longer shared with Uxbridge trains. The GC commenced a full suburban service to Aylesbury from 1905.

Below:
With four days to go until closure of the line as a through route, 'Black 5' No 44858, which had the dubious honour of hauling the last Liverpool to Marylebone mail from Leicester Central to Woodford Halse (on the 3/4 September 1966) leaves Harrow on the 08.15 Nottingham to Marylebone on 31 August 1966. *Bill Pigott*

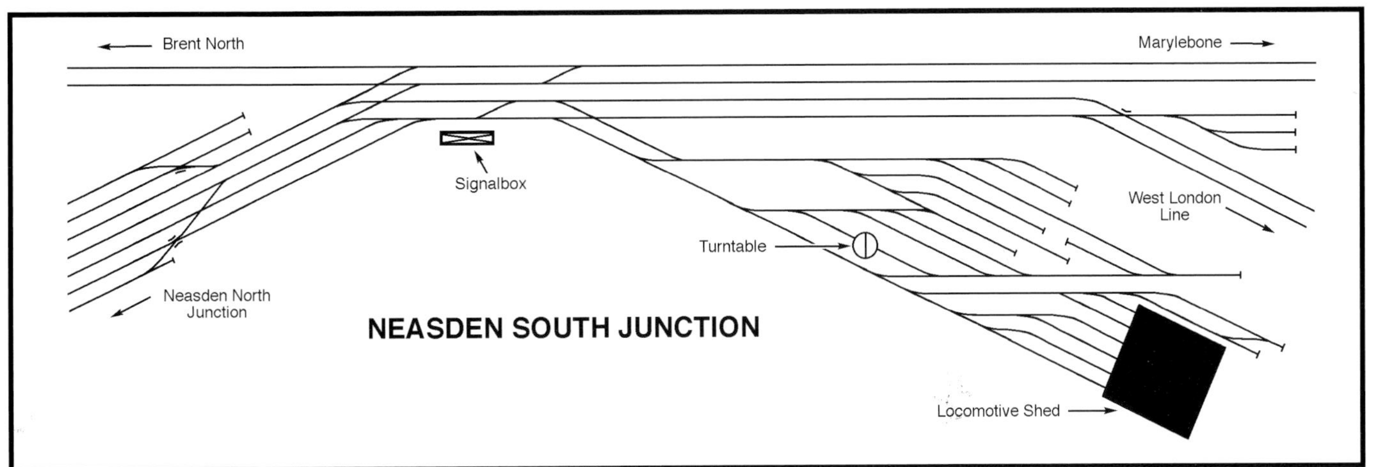

Neasden South Junction

The junction of the line to Northolt Junction and the GW/GC joint line was situated at Neasden South Junction. Brent North Junction came first on a southbound journey and allowed access into the substantial freight yards at Neasden.

Below:
A rebuilt 'Royal Scot', No 46125 *3rd Carabinier*, passes a northbound Bakerloo train on its way to Stanmore (before the Jubilee Line took over the route) at Neasden South Junction on 26 October 1965 with the 14.38 from Marylebone to Nottingham. The bridge carrying the West London line can be seen just behind the train, and the link to it and Neasden shed is in the bottom right-hand corner of the photograph. *Brian Stephenson*

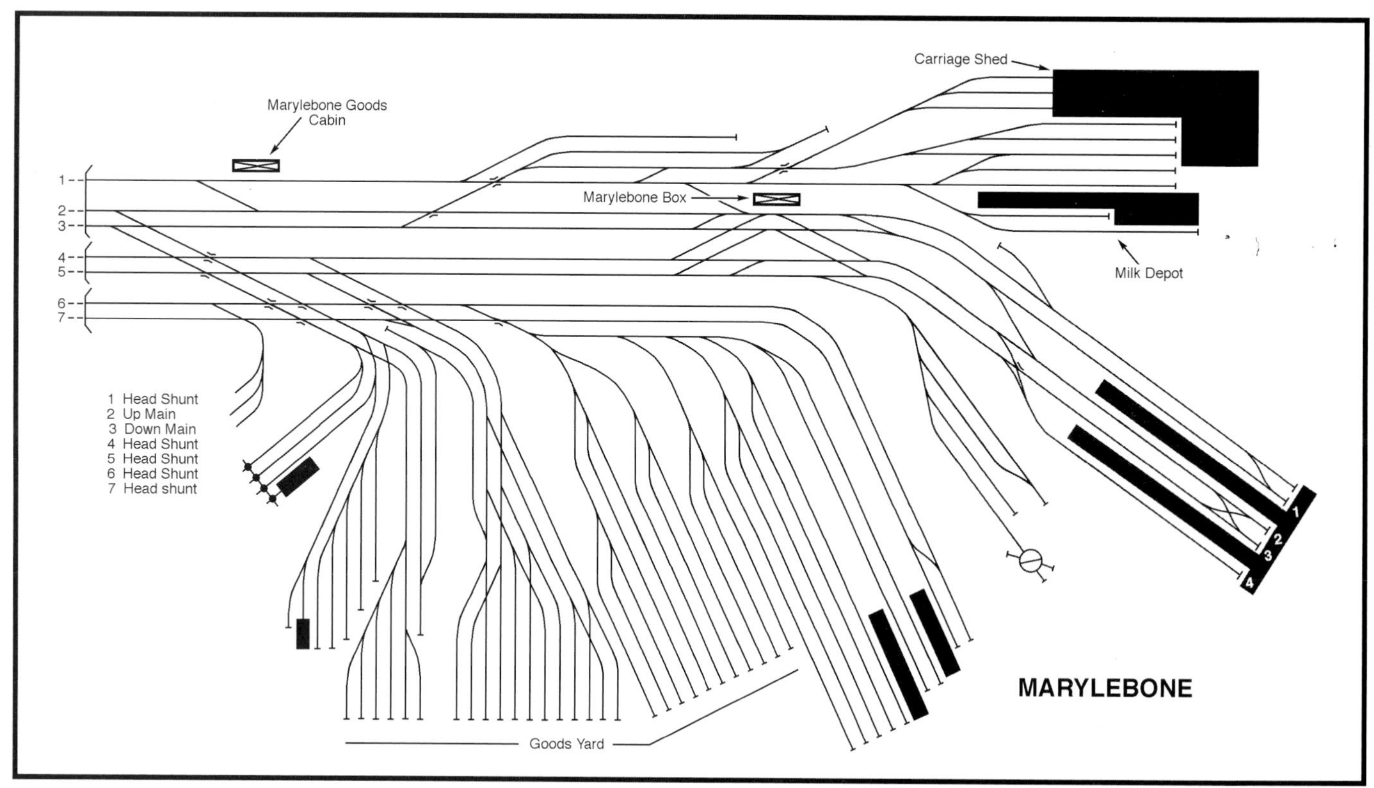

Marylebone

A trip to Marylebone station reveals almost half a terminus as only the eastern side seems to have been completed. In fact, a larger station was planned to have extra platforms that would align with the length of the concourse. The tunnels that lead to Marylebone allowed for four tracks but only two were ever used as far as Canfield Place where the GC joined the Metropolitan formation to Harrow. However, despite a terminus with only four platforms the goods depot was laid out to the west on a large scale. Carriage sheds were constructed to the east just before the station throat, together with milk sidings and facilities for loading horses. Locomotive servicing facilities were provided, but the main motive power was based at Neasden.

After Neasden depot closed in 1962 engines were transferred to Cricklewood, but following the closure of the LMR's London depots to steam some locomotives were stabled at Marylebone diesel depot. The allocation on 30 May 1966 was — DMUs excepted — 'Black 5' No 45426 and diesel locomotives Nos D5016, D5140 and D3051.

Marylebone survives in even smaller form today but in some respects looks better than ever. The goods sidings have all gone, as have the carriage sheds, but more trains than ever before use the station and services now run as far as Birmingham Snow Hill.

Left:
Looking at the station throat area at Marylebone, the entrance from Lord's Tunnel can be seen together with the DMU sidings and fuelling point. The former carriage sheds are to the right beyond the oil tanks, and the goods yards were situated where the cars are now parked, having been built on. A Class 115 DMU arrives from Aylesbury on 5 July 1984. A train of Metropolitan Line 'A60' stock is visible on its way from Baker Street to the suburbs in the background.
J. G. Glover

Above:
Class 5 No 45324 moves off the turntable at Marylebone prior to hauling the 16.38 semi-fast to Nottingham on 1 August 1966. The turntable was situated just to the north of Rossmore Road bridge and the station can just be seen through the bridge on the left. Neasden depot had closed by this time and locomotives were merely serviced at Marylebone. *B. H. Jackson*

Right:
Leicester-based 'A3' No 60102 *Sir Frederick Banbury* rolls off the turntable at Marylebone prior to working the down 'Master Cutler'. The station can be seen in the background through the arches of Rossmore Road bridge. The servicing and turning facilities at Marylebone avoided the need for the lengthy trip to Neasden depot. As well as the turntable there was a small coaling plant and inspection pits. *Ian Allan Library*

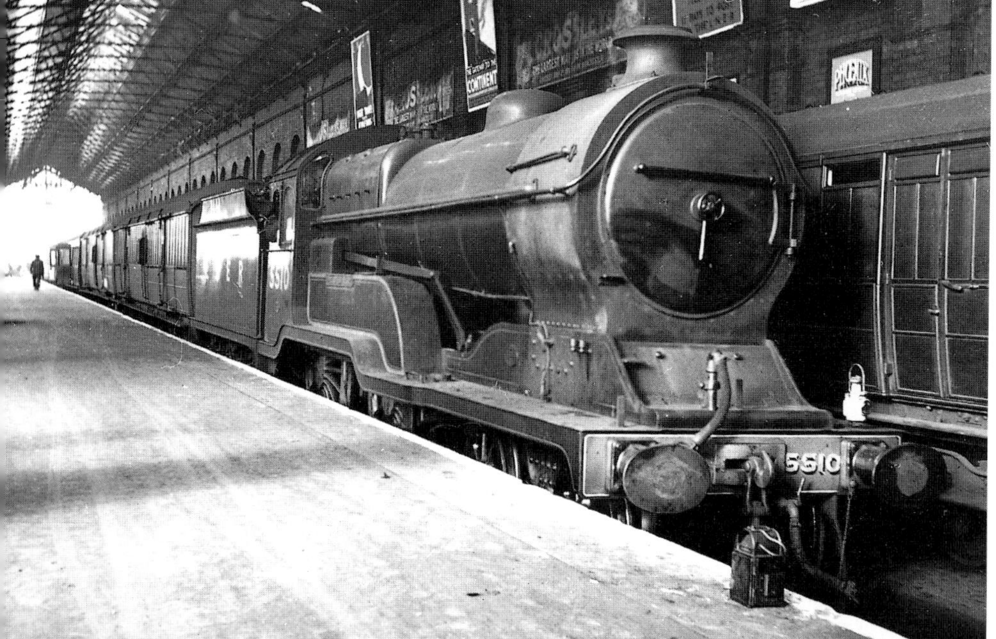

Left:
GC 'Director' No 5510 *Princess Mary* has arrived at Marylebone with an express from Manchester in 1935.
C. R. L. Coles/Rail Archive Stephenson

Left:
'V2' No 60876 waits for the departure time of 6.18pm at Marylebone with the down 'Master Cutler' for Sheffield on 6 May 1958. The station box can clearly be seen as well as the backs of houses which illustrates well how Marylebone was squeezed into a residential area. The 'Cutler' would take the High Wycombe route to the North. The locomotive carries the shed plate 14D, the then new LMR code for Neasden; the LMR having taken over the GC route in February that year. The 'Master Cutler' name was transferred to the new ER Pullman service from King's Cross via Retford as from 14 September 1958.
T. G. Hepburn/Rail Archive Stephenson

Left:
A rare photograph taken in Marylebone goods yard showing the first of the Clayton Bo-Bo diesel electrics, ready for inspection by BR Board staff who were based at 222 Marylebone Road, the former Great Central Hotel. Parcels vans can be seen behind the locomotive which is in 'ex-works' condition.
Ian Allan Library

Tunnels and Viaducts

Space has not permitted a detailed structure by structure analysis of every station and tunnel on the London Extension. However, whilst vast engineering operations were undertaken to construct the major stations at Nottingham Victoria and Marylebone, these locations have been covered in the earlier sections of the book. This section covers the major viaducts and tunnels that the Great Central had to build to get to London. Other railways had usually 'bagged' the cheapest ways of entering towns and indeed engineering their routes to and from them. Being the last main line, the Great Central had to take the best route that was left. However, this meant that the railway tended to arrive in almost dramatic style with vast, deep cuttings, long tunnels and graceful viaducts all built in engineers' blue brick that was intended to last for much longer than 67 years. This section covers some of the most outstanding features other than the station areas — these being the main tunnels and viaducts that were such a feature of the London Extension — many of which survive today.

Below:
A BR Standard Class 5 heads the 14.38 semi-fast train from Marylebone to Nottingham Victoria out of the three-track eastern Lord's Tunnel (the line, far left, is a headshunt) and into St John's Wood Tunnel, in the first week of August 1964. The lines to the right are the headshunts for Marylebone goods yard, originally intended as main lines to the north, but never developed as such. *R. L. Sewell*

Lord's Tunnel

Leaving Marylebone trains passed through three tunnels: Lord's; St John's Wood; and Hampstead. Lord's Tunnel is 237yd long and has one tunnel bored for three tracks and two tunnels bored for double track. However, the western pair were used only for headshunts out of Marylebone station and Marylebone goods yard. Originally the GC had expected to have four main lines approaching Marylebone and thus built its requirements as such, with the third bore purely as a headshunt. Traffic had been expected to grow and it was thought the extra capacity would be needed. The construction in advance of the traffic materialising would also save bothering Lord's Cricket Ground again — whose sacred turf had been disturbed in the building of the railway, despite work being carried out in the non cricketing season from August 1896 to May 1897. In the event, one pair of tracks was sufficient for main line and suburban services with the next bores staying as headshunts. The north end of Lord's Tunnel, complete with its three bores, is well illustrated in this photograph looking down from the short gap that separates it from St John's Wood Tunnel, 1,279yd long. At its northern end the LNWR main line into Euston is crossed on a double-track, 118ft three-span girder bridge, situated just in front of the portals of Primrose Hill Tunnel. After the brief break comes the 667yd Hampstead Tunnel which ends at Canfield Place. Canfield Place had a small signalbox (originally worked by the Metropolitan) that controlled a trailing crossover and closed on 1 December 1968.

Brackley Viaduct

Brackley Viaduct was necessary to cross the River Great Ouse's flood plain just south of the town of Brackley. The viaduct comprised 22 arches and was 756ft long. Two cuttings to the north and south of the town had to be excavated and the material was used to build the approach embankments. The southern end of the viaduct consisted of girder spans, owing to difficulties encountered with the clay beds on which the viaduct was to stand. The structure had the last laugh in 1978 — refusing to collapse after the demolition charges had been fired. This led to its demolition being carried out piecemeal, the Great Central's high quality engineers' blue brick intending to be around much longer than the 67 years of use it actually had. How marvellous it would have been to see Class 92 locomotives with Continental loading gauge wagons crossing Brackley Viaduct on their way from Manchester to Paris!

Above:
In 1959, there was still a full Sunday passenger service on the London Extension. 'B1' No 61078 has just crossed the viaduct with a Sunday service from Woodford Halse heading towards Aylesbury on 1 March 1959. *Mike Mitchell*

Left:
Before the '9F' era arrived, the Annesley to Woodford services were worked by more traditional Great Central motive power. 'O4' 2-8-0, No 63722 storms out of the southern portal (leaving the bore full of smoke) on 14 May 1949. The brickwork proudly proclaims construction was completed in 1897, work having commenced on 18 February 1895 and finished on 22 May 1897. *H. Weston*

Catesby Tunnel

The owner of Catesby House, where the plan was made to blow up the Houses of Parliament in the Gunpowder Plot, refused permission to allow the Great Central to build one of its long and impressive cuttings through his land. This necessitated the building of the 2,997yd-long Catesby Tunnel, the longest on the London Extension, and on a ruling gradient of 1 in 176 from north to south. The tunnel was wet in parts, but constructed of engineers blue brick with approximately 30 million bricks. Despite four ventilation shafts it was notoriously smoky as it tended to hold the exhaust from the 'Runners' that had passed through on their way from Annesley to Woodford. The wet patches could also give impromptu showers to those crews working tender first! The tunnel is still extant today, as is bridge No 488 at the north portal (on which can be seen the chips taken out of the brickwork from the fire irons of locomotive tenders whose coal had been overloaded!) and the 12-arch Catesby Viaduct is beyond this.

Right:
An Annesley '9F', No 92094, on a typical 'Runner' or 'Windcutter' from Annesley to Woodford storms towards Rugby Central off the Birdcage Bridge over the former LNWR main line on 17 October 1964. *P. H. Wells*

Rugby — the Birdcage Bridge

To the north of the Birdcage was an impressive viaduct of 14 arches and two plate girder bridges that took the GC over the LNWR's sidings, main lines and Peterborough route. This was followed to the north of the brick arches by a 392ft girder bridge over the Oxford Canal. The Birdcage itself followed the two plate girders and comprised three lattice girder bridges 375ft in length. A small plate girder of 40ft then followed. Two spans of the Birdcage still stand today — it being far too difficult to demolish following the electrification of the West Coast main line in the1960s. The Birdcage Bridge and viaducts beyond dipped on a falling gradient of 1 in 176 from Rugby northwards for a mile and a quarter before a climb up to Lutterworth. Not surprisingly, up trains, having descended from just south of Lutterworth through Shawell to Rugby, passed over the Birdcage at high speed, unlike trains on the LNWR which had severe speed checks until comparatively recently. The Birdcage was the site of the famous signal gantry, paid for by the Great Central, situated on the west side of the bridge that controlled the east end of the LNWR station. Between the Birdcage and the station was a signalbox called Rugby Cattle Sidings that closed on 16 August 1963.

Below:
Looking at the tunnel entrance, the soot marks from up trains can be seen blackening the southern portal. The climb does not seem to be bothering 'B1' No 61206 as it hurries an 'Ord' from Leicester to Marylebone away from the station stop at Ashby Magna on 29 August 1959.
Barry Hilton

Ashby Magna Tunnel

Ashby Magna Tunnel was really a rather long bridge, 92yd in length (bridge No 414) and is located south of Ashby Magna station. It was situated on a 1 in 176 falling gradient from the summit of Ashby Bank that was situated roughly half way between Lutterworth and Ashby Magna, a descent that started virtually at Leicester South Goods.

Leicester Viaducts

The Great Central accessed Leicester by a series of viaducts which were expensive to build and, as with Nottingham, meant that many houses had to be demolished. South of Leicester Central the line crossed Bath Lane on a vast 88ft-long girder bridge, followed by a span over the River Soar. Viaducts and other bridges took the line on to Leicester North Goods on a falling gradient.

Above:
Rebuilt 'Patriot' No 45529 *Stephenson* gets away from Leicester Central and crosses the River Soar with a typical GC rousing start on 28 December 1963. The train is the 11.15am empty newspaper vans and parcels that had worked up to Nottingham the night before.
Horace Gamble

Loughborough Midland Bridge

Just north of Loughborough Central the line crossed the Grand Union Canal and then passed over the Midland Railway's line to St Pancras. The bridge was 160ft long, consisted of four spans and was of skew girder construction. Unfortunately this bridge has now been demolished thus severing the preserved Great Central line from Loughborough to Leicester North from the route north, which is still extant as a long single-track siding to Rushcliffe Halt and British Gypsum's works at Hotchley Hill. This connection was built in the 1970s down from the GC to the Midland to allow access to the line through Weekday Cross to be closed, freights previously having reversed on a short spur inside Nottingham Victoria and then ran south to access Hotchley Hill from the north. Freight trains are now running again on this southern section, which is expected to be owned and maintained by Great Central Nottingham, with track access being provided to English Welsh & Scottish Railways for freight traffic. The GCN is restoring the line northwards from Rushcliffe Halt to Ruddington, where the old MoD depot is being converted into a wonderful heritage centre of trains, buses and models and is building a new northern terminus with signals controlled by the former Neasden South signalbox. It is the intention to rebuild this bridge on a slightly different alignment to allow through running to take place again. Anyone who doubts the determination or practicality of this should pay a visit to these two Great Central Railways which have already turned 'impossible' dreams into realities. A 17-mile preserved main line with a Railtrack connection at Loughborough is now a very real possibility. Even better — become a member of Great Central Nottingham or the Main Line Steam Trust and support the determination for yourself.

Below left:
BR Standard Class 5 No 73010 crosses the Midland main line as it leaves Loughborough Central with a Portsmouth-Nottingham train on 10 August 1963. *T. G. Hepburn/Rail Archive Stephenson*

Above:
In 1962, the motive power of the London Midland Region was taking hold and here, a 'Black 5', No 44932 blasts away from Loughborough with the 12.25pm from Marylebone to Nottingham on 9 September 1962. These trains were still of reasonable length at this time, but the service was made less attractive by a management that wanted rid of the line a few months later when all the semi-fasts bar one were reduced to four coaches and the 12.25pm and its return became the preserve of a non-gangway four-car DMU. *Mike Mitchell*

Loughborough Soar Viaduct

The railway climbs up from the Midland bridge at 1 in 176 to the impressive Soar Viaduct which is 160yd long and consists of 11 arches. The high embankments at either end were built using spoil from East Leake and Barnston cuttings to the north, some 300,000cu yd in all.

B6

Left:
With the north portal in the background, Brush Type 4 No D1766 heads the Poole to Newcastle cross-country service towards East Leake on 10 August 1966. *Tom Boustead*

Barnston Tunnel

East Leake, or Barnston, Tunnel is 99yd long and approached by deep cuttings, to the south of which was Barnston Lime Siding controlled by a ground frame and which had access from the down line only. Barnston Tunnel's north portal was the start of the 1 in 176 descent to Loughborough and a similar descent in the opposite direction to Ruddington.

Trent Bridge

The approach to Nottingham was by a series of massive viaducts and bridges firstly over the River Trent, followed by a viaduct through the Meadows and over the Midland station before tunnelling into Nottingham Victoria. The river was crossed by two sets of three lattice girder bridges with a total length of 336ft, having been approached on a viaduct of seven arches. Once over the Trent, immediately Trent Boulevard was crossed on a 66ft girder structure.

Left:
This photograph is not a particularly inspiring one. After the main line had closed south of Rugby in September 1966 a DMU service began between Nottingham Victoria and Rugby Central. After the 'Vic' had closed in September 1967, and Arkwright Street had been hastily reopened as the northern terminus, the track was rationalised south of Nottingham with the closure of Queen's Walk Sidings and Nottingham Goods South signalbox — seen here in a dilapidated condition. A three-car Cravens DMU runs south on a Rugby service on 2 September 1967. *T. G. Hepburn/Rail Archive Stephenson*

Bulwell Viaduct

Bulwell Viaduct crossed the River Leen, the main Hucknall to Bulwell road and the Midland Railway's line to Mansfield and was 420yd long on 26 arches. Constructed with over six and a half million blue bricks, it was demolished in stages, the last portion going in 1989.

Above:
As can be seen here, the viaduct started at the bottom of a dip at its southern end, with the viaduct itself being on a climb towards Hucknall of 1 in 130. 'Black 5' No 45217 heads an excursion to Wembley off the viaduct on 27 April 1963. *Tom Boustead*

ACCELERATED SERVICE OF THROUGH EXPRESS TRAINS

BETWEEN

LONDON (MARYLEBONE), LEICESTER, NOTTINGHAM, YORK, SHEFFIELD, LEEDS, HUDDERSFIELD, HALIFAX, BRADFORD, AND MANCHESTER,

BY THE NEW ROUTE.

STATIONS	WEEK DAYS											SUNDAYS			
	Newspaper Express	BREAKFAST AND LUNCHEON CAR EXPRESS	LUNCHEON CAR EXPRESS	LUNCHEON CAR EXPRESS	LUNCHEON CAR EXPRESS	RESTAURANT CAR EXPRESS	RESTAURANT CAR EXPRESS	RESTAURANT CAR EXPRESS	DINING CAR EXPRESS	Express	Express	LUNCHEON CAR EXPRESS	Express A	Express	
Marylebone,	morn	morn	morn	aft	aft	aft	aft	aft	aft	aft	aft	morn	aft	aft	
LONDON ....dep	2 45	8 45	10 0	12 15	1 40	3 25	4 0	4 30	5 40	7 30	10 0	11 20	5 0	1145	....
Leicester (Central) ......arr	4 54	10 54	12 8	2 28	3 40	5 22	6 20	6 33	7 53	10 36	12 21	1 30	7 22	2 24	....
Nottingham (Victoria).. „	5 26	11 29	12 40	3 4	4 11	5 56	6 57	7 5	8 25	11 56	12 55	2 7	7 55	3 7	....
York .... „	9 18	1 32	3 6	....	7 40	....		....	....		2 55	....	....		....
Sheffield (Victoria) ...... „	6 20	12 22	1 32	3 58	5 1	6 33	....	8 0	9 17	....	2 0	3 3	8 50	....	....
Leeds (Central) .... „	7 43	2 0	2 48	....	6 14	7 36	....	....	10 29	....	....	....	....	....	....
Huddersfield.............. „	10 26	1 33	2 26	5 6	6 17		....	9 8	10 5	....	....	....	10 24	....	....
Halifax .... „	11 8	2 7	3 5	5 41	6 54	....	....	9 32	10 33	....	....	....	10 52	....	....
Bradford (Exchange) ... „	11 4	2 11	2 52	6 13	6 54	....	....	10 12	10 50	....	....	....	11 23	....	....
Manchester .... „ (London Road)	7‡35	1 32	2 50	5 15	6 15	....	....	9 10	10 35	....	3 30	4 15	10 0	....	....

STATIONS	WEEK DAYS												SUNDAYS			
	Express	BREAKFAST CAR EXPRESS	Express	BREAKFAST AND LUNCHEON CAR EXPRESS	BREAKFAST AND LUNCHEON CAR EXPRESS	LUNCHEON CAR EXPRESS	LUNCHEON CAR EXPRESS	RESTAURANT CAR EXPRESS	Express	RESTAURANT CAR EXPRESS	DINING CAR EXPRESS	Express	Express	Express	LUNCHEON CAR EXPRESS	Express A
London Road,	morn	morn	morn	morn	morn	morn	aft	aft	aft	aft	aft	aft	morn	morn	aft	aft
Manchester ....dep	....	....	6 23	....	8 25	10 0	12 30	2 15	....	3 45	5 0	1020	....	....	12 30	5 30
Bradford (Exchange) ... „	....	....	6 3	....	7 28	10 7	11 57	1 22	....	2 45	5 0	9 35	....	....	....	4 0
Halifax .... „	....	....	5 50	....	7 58	9 52	11 56	1 15	....	2 55	4 48	9 47	....	....	....	4 28
Huddersfield.............. „	....	....	6 35	....	8 28	10 33	12 30	2 0	....	3 30	5 28	1017	....	....	....	5 0
Leeds (Central) .... „	....	....	....	7 40	....	9 20	11 40	....	2 41	3 32	....	9 44	....	....	....	....
Sheffield (Victoria) ...... „	....	5*45	7 42	8 50	9 36	11 20	1 40	3 18	....	4 53	6 21	1146	....	9 35	1 40	6 42
York .... „	....	....	....	....	....	9 25	11 40	....	2 47	....	....	9 45	....	....	....	....
Nottingham (Victoria).. „	5 35	7 45	8 39	....	10 28	12 12	2 32	4 9	4 52	5 45	7 13	1243	....	1130	2 35	7 40
Leicester (Central) ..... „	6 30	8 20	9 17	....	10 58	12 48	3 9	4 40	5 40	6 23	7 46	1 20	6 30	1212	3 13	8 17
LONDON ....arr (Marylebone)	9 50	10 20	1140	12 0	1 10	3 5	5 43	6 42	8 0	8 40	9 50	3 40	9 50	2 59	5 25	10 35

A Dinners are served to First and Third class Passengers at the usual tariff.

* Passengers from Sheffield change at Nottingham. ‡ Central Station.

Attendants travel with the Breakfast, Luncheon, Dining, and Restaurant Car Trains.

GREAT CENTRAL RAILWAY COMPANY'S

QUICK ROUTE TO

Hamburg, Antwerp, Rotterdam, and the Continent, via Grimsby.

This Company's New, Fast, and Powerful Steamers leave Grimsby for Hamburg and Hamburg for Grimsby daily, Sundays excepted—average passage, 32 hours.

For Antwerp every Monday, Wednesday, and Saturday; returning from Antwerp every Tuesday, Thursday, and Saturday—average passage, 22 hours.

For Rotterdam every Wednesday and Saturday; returning from Rotterdam every Tuesday and Saturday—average passage, 17 hours.

The Steamers carry a Steward and Stewardess, and Special Accommodation for Ladies is provided.

For further particulars see Continental Programme.

☞ **Parliamentary Tickets are issued by all Trains on the Great Central Railway.**

Above: GC main line express timetable for summer 1903.

3. Express Passenger Services

The Great Central Era — 1899 to 1923

Passenger services started on the London Extension on Wednesday, 15 March 1899. The first trains were the 2.15am from Manchester London Road and the 5.15am from Marylebone. Other expresses that ran on that day were the 9.15am, 1.15pm, 5.15pm and 10.15pm down and 10am, 2pm, 5pm and 5.30pm up. The trains certainly offered a high quality service, with restaurant cars for first and third class passengers on the 9.15am and 5.15pm from Marylebone and 10am and 5pm from Manchester, buffet cars on the 1.15pm down and 2pm up services. There was also a Sunday service, with two trains in each direction leaving Marylebone at 11am and 4.15pm and 12.30pm and 5pm from Manchester. The new Nottingham Victoria station was not yet open (it opened in 1900) so until then trains stopped at Arkwright Street. How ironic it should be that after Nottingham Victoria's closure in 1967 that Arkwright Street should be temporarily reopened to serve the rump DMU service to Rugby.

One of the most famous GC trains that continued up to the end of express services was introduced on 19 October 1899. The 'Newspaper' was chartered by the Daily Mail and left Marylebone at

Below:
An early view of Marylebone sees 'D10' 'Director' class No 431 *Edwin A. Beazley* and Class C4 Atlantic No 262 waiting to leave with the 3.15pm express to Sheffield on 1 November 1919. It was this train that was known as the 'Sheffield Special' and carried a dining car. The 'D10s' were ten in number, Nos 429 to 438, and were the original 'Director' class built at Gorton in 1913. The 'C4' in this photograph was built at Gorton in 1906.
LCGB Ken Nunn Collection/Rail Archive Stephenson

2.30am, arriving in Manchester at 7am. Another newspaper train left Marylebone at 5.15am and arrived in Leicester at 7.15am. August 1899 saw the introduction of the 5.20pm from Marylebone which left the main line at Woodford South and travelled over to the East and West Junction line where it terminated at Byfield at 7.36pm, where there was a connection for Stratford-upon-Avon. By September this train reversed at Woodford and went via the station and Woodford No 4 to the East and West Junction line at Woodford West Junction. The train never travelled via the south cord again, which remained unused latterley except for the storage of wagons.

Sam Fay became General Manager in 1902. His predecessor William Pollitt had introduced through expresses which began daily running from Marylebone to Huddersfield, Halifax and Bradford on 1 May 1900. Fay continued Pollitt's expansion of services not only on the London express services, but also on cross-country services and through services from Marylebone to Stratford-upon-Avon. This desire for non-stop running between Sheffield and Marylebone saw the installation of water troughs at Charwelton, just north of Woodford Halse, which were completed by 1 July 1903. This initially allowed one train each way to make a non-stop run, taking only 3hr 10min on the up journey and 3hr 8min on the down. A new Wakefield train, the 8.2am, that carried through coaches from Leeds and had connections from the GC's hinterland of Barnsley, Hull and Lincolnshire was introduced, arriving at Marylebone 12.22pm and returning at 3.25pm from Marylebone. This train conveyed a slip coach which was detached at Nottingham to provide connections for stations to Leicester, and in the down direction, a coach was slipped at Leicester for Nottingham and Grimsby.

Also in 1903, the 2.45am Marylebone to Manchester 'Newspaper', along with connections from Manchester to Bournemouth, were re-routed to Manchester Central to provide better connections to the GC's Cheshire Lines which did not run into London Road. Further improvements to the London services were an acceleration to the timetable, with the non-stop Sheffield to London service being only three hours. In July 1904 the 3.25pm to Sheffield's schedule was only 2hr 57min, and it was extended to Manchester, arriving in only 3hr 50min. The 6.20pm from Marylebone replaced the 5.40pm and ran non-stop to Nottingham in only 2hr 13min, arriving at Manchester at 10.35pm, only 4hr 15min.

The opposite direction saw the introduction of an 11.25am from

Manchester which ran the 103 miles from Leicester to London in only 105 minutes, after a departure from Leicester at 1.45pm. From Marylebone there were expresses at 2.45, 5.15, 8.45 and 10am, 12.15, 1.40, 4.00, 4.35, 5.25, 6.20 and 10pm, all taking the Aylesbury and Metropolitan line. These trains were tightly timed, the best journey to Sheffield being only 3hr 2min. The up service had an even faster schedule from Sheffield to London leaving at 7.38, 8.50, 9.36 and 11.20am, 12.33, 1.40, 3.18, 4.53, 6.21 and 11.46pm, with the quickest train arriving at Marylebone in only 2hr 57min. Trains were light, some being only four coaches, and by 1904 the Robinson Atlantics were becoming the main source of motive power, taking over from the Pollitt 4-4-0s.

Cecil J. Allen wrote highly of these services in *Trains Illustrated* magazine. On one occasion, in summer 1912, a journey was made on the 2.40am newspaper express behind Atlantic No 363, driven by Driver Bailey of Neasden. The train comprised four coaches and two vans, a total of 140 tons. The train ran fast to Brackley, where a stop was made, but not advertised for passengers, with mile-a-minute timings for the rest of the journey to Nottingham Arkwright Street. The train then ran to Sheffield and arrived there in 3hr 12min for the 164.7 miles. Harrow was passed in 11min 47sec, Aylesbury in 42min 14sec and Brackley Central reached in 62min, speeds being no lower than 60mph between Finmere and Brackley. A van was detached there and the train went on, passing Culworth Junction at 79mph, 82mph at Braunston & Willoughby, reaching Rugby in 23min 10sec for the 23.9 miles from Brackley. From Rugby, Ashby Magna was passed in 11min 29sec, speed increasing to 82mph at Whetstone, the 19.9 miles from Rugby being covered in only 19min 58sec. The Leicester to Nottingham section saw even faster running, Loughborough Central being passed at 83mph with an arrival at Arkwright Street in 21min 22sec for 22½ miles.

In 1906, four expresses (three Manchesters and the Bradford) were switched from the Met and GC Joint (which had become very congested) to travel via High Wycombe and the GW/GC joint line. The Stratford-upon-Avon service was not forgotten and the 6.20pm from Marylebone carried a coach that was slipped at Woodford from 1 July 1907. By the winter, the Stratford through coach and other connections took only 2hr 5min. Amazingly, there was even a slip coach for Amersham and Great Missenden off the 1.40pm express on Saturdays only. The 3.15pm Marylebone to Sheffield and Manchester Central (for Warrington and Liverpool) also carried slip coaches for Bradford and Huddersfield, slipped at Penistone. By 1910 traffic was growing sufficiently to see an even further improvement to the London Extension's express services. The precursor of the 'Master Cutler', the 7.20am from Sheffield, Chesterfield, Nottingham and Leicester was introduced, serving breakfast. The run was non-stop from Leicester to Marylebone, and in 1914 there were seven services that ran more than 100 miles, including a slip coach. This meant that trains had to accomplish their journeys in 'even time' (a practice that went on well into Eastern Region days), and average speeds in 1914 were in the mid 50s. The London expresses were certainly amongst the fastest trains in the country. Promoted by innovative advertising such as, 'The Great Central Railway is the Line of Health' and posters depicting the company's numerous steamship services, an image of speed and sophistication was built up that attracted a strong clientele who returned time and time again. Whether they really made money was questioned by the GC hierarchy. J.G. Robinson, putting a report together on the locomotive building programme in 1910 demonstrated that the revenue from expresses did not yield more than 2s 2d (11p) per mile. Expenses were 3s 6d (17½ p). This cemented the theory that, even right through to BR days the GC had to prioritise on its capacity as a freight carrier. Lose that and the London Extension would not be viable. That is exactly what happened in 1965 as through freight services were withdrawn. Within two years the line had closed.

World War 1 had a dramatic effect on the Great Central, not least because its operations came under control of the Railway Executive Committee and its ships were commandeered for war service. Ordinary train services were reduced as priority was given to freight and troop movements. At the same time excursion and cheap travel offers were withdrawn and in 1918 fares were increased by 50 per cent.

By 1919, services were recovering and the newer 'Directors' and 'Sam Fay' 4-6-0s were starting to make an impact on London services, and the GC, unlike many other railways, ran expresses with a train engine only. A slip coach for Brackley was introduced on the 6.10pm down Bradford express. The summer of 1922 saw a through dining car train from Mansfield, leaving at 8.12am and arriving at 11.10am, the down working leaving London at 4.55pm.

Left:
Robinson's very first 4-4-0 for the Great Central was the 'D9' class which consisted of 40 locomotives introduced from 1902. They were rebuilt between 1913 and 1926 with boilers having a diameter of 5ft 0in, superheating and an increased cylinder diameter of up to 19in. The tenders carried 4,000gal of water and 6 tons of coal. In LNER days they were painted green until 1928, and following the Grouping many appeared on the GE Section. No 1024 was built by Sharp, Stewart in 1902 and is seen leaving Marylebone with an express for Sheffield in the early 1900s.
Real Photographs/Rail Archive Stephenson

The LNER Takes Over — 1923 to 1947

Much the same service was continued by the LNER. Traffic stayed relatively static in the 1920s, but the 1930s saw growth and this meant that expresses were strengthened from the small GC flyers that had preceded them. This presented much heavier loads for the GC Atlantics — mainly from Leicester — that were rostered for the work, these locomotives still dominating express work despite the introduction of the 'Directors'. In typical Leicester tradition the Atlantics were pushed hard and Cecil J. Allen believed the toughest task was the 6.20pm Marylebone to Bradford. In 1928 he travelled behind No 6092 driven by Driver Muxloe with a train of 272 tons from Marylebone that detached stock at Finmere and Woodford. Travelling via High Wycombe, 55mph was attained on the 1 in 175/1 in 254 past Gerrards Cross and 49mph on Saunderton Bank. Finmere Bank was taken at 57mph, and 60mph was recorded up towards Brackley. However, on the downhill stretches the speeds were even more impressive with Haddenham being passed at 75mph and Braunston at 80mph. Leicester Central was reached in 111min 50sec from Marylebone. The 66 miles from Princes Risborough to Whetstone were completed in only 61½min.

On another occasion, with No 5361, and a heavier train, Allen recorded the Princes Risborough to Whetstone stretch in only 61 minutes with speeds as high as 85mph at Braunston and 80mph at Whetstone. He described the typical GC style of 'dashing through the suburbs of Leicester at top speed, often well over 70mph, until the station was pretty well in sight, and having the brakes slammed on to make a very quick stop'. The 6.20pm was also recorded leaving Leicester with GC Atlantic No 5267 and GN Atlantic No 4420 as pilot. By Birstall, 52mph had been reached, 83mph at Loughborough, 64mph up the climb to Barnston Tunnel and 82mph at Ruddington. Arkwright Street was passed in 20min and Nottingham Victoria in 22½ min from Leicester. Nottingham to Leicester was one of the most exciting parts of the GC in terms of speed. The GN may have had York to Darlington, but this was just as good! Interestingly enough, Allen recorded no outstanding runs with the 'Sam Fay' class that were introduced from 1912. He blamed their alledged inadequate fireboxes, which were the same size as 'Directors', and ideal for that class, but with larger cylinders and boilers, the 'Sam Fays' were not as good in steaming capacity. The same could be said of the 'Lord Faringdons', the other big GC 4-6-0 passenger locomotive, although Cecil J. Allen recorded a very fast run with one; *Lord Faringdon* itself, on the 3.20pm from Marylebone, passing Neasden at over 70mph, 67mph at Pinner, with the 1 in 105 climb up from Rickmansworth at 39mph. On the descent from Dutchlands, 75mph was reached with an 'on time' arrival at Leicester of 108min 55sec for the 103.1 miles. The load was 230 tons gross. Another trip with No 1164 and a train on the 3.20pm was initially more exciting. Moor Park was passed at 70mph with the curve at Rickmansworth being negotiated at 50mph! This was lost on the

Above:
Running parallel to the electrified Metropolitan Line at Willesden Green, Class B3 4-6-0, No 6165 *Valour*, the Great Central's mobile war memorial to those employees who gave their lives in World War 1, heads an excursion back to Sheffield from Marylebone in 1936. The 'B3s' were known as the 'Lord Faringdon' class and were six in total, all superheated. They were completed between 1917 and 1921. In general, they were similar to the 'Sam Fay' class of 4-6-0, but they were sluggish and heavy coal consumers. Nos 6166 and 6168 were fitted with Caprotti valve gear by Gresley and in 1943, No 6166 was entirely rebuilt to look like a 'B1'. *E. R. Wethersett/Real Photographs*

climb to Amersham with speed dropping to only 33mph. However, the rest of the journey was uneventful, Leicester being reached in 108min 25sec.

People had more money to spend in the 1930s and excursion tickets which had previously been valid only on special trains were suddenly made available on normal services. Trains were lengthened to 10 coaches and even more as demand dictated. Motive power did see a change away from the traditional GC types to the new 'B17' class of 4-6-0 which was trialled on the expresses from 1933 and actually shedded at Gorton in the first instance. Having proved themselves, three 'B17s' were sent to Neasden at the end of 1934; Nos 2834, 2842 and 2824 replacing three GC 'B3' 4-6-0s. They lasted a year before being transferred north again and at the same time the first batch of a new series of 'B17s', named after football clubs, was ordered for GC line express services. The first shed to receive a batch of 'Footballers' was Leicester, a shed that was rapidly gaining a name for fast running in an inimitable GC style and, in contrast to the Midland — as GC men would boast. Nos 2848-55 were allocated there in stages from 3 March 1936. They replaced the famous 4-4-2 GC 'C4' Atlantics and ran the length of the London Extension on heavier loading trains. Neasden and Gorton also received some of these locomotives (Nos 2856-62) which in the main replaced the 'Director' class 4-4-0s. Two of these engines ended up at Woodford Halse, and others at Sheffield Darnall. The 'B17s' did not transform passenger services, most GC types being more than capable — indeed many GC locomotives were not scrapped but transferred to other LNER depots and were to last well into BR days. But they did allow longer and heavier trains to be introduced to cater for the increased demand.

The ongoing development of passenger services brought about a demand for even stronger motive power. 'A3' Pacific No 4480 *Enterprise* was tested in August 1938 and in September, when arrangements had been made to strengthen and extend turntables at Marylebone and Leicester, No 2558 *Tracery* was allocated to Gorton for working on London Extension services. This locomotive was supplemented by other Pacifics sent to Neasden, Leicester and Gorton. Before the 'B17' and 'A3' era began in earnest the GC 'Directors' still proved to be excellent performers, with Cecil J. Allen recording a run on the 3.15pm 'Sheffield Special' in 1935. The load of the train had increased from GC flyer days from four bogies up to seven or eight and on this occasion the train engine was 'Director' No 5510 *Princess Mary* with eight coaches weighing 276 tons tare. Another carriage was added at Nottingham to make the total 330 tons gross. Neasden was passed at 67mph, Harrow at 50mph, and Aylesbury at an astonishing 75mph — 45min 4sec from Marylebone, right on time. From there speeds were no less than 55mph up the banks with 70mph at Calvert. Woodford was passed in 74min 15sec, 80mph was recorded at Braunston, 52mph at Lutterworth, and 83mph at Whetstone, giving an arrival at Leicester Central 2½min early in 105min 42sec. This was only 70min for the 74.8 miles from Amersham to Whetstone. Leicester to Nottingham was accomplished virtually in 'even time', Loughborough and Gotham being passed at 75mph. North of Nottingham Victoria the line undulated through a mining area with many speed restrictions but No 5510 with 330 tons in tow passed Bulwell Common at 52mph, 45mph by Kirkby South Junction and once past Pilsley averaged 81.2mph from Heath to Killamarsh with 90mph through Staveley Town. The 38.2 miles from Nottingham to Sheffield was run to the booked time of 45min 17sec. It is amazing to note that this sort of performance was a regular occurrence on the GC.

Cecil J. Allen also travelled behind the then new 'B17s' including No 2851 *Derby County* on the 6.20pm from Marylebone to Bradford in 1936. For him, it was a good chance to compare the performance

Below:
The Class C5 Atlantics were four locomotives, built at Gorton between 1905 and 1906, and were three-cylinder compounds using the Smith system. All retained green livery until 1928, so No 5259 *King Edward VII*, does not have long to run before it was painted black. It is seen in March of that year passing Neasden South Junction (the joint line coming in from the left) on a Manchester to Marylebone express. The Met signalbox for their suburban line can be seen to the right of the photograph. *F. R. Hebron/Rail Archive Stephenson*

Table 2— *Continued*

SCOTLAND, NEWCASTLE, YORK, CLEETHORPES, HULL, LIVERPOOL, MANCHESTER, BRADFORD, HUDDERSFIELD, SHEFFIELD, NOTTINGHAM, LEICESTER, and LONDON

Week Days

Miles from London Rd.	Station	1	2	3	4	5	6	7	8	9	10	11	12	13	14	15	16	17	18	19	20	21	22	23	24	25	26	27	28	29	30
		mrn	mrn	mrn	mrn	mrn	mrn	mrn	aft	mrn	mrn	mrn	mrn	mrn	mrn	mrn	mrn	aft	mrn	non	aft	mrn	aft	aft	aft	aft	aft	aft	aft	mrn	aft
	57 Liverpool (Central) dep	..	..	..	..	..	..	..	10∥30	..	..	..	5r5	..	..	7K17	7K17	..	..	..	..	10K30	..	..	..	2 30	..	..	..	..	..
	57 Warrington (Central) "	..	..	..	..	..	..	..	11∥22	..	..	..	6r33	..	..	8K44	8K44	..	..	..	..	11K0	..	..	..	3 0	..	..	..	..	..
	57 Stockport (Tiv. Dale) "	..	..	..	..	..	..	..	..	..	..	..	6y51	..	..	..	..	..	..	..	..	..	..	..	..	..	..	..	..	..	..
	57 Manchester (Cen.) dep	..	..	..	..	..	..	..	mrn	..	..	..	7r43	..	..	..	..	..	..	..	..	..	..	..	..	3r30	..	..	..	..	..
	67 " (London Rd.) "	..	..	..	..	..	..	..	1 40	..	..	..	8 20	..	..	9 45	9 45	..	..	..	..	12 25	..	..	..	3 50	..	..	..	..	5 0
—	76 Oldham (Clegg St.) dep	..	..	..	..	..	..	..	..	..	..	..	8 0	..	..	9 17	9 17	..	..	..	..	12 7	..	..	..	1S56	..	..	..	..	4 30
—	75 Stalybridge "	..	..	..	..	..	..	..	..	..	..	..	7 52	..	..	8 32	8 32	..	..	..	..	..	..	..	..	..	..	..	..	..	..
—	75 Ashton (Oldham Rd.) "	..	..	..	..	..	..	..	..	..	..	..	8 15	..	..	9 26	9 26	..	..	..	..	12 16	..	..	..	2S6	..	..	..	..	4 38
—	67 Guide Bridge dep	..	..	..	..	..	..	..	..	..	..	..	8 32	..	..	9 56	9 56	..	..	..	..	12c37	..	..	..	4 1	..	..	..	..	5 11
—	67 Glossop (Central) dep	..	..	..	..	..	..	..	..	..	..	..	8V9	..	..	9V28	9V28	..	..	..	..	12EV46		..	..	..	..	..	..	..	..
—	Bradford (Exch.) dep	..	..	..	..	..	..	..	..	..	..	..	7 8	..	..	8 38	8 38	..	..	..	..	10S43	..	..	..	..	..	..	..	..	4 9
—	Halifax (Old) "	..	..	..	..	..	..	..	..	..	..	..	7 45	..	..	8 28	8 28	..	..	..	..	10S20	..	..	..	..	..	..	..	..	4 5
—	Huddersfield "	..	..	..	..	..	..	..	..	..	5 47	..	8 16	..	..	10 0	10 0	..	..	..	..	12S14	..	..	..	..	..	..	..	..	5 0
—	67 Barnsley U 73 "	..	..	..	..	..	..	..	..	..	6 3	..	8 10	..	..	..	..	..	..	..	..	..	..	..	2 0	2 18	..	..	..	..	5 5
	67 Penistone dep	..	..	..	..	..	..	..	2 34	..	6 50	..	9 21	..	..	1041	1041	..	..	..	..	1F27	..	..	2 5	4 46	..	..	..	..	6 15
—	.03 Aberdeen dep	..	..	..	..	..	..	..	..	..	..	..	6R40	..	..	..	..	..	..	..	..	..	..	..	..	..	..	..	..	6 10	..
—	.0 Dundee (Tay Bridge) "	..	..	..	..	..	..	..	..	..	..	..	8R37	..	..	..	..	..	..	..	..	..	..	..	..	..	..	..	..	8 5	..
—	03 Glasgow (Queen St.) "	..	..	..	..	..	..	..	..	..	..	..	8Z45	..	..	..	..	..	..	..	..	..	..	..	..	..	..	..	..	8 25	..
—	03 Edinburgh (Wav.) "	..	..	..	..	..	..	..	..	..	aft	..	10Z20	..	..	..	..	..	..	..	..	..	..	..	..	..	..	..	..	10 0	..
—	03 Newcastle "	..	..	..	..	..	..	..	..	..	10Zy45	..	1a10	..	..	..	..	..	..	..	..	9 50	..	..	..	..	..	..	..	12p55	..
—	.0 Scarborough (Cen.) "	..	..	..	..	..	..	..	..	..	..	..	..	..	..	..	..	..	..	..	..	10 43	..	..	..	..	..	..	..	1 5	..
—	.25 Harrogate 83 "	..	..	..	..	..	..	..	..	..	8n44	..	..	..	..	..	..	..	..	..	..	9n10	..	..	11C15	..	..	..	..	1n20	3n19
—	114 York 1 "	..	..	..	..	..	..	..	..	..	12ay55	..	3H10	..	..	..	..	..	..	..	..	12p10	..	..	..	..	..	..	..	2y1	..
—	.8 Hull "	..	..	..	..	..	..	..	..	..	..	..	6 13	..	..	..	..	..	..	..	..	9u45	..	..	1235	..	..	..	..	1y40	4 15
—	67 Doncaster (Central) "	..	..	..	..	..	..	..	..	..	1y47	..	8 32	..	..	..	..	..	..	..	..	11uh12	..	..	2 10	..	..	..	..	3y40	5 30
—	67 Rotherham T 114 dep	..	..	..	..	..	..	..	..	..	..	..	9 1[illegible]	..	..	..	..	..	..	..	..	1 27	..	..	2 51	..	..	..	..	..	6 1
—	67 Cleethorpes dep	..	..	..	..	..	..	..	..	..	..	..	5H50	..	..	..	..	..	..	..	..	10a45	..	..	..	..	..	..	..	2 20	3H5
—	67 Grimsby Town "	..	..	..	..	..	..	..	..	..	..	..	6H12	..	..	..	..	..	..	..	..	11 5	..	..	..	..	..	..	..	2 41	3H26
—	67 Lincoln "	..	..	..	..	..	..	..	..	..	..	..	7 23	..	..	..	..	..	..	..	..	10a50	..	..	2 28	..	..	..	..	..	..
—	67 Retford "	..	..	..	..	..	..	..	..	..	6 30	..	8 15	..	..	..	..	..	..	..	..	12B55	..	..	3B15	..	..	..	..	4B50	6B0
—	Sheffield (Victoria) dep	..	..	..	..	..	..	..	6 15	..	7 55	..	9 55	..	..	11 5	11 5	..			..	2 0	..	..	4 0	5 10	..	..	..	5 40	6 55
42¾	Darnall for Handsworth	..	..	..	..	..	..	..	6 22	..	8 1	..	10 1	..	..	..	..	..			..	..	..	..	4 7		..	..	..	5 46	7 1
46¼	Woodhouse	..	..	..	..	..	..	..	6 31	..	8 8	..	10 8	..	..	..	..	..			..	2 10	..	..	4 14		..	..	..	5 53	7 8
47¾	Beighton	..	..	..	..	..	..	..	6 35	..	8 12	..	1013	..	..	..	..	..			..	..	..	..	4 19		..	..	..	5 58	7 13
49½	Killamarsh	..	..	..	..	..	..	..	6 42	..	8 17	..	1018	..	..	..	..	..			..	2S18	..	..	4 24		..	..	..	6 3	7 18
51½	Eckington and Renishaw	..	..	..	..	..	..	..	6 48	..	8 22	..	1023	..	..	..	..	..			..	2S23	..	..	4 2[illegible]		..	..	..	6 8	7 23
53½	Staveley Town	..	6 10	..	..	..	..	..	6 55	..	8 27	..	1029	..	..	1128	1128	..	1140	12 0	..	2†23	2 30	..	4 37		..	..	..	6 14	7 31
54¾	Staveley Works R	..	6 15	..	..	..	..	..	7 0	..	8 32	..	1034	..	..			..	1145	12 5	..	..	2 35	..	4 42		..	..	..	6 19	7 36
56½	Sheepbridge P	..	6 20	..	..	..	..	..	7 5	..	8 37	..	1039	..	..			..	1150	1210	..	..	2 40	..	4 47		..	..	..	6 24	7 41
58¼	Chesterfield (Central) arr	..	6 24	..	..	..	..	..	7 9	..	8 41	..	1043	..	..			..	1154	1214	..	2†33	2 44	..	4 51		..	..	..	6 28	7 45
	Chesterfield (Central) dep	..	Stop	..	..	..	..	..	7 14	..	..	..	1044	..	..			..	Stop	Stop	..	2†35	Stop	..	4 58		..	..	..	6 31	Stop
60¾	Grassmoor ¶	..		..	..	..	..	..	..	..	..	..	..	..	..			..			..	..		..	..		..	..	..	..	
59	Heath	..	..	..	..	..	..	..	7 28	..	..	..	1058	..	..			..	..	..	..	..	..	..	5 11		..	..	..	6 45	..
61½	Pilsley	..	..	..	..	..	..	..	7 34	..	..	..	11 4	..	..			..	..	..	..	..	..	..	5 17		..	..	..	6 51	..
63	Tibshelf Town	..	..	..	..	..	..	..	7 39	..	..	..	11 8	..	..			..	..	..	..	2†55	..	..	5 22		..	..	..	6 56	..
67¾	Kirkby Bentinck	..	..	..	..	..	..	..	7 48	..	..	..	1117	..	..			..	..	..	..	3†4	..	..	5 31		..	..	..	7 6	..
—	66 Lincoln dep	..	..	..	..	..	..	..	..	..	..	..	..	..	..			..	..	..	..	..	..	..	..		12T37	..	..	..	..
—	Mls Ollerton dep	..	..	..	..	..	..	..	..	..	..	..	..	..	..			..	..	..	..	..	..	..	..		1T25	..	..	..	..
—	1½ Edwinstowe	..	..	..	..	..	..	..	..	7 47	..	..	..	..	..			..	..	..	..	..	..	..	..		1T29	..	..	..	..
—	8½ Mansfield (L·N·E·R) arr	..	..	..	..	..	..	..	..	8 1	..	..	..	..	..			..	..	..	..	..	..	..	..		2T1	..	..	..	..
	Mansfield (L·N·E·R) dep	..	..	..	..	..	..	7 14	..	8 5	..	..	..	1124	..			..	..	..	1 48	..	..	..	..		5 48	..	6 42	..	..
—	11½ Sutton-in-Ashfield (C.)	..	..	..	..	..	..	7 22	..	8 13	..	..	..	1132	..			..	..	..	1 56	..	..	..	..		5 56	..	6 50	..	..
—	13 Kirkby-in-Ashfield (C.)	..	..	..	..	..	..	7 28	..	8 19	..	..	..	1138	..			..	..	..	2 2	..	..	..	..		6 2	..	6 56	..	..
73¾	Hucknall (Central)	..	..	..	..	..	..	7 40	8 3	8 33	..	..	1132	1150	..			..	..	..	2 14	3†15	..	..	5 46		6 18	..	7 8	7 20	..
76¼	Bulwell Common	..	..	..	..	..	..	7 46	8 9	8 39	..	..	1138	1156	..			..	..	..	2 20	3†21	..	..	5 52		6 24	..	7 14	7 28	..
78	New Basford	..	..	..	..	..	..	7 51	8 14	8 44	..	..	..	12 1	..			..	..	..	2 25	..	..	..	..		6 29	..	7 19	..	..
		1	2	3	4	5	6	7	8	9	10	11	12	13	14	15	16	17	18	19	20	21	22	23	24	25	26	27	28	29	30
79¾	Nottingham (Victoria) arr	..	..	..	..	..	..	7 55	8 18	8 48	..	..	1140	12 5	..	1 12	1212	..	..	aft	2 29	3†29	..	..	6 0	6 11	6 33	..	7 23	7 35	..
	Nottingham (Victoria) dep	..	..	..	..	..	6 25	8 0	Stop	..	..	9 30	..	..		1217	1217	..	..	1253	Stop	3†34	..	5 45	..	6 16	..	..	Stop	..	..
80½	Arkwright Street	..	..	..	..	..	6 28	8 3		..	..	9 33	..	..		..	..	..	..	1258		..	..	5 48	..	..	..	..		..	..
84	Ruddington	..	..	..	..	..	6 35	8 10	..	..	..	9 40	..	..		..	..	..	..	1 5	..	..	..	5 56	..	..	..	..	..	..	..
87¼	Rushcliffe Halt	..	..	..	..	..	6 41	8 16	..	..	..	9 46	..	..		..	..	..	..	1 11	..	..	..	6 2	..	..	..	..	..	..	..
88¾	East Leake	..	..	..	..	..	6 46	8 21	..	..	..	9 51	..	..		..	..	..	..	1 16	..	..	..	6 7	..	..	..	..	..	..	..
93	Loughborough (Central)	..	..	..	..	..	6 56	8 30	..	..	..	10 1	..	..		1238	1238	..	..	1 26	..	3†56	..	6 18	..	6 37	..	..	..	..	..
95¼	Quorn and Woodhouse	..	..	..	..	..	7 1	8 35	..	..	..	10 6	..	..		..	..	..	..	1 31	..	..	..	6 23	..	..	..	..	..	..	..
98	Rothley	..	..	..	..	..	7 7	8 41	..	..	..	1012	..	..		..	..	..	..	1 37	..	..	..	6 29	..	..	..	..	..	..	..
100¼	Belgrave and Birstall	..	..	..	..	..	7 13	8 47	..	..	..	1018	..	..		..	..	..	..	1 43	..	..	..	6 35	..	..	..	..	..	..	..
103	Leicester (Central) arr	..	..	..	..	..	7 17	8 51	..	..	..	1022	..	..		1254	1254	..	..	1 47	..	4†12	aft	6 39	..	6 53	..	..	..	..	..
	Leicester (Central) dep	6 20	..	..	..	..	7 30	Stop	..	..	..	..	..	..	1155	1259	1259	..	..	1 52	..		5 22	Stop	..	6 58	..	7 7	..	..	..
107¾	Whetstone	6 29	..	..	..	..	7 39		..	..	..	..	..	..	12 4	..	..	..	..	2 1	..		5 32		..	..	..	7 16	..	..	..
112¼	Ashby Magna	6 39	..	..	..	..	7 49		..	..	..	..	..	..	1214	..	..	..	..	2 11	..		5 43	..	..	..	..	7 26	..	..	..
116	Lutterworth	6 48	..	..	..	..	7 59	..	..	..	..	..	..	..	1223	..	1 21	..	..	2 20	..		5 53	..	..	7 17	..	7 36	..	..	..
122¼	Rugby (Central)	6d58	..	..	..	..	8 11	..	..	..	..	..	..	..	1233	1 29	1 33	..	..	2 32	..		6 3	..	..	7 29	..	7 48	..	..	..
127¼	Braunston and Willoughby	..	..	..	..	..	8 20	..	..	..	..	..	..	..	..	..	..	..	..	2 41	..		..	..	..	..	..	7 57	..	..	..
134¼	Charwelton	..	..	..	..	..	8 33	..	..	..	..	..	..	..	..	..	..	..	..	2 54	..		..	..	..	..	..	8 10	..	..	..
137	Woodford and Hinton arr	7 35	..	..	..	..	8 38	..	..	..	..	..	..	..	..	1 49	1 53	..	..	2 59	..		..	..	..	7 49	..	8 15	..	..	..
161	9 Stratford-on-Avon arr	..	..	..	..	..	..	..	..	..	..	..	..	..	..	..	..	..	..	..	..		..	aft	..	8 50	..	..	..	..	..
—	Woodford & Hinton dep	..	..	..	..	..	8 50	..	..	..	..	..	..	..	..	..		..	..	..	..		..	5 30	..	..	..	..	..	..	..
141	Eydon Road Halt	..	..	..	..	..	9 1	..	..	..	..	..	..	..	..	..		..	..	..	..		..	5 39	..	..	..	..	..	..	..
144½	Chalcombe Road Halt	..	..	..	..	..	9 8	..	..	..	..	..	..	..	..	..		..	..	..	..		..	5 47	..	..	..	..	..	..	..
14[illegible]	Banbury arr	..	..	..	..	..	9 17	..	mrn	..	..	..	..	..	..	..		..	..	..	..		..	5 57	..	..	..	..	..	..	aft
—	Mls Banbury dep	..	..	..	..	..	..	..	10 0	..	..	..	..	..	..			..	..	..	..		..	Stop	..	6 25	..	..	..	..	8 50
—	3½ Chalcombe Road Halt	..	..	..	..	..	..	..	10 8	..	..	..	..	..	..			..	..	..	..		..		..	6 33	..	..	..	..	..
—	7 Eydon Road Halt	..	..	..	..	..	..	..	10 16	..	..	..	..	..	..			..	..	..	..		..		..	6 41	..	..	..	..	..
—	11 Woodford & Hinton arr	..	..	..	..	..	..	..	10 24	..	..	..	..	..	..	..		..	..	..	..		..		..	6 49	..	..	..	..	9 8
—	9 Stratford-on-Avon dep	..	mrn	..	..	..	..	..	..	..	..	..	..	..	..	..	..	..	..	..	..	..	..		..	6 20	..	..	..	..	..
—	Woodford and Hinton dep	..	7 40	..		..	9 5	..	..	..	..	..	..	..	..	1 52	1 56	..		3 7	..	..	..		..	7 52	..	..	..	..	..
140	Culworth	..	7 47	..		..	9 12	..	..	..	..	..	..	..	..	..	..	..		3 14	..	..	..		..	..	..	..	..	..	..
143¼	Helmdon, for Sulgrave	..	7 55	..		..	9 20	..	..	..	..	..	..	..	..	..	..	..		3 22	..	..	..		..	..	..	..	aft	..	..
146¾	Brackley (Central)	..	8 3	..		..	9 28	..	..	..	..	..	..	..	..	..	2 12	..		3 30	..	..	..		..	8 8	..	..	8 20	..	..
151¼	Finmere	..	8 12	..		..	9 38	..	..	..	..	..	..	..	..	..	..	..		3 40	..	..	..		..	..	..	..	8 30	..	..
157¼	Calvert	..	8 22	..		..	9 49	..	..	..	..	..	..	..	..	..	..	..		3 51	..	..	..		..	..	..	..	8 41	..	..
162	Quainton Road	..	8 30	..		..	9 57	mrn	..	..	..	..	..	..	..	..	..	..		3 59	aft	..	..		..	..	..	..	..	..	..
168¾	Aylesbury	..	8 40	..		8 55	10 7	1040	..	..	..	..	..	..	..	2 31	2 40	3 15		4 9	4 50	..	..		..	8 36	..	..	..	..	..
192¾	Northwood	..	..	..		..	1120	..	..	..	..	..	..	..	..	..	..	..		5 34	..	..	..		..	..	..	..	..	..	..
196¾	Harrow on the Hill	..	..	..		..	1134	..	..	..	..	..	..	..	..	..	..	..		5 48	..	..	..		..	9 23	..	..	..	..	..
163¾	Wotton	..	..	8 26	..	..	..	..	..	..	..	..	..	..	..	..	..	..	aft	..	..	..	..	aft	..	..	..	..	8 52	..	..
169	Haddenham (Bucks)	..	..	8 36	8 53	..	..	..	..	..	..	..	..	..	..	..	..	..	2 56	..	..	..	..	7 17	..	..	..	..	9 2	..	..
171¼	Ilmer Halt	..	..	8 42	8 58	..	..	..	..	..	..	..	..	..	..	..	..	..	3 2	..	..	..	..	7 22	..	..	..	..	9 8	..	..
174½	Princes Risborough arr	..	..	8 52	9 5	9 13	..	11 0	..	..	..	..	..	..	..	..	..	3 32	3 11	..	5 8	..	..	7 28	..	..	..	..	9 14	..	..
182¾	High Wycombe "	..	..	9 11	9 21	9§18	..	1118	..	..	..	..	..	..	..	..	..	3 53	3 27	..	5 28	..	..	8 13	..	..	..	..	9 35	..	..
206	London (Marylebone) "	..	9 45	10 22	..	..	1151	..	..	..	..	..	..	..	..	3 30	3 44	..	4 4	6 5	..	..	..	..	..	9 40	..	..	1048	..	..

Column notes (printed vertically in the columns): Col. 14 — Saturdays only. Col. 15 — Except Saturdays; TC and Buffet Car, Manchester (L. Rd.) to Marylebone. Col. 16 — Saturdays only; TC and Buffet Car, Manchester (L. Rd.) to Marylebone. Col. 18 — Except Saturdays; One class only. Col. 19 — Saturdays only. Col. 21 — TC and Buffet Car, Manchester (Lon. Rd.) to Leicester (Central). Col. 23 — One class only. Col. 25 — TC and Buffet Car, Manchester (Lon. Road) to Marylebone. Col. 4 — One class only.

A For particulars of London Suburban Services, see Suburban Time Table.
A Dep. 9 41 aft. on Suns. via Leeds (City) and York
a Mrn
B Change at Woodhouse.
C Via Leeds Cen. & Doncaster
c 5 mins. later on Sats.
d Dep. 7 15 mrn
E Except Saturdays
F 4 mins. later Sats.
H Via Doncaster
K Via Manchester (Central) and (London Rd). Passengers cross the town at own expense
k Dep. Doncaster 12 15 aft. on Sats.
H Via Godley Junction
n Via Holbeck and Doncaster
P Sheepbridge and Brimington
p Aft
R Station for Barrow Hill
R Except Sat ngts. Dep. Aberdeen 6 10 and Dundee T.B.) 8 12 aft on Sundays
r Change at Guide Bridge
S Saturdays only
T Rotherham and Masboro'
T Via Warsop
TC Through Carriage
U Barnsley (Court House)
U Thurs. and Sats.
u Via Retford except on Sats.
V Change at Dinting.
y Via Retford
Z Except Saturday nights but applies on Sunday nights
† 6 mins later on Sats
§ Change at Princes Risborough
∥ Via Manchester (Central) & (London Rd). Passengers cross the town at own expense. Dep Liverpool 9 45 and Warrington 10 26 aft. on Suns.
¶ Station closed.

Left:
The LNER wartime timetable for 28 October 1940.

Above:
The first LNER design to make an impact on GC line passenger services were the 'B17s' which were introduced from 1936. No 2851 *Derby County* makes an impressive sight as it leaves Nottingham Victoria with an express from Liverpool to Leicester on 1 August 1937. The train is about to enter the short tunnel to exit the station. The photographer is standing just by the tunnel mouth.
T. G. Hepburn/Rail Archive Stephenson

of these locomotives with the Robinson Atlantics which had been the usual power, along with other traditional GC types. With a load of seven coaches, 255 tons gross, the 1 in 100 up through Canfield Place to Neasden saw speeds of 40mph and Neasden South Junction was passed in only 8min. The train was routed via High Wycombe which was passed in only 35min 7sec and on time. Once through Princes Risborough the train virtually took off into the Vale of Aylesbury, passing Haddenham at 82mph and achieving an average of 74mph from Princes Risborough to Haddenham. The train had, at one time, slipped coaches at Finmere and Woodford, but these had been replaced by station stops. Finmere, 59 miles from Marylebone, was reached in 65min 17sec and Woodford in only another 16min 21sec for the 14.6 miles. On the run to Leicester, Braunston & Willoughby was passed at 85mph, Rugby at 71mph, and Whetstone at 88mph. These trains were heavier than the earlier GC flyers and No 2859 *Sheffield United* with Driver Newall of Leicester took a nine-coach train of 325 tons non-stop from Marylebone to Finmere in only 63min 14sec. The same train travelled from Woodford to Leicester in only 32min 55sec, passing Braunston & Willoughby at 85mph and Whetstone again at 88mph.

Driver Newall continued the fine reputation of Leicester shed with a train of 11 coaches of 400 tons, that was checked (as it usually was — causing much caustic comment about the GW or 'Gas Works Railway' from GC crews!) behind the 6.10pm Paddington to Wolverhampton on the GW/GC joint line. On this occasion, the 6.18pm from Marylebone, later the 'Master Cutler', with 'B17' power reached Finmere in 67min 53sec, running from Finmere to Woodford in only 17min 42sec while the 34 miles from Woodford to Leicester took only 32min 18sec, with 89mph at Whetstone before the 'GC' stop at Leicester Central. Another run was even better, this time double-headed (a practice that was not encouraged on the thrifty Great Central, even in BR days, unlike on the Midland) with 'B17s' Nos 2855 and 2842 on the front of 13 coaches for 475 tons. The 34 miles from Woodford Halse to Leicester were run in only 31min 5sec, with 82mph at Braunston & Willoughby, and 92mph at Whetstone.

As well as the 'A3s' the new 'V2' 2-6-2s became regular performers on the GC — right up to the end of passenger services, and many would say that these locomotives, more than the 'A3s', were the most successful performers on the GC. Another Cecil J. Allen run, with Driver Tetlow in charge, saw the 6.18pm from Marylebone, consisting of seven coaches, delayed once again by the tardy performance of the 6.10pm from Paddington to Birmingham. This caused a 3½min late departure from Woodford that would have been worse had there not been some impressive driving and firing. Princes Risborough to milepost 155, 19½ miles, was covered at an average speed of 80.5mph and on leaving Woodford another burst of speed was made to pass Staverton Road at 81mph, Braunston at 90mph, over the hump at Rugby at 76mph, and climbing to Lutterworth at 65mph. By Whetstone, the train was running at 88mph which gave the impressive figure for Staverton Road to Leicester South Goods at an average of 79.3mph for 26.9 miles.

With 'B17' and 'A3' haulage continuing through the war, when the normal express timetable was decimated and trains dominated by the military, the line suffered from an austere wartime maintenance package that saw speed restrictions being enforced rather than instant repairs. The GC was also dominated by freight services during this period and by the end of the war, as with the rest of the system, much remained to be done to restore a normal express service to anything like the timings that had been achieved in 1939. But many would argue that the best was yet to come. As the wartime restrictions were gradually lifted and locomotives given thorough overhauls, some of the best express performances were achieved by GC crews with their glorious 'A3s'.

British Railways Eastern Region 1947-58

After the end of World War 2, a new machine, the Thompson 'B1' 'Springbok' 4-6-0, was allocated to the line. Despite coping with the passenger services that were on offer to them in this postwar period, trains became more heavily loaded and the 'B1s' began to struggle with the fast point-to-point timings required of them, as well as with the speed restrictions and track condition north of Nottingham. The solution would most probably have been the transfer of 'V2' 2-6-2 'Green Arrows' *en masse* to the line, but instead, 'A3' Pacifics that had been working on the line before the war made a return. At the same time, to help relaunch the express passenger services, from September 1947 the 6.25pm from Marylebone to Sheffield Victoria and the up working, the 7.40am from Sheffield to Marylebone were given the name the 'Master Cutler'. A year later another named train was launched, the 'South Yorkshireman' — the 10am from Bradford and Sheffield to Marylebone, the down working being the 4.50pm from Marylebone. By 1949 there had been an influx of 'A3s' to work the express service which ran as follows with few timetable changes up to their withdrawal in January 1960:

Left:
Blue-liveried 'A3' No 60052 *Prince Palatine*, arrives at Nottingham with the up 'Master Cutler' in 1950. *T. G. Hepburn/Ian Allan Library*

Below:
'A3' Pacific No 60050 *Persimmon* approaches Princes Risborough with the down 'Master Cutler' on Whit Monday, 21 May 1956. The train is passing Saunderton Summit — the up line can be seen parting from the down on the left, which allowed London-bound trains an easier passage through the Chilterns. The train is loaded to 11 coaches — a mixture of LNER and BR Mk 1s all in carmine and cream livery. At this time, the train usually ran with nine coaches — the front two had possibly been added for the extra traffic generated by the Bank Holiday.
C. R. L. Coles/Ian Allan Library

Above:
The 'A3s' never had a complete monopoly on the expresses and this is evident as 'V2' No 3650 arrives at Nottingham Victoria with the 8.25am from Manchester London Road (the 10.44am from Nottingham to Marylebone) on 5 August 1946. The 'V2' still carries the black livery applied to these locomotives during the war. *T. G. Hepburn/Rail Archive Stephenson*

Below :
Further south, No 60049 *Galtee More* takes a dip on Charwelton water troughs with the up 'South Yorkshireman' in 1952. The 'Yorkshireman' was the other named train introduced to the London Extension after the war. *H. Gordon Tidey/Real Photographs*

Up Trains

7.40am	Sheffield to Marylebone — the 'Master Cutler' — via High Wycombe
8.30am	Manchester to Marylebone — via Aylesbury
10am	Bradford/Sheffield to Marylebone — the 'South Yorkshireman' — via Aylesbury
2.10pm	Manchester to Marylebone — via Aylesbury
4.5pm	Manchester to Marylebone — via Aylesbury
9.30pm	Liverpool (and 10.25pm ex-Manchester) to Marylebone Mail — via Aylesbury

Down Trains

1.45am	Marylebone to Sheffield 'Newspaper' — via Aylesbury
10am	Marylebone to Manchester — via Aylesbury
12.15pm	Marylebone to Manchester — via High Wycombe
3.20pm	Marylebone to Manchester — via Aylesbury
4.50pm	Marylebone to Bradford — the 'South Yorkshireman' — via Aylesbury
6.18pm	Marylebone to Sheffield — the 'Master Cutler' — via High Wycombe
10pm	Marylebone to Manchester and Liverpool Mail — via Aylesbury

In 1949 the Eastern Region transferred 'A3s' Nos 60048, 60049, 60053 (replaced by 60052 in May 1949), 60054, 60061 and 60090 (replaced by 60102 in May 1949) to Leicester shed and Nos 60050, 60051 and 60111 to Neasden. Other variations followed in the 1950s which saw Nos 60103, 60106 and 60107 allocated to Leicester. The Pacifics immediately made an impact on services in terms of reliability and style, but the Midland services to Nottingham and Leicester were still faster and more frequent. Manchester to London passengers found the former LNWR main line expresses quicker, but the GC line services did establish a reputation for business travellers that attracted a regular and loyal clientele — much to the annoyance of the London Midland Region's management. However the writing appeared to be on the wall for the GC line expresses as car ownership rapidly expanded in the 1950s — as well as the development of competing rail services. The expresses had been reduced from eleven or twelve coaches down to a standard nine. Despite the 'Master Cutler' loading relatively well the other expresses only averaged about 80 passengers per train. By this time the ownership of the route came under close scrutiny. The Eastern Region realised that the 'A3s' would be better employed on the GN main line and by September 1957 they had gone, being replaced by the 'V2s', whose smaller driving wheels seemed more suited to the fast starts that the GC line timetables required. Then, from February 1958, the GC was transferred to the London Midland Region — an almost inevitable occurrence as the line ran deep into its territory.

Table 2— *continued*

LONDON, LEICESTER, NOTTINGHAM, SHEFFIELD, HUDDERSFIELD, BRADFORD, MANCHESTER, LIVERPOOL, HULL, CLEETHORPES, YORK, NEWCASTLE, and SCOTLAND

Week Days—*continued*

Station	1	2	3	4	5	6	7	8	9	10
	p.m	p.m B	p.m	p.m		p.m	p.m B	p.m B	p.m B	p.m B
Notes	Saturdays only			Runs 24th June to 9th September inclusive; Saturdays only; Buffet Car Ramsgate dep. 12 28 p.m. to		RG Marylebone to Manchester (Lon. Rd.)		Except Saturdays		
LONDON (M'lebone) . dep	1 38	2§20	..		..	3 20	..	..	3§50	..
High Wycombe ...... "	..	3§43	..		..	..	3 43	..	..	4 52
Princes Risborough . "	..	4 10	..		..	..	4 3	..	..	5 12
Ilmer Halt	..	4 15	..		..	..	..	..	..	..
Haddenham (Bucks.)	..	4 20	..		..	..	..	..	..	..
Wotton	..	..	..		..	..	..	..	..	..
Harrow on the Hill	1 57	Stop	..		..	3 39	..	..	4§8	..
Northwood	2 11	..	..		..	..	..	..	4§20	..
Aylesbury	3 17	..	..		..	4 22	4 20	5 25	5§23	5 30
Quainton Road	3 27	..	..		..	..	..	5 35	5§33	..
Calvert	3 37	..	..		..	..	Stop	5 43	Stop	Stop
Finmere	3 47	..	..		..	..	..		..	..
Brackley (Central)	3 57	..	..		..	4 50	..		..	..
Helmdon, for Sulgrave	4 5	..	..		..	..	..		..	..
Culworth	4 14	..	..		..	..	..		..	..
Woodford Halse .... arr	4 20	p.m	..	4 34	..	5 4	..		..	..
Woodford Halse ...... dep		4 45	..		..	..	..		..	..
Eydon Road Halt		4 54	..		..	..	..		..	..
Chalcombe Road Halt		5 2	..		..	..	..		..	..
Banbury .... arr		5 15	..		..	..	..		..	..
Banbury .... dep		Stop	..		..	..	..		..	..
Chalcombe Road Halt		..	..		..	..	..		..	..
Eydon Road Halt		..	..		..	..	..		..	..
Woodford Halse .... arr		..	..		..	..	..	Stop	..	p.m
Woodford Halse .... dep		..	..	4 37	..	5 6	..	..	..	5 30
Charwelton	..	..	..	..	..	..	..	..	..	5 36
Braunston and Willoughby	..	..	..	..	..	..	..	..	..	5 47
Rugby (Central)	..	..	..	5* 0	..	5 28	..	..	..	5*58
Lutterworth	..	..	..	5*14	..	..	..	..	..	6 11
Ashby Magna	..	..	..	..	..	..	..	..	..	6 19
Whetstone	..	..	..	..	..	..	..	..	..	6 28
Leicester (Central) arr	..	..	..	5 34	..	5 51	..	..	p.m	6 36
Leicester (Central) dep	..	..	5 20	5 39	..	5 56	..	..	6 15	..
Belgrave and Birstall	..	..	5 25	..	..	..	..	..	6 20	..
Rothley	..	..	5 31	..	..	..	..	..	6 26	..
Quorn and Woodhouse	..	..	5 37	..	..	..	..	..	6 32	..
Loughborough (Central)	..	..	5*44	5*55	..	6 11	..	..	6u40	..
East Leake	..	..	5 52	..	..	..	..	..	6 48	..
Rushcliffe Halt	..	..	5 55	..	..	..	..	..	..	..
Ruddington	..	..	6 2	..	..	..	..	..	6 57	..
Arkwright Street	..	..	6 9	..	..	..	..	..	7 4	..
Nottingham (Victoria) arr	..	p.m	6 12	6 17	..	6 30	p.m	p.m	7 7	..
Nottingham (Victoria) dep	..	5 56	..		..	6 33	6 40	6 48	..	..
New Basford	..	..	..		..		6 45	6 53	..	..
Bulwell Common	..	..	..		..		6 50	6 58	..	..
Hucknall (Central)	..	6 8	..		..		6 56	7 4	..	..
Kirkby-in-Ashfield (Cen.)	..	..	..		..		..	7 20	..	..
Sutton-in-Ashfield (Cen)	..	..	..		..		..	7 25	..	..
Mansfield (E.R.) arr	..	..	..		..		..	7 30	..	..
Mansfield (E.R.) dep	..	..	..		..		..	7 33	..	..
Edwinstowe	..	..	..		..		..	7 49	..	..
Ollerton .... arr	..	..	..		..		..	..	..	..
79 LINCOLN .... arr	..	..	..		..		..	..	..	..
Kirkby Bentinck	..	6 22	..		..		7 11	..	..	..
Tibshelf Town	..	6 32	..		..		7 21	..	..	..

Station	11	12	13	14	15	16	17	18	19	20	21
		p.m B	p.m B	p.m	p.m		p.m	p.m B	p.m B	p.m B	p.m
Notes			Saturdays only; To Brackley, arr. 7 12 p.m	THE SOUTH YORKSHIREMAN RG Marylebone to Bradford				Saturdays only; From Marylebone, dep. 4 45 p.m	Except Saturdays		
LONDON (M'lebone) . dep	..	4 20	4 45	4 50	..	..	5 0	..	5 22	..	6 8
High Wycombe ...... "	..	5 23	5 55	..	..	..	..	..	..	6§k24	..
Princes Risborough . "	..	5 41	6 18	..	..	..	..	..	..	6 50	..
Ilmer Halt	..	..	..	..	..	..	..	..	..	..	..
Haddenham (Bucks.)	..	5 49	6 29	..	..	..	..	..	..	..	..
Wotton	..	..	6 41	..	..	..	..	6 41	..	..	..
Harrow on the Hill	..	..		..	..	..	..	..	5 40	..	..
Northwood	..	..		..	..	..	..	..	5 52	..	6 36
Aylesbury	..	..		5 49	..	..	6 18	..	6 55	7 8	7j34
Quainton Road	..	..		..	..	..	6 28	..	7 5	..	7j44
Calvert	..	..			..	..	6 38	6 53		..	7j54
Finmere	..	..			..	..	6 48	7 3		..	8j 4
Brackley (Central)	..	..			..	..	6 59	7 12		..	8j15
Helmdon, for Sulgrave	..	..			..	..	7 8			..	..
Culworth	..	..			..	..	7 16			..	Cc
Woodford Halse .... arr	..	..			..	..	7 22			..	8j31
Woodford Halse ...... dep	..	..			..	..	Stop			..	..
Eydon Road Halt	..	..			..	..	..			..	..
Chalcombe Road Halt	..	..			..	..	..		..	..	..
Banbury .... arr	..	..			..	..	..		..	..	..
Banbury .... dep	..	..			5 50	..	..		..	..	..
Chalcombe Road Halt	..	..			5 59	..	..		..	..	..
Eydon Road Halt	..	..			6 7	..	..		..	..	..
Woodford Halse .... arr	..	..			6 15	..	p.m		..	..	..
Woodford Halse .... dep	..	..	..		Stop	..	7 5		..	..	..
Charwelton	..	..	..		..	..	7 11		..	..	..
Braunston and Willoughby	..	..	..		..	..	7 22		..	..	..
Rugby (Central)	..	..	..		..	..	7 32		..	..	..
Lutterworth	..	..	..		..	..	7 44		..	..	..
Ashby Magna	..	..	..		..	..	7 52		..	..	..
Whetstone	..	..	..		..	..	8 1	..	..	..	..
Leicester (Central) arr	..	..	..	7 0	p.m	..	8 9	..	..	..	..
Leicester (Central) dep	..	..	..	7 5	7 12	..	Stop	..	..	..	..
Belgrave and Birstall	..	..	..	..	7 17	..	..	..	..	..	..
Rothley	..	..	..	..	7 23	..	..	..	..	..	..
Quorn and Woodhouse	..	..	..	..	7 29	..	..	..	..	..	..
Loughborough (Central)	..	..	..	..	7*36	..	..	..	..	..	..
East Leake	..	..	..	..	7 44	..	..	..	..	..	..
Rushcliffe Halt	..	..	..	..	7 47	..	..	..	..	..	..
Ruddington	..	..	..	..	7 56	..	..	..	..	..	..
Arkwright Street	..	..	..	..	8 4	..	..	..	..	..	..
Nottingham (Victoria) arr	..	..	..	7 33	8 7	..	..	..	..	..	..
Nottingham (Victoria) dep	..	..	..	7 36	..	..	..	..	..	..	..
New Basford	..	..	..	..	..	..	..	..	..	..	..
Bulwell Common	..	..	..	..	..	..	..	..	..	..	..
Hucknall (Central)	..	..	..	..	..	..	..	..	..	..	..
Kirkby-in-Ashfield (Cen.)	..	..	..	..	..	..	..	..	..	..	..
Sutton-in-Ashfield (Cen)	..	..	..	..	..	..	..	..	..	..	..
Mansfield (E.R.) arr	..	..	..	..	..	..	..	..	..	..	..
Mansfield (E.R.) dep	..	..	..	..	..	..	..	..	..	..	..
Edwinstowe	..	..	..	..	..	..	..	..	..	..	..
Ollerton .... arr	..	..	..	..	..	..	..	..	..	..	..
79 LINCOLN .... arr	..	..	..	..	..	..	..	..	..	..	..
Kirkby Bentinck	..	..	..	..	..	..	..	..	..	..	..
Tibshelf Town	..	..	..	..	..	..	..	..	..	..	..

Station	22	23	24	25	26	27	28	29	30	31
	p.m.	p.m	p.m B		p.m B	p.m	p.m		p.m	p.m B
Notes	Except Saturdays; THE MASTER CUTLER RG Marylebone to Sheffield	Saturdays only; THE MASTER CUTLER. RG Marylebone to Sheffield	Except Saturdays				Runs 8 minutes later on Fridays and Saturdays		Runs 8 minutes later on Fridays and Saturdays	Except Saturdays
LONDON (M'lebone) . dep	6 15	6 15	6 22	..	..	..	..	..	..	8 20
High Wycombe ...... "			7 11	..	..	..	..	..	..	9 15
Princes Risborough . "			7 32	..	8 10	..	..	..	..	9 36
Ilmer Halt			Vv	..	Vv	..	..	..	..	..
Haddenham (Bucks.)			7 43	..	8 20	..	..	..	..	9 46
Wotton			7 53	..	Stop	..	..	..	..	9 53
Harrow on the Hill			..	..	..	..	..	..	..	..
Northwood			..	..	..	..	..	..	..	..
Aylesbury			..	..	..	..	..	..	..	..
Quainton Road			..	..	..	..	..	..	..	..
Calvert			Vv	..	..	..	..	..	..	1010
Finmere			Vv	..	..	..	..	..	..	1020
Brackley (Central)			8 25	..	..	..	..	..	..	1029
Helmdon, for Sulgrave				..	..	..	..	..	..	
Culworth				..	..	..	..	..	..	
Woodford Halse .... arr				..	..	..	..	..	..	
Woodford Halse ...... dep				..	..	..	..	..	..	
Eydon Road Halt				..	..	..	..	..	..	
Chalcombe Road Halt				..	..	..	..	..	..	
Banbury .... arr				..	..	..	..	..	..	
Banbury .... dep			..	..	..	..	..	..	..	..
Chalcombe Road Halt			..	..	..	..	..	..	..	..
Eydon Road Halt			..	..	..	..	..	..	..	..
Woodford Halse .... arr			..	..	..	..	..	..	..	..
Woodford Halse .... dep			..	..	..	..	..	..	..	..
Charwelton			..	..	..	..	..	..	..	..
Braunston and Willoughby			..	..	..	..		..		..
Rugby (Central)	8 8	8 8	..	..	..	8 30		..		..
Lutterworth	..	..	..	..	..	8 42		..		..
Ashby Magna	..	..	..	..	..	8 50		..		..
Whetstone	..	..	..	..	..	8 59		..		..
Leicester (Central) arr	8 31	8 31	..	..	p.m	9 7		..		..
Leicester (Central) dep	8 36	8 36	..	..	8 55	..		..		..
Belgrave and Birstall	..	..	..	..	9 0	..		..		..
Rothley	..	..	..	..	9 6	..		..		..
Quorn and Woodhouse	..	..	..	..	9 12	..		..		..
Loughborough (Central)	..	..	..	..	9 19	..		..		..
East Leake	..	..	..	..	9 27	..		..		..
Rushcliffe Halt	..	..	..	..	..	..		..		..
Ruddington	..	..	..	..	9 37	..		..		..
Arkwright Street	..	..	..	..	..	..	..	..	..	..
Nottingham (Victoria) arr	9 4	9 4	..	..	9 47	..	..	..	..	..
Nottingham (Victoria) dep	9 8	9 8	..	..	..	..	9 55	..	10 7	..
New Basford	..	..	..	..	..	..	..	..	..	..
Bulwell Common	..	..	..	..	..	..	10 3	..	..	..
Hucknall (Central)	..	..	..	..	..	..	10 9	..	10 19	..
Kirkby-in-Ashfield (Cen.)	..	..	..	..	..	..	..	..	10 33	..
Sutton-in-Ashfield (Cen)	..	..	..	..	..	..	..	..	10 38	..
Mansfield (E.R.) arr	..	..	..	..	..	..	..	..	10 43	..
Mansfield (E.R.) dep	..	..	..	..	..	..	..	..	..	..
Edwinstowe	..	..	..	..	..	..	..	..	..	..
Ollerton .... arr	..	..	..	..	..	..	..	..	..	..
79 LINCOLN .... arr	..	..	..	..	..	..	..	..	..	..
Kirkby Bentinck	..	..	..	..	..	..	1027	..	..	..
Tibshelf Town	..	..	..	..	..	..	1037	..	..	..

	1	2	3	4	5	6	7	8	9	10	11	12	13	14	15	16	17	18	19	20	21	22	23	24	25	26	27	28	29	30	31
Pilsley	..	6 37	..	dep. 12 10 p.m. and Margate Nottingham, see page 35	..	..	7 26	..	..	..	..	..	..	..	..	..	..	..	..	..	..	Except Saturdays. THE MASTER CUTLER	Saturdays only THE MASTER CUTLER	..	..	..	..	1042	..	..	..
Heath	..	6 43	..		..	..	7 32	..	..	..	..	..	..	..	..	..	..	..	..	..	..			..	..	..	..	1048	..	..	..
Chesterfield (Central) arr	..	6 55	..		..	..	7 44	..	..	..	..	..	..	..	..	..	p.m	..	..	..	..			..	..	..	..	11 1	..	..	..
Chesterfield (Central) dep	..	..	..		..	..	..	..	..	..	..	..	..	..	..	..	8 25	..	..	..	..			..	..	..	..	Runs 8 minutes later on Fridays and Saturdays	..	..	..
Sheepbridge P	..	..	..		..	..	..	..	..	..	..	..	..	..	..	..	8 29	..	..	..	..			..	..	..	..		..	..	..
Staveley Works R	..	..	..		..	..	..	..	..	..	..	..	..	..	..	..	8 34	..	..	..	..			..	..	..	..		..	..	..
Staveley Town	..	..	..		..	..	..	..	..	..	..	..	..	..	..	..	8 41	..	..	..	..			..	..	..	..		..	..	..
Eckington and Renishaw	..	..	..		..	..	..	..	..	..	..	..	..	..	..	..	8 46	..	..	..	..			..	..	..	..		..	..	..
Killamarsh	..	..	..		..	..	..	..	..	..	..	..	..	..	..	..	8 51	..	..	..	..			..	..	..	..		..	..	..
Beighton	..	..	..		..	..	..	..	..	..	..	..	..	..	..	..	8S56	..	..	..	..			..	..	..	..		..	..	..
Woodhouse	..	..	..		..	..	..	..	..	..	..	..	..	..	..	..	8r59	..	..	..	..			..	..	..	..		..	..	..
Darnall, for Handsworth	..	..	..		..	..	..	..	..	..	..	..	..	..	..	..	9r7	..	..	..	..			..	..	..	..		..	..	..
Sheffield (Victoria) arr	..	..	..		..	7 32	..	..	..	..	..	..	..	8 35	..	..	9r12	..	..	..	..	10 11	1011	..	..	..	..		..	..	..
80 Retford arr	..	..	..		..	..	..	..	..	..	..	..	..	9N37	..	..	..	..	..	..	..	11 12	1112	..	..	..	..		..	..	..
80 Lincoln "	..	..	..		..	..	..	..	..	..	..	..	..	..	..	..	..	..	..	..	..	..	..	..	..	..	..		..	..	..
80 Grimsby Town "	..	..	..		..	..	..	..	..	..	..	..	..	..	..	..	..	..	..	..	..	..	..	..	..	..	..		..	..	..
80 Cleethorpes "	..	..	..		..	..	..	..	..	..	..	..	..	..	..	..	..	..	..	..	..	..	..	..	..	..	..		..	..	..
80 Rotherham T 104 arr	..	..	..	..	..	..	..	..	..	..	..	..	..	9b11	..	..	..	..	..	..	..	..	..	..	..	..	..	..	..	..	..
80 Doncaster (Central) arr	..	..	..	..	..	..	..	..	..	..	..	..	..	9b39	..	..	..	..	..	..	..	12y 9	12y9	..	..	..	..	..	..	..	..
103 Hull "	..	..	..	..	..	..	..	..	..	..	..	..	..	11i 9	..	..	..	..	..	..	..	2y32	..	..	..	..	..	..	..	..	..
104 York 1 "	..	..	..	..	..	..	..	..	..	..	..	..	..	12[illegible]g32		..	..	..	..	..	..	1y 1	1y 1	..	..	..	..	..	..	..	..
Harrogate 97 "	..	..	..	..	..	..	..	..	..	..	..	..	..	11U52	..	..	..	..	..	..	..	4L54	..	..	..	..	..	..	..	..	..
Scarborough (Cen. "	..	..	..	..	..	..	..	..	..	..	..	..	..	..	..	..	..	..	..	..	..	5 32	5 35	..	..	..	..	..	..	..	..
Newcastle "	..	..	..	..	..	..	..	..	..	..	..	..	..	2g32	..	..	..	..	..	..	..	3 0	3 0	..	..	..	..	..	..	..	..
Edinburgh (Wav.) "	..	..	..	..	..	..	..	..	..	..	..	..	..	5g39	..	..	..	..	..	..	..	6 8	6 8	..	..	..	..	..	..	..	..
Glasgow (Queen St.) "	..	..	..	..	..	..	..	..	..	..	..	..	..	7 38	..	..	..	..	..	..	..	7 38	9 3	..	..	..	..	..	..	..	..
Dundee (Tay Bridge) "	..	..	..	..	..	..	..	..	..	..	..	..	..	8 25	..	..	..	..	..	..	..	8 57	9 19	..	..	..	..	..	..	..	..
Aberdeen "	..	..	..	..	..	..	..	..	..	..	..	..	..	..	..	..	..	..	..	..	..	11 16	1122	..	..	..	..	..	..	..	..
80 Penistone arr	..	..	..	..	..	8 0	..	..	..	..	..	..	..	9 3	..	..	..	..	..	..	..	10R53	11 8	..	..	..	..	..	..	..	..
80 Barnsley U 87 arr	..	..	..	..	..	8 37	..	..	..	..	..	..	..	..	..	..	..	..	..	..	..	..	..	..	..	..	..	..	..	..	..
Huddersfield "	..	..	..	..	..	..	..	..	..	..	..	..	..	9 33	..	..	..	..	..	..	..	11L34	1149	..	..	..	..	..	..	..	..
Halifax (Old) "	..	..	..	..	..	..	..	..	..	..	..	..	..	10 37	..	..	..	..	..	..	..	..	..	..	..	..	..	..	..	..	..
Bradford (Exch.) "	..	..	..	..	..	..	..	..	..	..	..	..	..	10 14	..	..	..	..	..	..	..	..	..	..	..	..	..	..	..	..	..
80 Glossop (Central) arr	..	..	..	..	..	8m38	..	..	..	..	..	..	..		..	..	..	..	..	..	..	..	..	..	..	..	..	..	..	..	..
80 Guide Bridge arr	..	..	..	..	..	8 40	..	..	..	..	..	..	..	THE SOUTH YORKSHIREMAN	..	..	..	..	..	..	..	11R41	1156	..	..	..	..	..	..	..	..
90 Ashton (Oldham Rd.) arr	..	..	..	..	..	9 56	..	..	..	..	..	..	..		..	..	..	..	..	..	..	..	..	..	..	..	..	..	..	..	..
89 Stalybridge "	..	..	..	..	..	..	..	..	..	..	..	..	..		..	..	..	..	..	..	..	..	..	..	..	..	..	..	..	..	..
90 Oldham (Clegg St.) "	..	..	..	..	..	10 5	..	..	..	..	..	..	..		..	..	..	..	..	..	..	..	..	..	..	..	..	..	..	..	..
80 Manchester (L.Rd.) arr	..	..	..	..	..	8 55	..	..	..	..	..	..	..		..	..	..	..	..	..	..	11R58	1213	..	..	..	..	..	..	..	..
80 " (Central) "	..	..	..	..	..	..	..	..	..	..	..	..	..		..	..	..	..	..	..	..	..	..	..	..	..	..	..	..	..	..
80 Stockport (Tiv. Dale) arr	..	..	..	..	..	..	..	..	..	..	..	..	..		..	..	..	..	..	..	..	..	..	..	..	..	..	..	..	..	..
80 Warrington (Cen.) "	..	..	..	..	..	9K51	..	..	..	..	..	..	..		..	..	..	..	..	..	..	..	..	..	..	..	..	..	..	..	..
80 Liverpool (Cen.) "	..	..	..	..	..	10K22	..	..	..	..	..	..	..		..	..	..	..	..	..	..	..	..	..	..	..	..	..	..	..	..

A For particulars of London Suburban Services, see Table 13
a a.m.
b Arr. Rotherham 9 26 and Doncaster 9 57 p.m. on Saturdays
Cc Stops on Fridays only when required to set down from Marylebone on notice to the Guard at Marylebone
E Except Saturdays
g 9 mins. later on Saturdays
H Via Doncaster
i Arr. 11 19 p.m. on Fridays and Saturdays
j 4 mins. later on Saturdays
K Via Manchester (Lon. Rd.) and (Central). Passengers cross the town at own expense
k Dep. 6 15 p.m. on Saturdays
L Arr. 11 49 p.m. on Fridays
L Via Retford, Doncaster, and Holbeck. Except Suns.
m Change at Dinting. Arr. 8 53 p.m. on Saturdays
N 4 minutes later on Fridays and Saturdays
P Sheepbridge & Brimington
p p.m.
R Station for Barrow Hill
R 15 minutes later on Fridays
RC Restaurant Car
r 3 mins. later on Saturdays
S Saturdays only
T Rotherham and Masboro'
TC Through Carriages
Vv Stops when required to set down on notice being given to the Guard
U Barnsley (Court House)
U Via Doncaster and Holbeck
u Arr. 4 minutes *earlier*
y Via Retford
* Arr. 3 minutes *earlier*
§ Change at Princes Risboro'
Ⓐ Third class only

Above:
BR Eastern Region express timetable 5 June to 24 September 1950.

Left: 'V2' No 60831 from Leicester shed arrives at Nottingham with the 2.20pm from Manchester to Marylebone on 8 April 1953. The first vehicle in the train is a six-wheel bogie restaurant car which has not yet been painted in the new BR livery.
J. P. Wilson/Rail Archive Stephenson

Right:
At this time, 'B1s' still appeared regularly on expresses and No 61187 is seen heading the nine-coach 12.15pm from Marylebone to Manchester near Denham and Harefield on the GW/GC joint line on 6 June 1958. GC line expresses were pretty much standardised on nine-coach formations, but reliefs did run, especially on summer weekends.
E. R. Wethersett/Real Photographs

British Railways London Midland Region 1958-69

The 'V2s' were not liked by the LMR which saw them as 'foreign' locomotives and soon allocated its own motive power to the line in the form of 'Black 5s' together with a few of the new BR Standard Class 5s. These 4-6-0s excelled in the hands of GC crews as did the new '9F' 2-10-0 freight locomotives that were used on expresses when other power was short. There are many stories about '9Fs' on GC expresses; suffice it to say that speeds in the 90s were common and it was not long before the new owners restricted them to just 60mph! The line's controllers would also regularly 'borrow' an Eastern Region locomotive that had worked in on an inter-regional freight service and use it on an express turn to and from Marylebone, having reported it as 'failed'! But with the advent of 'London Midlandisation', as it was known, the 'Master Cutler' was transferred to King's Cross, where it became a diesel-hauled Pullman service that ran to Sheffield via Retford. The expresses had continued to run, one even in the path of the 'Cutler's', but the LMR had other ideas and on 2 January 1960, they were withdrawn and replaced by a semi-fast service of just three trains in either direction with no catering facilities. These were proposed to be four-car non-corridor DMUs leaving Marylebone at 8.40am, 12.40pm and 4.30pm. In the up direction departures from Nottingham were at 8.40am, 12.25pm and 5.15pm. However, no crews had been trained on the diesels and the semi-fasts were six-coach formations with steam haulage. In any case, in the early 1960s, the LMR was planning to use the route as a cross-country line and withdraw all London to Nottingham services and close all the local stations.

Services were dominated by 'Black 5s' allocated to Annesley shed, but occasionally 'B1s' from Colwick and BR Standard classes were used, which were still driven in 'GC' style and had brisk point-to-point timings. Sunday services continued from Nottingham to Marylebone

Below:
The take-over of the GC by the LMR in February 1958 soon brought that region's motive power onto the scene. This is evident as the up 'South Yorkshireman' is seen leaving Aylesbury with 'Black 5' No 44842 in charge. Even the headboard was changed from ER blue to maroon, as were the station signs. Thankfully, Aylesbury South cabin is now preserved in working order at Swithland on today's Great Central Railway. The date is 8 November 1958. *Mike Mitchell*

Right:
By 1965, this is what had replaced the expresses. Originally six coaches, the three replacement semi-fasts had been reduced to four coaches to make them even less attractive to passengers. Sidings were being lifted and there were only a few more weeks left of the Annesley to Woodford 'Runners'. BR Standard '5' No 73004 heads the 14.38 from Marylebone to Nottingham away from Lutterworth on 22 May 1965. The new M1 motorway, still to be opened, looms on the left of the photograph. *Mike Mensing*

Below right:
The last day at Woodford. The yards to the north of the station were being demolished and track lifted and the 'Banbury Motor' was replaced by buses in April 1966. The 'Runners' had ended the previous year and passing through Woodford on one of the semi-fasts was a sobering experience, especially for the train crews. The last up 5.15pm from Nottingham to Marylebone, hauled by 'Black 5' No 44984, complete with wreath, pauses at Woodford on 3 September 1966. At that time there were locals in the village who could remember the opening of the railway in 1899 and were there to see it close. No 44984 had the dubious distinction of working the last Marylebone to Manchester and Liverpool mails at 22.45 from Marylebone on the same evening. How apt that the very last train should be one from Marylebone to Manchester. *Author's Collection*

Table 116 — Weekdays

Nottingham and Leicester to London Marylebone

Miles	Station		A MX	E MX	G MO	B MO	V MX [sleeper]	X MO [sleeper]	J MX	H MO [sleeper]	R MX [sleeper]		Y [sleeper]		
	SHEFFIELD VICTORIA	d	..	00 09	..	..	..	..	00 45	..	..	..	..	..	..
	NOTTINGHAM VICTORIA	a	..	01 20	..	..	..	..	01 58	..	..	..	..	..	..
0	NOTTINGHAM VICTORIA	d	..	01 33	..	..	..	..	02 15	..	..	..	..	07 40	08 15
9	EAST LEAKE	d	..	..	..	..	..	..	..	..	..	..	..	07 54	08 29
13½	LOUGHBOROUGH CENTRAL	a	..	01 52	..	..	..	..	..	..	..	..	..	08 02	08 37
	LOUGHBOROUGH CENTRAL	d	..	01 53	..	..	..	..	..	..	..	..	..	08 04	08 38
23½	LEICESTER CENTRAL	a	..	02 08	..	..	..	..	02 46	..	..	..	..	08 17	08 49
	LEICESTER CENTRAL	d	..	02 23	..	..	..	..	03 05	..	..	..	..	08 20	08 52
32½	ASHBY MAGNA	d	..	..	..	..	..	..	..	..	..	..	..	08 36	09 08
36½	LUTTERWORTH	d	..	..	..	..	..	..	..	..	..	..	..	08 45	09 17
43½	RUGBY CENTRAL	a	..	02 48	..	..	..	..	..	..	..	..	..	08 55	09 26
	RUGBY CENTRAL	d	..	02 52	..	..	..	..	..	..	..	..	..	..	09 30
57½	WOODFORD HALSE	a	..	03 15	..	..	..	..	03 50	..	..	..	..	..	09 50
—	WOODFORD HALSE	d	00 12	03 17	..	..	..	..	..	..	..	07t47	..	..	10t17
68½	BANBURY	a	00 33	03 38	..	..	..	..	..	..	..	08t11	..	..	10t41
	BANBURY	d	..	..	..	..	..	..	..	..	..	..	..	..	09t45
—	WOODFORD HALSE	a	..	..	..	..	..	..	..	..	..	..	..	..	09t49
—	WOODFORD HALSE	d	..	..	..	..	..	..	03 55	..	..	..	..	..	09 52
64½	BRACKLEY	d	..	..	..	..	..	..	..	..	..	..	..	..	10 06
88½	AYLESBURY	a	..	..	..	..	..	..	04s42	..	..	..	..	..	10 29
95	120 PRINCES RISBOROUGH	a	..	..	..	..	..	..	07 14	..	..	..	..	..	11 10
103	120 HIGH WYCOMBE	a	..	..	..	..	..	..	07 28	..	..	..	..	..	12 48
117½	HARROW ON THE HILL	a	..	..	..	..	..	..	..	..	..	..	..	..	11 09
126½	LONDON MARYLEBONE	a	..	..	04 40	04 43	05 10	05 30	05 42	05 47	05 57	..	06 20	..	11 25

Station				Q [⌶]	L [⌶]
SHEFFIELD VICTORIA	d	..	..	11 37	11 37
NOTTINGHAM VICTORIA	a	..	..	12 45	12 45
NOTTINGHAM VICTORIA	d	12 25	..	12 48	12 48
EAST LEAKE	d	12 38	..	..	..
LOUGHBOROUGH CENTRAL	a	12 44	..	13 05	13 05
LOUGHBOROUGH CENTRAL	d	12 47	..	13 07	13 07
LEICESTER CENTRAL	a	13 00	..	13 20	13 20
LEICESTER CENTRAL	d	13 05	..	13 23	13 23
ASHBY MAGNA	d	13 17	..	..	..
LUTTERWORTH	d	13 25	..	..	..
RUGBY CENTRAL	a	13 33	..	13 46	13 46
RUGBY CENTRAL	d	13 35	..	13 49	13 49
WOODFORD HALSE	a	13 53	..	..	..
WOODFORD HALSE	d	..	13t17	..	..
BANBURY	a	..	13t41	14 28	14 28
BANBURY	d	12t30	..	..	..
WOODFORD HALSE	a	12t54	..	..	..
WOODFORD HALSE	d	13 54	..	..	..
BRACKLEY	d	14 06	..	..	..
AYLESBURY	a	14 27	..	..	..
120 PRINCES RISBOROUGH	a	15b35	..	..	..
120 HIGH WYCOMBE	a	16e04	..	..	..
HARROW ON THE HILL	a	15 29	..	..	..
LONDON MARYLEBONE	a	15 18	..	..	..

Heavy figures denote through carriages; light figures denote connecting services
For general notes see page 4

For complete service between Aylesbury and London Marylebone see Table 120

A Through carriages to Swindon arr. 02 20
E Through carriages from York dep 22 22 SX to Swindon arr. 05 45
G Through carriages from Manchester Piccadilly dep. 23 50 Sun
H [sleeper] and through carriages from Manchester Piccadilly dep. 01 00
J Through carriages from Manchester Central dep. 23 05 SX
L From 6 September. [⌶] and through carriages from York dep. 10 08 to Bournemouth West arr. 18 44
Q Until 4 September, [⌶] and through carriages from Newcastle dep. 08 30 to Bournemouth West arr. 18 44 SX, 18 35 SO
R [sleeper] and through carriages from Manchester Piccadilly dep 01 00
B Through carriages from Liverpool Lime Street dep. 23 55 Sun
V [sleeper] and through carriages from Glasgow Central dep. 19 00 SX
X [sleeper] and through carriages from Glasgow Central dep. 19 00 Sun
Y [sleeper] and through carriages from Liverpool Lime Street dep. 00 30
b On Saturdays arr. Princes Risborough 15 40
e On Saturdays arr. High Wycombe 15 58
s Stops to set down only
t By omnibus

Table 116 — Weekdays

Nottingham and Leicester to London Marylebone

Station			SX	SO	SX	SX	C FSX	D FSO
SHEFFIELD VICTORIA	d	..	..	..	..	..	20 55	20 55
NOTTINGHAM VICTORIA	a	..	..	..	..	..	22 09	22 09
NOTTINGHAM VICTORIA	d	17 15	18 15	..	..	..	22 22	22 22
EAST LEAKE	d	17 29	18 29	..	..	..	..	..
LOUGHBOROUGH CENTRAL	a	17 37	18 37	..	..	..	22 41	22 41
LOUGHBOROUGH CENTRAL	d	17 39	18 39	..	..	..	22 43	22 43
LEICESTER CENTRAL	a	17 50	18 52	..	..	..	22 58	22 58
LEICESTER CENTRAL	d	17 54	18 55	..	..	..	23 12	23 12
ASHBY MAGNA	d	18 10	19 11	..	..	..	..	..
LUTTERWORTH	d	18 19	19 20	..	..	..	..	23 32
RUGBY CENTRAL	a	18 28	19 30	..	..	..	23 41	23 41
RUGBY CENTRAL	d	18 29	..	..	..	..	23 47	23 47
WOODFORD HALSE	a	18 49	..	..	..	..	00 10	00 10
WOODFORD HALSE	d	18t57	..	..	..	..	00 12	00 12
BANBURY	a	19t20	..	..	..	..	00 33	00f33
BANBURY	d	17t45	..	21 10	21 16	23 50	..	..
WOODFORD HALSE	a	18t09	..	21 32	21 38	00 12	..	..
WOODFORD HALSE	d	18 51	..	..	..	..	..	..
BRACKLEY	d	19 04	..	..	..	..	..	..
AYLESBURY	a	19 27	..	..	..	..	..	..
120 PRINCES RISBOROUGH	a	19b55	..	..	..	..	..	..
120 HIGH WYCOMBE	a	20c57	..	..	..	..	..	..
HARROW ON THE HILL	a	20 09	..	..	..	..	..	..
LONDON MARYLEBONE	a	20 25	..	..	..	..	..	..

Sundays

Station		J		K	L	R [sleeper]	U [sleeper]	H [sleeper]	Y
SHEFFIELD VICTORIA	d	..	..	00 09	00 24	..	..	..	..
NOTTINGHAM VICTORIA	a	..	..	01 20	01 37	..	..	..	..
NOTTINGHAM VICTORIA	d	..	..	01 33	01 52	..	..	..	..
EAST LEAKE	d	..	..	..	..	..	..	..	..
LOUGHBOROUGH CENTRAL	a	..	..	01 52	..	..	..	..	..
LOUGHBOROUGH CENTRAL	d	..	..	01 53	..	..	..	..	..
LEICESTER CENTRAL	a	..	..	02 08	02 25	..	..	..	..
LEICESTER CENTRAL	d	..	..	02 23	02 40	..	..	..	..
ASHBY MAGNA	d	..	..	..	..	..	..	..	..
LUTTERWORTH	d	..	..	..	..	..	..	..	..
RUGBY CENTRAL	a	..	..	02 48	..	..	..	..	..
RUGBY CENTRAL	d	..	..	02 52	..	..	..	..	..
WOODFORD HALSE	a	..	..	03 15	03 26	..	..	..	..
WOODFORD HALSE	d	00 12	..	03 17	..	..	..	..	..
BANBURY	a	00 35	..	03 38	..	..	..	..	..
BANBURY	d	..	00 20	..	..	..	..	..	..
WOODFORD HALSE	a	..	00 45	..	..	..	..	..	..
WOODFORD HALSE	d	..	..	..	03 28	..	..	..	..
BRACKLEY	d	..	..	..	..	..	..	..	..
AYLESBURY	a	..	..	..	..	..	..	..	..
120 PRINCES RISBOROUGH	a	..	..	..	..	..	..	..	..
120 HIGH WYCOMBE	a	..	..	..	..	..	..	..	..
HARROW ON THE HILL	a	..	..	..	..	..	..	..	..
LONDON MARYLEBONE	a	..	..	..	05 06	05 26	05 56	06 10	08 20

Heavy figures denote through carriages; light figures denote connecting services
For general notes see page 4

For complete service between Aylesbury and London Marylebone see Table 120

C Through carriages from York dep. 18 40 (from 5 July to 2 September through carriages from Scarborough Central dep. 17 28) to Swindon arr. 02 20
D Through carriages from York dep. 18 40 FO, 18 46 SO (from 3 July to 4 September through carriages from Scarborough Central dep. 17 28) to Swindon arr. 02 20
J Through carriages to Swindon arr 02 20
K Through carriages from York dep. 22 22 SO to Bristol Temple Meads arr. 07 45
L Through carriages from Manchester Central dep. 22 50 SO
H [sleeper] and through carriages from Manchester Piccadilly dep. 01 00
X [sleeper] and through carriages from Glasgow Central dep. 19 00 SO
U [sleeper] and through carriages from Liverpool Lime Street dep. 00 30
Y Through carriages from Glasgow Central dep 22 20 SO
b On Saturdays arr. Princes Risborough 20 50
c On Saturdays arr. High Wycombe 21 07
f On Sunday mornings arr. Banbury 00 35
t By Omnibus

Table 116 — Weekdays

London Marylebone to Leicester and Nottingham

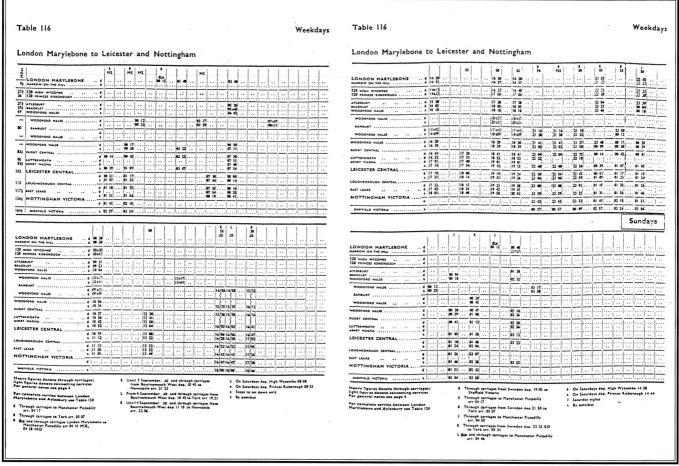

Miles	Station		A MX	B MX	MX	D [sleeper]		MX			
	LONDON MARYLEBONE	d	..	..	..	00 15	01 40	..	..	03 40	..
9½	HARROW ON THE HILL	d	..	..	..	..	..	..	..	..	..
27½	120 HIGH WYCOMBE	d	..	..	..	..	..	..	..	..	..
36	120 PRINCES RISBOROUGH	d	..	..	..	..	..	..	..	..	..
37½	AYLESBURY	d	..	..	..	..	..	..	..	05 20	..
59½	BRACKLEY	d	..	..	..	..	..	..	..	05s48	..
69	WOODFORD HALSE	a	..	..	..	..	..	..	..	06 02	..
—	WOODFORD HALSE	d	..	..	00 12	..	..	03 17	..	..	07t47
80	BANBURY	a	..	..	00 33	..	..	03 38	..	..	08t11
	BANBURY	d	..	..	..	..	..	..	..	..	..
—	WOODFORD HALSE	a	..	..	..	..	..	..	..	..	..
—	WOODFORD HALSE	d	..	00 17	..	..	..	..	..	06 50	..
83½	RUGBY CENTRAL	a	..	00 38	..	..	03 22	..	..	07 11	..
	RUGBY CENTRAL	d	00 14	00 42	..	..	03 23	..	..	07 20	..
90	LUTTERWORTH	d	..	..	..	..	..	..	..	07 31	..
93½	ASHBY MAGNA	d	..	..	..	..	..	..	..	07 40	..
103	LEICESTER CENTRAL	a	00 39	01 07	..	..	03 47	..	..	07 54	..
	LEICESTER CENTRAL	d	00 51	01 17	..	..	..	..	07 30	08 00	..
113	LOUGHBOROUGH CENTRAL	a	01 07	01 33	..	..	..	..	07 44	08 14	..
	LOUGHBOROUGH CENTRAL	d	01 10	01 35	..	..	..	..	07 45	08 16	..
117½	EAST LEAKE	d	..	..	..	..	..	..	07 54	08 25	..
126½	NOTTINGHAM VICTORIA	a	01 31	01 56	..	..	..	..	08 10	08 41	..
	NOTTINGHAM VICTORIA	d	01 41	02 10	..	..	..	..	..	..	..
164½	SHEFFIELD VICTORIA	a	02 57	03 24	..	..	..	..	..	..	..

Station			SO		K SX [⌶]	L [⌶]	N SO [⌶]
LONDON MARYLEBONE	d	08 38	..	..	..	..	..
HARROW ON THE HILL	d	08 58	..	..	..	..	..
120 HIGH WYCOMBE	d	08c30	..	..	..	..	..
120 PRINCES RISBOROUGH	d	08e45	..	..	..	..	..
AYLESBURY	d	09 31	..	..	..	..	..
BRACKLEY	d	09 53	..	..	..	..	..
WOODFORD HALSE	a	10 04	..	..	..	..	..
WOODFORD HALSE	d	10t17	..	13t17	..	..	..
BANBURY	a	10t41	..	13t41	..	..	..
BANBURY	d	09t25	..	..	14 58	14 58	15 33
WOODFORD HALSE	a	09t49	..	..	..	..	..
WOODFORD HALSE	d	10 06	..	..	..	..	..
RUGBY CENTRAL	a	10 24	..	..	15 35	15 35	16 13
RUGBY CENTRAL	d	10 27	12 30	..	15 38	15 38	16 16
LUTTERWORTH	d	10 36	12 41	..	..	..	..
ASHBY MAGNA	d	10 42	12 50	..	..	..	..
LEICESTER CENTRAL	a	10 55	13 04	..	16 02	16 02	16 41
LEICESTER CENTRAL	d	10 59	13 08	..	16 06	16 06	16 47
LOUGHBOROUGH CENTRAL	a	11 12	13 22	..	16 20	16 20	17 03
LOUGHBOROUGH CENTRAL	d	11 13	13 23	..	16 23	16 23	17 05
EAST LEAKE	d	11 20	13 32	..	..	..	..
NOTTINGHAM VICTORIA	a	11 35	13 49	..	16 43	16 43	17 26
NOTTINGHAM VICTORIA	d	..	..	..	16 47	16 47	17 30
SHEFFIELD VICTORIA	a	..	..	..	18 00	18 00	18 46

Heavy figures denote through carriages; light figures denote connecting services
For general notes see page 4

For complete service between London Marylebone and Aylesbury see Table 120

A Through carriages to Manchester Piccadilly arr. 04 17
B Through carriages to York arr. 05 07
D [sleeper] and through carriages London Marylebone to Manchester Piccadilly arr 04 41 MX, 04 58 MO
K Until 3 September. [⌶] and through carriages from Bournemouth West dep. 10 45 to Newcastle arr. 21 23
L From 6 September. [⌶] and through carriages from Bournemouth West dep. 10 45 to York arr 19.31
N Until 4 September. [⌶] and through carriages from Bournemouth West dep 11 10 to Newcastle arr. 22 06
c On Saturdays dep. High Wycombe 08 08
e On Saturdays dep. Princes Risborough 08 21
s Stops to set down only
t By omnibus

Table 116 — Weekdays

London Marylebone to Leicester and Nottingham

Station			SX	SO	SX	B FO	B FSX	B SO	G SX	H SX	J SO
LONDON MARYLEBONE	d	14 38	..	16 38	16 38	..	..	..	21 55	..	22 45
HARROW ON THE HILL	d	14 57	..	16 57	16 57	..	..	..	21 22	..	22 22
120 HIGH WYCOMBE	d	14b15	..	16 52	16 48	..	..	..	22 25	..	22 25
120 PRINCES RISBOROUGH	d	14e32	..	17 06	17 06	..	..	..	22 38	..	22 38
AYLESBURY	d	15 38	..	17 38	17 38	..	..	..	23 04	..	23 39
BRACKLEY	d	16 05	..	18 05	18 05	..	..	..	23 32	..	00 04
WOODFORD HALSE	a	16 18	..	18 18	18 18	..	..	..	23 46	..	00 18
WOODFORD HALSE	d	..	..	18t57	18t57	..	..	..	..	..	..
BANBURY	a	..	..	20t21	20t21	..	..	..	..	..	..
BANBURY	d	15t45	..	17t45	17t45	21 16	21 16	21 10	..	23 50	..
WOODFORD HALSE	a	16t09	..	18t09	18t09	21 38	21 38	21 32	..	00 12	..
WOODFORD HALSE	d	16 20	..	18 20	18 20	21 41	21 41	21 37	23 48	00 17	00 20
RUGBY CENTRAL	a	16 39	..	18 39	18 39	22 02	22 02	21 58	00 09	00 38	00 39
RUGBY CENTRAL	d	16 41	17 20	18 41	18 41	22 09	22 09	22 25	00 14	00 42	00 41
LUTTERWORTH	d	16 52	17 31	18 52	18 52	22 22	..	22 18	..	..	..
ASHBY MAGNA	d	17 01	17 40	19 01	19 01	..	..	..	..	..	..
LEICESTER CENTRAL	a	17 15	17 54	19 15	19 15	22 40	22 40	22 36	00 39	01 07	01 05
LEICESTER CENTRAL	d	17 19	18 00	19 19	19 24	22 50	22 50	22 43	00 51	01 17	01 10
LOUGHBOROUGH CENTRAL	a	17 31	18 14	19 31	19 36	23 06	23 06	22 59	01 07	01 33	01 24
LOUGHBOROUGH CENTRAL	d	17 33	18 15	19 33	19 38	23 08	23 08	23 01	01 10	01 35	01 26
EAST LEAKE	d	17 42	18 24	19 42	19 47	..	..	..	..	..	..
NOTTINGHAM VICTORIA	a	18 01	18 40	19 58	20 03	23 29	23 29	23 22	01 31	01 56	01 46
NOTTINGHAM VICTORIA	d	..	..	..	..	23 43	23 43	23 33	01 41	02 10	01 51
SHEFFIELD VICTORIA	a	..	..	..	..	00 57	00 57	00 49	02 57	03 24	03 04

Sundays

Station			J	K	L [sleeper]		
LONDON MARYLEBONE	d	..	..	..	00 15	00 40	..
HARROW ON THE HILL	d	..	..	..	..	23f37	..
120 HIGH WYCOMBE	d	..	..	..	..	..	..
120 PRINCES RISBOROUGH	d	..	..	..	..	..	..
AYLESBURY	d	..	..	..	..	01 38	..
BRACKLEY	d	..	00 04	..	..	..	..
WOODFORD HALSE	a	..	00 18	..	..	02 15	..
WOODFORD HALSE	d	00 12	..	..	..	..	03 17
BANBURY	a	00 35	..	..	..	..	03 38
BANBURY	d	..	..	00 20	..	..	..
WOODFORD HALSE	a	..	..	00 45	..	..	..
WOODFORD HALSE	d	..	00 20	00 47	..	02 18	..
RUGBY CENTRAL	a	..	00 39	01 08	..	02 36	..
RUGBY CENTRAL	d	..	00 41	01 13	..	02 38	..
LUTTERWORTH	d	..	..	..	..	02 56	..
ASHBY MAGNA	d	..	..	..	..	..	..
LEICESTER CENTRAL	a	..	01 05	01 38	..	03 13	..
LEICESTER CENTRAL	d	..	01 10	01 48	..	03 23	..
LOUGHBOROUGH CENTRAL	a	..	01 24	02 04	..	..	..
LOUGHBOROUGH CENTRAL	d	..	01 26	02 07	..	..	..
EAST LEAKE	d	..	..	..	..	..	..
NOTTINGHAM VICTORIA	a	..	01 46	02 28	..	03 55	..
NOTTINGHAM VICTORIA	d	..	01 51	02 43	..	..	..
SHEFFIELD VICTORIA	a	..	03 04	03 58	..	..	..

Heavy figures denote through carriages; light figures denote connecting services
For general notes see page 4

For complete service between London Marylebone and Aylesbury see Table 120

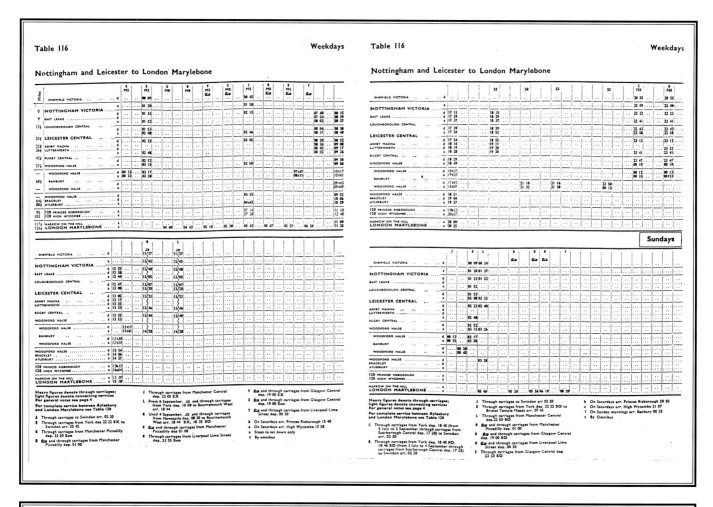

B Through carriages from Swindon dep. 19 05 to Sheffield Victoria
G Through carriages to Manchester Piccadilly arr 04 17
H Through carriages from Swindon dep 21 50 to York arr. 05 07
J Through carriages to Manchester Piccadilly arr. 04 20
K Through carriages from Swindon dep. 22 25 SO to York arr. 05 34
L [sleeper] and through carriages to Manchester Piccadilly arr. 04 46
b On Saturdays dep. High Wycombe 14 30
e On Saturdays dep. Princes Risborough 14 44
f Saturday nights
t By omnibus

Left:
Table 116 BR LMR semi-fast service 14 June 1965 to 17 April 1966.

Above:
The semi-fasts were supplemented by two local trains for commuters which ran between Nottingham and Rugby only. The 07.40 from Nottingham has just arrived at Rugby at 08.55 behind 'Black 5' No 45426 in March 1966. *Andrew Muckley*

at 9.50am, 3.50pm and 7.50pm, with down services leaving Marylebone at 10.10am, 1.25pm and 6.15pm. The LMR continued the rundown with the withdrawal of the Sunday trains on 10 March 1963 (all local services having been withdrawn seven days earlier). The semi-fasts had also been hauled by 'Royal Scot' 4-6-0s which had been displaced by diesels on the West Coast main line. The first batch was allocated to Annesley but after being repaired, along with some 'Britannia' Pacifics, they were transferred away. It soon became clear that the LMR was putting all its 'worst' locomotives onto the GC, but these were being used on 'express' type duties on the overnight sleepers that ran out of Marylebone during the West Coast main line electrification, as well as the Liverpool mails and the 'Newspaper'. Leicester was allocated two 'Royal Scots' in June 1962 and at the same time Neasden shed closed as DMUs totally dominated Marylebone suburban services. Its allocation of 'Britannias' that had been drafted in to work the heavier overnight trains in 1962, Nos 70014, 70048 and 70049, were transferred to Annesley, a depot that had acquired further batches of 'Royal Scots' to work GC line services. By the end of 1962, more 'London Midlandisation' saw all Woodford's 'B1s' replaced by 'Black 5s' and the Annesley 'Britannias' replaced by 'Royal Scots' in the shape of Nos 46111, 46143, 46153 and 46158. The overnight West Coast diversion services had seen more LMR power in the form of 'Jubilees', which were one of the few 'foreign' locomotive types liked by GC crews.

In 1963, LMS locomotives dominated the scene and even the 8.38am from Marylebone to Nottingham and the 12.25pm return working consisted of a four-car DMU. The semi-fast passenger services were run down even further from the summer of that year; with most of the local stations now closed they were reduced to four coaches only, except the 5.15pm Nottingham to Marylebone which had seven, returning three coaches to London that had come down on the newspaper working the night before. More 'Scots' had arrived at Annesley (Nos 46125, 46126 and 46167) to replace their worn out sisters, which were withdrawn (Nos 46101, 46111 and 46169). At the same time, rebuilt 'Jubilee' No 45735 *Comet* was allocated to Annesley.

Woodford depot closed in June 1964, and as Neasden had also shut, responsibility for motive power at the southern end of the line was passed to Willesden. But Willesden closed to steam a few months later and with Annesley crews not being trained on diesels, trains were worked out and back to Marylebone — a 260-mile round trip with one tender of coal. 'Britannias' with high capacity tenders were reintroduced for this and based at Banbury. Annesley's allocation of passenger and mixed traffic power was being swiftly reduced and could no longer provide cover for any 'Britannias' that may have failed on a semi-fast. Colwick was usually called upon to provide a replacement which did at least bring an Eastern locomotive to the line, and after Annesley closed in December 1965, its allocation was transferred there.

It seems almost unbelievable that the LMR allowed services to sink to the depth that they were now at. Failures amongst the badly maintained and worst LMR engines that could be found were high and delays were inevitable. As most of the lines' signalboxes had been closed by 1965, block sections were long, and if a failure occurred between boxes, it was reported that crews had to walk to farm houses to call for assistance. It is left to the reader to draw conclusions and opinions about the deliberate run down of GC services. It certainly worked and the LMR were able to withdraw the semi-fast services — all freight had gone by this time — and the remaining York-Bournemouth train as well as the overnight mails from the night of 3/4 September 1966. The following week track lifting commenced south of Rugby. No one at the LMR wanted to allow any chance of a possible GC comeback some time in the future!

A local service remained, operated by DMUs from Rugby to Nottingham Victoria, until the 'Vic' was closed in September 1967 and Arkwright Street was hastily reopened. Guards issued tickets on the trains which called at Lutterworth, Ashby Magna, Leicester, Loughborough, East Leake and Nottingham. Not surprisingly, the service was not marketed at all, except with some timetable handbills, and it was withdrawn from 5 May 1969. Only the Marylebone suburban service remained and a chance to preserve a portion between Nottingham and Leicester. The rest, as they say, is history.

Left:
BR LMR Nottingham to Rugby service 1 January 1968 until further notice.

Train Service

Nottingham Arkwright Street and Rugby Central.

on and from 1 January 1968 the following service will operate.

					SO			SX
NOTTINGHAM Arkwright St.	dep.	07 50	08 22	12 27	13 55	16 17	17 34	18 52
EAST LEAKE	dep.	08 03	08 35	12 40	14 08	16 30	17 47	19 05
LOUGHBOROUGH Central	arr.	08 10	08 42	12 47	14 15	16 37	17 54	19 12
,, ,, ...	dep.	08 11	08 43	12 48	14 16	16 38	17 55	19 13
LEICESTER Central	arr.	08 24	08 56	13 01	14 29	16 51	18 08	19 26
,, ,, ...	dep.	08 26	08 58	13 03	14 31	16 53	18 10	19 28
ASHBY MAGNA	dep.	08 41	09 13	13 18	14 46	17 08	18 25	19 43
LUTTERWORTH	dep.	08 48	09 20	13 25	14 53	17 15	18 32	19 50
RUGBY Central	arr.	08 57	09 29	13 34	15 02	17 24	18 41	19 59

					SO			SX	
RUGBY Central	dep.	—	07 11	10 30	12 30	15 05	16 20	17 37	18 55
LUTTERWORTH	dep.	—	07 20	10 39	12 39	15 14	16 29	17 46	19 04
ASHBY MAGNA	dep.	—	07 28	10 47	12 47	15 22	16 37	17 54	19 12
LEICESTER Central	arr.	—	07 41	11 00	13 00	15 35	16 50	18 07	19 25
,, ,, ...	dep.	07 10	07 43	11 02	13 05	15 37	16 55	18 12	19 30
LOUGHBOROUGH Central	arr.	07 21	07 54	11 13	13 16	15 48	17 06	18 23	19 41
,, ,, ...	dep.	07 22	07 55	11 14	13 17	15 49	17 07	18 24	19 42
EAST LEAKE	dep.	07 30	08 03	11 22	13 25	15 57	17 15	18 32	19 50
NOTTINGHAM Arkwright St.	arr.	07 42	08 15	11 34	13 37	16 09	17 27	18 44	20 02

Notes: SO—Saturday only. SX—Saturdays excepted.

This service will provide SECOND CLASS accommodation only.

Passengers will be able to obtain tickets, **between stations served by this Service only,** from the Guard in charge of the train.

Accommodation will be provided for the conveyance of cycles, perambulators, etc., accompanied by passengers, who will be responsible for the removal of these articles from the stations.

Unaccompanied traffic will not be conveyed.

Season tickets, **between stations served by the Service only,** will be issued at Nottingham Midland, Leicester London Road and Rugby Midland Stations.

From:	**Notting-ham**		**East Leake**		**Lough-boro Cen.**		**Leicester Central**		**Ashby Magna**		**Lutter-worth**		**Rugby Central**	
To:	S	R	S	R	S	R	S	R	S	R	S	R	S	R
Nottingham ...	–	–	2/6	3/9	3/9	5/–	6/3	7/6	8/9	11/–	9/9	13/6	11/9	16/–
East Leake	2/6	3/9	–	–	1/4	2/6	4/3	5/6	6/6	10/–	7/9	12/–	9/6	14/6
Loughboro Central	3/9	5/–	1/4	2/6	–	–	2/9	4/6	5/6	9/–	6/3	11/3	8/3	14/3
Leicester Central ...	6/3	7/6	4/3	5/6	2/9	4/6	–	–	2/9	4/9	4/–	6/3	5/6	9/–
Ashby Magna ...	8/9	11/–	6/6	10/–	5/6	9/–	2/9	4/9	–	–	1/2	2/3	3/–	5/6
Lutterworth ..	9/9	13/6	7/9	12/–	6/3	11/3	4/–	6/3	1/2	2/3	–	–	2/–	3/9
Rugby Central ...	11/9	16/–	9/6	14/6	8/3	14/3	5/6	9/–	3/–	5/6	2/–	3/9	–	–

The return fare quoted above is that for Cheap Day Return.

London Midland Region

Issued by British Railways
Divisional Manager, Furlong House,
Middle Furlong Road, Nottingham.

AD136X BR 35000 December, 1967

Below:
The Rugby to Nottingham section lived on for a further 2½ years until that section was also closed. It was terminated at the hastily reopened Arkwright Street after Nottingham Victoria was closed in September 1967. The track to the south of Rugby was started on by the demolition men the week after closure, stop blocks being erected — the contracts were even signed before the service ceased. The replacement DMUs' guards sold tickets on the train which stopped at Lutterworth, Ashby Magna, Leicester, Loughborough, East Leake and Nottingham Victoria, later Arkwright Street. A DMU waits to leave for Nottingham on 7 September 1966, a week after closure of the line to the South. *Andrew Muckley*

4. Cross-Country Passenger Services

The MS&L and Great Central Era

It could be argued that cross-country passenger services on the Great Central's London Extension were more important than the expresses it ran to and from the capital. This potential had been realised during construction of the line and was to be the source of vast amounts of freight and parcels traffic in addition to passenger services. In 1896, a route was surveyed to link the Great Western and the London Extension between Banbury, on the Paddington-Birmingham Snow Hill-Birkenhead main line, and Woodford Halse. The Great Western seemed more anxious to get this route built than the Manchester: Sheffield & Lincoln, even lending them the £300,000 needed at a favourable rate of interest of only 3%.

The line took 2½ years to build and was in typical GC style with deep cuttings and confident blue brick bridges for any roads that it crossed — most of which can still be seen today. It left Banbury north of the station and yards (which were expanded to cope with the extra traffic that was expected to be generated) and from Banbury Junction ran Northeast towards Woodford through two tiny halts which were later added at Chacombe Road and Eydon Road before joining the GC at Culworth Junction. It was officially opened for freight traffic on 1 June 1900, with passenger services starting on 13 August. At first there were only two trains, both worked by the Great Western from Oxford to Leicester using its own locomotives.

From Banbury Junction the line climbed for 4½ miles where it dipped down at 1 in 176 to a roughly level section to Culworth Junction. The line in total was 8¼ miles long. This proved very successful, but it was not until the arrival of the Fay era that the Great Central joined the Great Western in fully exploiting the potential of the cross-country service both for passengers and freight. The Great Western expanded the Oxford to Leicester service with coaches that ran through in the summer from Southampton. Fay, however, was much more ambitious (as indeed he had been in exploiting the through services on the Midland & South Western Junction line where he had been General Manager from 1892) and started to introduce longer distance cross-country passenger trains, the first of these being the classic Bournemouth to Newcastle service. This train ran right through until closure in 1966, with some wartime exceptions and a brief period as a Fridays and Saturdays only service. Through coaches (a convenient facility now vanished from Britain's railways) were also provided from Manchester, Bradford and Huddersfield. In 1903 this train left Bournemouth at 9.40am and ran as far as Nottingham where the Newcastle coaches (arriving 10.10pm) split from the Bradford and Manchester coaches arriving at 8.4pm and 7.20pm respectively. The return train started at Newcastle which it left at 7.5am and arrived in Bournemouth at 5.53pm. As well as Nottingham, Sheffield was a centre of cross-country services but Fay introduced more trains and by the end of 1902 a service from York to Southampton was also added, running via the Didcot, Newbury & Southampton line. This was followed in 1903 by a service to the South East of England with a train to Dover via Reading and another through train in the summer of 1904 which ran to Bath and Bristol and then on to Torbay. In some cases, trains connected with services to and from Stratford-upon-Avon at Woodford & Hinton (later Woodford Halse). The trains via Stratford came from Redditch, Broom Junction and Stratford on the Stratford & Midland Junction's line from Stratford Old Town.

The confidently titled 'Improved Service' for cross-country trains is shown overleaf and dates from 1903.

Right:
Great Central '9Q' class 4-6-0 No 468 races past Rushcliffe on the York to Southampton cross-country express in 1922. This train ran via Rotherham, Nottingham and Leicester, Culworth to Oxford and Winchester via the Didcot, Newbury & Southampton line and conveyed through coaches from Scarborough in the summer. It terminated at Southampton Docks. *Real Photographs*

Following pages:
GCR summer timetables for 1903, for both the cross country services and connections to Stratford-upon-Avon.

NEW ROUTE TO STRATFORD-ON-AVON.

TRAIN SERVICE

BETWEEN

LONDON (Marylebone) & STRATFORD-ON-AVON, &c.

Via WOODFORD and HINTON.

For Local Trains see pages	STATIONS		WEEK DAYS mrn	mrn	aft	aft	aft
14 to 25	**LONDON** (Marylebone)	dep	7 10	10 0	12 15	4 0	5 40
	Harrow-on-the-Hill	"	7 26	...	11 51	4 15	5 26
	Aylesbury	"	8 9	10 51	1 5	4 54	6 5
	Brackley	"	8 53	...	1 32	5 21	6 39
	WOODFORD AND HINTON	arr	9 17	11 28	1 47	5 34	7 8
...	WOODFORD AND HINTON	dep	9 20	11 45	1 50	5 40	7 25
...	Byfield	arr	9 25	11 50	1 51	.	7 41
...	Fenny Compton	"	9 46	12 3	B	B	7 56
...	Kineton	"	9 59	12 16	2 17	6 6	8 8
...	Ettington	"	10 8	12 24	2 25	6 14	8 17
...	**STRATFORD-ON-AVON**	"	10 20	12 35	2 35	6 25	8 30
...	Binton	"	10 33	2 3	5 43		
...	Bidford	"	10 41	2 11	5 51	.	.
...	Broom Junction	"	10 48	2 18	5 58	...	...
...	Alcester	"	11 9	2 40	6 23	.	.
...	Studley	"	11 20	2 51	6 35	...	...
...	REDDITCH	"	11 28	2 58	6 42	.	.

Through Carriage, London (Marylebone) to Stratford-on-Avon (10 0 mrn and 5 40 aft from London).

STATIONS		WEEK DAYS mrn	mrn	mrn	aft	aft	aft
REDDITCH	dep	.	7 42	10 32	2 5	.	5 43
Studley	"	...	7 50	10 39	2 12	...	5 51
Alcester	"	.	8 0	10 50	2 22	.	6 1
Broom Junction	"	...	8 17	11 10	2 37	...	6 17
Bidford	"	.	8 22	11 15	2 42	.	6 22
Binton	"	...	8 30	11 23	2 50	...	6 30
STRATFORD-ON-AVON	"	8 15	8 45	12 15	3 0	4 30	6 55
Ettington	"	8 25	8 56	12 25	3 10	4 40	7 6
Kineton	"	8 33	9 7	12 34	3 18	4 48	7 17
Fenny Compton	"	A	9 19	12 43	3 29	A	7 30
Byfield	"	.	9 40	1 5	3 41	.	7 43
WOODFORD AND HINTON	arr	8 57	9 45	1 10	3 50	5 15	7 52
WOODFORD AND HINTON	dep	9 1	9 59	1 33	4 0	5 20	8 27
Brackley	arr	9 51	1012	1 46	4 15	...	...
Aylesbury	"	.	1047	2 12	4 48	5 53	.
Harrow-on-the-Hill	"	...	...	4 5	5 28	...	...
LONDON (Marylebone)	"	1020	1140	3 5	5 43	6 42	9 50

A Stops when required to take up Passengers. B Stops when required to set down Passengers.

LIVERPOOL, MANCHESTER, BRADFORD, HALIFAX, HUDDERSFIELD, SCARBOROUGH, YORK, GRIMSBY, SHEFFIELD, NOTTINGHAM, LEICESTER, RUGBY, AND STRATFORD-ON-AVON, &c.

VIA WOODFORD AND HINTON.

For Local Trains see pages	STATIONS		WEEK DAYS mrn	mrn	mrn	aft	aft	aft	
14 to 25	MANCHESTER (London Rd.)	dep	.	8 25	10 0	.	2 15	3 45	.
	Oldham (Clegg Street)	"	...	8 13	9 39	...	1 37	3 17	...
	Stalybridge	"	.	8 15	9 43	.	1 55	3 10	.
	Guide Bridge	"	...	8 36	10 10	...	2 25	3 55	...
	LIVERPOOL (Central)	"	.	5 15	8 35	.	1 0	1 33	.
	Warrington (Central)	"	...	5 46	9 8	...	1 27	1 59	...
	Stockport (Tiviot Dale)	"	.	6 13	9 45	.	1 55	2 32	.
	BRADFORD (Exchange)	"	...	7 28	10 7	...	1 22	2 45	...
	HALIFAX	"	.	7 58	9 52	.	1 15	2 55	.
	HUDDERSFIELD	"	...	8 28	10 33	...	2 0	3 30	...
	Barnsley (Court House)	"	.	8 31	9 43	.	2 0	3 48	.
	Penistone	"	...	9 16	10 50	...	2 46	4 32	...
	GRIMSBY TOWN	"	.	6 55	8 16	.	1 45	.	.
	Gainsboro'	"	...	7 41	9 28	...	2 36	...	...
	Lincoln	"	.	6 55	9 15	.	mrn	12 30	.
	Scarborough	"	...	...	8 0	...	9 15	1A30	...
	York	"	.	6 45	9 25	.	11 40	2 47	.
	Doncaster	"	...	8 15	9 0	...	...	4 3	...
	Leeds (Central)	"	.	7 40	9 20	.	11 40	3 32	.
	Wakefield (Westgate)	"	...	8 2	9 41	...	11 59	3 52	...
							aft		
	Rotherham and Masboro'	"	.	8 50	10 35	.	2 20	4 34	.
	SHEFFIELD (Victoria)	"	5 45	9 36	11 20	...	3 18	4 53	...
	Chesterfield	"	6 31	9 0	10 35	.	2 40	.	.
	NOTTINGHAM (Victoria)	"	7 45	10 28	12 12	12 21	4 9	5 45	...
	Loughboro' (Central)	"	8 4	10 15	12 31	12 50	4 0	6 5	.
	LEICESTER (Central)	"	8 20	10 58	12 48	1 15	4 40	6 23	...
	Lutterworth	"	7 46	10 38	.	1 41	3 29	6 42	.
	Rugby	"	8 43	10 51	1 13	1 51	3 40	6 52	...
	WOODFORD AND HINTON	arr	9 0	11 39	1 31	2 15	5 18	7 11	.
...	WOODFORD AND HINTON	dep	9 20	11 45	1 50	2 40	5 40	7 25	...
...	Byfield	arr	9 25	11 50	1 54	2 52	.	7 41	.
...	Fenny Compton	"	9 46	12 3	B	3 4	B	7 56	...
...	Kineton	"	9 59	12 16	2 17	3 16	6 6	8 8	.
...	Ettington	"	10 8	12 24	2 25	3 28	6 14	8 17	...
...	**STRATFORD-ON-AVON**	"	10 20	12 35	2 35	3 40	6 25	8 30	.
...	Binton	"	10 33	2 3		5 43			...
...	Bidford	"	10 41	2 11	.	5 51	.	.	.
...	Broom Junction	"	10 48	2 18	...	5 58	...	...	...
...	Alcester	"	11 9	2 40	.		.	.	.
...	Studley	"	11 20	2 51	...	...	...	...	...
...	REDDITCH	"	11 28	2 58	.	.	.	.	.

STATIONS		WEEK DAYS mrn	mrn	mrn	aft	aft
REDDITCH	dep	.	7 42	10 32	2 5	5 43
Studley	"	...	7 50	10 39	2 12	5 51
Alcester	"	.	8 0	10 50	2 22	6 1
Broom Junction	"	...	8 17	11 10	2 37	6 17
Bidford	"	.	8 22	11 15	2 42	6 22
Binton	"	...	8 30	11 23	2 50	6 30
STRATFORD-ON-AVON	"	8 15	8 45	12 15	4 30	6 55
Ettington	"	8 25	8 56	12 25	4 40	7 6
Kineton	"	8 33	9 7	12 34	4 48	7 17
Fenny Compton	"	D	9 19	12 46	D	7 30
Byfield	"	.	9 40	1 5	.	7 43
WOODFORD AND HINTON	arr	8 57	9 45	1 10	5 15	7 52
WOODFORD AND HINTON	dep	9 18	9 57	1 48	5 36	8 20
Rugby	arr	9 46	10 17	2 6	5 55	8 46
Lutterworth	"	9 56	10 27	2 40	6 5	8 56
LEICESTER (Central)	"	10 22	10 44	2 28	6 20	9 21
Loughboro' (Central)	"		11 12	2 45	6 37	10 [illegible]
NOTTINGHAM (Victoria)	"	...	11 29	3 4	6 57	10 56
Chesterfield	"	.	2 9	4 10	8 [illegible]	mrn
SHEFFIELD (Victoria)	"	...	12 22	3 58	8 0	2 0
Rotherham and Masboro'	"	.	12 36	4 22	8 33	1 55
Wakefield (Westgate)	"	...	1 40	5 54	10 9	...
Leeds (Central)	"	.	2 0	6 14	10 29	.
Doncaster	"	...	2 6	5 3	9 15	...
York	"	.	1 32	6 33	10 15	2 55
Scarborough	"	...	3 5	7 2	11 33	5 35
Lincoln	"	.	2 15	5 25	.	.
Gainsboro'	"	...	1 16	5 18	...	4 † 2
GRIMSBY TOWN	"	.	2 10	6 13	.	5 † 2
Penistone	"	...	12 47	4 25	8 26	2 33
Barnsley (Court House)	"	.	1 17	5 32	8 57	.
HUDDERSFIELD	"	...	1 33	5 6	9 8	...
HALIFAX	"	.	2 7	5 41	9 32	.
BRADFORD (Exchange)	"	...	2 11	6 13	10 12	...
Stockport (Tiviot Dale)	"	.	1 52	5 23	.	4 5
Warrington (Central)	"	...	2 18	6 3	...	4 37
LIVERPOOL (Central)	"	.	2 45	6 35	.	5 5
Guide Bridge	"	...	1 22	5 6	9 0	3 17
Stalybridge	"	.	1 38	6 7	9 26	.
Oldham (Clegg Street)	"	...	1 50	5 27	9 26	...
MANCHESTER (London Rd.)	"	.	1 32	5 15	9 10	3 30

A Until July 11th leaves at 1-20 aft. B Stops when required to set down Passengers.
D Stops when required to take up Passengers on notice being given at the Station.
† Not on Sunday mornings.

IMPROVED SERVICE.

North and Midlands to the South and West of England, via Banbury and Oxford.

MANCHESTER, LIVERPOOL, BRADFORD, LEEDS, HALIFAX, HUDDERSFIELD, EDINBURGH, HINTON, BANBURY, OXFORD, READING, GUILDFORD, HASTINGS, BRISTOL,

For Local Trains see Pages	UP		WEEK DAYS morn	morn	morn (Through Corridor Carriages Liverpool, Manchester (Central), and Bradford to Southampton and Bournemouth.)	morn (Breakfast and Luncheon Corridor Car Express, Newcastle, Sunderland, and York to Oxford, Southampton, and Bournemouth.)		morn (Through Train, Leicester to Southampton, via Banbury, Oxford, and Winchester.)	aft	aft (Restaurant Corridor Car Express York to Oxford, Winchester, and Southampton Docks, via Rotherham, Nottingham, Leicester, and Banbury; also from Scarborough, commencing July 13th.)	aft	aft (Through Train, Leicester to Banbury and Oxford.)	aft
20/55	M'CHESTER Cen.	dep	....	....	9 20	....	....	....	....	....	....	7 20	....
	M'CHESTER L.Rd.	„	..	6 23	9 10	..	..	10 0	12 30	2 15	3 45	6 50	..
67	Oldham (Clegg Street)...	„	....	6 2	8 55	....	....	9 39	12 2	1 37	3 17	6 57	....
60	Stalybridge	„	..	6 15	8 42	..	..	9 43	11 50	1 55	3 10	7 2	..
20/25	Guide Bridge	„	....	6 35	9 37	....	....	10 10	12 40	2 25	3 55	7 37	....
37	LIVERPOOL (Central)	„	..	5 15	8 30	..	..	8 35	11 20	1 0	1 33	6 30	..
	Warrington (Central) ...	„	....	5 46	8 55	....	....	9 8	11 45	1 27	1 59	6 55	....
	Stockport (Tiviot Dale)...	„	..	6 13	..	..	..	9 45	12 20	1 55	2 32	6 25	..
43	BRADFORD (Exch.)...	„	....	6 3	8 45	....	....	10 7	11 57	1 22	2 45	6 20	....
	HALIFAX	„	..	5 50	8 36	..	..	9 52	11 56	1 15	2 55	6 50	..
	HUDDERSFIELD	„	....	6 35	9 28	....	....	10 33	12 30	2 0	3 30	7 18	....
40, 49	Barnsley (Court House)	„	..	6 25	9 38	..	..	..	12 20	2 0	3 48	7 38	..
20/25	Penistone	„	....	7 21	10 15	....	....	10 50	1 20	2 46	4 32	8 14	....
46	Hull (Paragon)	„	..	..	6 35	..	..	..	10 55	12 5	3 0	6 15	..
30 to 33	Grimsby Docks	„	....	....	8 0	....	....	....	11 55	1 40	....	4 16	....
	GRIMSBY (Town)	„	..	..	8 16	..	..	..	12 0	1 45	..	4 25	..
	Gainsborough	„	....	....	9 28	....	....	....	12 50	2 36	....	5 47	....
	Lincoln	„	..	..	9 15	..	..	..	11 25	12 30	..	6 18	..
	Retford	„	....	6 10	9 52	....	....	....	12 0	1 20	2 52	7 35	....
	Worksop	„	..	6 28	10 4	..	..	..	1 20	3 3	3 10	7 53	..
	Shireoaks	„	....	6 33	9 5	....	....	....	11 13	1 43	4 2	7 58	....
	Kiveton Park	„	..	6 42	9 14	..	..	..	12 22	1 52	4 10	8 7	..
46	Doncaster	„	....	6 0	9 0	....	....	....	11 58	3 15	4 3	....	9 50
22	Edinburgh	„	..	..	..	..	..	..	..	10 0	..	..	2 50
	Newcastle	„	....	....	....	7 5	....	....	9 30	12 40	....	....	7 20
	Sunderland	„	..	..	..	7 27	..	..	9 11	11 57	..	..	6 40
	Scarborough	„	....	....	8 10	8 0	....	....	9 15	1D30	....	....	8 10
	York	„	..	..	..	9 25	..	..	11 40	2 47	..	..	9 45
	Leeds (Central)	„	....	....	9 20	....	....	....	11 40	2 41	3 32	....	9 44
	Wakefield (Westgate)...	„	..	..	9 41	..	..	..	11 59	3 0	3 52	..	10 4
48	Rotherham & Masboro'...	„	....	6 57	....	10 25	....	10 35	1 7	3 51	4 34	....	11 2
	SHEFFIELD (Victoria)	„	..	7 42	10 35	..	..	11 20	1 40	3 18	4 53	9 5	..
20 to 25	Chesterfield	„	....	6 31	10 35	....	....	....	12 22	2 40	....	10 0	....
	NOTTINGHAM (Victoria)	arr	..	8 36	11 23	11 28	..	12 10	2 30	4 50	5 43	11 3	12A5
		dep	5 35	8 39		11 33	....	12 12	2 32	4 52	5 45		12A10
													morn
	LEICESTER (Central)	„	6 30	9 17		12 3		12 55	3 9	5 25	6 23		12A50
	Rugby (Central)	„	7 10	9 40		12 28		1 21	3 40	5 51	6 52		....
	Woodford & Hinton	arr	7 36	9 58		..		..	3 59	..	7 11		..
		dep	7 55	10 45		....		....	4 38	....	7 15		....
	G. W. Rly. Banbury	arr	8 15	11 5		1 0		1 58	4 58	6 26	7 35		2A0
		dep	8 30	11 35		1 2		2 0	5 15	6 27	7 40		2A7
	OXFORD	arr	8 59	12 5		1 32		2 28	5 45	6 56	8 10		2A37
		dep	9 5	12 10	1 52	2 12		2 33	5 52	7 0	9 20		2A45
	Didcot	arr	9 49	12 43	..	..		2 56	6 20	7 16	10 3		7A38
...	Reading	„	9 43	12 55	....	2 45		3 57	6 28	8 0	10 0		8A40
...	S. E. & C. Rly. Reading	dep	9 55	1 15	..	2 55		4 18	6 40	9 25	10 55		..
...	Aldershot Town	arr	10 58	2 8	....	4 1		5 16	7 35	10 26	12 8		....
...	Guildford	„	11 4	2 8	..	3 39		5 16	7 41	..	..		..
...	Reigate	„	11 55	2 46	....	4 58		5 57	8 33	....	....		....
...	Tunbridge Wells	„	1 20	4 18	..	5 10		7 40	11 20	..	..		..
...	Hastings	„	2 28	5 24	....	6 20		8 50	12†3	....	....		....
...	Folkestone (Central) ...	„	3 2	..	..	5 47		9 46	12 17	..	..		..
...	Dover	„	3 23	....	....	6 0		10 5	12 29	....	....		....
...	D. & N. Rly. Didcot	dep	..	12 50	..	Stop		3 3	..	7 23	..		7A45
...	Newbury	arr	10§46	1 27	....			3 44	6§58	8 10	....		8A33
...	Winchester (Cheesehill)	„	11¶36	2*48	..	..		4*53	7¶53	9*19	..		10A4
...	Lambourn	„	12 20	2 40	....	....		5 5	7 55	..	....		....
...	G. W. Rly. Didcot	dep	10 5	1 35	..	..		3 20	6 31	8 30	10 40		..
...	Swindon	arr	10 37	2 35	....	....		4 5	7 2	9 35	11 15		3A30
...	BRISTOL (Temple M)..	„	11 57	4 7	..	..		5 35	8 27	11 5	1 0		4A45
...	EXETER (St. David's)..	„	1 50	6 18	....	....		7 35	10 30	....	2 59		8A32
...	TORQUAY	„	3 4	7 37	..	..		8 42	11 28	..	4 5		10A6
...	PLYMOUTH (Millbay)	„	3‡30	8 5	....			9 18	12 5	....	4‡34		10A55
...									aft				
...	WEYMOUTH	„	1§35	4§15	....			6 45	11 5	....	2 0		9A55
...	Basingstoke	arr	10 30	2 21	2 45	aft		5 55	7 17	8 57	10 43		9A27
...		dep	10 42	2 32	2 55	3 15		6 10	7 37	9 30	11 1		9A38
...	L. & S. W. Ry. Winchester (L. & S.W.)	arr	11 10	3 1	..	3 40		6 41	8 6	9 59	11 33		10A12
...	Eastleigh	„	11 23	3*6	3 28	4 12		5*12	8¶9	9*39	11 45		10A27
...	PORTSMOUTH (Town)	„	12 49	4 36	..	5 24		6*36	9 35	11 25	12 45		11A40
...	SOUTHAMPTON (Dks)	„	11 47	3*25	....	....		5*27	8*25	9*58	12 7		10A50
...	„ (West)	„	11 36	..	3 51	4 32	..	..	8 44	..	..		..
...	Lyndhurst Road	„	12 25	....	....	4 52	....	....	9 15	....	....		11A13
...	Brockenhurst	„	12 16	..	..	5 9	..	..	9 30	10 59	12 54		11A28
...	Christchurch	„	12 54	....	....	5 38	....	....	9 22	11 21	1 29		12A18
...	BOURNEMOUTH (C.)	„	12 43	..	4 42	5 53	..	6*57	9 36	11 33	1 41		12A30
...	„ (West)	„	1 18	....	4 52	6 6	....	....	9 52				
...	COWES (Boat)	„	3 10	4 50		7 10	..	7 10	9 50	..	..		

A Monday mornings excepted. **B** Will run during September only. **D** Until July 11th leaves at 1-20 aft.

* Via Didcot & Newbury. † Wednesdays only. ‡ North Road. § Via Reading. ¶ Via Reading and Newbury.

IMPROVED SERVICE.

South and West of England to the Midlands and the North, via Oxford and Banbury.

NEWCASTLE, YORK, SHEFFIELD, NOTTINGHAM, LEICESTER, WOODFORD AND WEYMOUTH, WINCHESTER, SOUTHAMPTON, PORTSMOUTH, BOURNEMOUTH, ETC.

For Local Trains see Page		DOWN	WEEK DAYS morn	midnight	morn		morn	morn		aft	aft	aft		
...	L. & S. W. Rly.	COWES (Boat) .... dep	..	..	..		7 0	9 40		1 30	..	3 40		..
...		BOURNEMOUTH (Wst) „	....	....	....		7 50	10 35		1 55	....	3 45		....
...		„ (C.) „	..	..	..		8 1	10 47		2 7	..	3 56		..
...		Christchurch .... „	....	....	....		7 12	10 55		....	....	3 24		....
...		Brockenhurst .... „	..	..	..		8 26	11 18		2 44	..	4 38		..
...		Lyndhurst Road .... „	....	....	....		8 13	10 49		3 1	....	4 52		....
...		SOUTHAMPTON (Wst) „	..	..	..		8 48	11 40		3 21	..	5 10		..
...		„ (Docks) „	....	....	7*5		9§7	11*50		3 15	....	5*28		....
...		PORTSMOUTH (Town) „	..	..	6 5		7*48	10 55		2 15	..	4 25		..
...		Eastleigh .... „	....	....	7*18		9§22	12*5		3 40	....	5*44		....
...		Winchester (L. & S. W.) „	..	..	7 21		9 27	12 13		3 58	..	5 51		..
...		Basingstoke .... arr	....	....	7 52		9 55	12 46		4 26	....	6 25		....
...		Basingstoke .... dep	..	..	8 0		10 0	1 20		4 35	..	6 42		..
...	G. W. Rly.	WEYMOUTH .... „	....	....	....		....	10 15		1‖15	....	4‖30		....
...		PLYMOUTH (Millbay) „	..	12 5	..		..	8 30		10 40	11‡45	3‡50		..
...		TORQUAY .... „	....	10B31	....		....	9 0		11 22	12 25	4 15		....
...		EXETER (St. David's) .. „	..	1 45	..		..	10 15		12 42	1 50	5 28		..
...		BRISTOL (Temple M.) „	....	3 40	7 45		....	12 0		3 0	4 15	7 24		....
...		Swindon .... „	..	6 35	9 2		9 15	1 40		4 10	..	8 45		..
...		Didcot .... arr	....	7 47	9 30		10 20	....		4 43	5 48	7 58		....
...	D. & N. Rly.	Lambourn .... dep	..	..	7 45		..	12 40		3 0	..	6 0		..
...		Winchester (Cheesehill) „	....	....	7*35		9§40	12*21		2*50	....	6*18		....
...		Newbury .... „	..	..	8 53		10‖29	1 25		3 57	..	7 22		..
...		Didcot .... arr	....	....	9 33		....	2 7		4 37	....	8 4		....
...	S. E. & C. Rly.	Dover .... dep	..	..	..		..	7 5		11 22	..	1 10		..
...		Folkestone (Central) ... „	....	....	....		....	7 23		11 39	....	1 22		....
...		Hastings .... „	..	..	..		..	8 0		11 18	..	2 17		..
...		Tunbridge Wells .... „	....	....	....		....	9 8		12 25	....	4 2		....
...		Reigate .... „	..	..	6 35		8 13	10 30		2 5	..	5 17		..
...		Guildford .... „	....	....	7 24		9 10	11 19		2 48	....	6 3		....
...		Aldershot Town .... „	..	..	7 30		8 50	11 16		2 50	..	6 6		..
...		Reading .... arr	....	....	8 29		10 9	12 22		3 41	....	6F59		....
...	G. W. Rly.	Reading .... dep	..	7 45	8 40		11 0	1 15		4 28	4 35	7 50		..
...		Didcot .... „	....	8 13	9 38		11 15	2 15		5 8	5 55	8 40		....
...		OXFORD .... arr	..	8 35	10 3		11 40	2 30		5 48	6 25	9 32		..
		OXFORD .... dep	....	9 5	10 15		11 48	2 55		5 53	6 28	9 45		....
		Banbury .... arr	..	9 34	10 43		12 20	3 24		6 22	7 25	10 25		..
		Banbury .... dep	8 30	9 36	10 45		1 8	3 26		6 24	7 47	10 30		....
		Woodford & Hinton .... arr	8 50	9 56	..		1 27	A		6 42	8 7	10 50		..
		Woodford & Hinton .... dep	9 18	9 57	....		1 48	A		7 10	8 20	10 52		....
14 to 18		Rugby (Central) .... arr	9 46	10 17	11 21		2 6	4 4		7 28	8 45	11 12		..
		LEICESTER (Central) „	10 22	10 44	11 48		2 28	4 30		7 53	9 21	11 38		....
		NOTTINGHAM (Victoria) „		11 29	12 28		3 4	5 3		8 25	10 56	12 55		..
		NOTTINGHAM (Victoria) dep	....	11 32	12 42	12 48	3 6	5 8	5 15	8 27	....	1 0	1 5	....
		Chesterfield .... arr	..	..	2 10	..	4 10	..	5 49	9 30	..	..	..	..
		SHEFFIELD (Victoria) „	....	12 22	1 32	....	3 58	5 58	....	9 17	....	....	2 0	....
48		Rotherham & Masboro' ... „	..	12 36	1 55	2 4	4 22	6 27	6 33	9 35	..	1 56	..	..
		Wakefield (Westgate) ... „	....	1 40	2 28	....	5 54	7 15	....	10 9	....	....	....	....
		Leeds (Central) .... „	..	2 0	2 48	..	6 14	7 36	..	10 29	..	..	..	..
		York .... „	....	1 32	....	3 6	....	....	7 40	....	....	2 55	....	....
15		Scarborough .... „	..	3 5	..	4C15	..	..	9 41	..	..	5 35	..	..
		Sunderland .... „	....	3 56	....	5 38	....	....	9 47	....	....	5 47	....	....
		Newcastle .... „	..	3 20	..	5 23	..	..	10 10	..	..	4 42	..	..
		Edinburgh .... „	....	6 15	....	8 5	....	....	4 0	....	....	7 15	....	....
44, 45		Doncaster .... „	..	2 6	2 26		5 8	7 0		10K40	..	6 21	..	..
		Kiveton Park .... „	....	1 34	....	....	6 4	7 59	....	9 59	....		....	....
		Shireoaks .... „	..	1 39	..	..	6 9	8 4	..	10 4	..	..	..	..
		Worksop .... „	....	12 40	2 5	....	4 45	6 39	....	10 9	....	....	3M28	....
26 to 29		Retford .... „	..	12 55	2 15	..	4 50	6 52	..	10 25	..	..	3M40	..
		Lincoln .... „	....	2 15	3 20	....	5 25	7 55	....	..	....	....	....	....
		Gainsborough .... „	..	1 16	3 2	..	5 18	7 19	..	10G52	..	..	4M2	..
		GRIMSBY (Town) ...... „	....	2 10	4 14	....	6 13	8 6	....	..	....	....	5M2	....
		Grimsby Docks .... „	..	2 20	4 23	..	6 20	8 13	..	....	..	..	5M7	..
44, 45		Hull (Paragon) .... „	....	....	3 55	....	....	8 28	....	1D27	....	....	....	....
14, 18		Penistone .... „	..	12 47	2 22	..	4 25	6 23	..	10 4	..	..	2 33	..
38, 49		Barnsley (Court House) .. „	....	1 17	2 48	....	5 32	7 34	....	10 40	....	....	....	....
		HUDDERSFIELD ...... „	..	1 33	2 26	..	5 6	7 12	..	10 5	..	..	3M7	..
42		HALIFAX .... „	....	2 7	3 5	....	5 41	8 17	....	10 33	....	....	....	....
		BRADFORD (Exch.) .... „	..	2 11	2 52	..	6 13	8 4	..	10 50	..	..	..	..
		Stockport (Tiviot Dale) ... „	....	1 52	3 18	....	5 25	....	....	10 58	....	....	4 5	....
36		Warrington (Central) ... „	..	2 18	3 54	..	6 3	7 48	..	11 24	..	..	4 37	..
		LIVERPOOL (Central) „	....	2 45	4 23	....	6 35	8 15	....	11 55	....	....	5 5	....
20, 24		Guide Bridge .... „	..	1 22	2 41	..	5 6	7 5	..	10 21	..	..	3 17	..
60		Stalybridge .... „	....	1 38	3 25	....	6 7	7 16	....	10 52	....	....	....	....
66		Oldham (Clegg Street) ... „	..	1 50	3 33	..	5 27	7 35	..	10 50	..	..	..	..
14, 18		M'CHESTER ... L. Rd. „	....	1 32	2 50	....	5 15	....	....	10 35	....	....	3 30	....
		M'CHESTER ... Cen. „	..	..	..	..	..	7 20	..	..	..	..	..	..

Through Train Oxford to Leicester, via Banbury.

Breakfast and Luncheon Corridor Car Express, Southampton, Winchester, and Oxford to York, via Leicester, Nottingham, and Rotherham; also to Scarborough, commencing July 11th.

Through Corridor Carriages, Bournemouth and Southampton to Bradford, Manchester (Central), and Liverpool.

Luncheon Corridor Car Express, Bournemouth, Southampton, and Oxford to York, Sunderland, and Newcastle.

Through Train, Oxford and Banbury to Leicester.

A Stops on Thursdays only. B Saturday nights excepted. C Until July 10th arrives at 5-34 aft. D Friday and Sunday mornings. F On Saturdays arrives at Reading at 7-28 aft. G Saturdays only. K Arrives at 10-59 aft. on Saturdays. M Sunday mornings excepted.

* Via Newbury and Didcot. ‡ North Road. § Via Newbury and Reading. ‖ Via Reading.

Right:
Great Central '8F' class 4-6-0 No 1096 heads the Newcastle to Swansea express at Rothley in 1922. To the rear of the train are Swithland Sidings with the lines parting to sweep around Rothley's island platform. It is wonderful to know that one can still travel on this section and that double track is about to be in operation once more.
Real Photographs

Fay also realised that shipping companies needed to move crews from port to port to take over their vessels. Ever keen to exploit the rapidly expanding railway network and use secondary routes to full advantage, he introduced another service in May 1906 — known to the railway as the 'Ports to Ports' — to meet this market. The train ran from Barry Docks via Cardiff, Cheltenham, Andoversford and Kingham to Newcastle with a portion for Hull, and was advertised from summer 1909. At Sheffield connections were made with Hull, Grimsby, Cleethorpes, Harwich, Lincoln and the East. These cross-country services had reached a zenith before the years immediately preceding the start of World War 1. The GC timetables of the period show that the services using the London Extension via Culworth Junction were as follows:

Barry Docks to Newcastle via Kingham
Bradford, Manchester and York to Bournemouth
Halifax, Huddersfield and Manchester to Bath and Bristol
Southampton to York
Sheffield to Swansea (Sundays Only)
Woodford to Southampton.

All of these trains carried through carriages from destinations such as Scarborough and the development of GC holiday services, reached a peak before World War 1 intervened. Through trains were strengthened and added to with additional through coaches as required. Destinations served were the traditional holiday resorts such as Blackpool, Aberystwyth, Ilfracombe, Skegness, Scarborough and Great Yarmouth, and a connection was made from Lymington Pier to the Isle of Wight by a Newcastle to Southampton train. As with most things GC, tradition lived on for a long time and many of these services survived until the early 1960s.

World War 1 saw the withdrawal of these holiday services and also most advertised cross-country workings, especially to and from ports as priority was given to troops sailing for the Western Front or the Middle East. The supply route to the Western Front passed through Richborough in Kent, where an Army depot was constructed for the purpose. The through workings that had previously serviced Dover and Deal in peacetime suddenly carried troops and were supplemented as necessary by many specials and goods services. The GC even had its own ambulance train to convey injured troops to hospitals in the North and the Midlands.

It took at least four years to get back to a normal service following the end of the war. The Southampton service was restored in 1921 but this time ran as far as Glasgow and Edinburgh instead of terminating at Newcastle upon Tyne. The Great Central dropped the Manchester connection for the Bournemouth train as there was a quicker service run by the Midland, from Manchester to Bournemouth via Birmingham and Bath Green Park (this train later becoming the 'Pines Express'), and the Dover connection was also withdrawn. The GC Bournemouth service also started to share rolling stock with its partner, the London & South Western. Any examination of this train, even in its last year of operation in 1966, will see that this arrangement continued right up until then, with the Southern Region providing green-liveried stock for one train, the Eastern stock for the other.

The Great Central had always been famous for its Penzance to Aberdeen through coaches attached to existing cross country services. These coaches ran from 1921 over a distance of 785 miles in less than 24hr providing access to restaurant car services en route and brought Great Western and North British coaches to opposite ends of the country courtesy of the GC. One could leave Aberdeen at 9.45am and arrive next morning in Penzance at 7.40am, the coaches being coupled to the Paddington to Penzance sleeper at Swindon. The northbound carriages left Penzance at 11am and arrived next day in Aberdeen at 7.40am, passengers having access to sleeping cars from York. Dining facilities were provided in both directions.

Right:
The London & South Western and the GC shared the rolling stock for the Bournemouth to Newcastle service, and on this occasion it is formed of LSWR coaches, the fourth of which is a restaurant car. Note the roof destination boards and the water trough storage tanks at Charwelton. Power is provided by a GC 'C4' 4-4-2 Atlantic No 5360 which would have taken over the train at Banbury. *Real Photographs*

The LNER Takes Over

The service pattern operated by the LNER following the Grouping in 1923 was very similar to that of the Great Central. The boat train service to Southampton (for Le Havre) was developed with the addition of a through carriage from Scarborough on Saturdays. The Bournemouth to York service continued as a through train and the 'Ports to Ports' train was given an additional through coach for Swansea.

World War 2 saw the cross-country services recast to include special troop trains which were all unadvertised for civilians as they were primarily for the use of the military. Trains in the public timetable were the Ashford (Kent) to Newcastle (departing Ashford at 8.45am and then travelling via Guildford, Reading and Oxford, arriving in Newcastle at 8.55pm with a return working leaving Newcastle at 8.15am and arriving Ashford at 8.32am) the evening Swindon to Sheffield, (Banbury depart 9.5pm with a Sheffield arrival at 12.34am, with a return working leaving Sheffield at 8.10pm passing Banbury at 12.6am, which carried through coaches from York) and a Banbury to York which left at 11.50pm and arrived in York at 8.9am the next day. This train ran about half an hour later on Saturday nights with its balancing working leaving York at 10pm and passing Banbury at 3.38am. On Sundays there was also a Swansea to Sheffield service that passed Banbury at 5.30pm with an arrival at Sheffield Victoria at 8.43pm. It ran south from Sheffield at 9.20am and passed Banbury at 12.29pm.

Inspection of the LNER wartime timetables will reveal statements that troops would get priority but, that subject to space being available, civilians would be carried. The Swindon to Sheffield service enabled a Leicester Central locomotive and crew to penetrate the Great Western as far as Swindon via Foxhall Junction and then have a fast run over the Vale of the White Horse as did the Sheffield to Swansea service that ran on Sundays. These arrangements continued until the closure of Leicester shed in 1963. The end of the war saw a return to the normal civilian service but the 'Ports to Ports', now a Newcastle to Swansea through service, was withdrawn although through coaches did remain but travelling via the Midland route through Birmingham. The long-standing overnight Sheffield to Swindon (known to GC men as the 'Penzance' — a throwback to the days of through coaches) and the Swindon to York services were retained.

Below:
On a special boat train working 'C5' Atlantic No 5364 *Lady Faringdon*, heads a train for Marylebone up through Saunderton on the GW/GC joint line in 1936. The Atlantics were common performers on all express workings along with other GC types until the advent of the 'B17s'. They were never totally displaced by the 'B17s' and World War 2 prolonged their lives. *Real Photographs*

Table 2 — LONDON, LEICESTER, NOTTINGHAM, SHEFFIELD, HUDDERSFIELD, BRADFORD, MANCHESTER, LIVERPOOL, HULL, CLEETHORPES, YORK, NEWCASTLE, and SCOTLAND

Week Days

Miles	Station	1	2	3	4	5	6	7	8	9	10	11	12	13	14	15
		mrn	mrn	mrn	mrn	mrn	mrn	mrn	mrn Ⓑ	mrn	mrn Ⓑ	mrn Ⓑ	mrn	aft	mrn Ⓑ	aft Ⓑ
	LONDON (M'lebone) . dep	..	..	3 45	..	..	..	..	6 15	8 15	8 30	..	9 50	..	..	1225
27¾	A High Wycombe ...... "	..	..	..	..	..	..	..	7 25	..	9 58	9F20	..	..	1150	..
36	Princes Risborough . "	..	..	..	..	..	..	..	7 46	..	1020	9 50	..	..	12 8	..
38¾	Ilmer Halt	..	..	..	..	..	..	..	..	..	1026	..	..	..	..	..
41½	Haddenham (Bucks.)	..	..	..	..	..	..	..	7 58	..	1032	..	..	..	..	..
46¾	Wotton	..	..	..	..	..	..	..	8 10	..	Stop	..	..	..	..	..
9¼	Harrow on the Hill	..	..	..	..	..	..	..	Stop	8 33	..	..	10 8	..	..	..
13½	A Northwood	..	..	..	..	..	..	..	..	8 47	..	..	..	..	..	..
37¾	Aylesbury	Except Mondays.	..	5 15	..	..	..	..	..	9 50	..	10 9	10 57	..	1227	1 48
44	Quainton Road	..	..	..	..	..	..	..	..	10 4	..	Stop	..	..	Stop	1 58
48¾	Calvert	..	..	..	..	..	..	..	..	1014	..	..	..	..	..	2 7
54½	Finmere	..	..	5U44	..	..	..	..	..	1024	..	..	..	..	..	2 17
59¼	Brackley (Central)	..	..	5U53	..	..	..	..	..	1034	..	..	..	..	..	2 26
62½	Helmdon, for Sulgrave	..	..	..	..	..	..	..	..	1042	..	..	..	..	..	..
66	Culworth	..	..	..	..	..	..	..	..	1051	..	..	..	..	..	..
69	Woodford and Hinton .. arr	..	..	6 10	..	..	..	..	..	1057	..	..	11 36	..	..	..
93¾	9 Stratford-on-Avon arr	..	..	Stop	..	..	..	..	..	..	..	..	..	..	..	..
—	Woodford and Hinton dep	3 20	..	..	..	..	8 50	..	..	..	..	..	..	..	..	..
73	Eydon Road Halt	..	..	..	..	..	9 1	..	..	..	..	..	..	..	..	..
76½	Chalcombe Road Halt	..	..	..	..	..	9 8	..	..	..	..	..	..	..	..	Saturdays only.
80	Banbury .... arr	3 38	..	..	..	..	9 17	..	..	..	..	..	..	..	..	..
—	Mls Banbury .... dep	Stop	..	..	..	..	Stop	..	..	1010	..	..	..	..	..	..
—	3¼ Chalcombe Road Halt	..	..	..	..	..	..	..	..	1018	..	..	..	..	..	..
—	7 Eydon Road Halt	..	..	..	..	..	..	..	..	1026	..	..	..	..	..	..
—	11 Woodford & Hinton arr	..	..	..	..	..	..	..	..	1034	..	..	..	..	..	..
—	9 Stratford-on-Avon dep	..	..	..	..	..	mrn	..	..	..	..	..	..	..	..	..
—	Woodford and Hinton .. dep	..	..	..	..	5 50	6 35	TC Leicester (Central) to Manchester (Lon. Rd.)	..	11 2	..	..	11 38	..	..	Stop
71½	Charwelton	..	..	..	..	5 55	6 40	..	..	11 7	..	..	..	..	..	..
78½	Braunston and Willoughby	..	..	..	..	6 8	6 53	..	mrn	1119	..	..	..	..	..	..
83¾	Rugby (Central)	..	..	..	..	6 17	7 1	..	7 30	1131	..	..	12B1	..	..	..
90	Lutterworth	..	..	..	..	6 29	..	..	7 42	1143	..	..	..	..	..	..
93¾	Ashby Magna	..	..	..	..	6 37	..	..	7 50	1151	..	..	..	..	..	..
98¼	Whetstone	..	..	..	..	6 46	..	..	7 59	12 0	..	..	..	..	..	..
103	Leicester (Central) .. arr	..	..	..	..	6 54	..	..	8 7	12 8	..	..	12 27	..	..	..
	dep	..	..	..	..	6 56	..	7 40	8 10	..	..	..	12 32	1238	..	..
105½	Belgrave and Birstall	..	..	..	..	7 1	..	..	8 15	Arrives Rugby 11 27 mrn	..	..	..	1243	..	..
108	Rothley	..	..	..	..	7 7	..	..	8 21	..	..	..	..	1249	..	..
110¾	Quorn and Woodhouse	..	..	..	..	7 13	..	..	8 27	..	..	..	..	1255	..	..
113	Loughborough (Central)	..	..	..	..	7 19	..	7 56	8 32	..	..	..	12 48	1N15	..	..
117½	East Leake	..	..	..	..	7 27	..	..	8 40	..	..	..	..	1 23	..	..
118½	Rushcliffe Halt	..	..	..	..	..	..	..	8 43	..	..	..	..	1 26	..	..
122	Ruddington	..	..	..	..	7 37	..	..	8 50	..	..	..	..	1 34	..	..
125½	Arkwright Street	..	..	..	..	7 44	..	8 17	8 57	..	..	..	..	1 41	..	..
126½	Nottingham (Victoria) arr	..	..	mrn	..	7 47	..	8 20	9 0	..	..	aft	1 8	1 44	aft	aft
	dep	..	..	6 0	6 15	..	..	8 26	Stop	..	..	1255	1 13	Stop	2 15	2 25
128	New Basford	..	..	6 5	6 20	..	..	..	..	..	..	1 0	..	..	2 20	2 30
129¾	Bulwell Common	..	..	6 10	6 25	..	..	8 34	..	..	..	1 5	..	..	2 25	2 35
132½	Hucknall Central	..	..	6 17	6 31	..	..	8 40	..	..	..	1 11	..	..	2 31	2 41
138	Kirkby-in-Ashfield (Cen.)	..	..	..	6 44	..	..	..	..	..	..	1 25	TC Marylebone to Manchester (L. Rd.)	..	..	2 57
139¾	Sutton-in-Ashfield (Cen.)	..	..	..	6 49	..	..	..	..	..	..	1 30	..	..	..	3 2
142¾	Mansfield (L.N.E.R.) arr	..	..	..	6 54	..	..	..	..	..	..	1 35	..	..	..	3 7
	dep	..	..	..	7 3	..	..	..	..	..	..	Stop	..	..	..	4T0
149½	Edwinstowe	..	..	..	7 19	..	..	..	..	..	..	..	..	..	..	4T45
151	Ollerton .... arr	..	..	..	7 44	..	..	..	..	..	..	..	..	..	..	4T52
172¼	66 Lincoln .... arr	..	..	..	8 27	..	..	..	..	..	..	..	..	..	..	5T34
138½	Kirkby Bentinck	..	..	6 34	..	..	..	8 52	..	..	..	..	..	..	2 48	..
143	Tibshelf Town	..	..	6 43	..	..	..	9 1	..	..	..	..	..	..	2 57	..

Miles	Station	16	17	18	19	20	21	22	23	24	25	26	27	28	29
		aft	aft	aft	aft Ⓑ	aft	aft	aft	aft Ⓑ	aft Ⓑ	aft	aft Ⓑ	aft	aft Ⓑ	aft
	LONDON (M'lebone) . dep	..	..	..	..	1 40	1 50	..	2 5	..	3 30	4h0	..	..	4 54
27¾	A High Wycombe ...... "	..	..	..	2 30	..	..	..	3 45	..	..	5 32	..	4 50	..
36	Princes Risborough . "	..	..	..	2 48	..	..	..	4 10	4 7	..	5 49	..	5 10	..
38¾	Ilmer Halt	..	..	..	..	..	..	..	4 15	..	..	..	..	..	..
41½	Haddenham (Bucks.)	..	..	..	..	..	..	..	4 21	..	..	5 57	..	..	..
46¾	Wotton	..	..	..	..	..	..	..	Stop	..	..	Stop	..	..	..
9¼	Harrow on the Hill	..	..	..	..	1 57	2 7	..	..	..	3 48	..	..	..	..
13½	A Northwood	..	..	..	..	2 11	2 23	..	..	..	..	..	..	..	..
37¾	Aylesbury	..	..	..	3 6	3 18	3 31	..	..	4 24	4 36	..	..	5 28	6 9
44	Quainton Road	..	..	..	Stop	3 28	3 41	..	..	Stop	..	..	..	Stop	6 19
48¾	Calvert	..	..	..	..	3 38	3 51	..	..	..	..	..	..	..	6 29
54½	Finmere	..	..	..	..	3 48	4 1	..	..	..	..	..	..	..	6 39
59¼	Brackley (Central)	..	..	..	..	3 58	4 11	..	..	..	5 6	..	..	..	6 50
62½	Helmdon, for Sulgrave	..	..	..	..	4 6	4 19	..	..	..	..	..	..	..	6 59
66	Culworth	..	..	..	..	4 15	4 28	..	..	..	..	..	..	..	7 7
69	Woodford and Hinton .. arr	..	..	..	..	4 21	4 34	..	..	..	5 21	..	..	..	7 13
93¾	9 Stratford-on-Avon arr	..	..	..	aft	..	..	..	..	..	..	..	..	..	9 27
—	Woodford and Hinton dep	..	..	..	3 25	..	..	..	..	..	5 32	..	..	..	Stop
73	Eydon Road Halt	..	..	..	..	..	..	..	..	..	5 41	..	..	..	..
76½	Chalcombe Road Halt	Saturdays only	..	..	..	..	..	..	..	..	5 49	..	..	..	..
80	Banbury .... arr	..	..	..	3 42	..	..	..	..	..	5 59	..	..	aft	..
—	Mls Banbury .... dep	..	..	1 27	Stop	Saturdays only	Except Saturdays	..	..	..	..	..	..	6 21	..
—	3¼ Chalcombe Road Halt	..	..	..	..	..	..	..	..	..	..	..	..	6 32	..
—	7 Eydon Road Halt	..	..	..	..	..	..	..	..	..	..	..	..	6 40	..
—	11 Woodford & Hinton arr	..	..	1 46	..	..	..	..	..	..	..	..	..	6 49	..
—	9 Stratford-on-Avon dep	..	..	..	..	..	..	..	..	..	..	aft	..	..	aft
—	Woodford and Hinton .. dep	1230	..	1 48	..	..	..	..	..	..	5 23	5 30	..	..	6 55
71½	Charwelton	..	..	..	..	..	Stop	..	..	..	..	5 35	..	..	..
78½	Braunston and Willoughby	..	..	..	..	..	..	..	..	..	..	5 48	..	..	..
83¾	Rugby (Central)	12A55	..	2B13	..	..	..	..	..	..	5B46	5 58	..	..	7B28
90	Lutterworth	1 7	..	..	..	Stop	..	..	..	..	..	6 11	..	..	7 40
93¾	Ashby Magna	1 15	..	..	..	..	..	..	..	..	..	6 19	..	..	7 48
98¼	Whetstone	1 24	..	..	..	..	..	..	..	..	..	6 28	..	..	7 57
103	Leicester (Central) .. arr	1 32	..	2 42	..	..	..	..	..	..	6 12	6 36	..	..	8 5
	dep	..	1 35	2 52	..	..	..	5 20	..	..	6 17	6 41	..	..	..
105½	Belgrave and Birstall	..	1 40	TC Ashford (Kent) dep. 8 45 mrn to Newcastle, via Guildford,	..	..	..	5 25	..	..	..	6 46	..	..	..
108	Rothley	..	1 46	..	..	..	..	5 31	..	..	..	6 52	..	..	..
110¾	Quorn and Woodhouse	..	1 52	..	..	..	..	5 37	..	..	..	6 58	..	..	..
113	Loughborough (Central)	..	2B0	3B9	..	..	..	5 42	..	..	6 33	7 5	..	..	..
117½	East Leake	..	2 8	..	..	..	..	5 50	..	..	..	7 13	..	..	..
118½	Rushcliffe Halt	..	2 11	..	..	..	..	5 53	..	..	..	7 16	..	..	..
122	Ruddington	..	2 18	..	..	..	..	6 0	..	..	..	7 25	..	..	..
125½	Arkwright Street	..	2 25	3 30	..	..	..	6 7	..	..	..	7 37	..	..	..
126½	Nottingham (Victoria) arr	..	2 28	3 33	..	aft	aft	6 10	aft	aft	6 53	7 40	..	..	..
	dep	..	..	3 36	..	4 35	5 45	..	6 22	6 30	6 58	..	From Nottingham dep 6 22 aft	..	..
128	New Basford	..	..	..	..	4 40	5 50	..	6 27	6 35	..	..	..	..	..
129¾	Bulwell Common	..	..	..	..	4 45	5 55	..	6 32	6 40	TC Marylebone to Manchester (L. Rd.)	..	..	..	..
132½	Hucknall Central	..	..	..	..	4 51	6 1	..	6 38	6 46	..	..	..	..	..
138	Kirkby-in-Ashfield (Cen.)	..	..	..	..	5 8	6 16	..	..	7 2	..	..	..	..	..
139¾	Sutton-in-Ashfield (Cen.)	..	..	..	..	5 13	6 21	..	..	7 7	..	..	..	..	..
142¾	Mansfield (L.N.E.R.) arr	..	..	..	..	5 18	6 26	..	..	7 12	..	..	..	..	..
	dep	..	..	..	..	Stop	..	..	..	7 15	..	..	..	..	..
149½	Edwinstowe	..	..	..	..	..	..	..	..	7 31	..	..	..	..	..
151	Ollerton .... arr	..	..	..	..	..	..	..	..	..	..	..	..	..	..
172¼	66 Lincoln .... arr	..	..	..	..	..	..	..	..	..	..	..	..	..	..
138½	Kirkby Bentinck	..	..	..	..	..	..	..	6 53	..	..	..	..	..	..
143	Tibshelf Town	..	..	..	..	..	..	..	7 3	..	..	..	..	..	..

Table 2—continued

Miles	Station	1	2	3	4	5	6	7	8	9	10	11	12	13	14	15
144¼	Pilsley	..	..	6 48	..	..	..	..	..	..	..	..	..	..	3 1	..
146½	Heath	..	..	6 54	..	..	..	..	..	..	aft	..	..	..	3 7	..
151½	Chesterfield (Central) arr	mrn	..	7 7	..	..	..	9 21	mrn	..	S	aft	..	..	3 20	..
	dep	5 40	6 50	7 9	..	..	..	9 22	9 30	..	1210	1 30	..	..	..	..
153½	Sheepbridge P	5 44	6 54	7 13	..	..	..	..	9 34	..	1214	1 34	..	..	..	..
155½	Staveley Works R	5 49	6 59	7 18	..	..	..	..	9 39	..	1219	1 39	..	..	..	..
152¼	Staveley Town	5 54	7 6	7 23	..	..	..	9 32	9 44	..	1224	1 44	1 57	..	..	..
154¾	Eckington and Renishaw	..	7 11	7 28	..	..	..	..	9 49	..	1229	..	..	..	..	..
156½	Killamarsh	..	..	7 33	..	..	..	..	9 54	..	1234	..	..	..	..	..
158½	Beighton	..	..	7 38	..	..	..	..	9 59	..	1239	..	..	..	..	..
159¾	Woodhouse	..	..	7 43	..	..	..	9 43	10 4	..	1244	..	..	..	..	..
162¾	Darnall, for Handsworth	..	..	7 50	..	..	..	..	1011	..	1251	..	..	..	..	..
164¾	Sheffield (Victoria) .... arr	..	..	7 55	..	..	..	9 53	1016	..	1256	..	2 19	..	..	..
187½	67 Retford .... arr	..	..	8Z34	..	..	..	..	1131	..	1Z45	..	4 19	..	..	..
208	67 Lincoln .... "	..	..	9 52	..	..	..	..	12z27	..	3 50	..	4 58	..	..	..
232½	67 Grimsby Town ..... "	..	..	10 19	10*19	..	..	1‖23	1 55	..	4 20	..	6*40	..	..	8‖23
235¾	67 Cleethorpes .... "	..	..	10 37	10*37	..	..	1‖40	2 12	..	4 45	..	6*57	..	..	8‖46
170¾	57 Rotherham T 114 .. arr	..	..	8 32	..	..	..	10 12	1235	..	..	..	2 57	..	..	..
175¾	67 Doncaster (Central) arr	..	..	..	..	..	..	10 45	1 9	..	2r23	..	3 20	..	..	..
216½	98 Hull .... "	..	..	..	..	..	..	12t46	2 33	..	3 56	..	6†38	..	..	..
211¼	114 York 1 .... "	..	..	9 40	..	..	..	12H57	..	..	..	..	4H20	..	..	..
231¾	125 Harrogate 89 ...... "	..	..	10 54	..	..	..	1n49	4L6	..	4L6	..	6 7	..	..	..
253¼	109 Scarborough (Cen.) "	..	..	11 22	..	..	..	4g15	..	..	Sats. only	..	6 25	..	..	..
291¾	103 Newcastle .... "	..	..	12p11	..	..	..	3 55	..	..	..	..	6 46	..	..	..
416¾	103 Edinburgh (Wav.) .. "	..	..	3 38	..	..	..	6 55	..	..	..	..	9 46	..	..	..
463¾	103 Glasgow (Queen St. "	..	..	5 5	..	..	..	8 34	..	..	..	..	..	..	..	..
475¾	103 Dundee (Tay Bridge) "	..	..	6 18	..	..	..	9 2	..	..	..	..	..	..	..	..
546¾	103 Aberdeen .... "	..	..	8 34	..	..	..	11 12	..	..	..	..	..	..	..	..
177¾	67 Penistone .... arr	..	..	8a47	..	..	..	10 25	12V4	..	1 52	..	2 50	..	..	..
184¾	67 Barnsley U 73 ..... arr	..	..	9 47	..	..	..	..	1f55	..	..	..	5 10	..	..	..
191	Huddersfield ...... "	..	..	10 21	..	..	..	12S36	12S36	..	3 0	..	5 51	..	..	..
201¾	Halifax (Old) ...... "	..	..	11 44	..	..	..	1S40	1S40	..	4 4	..	6 22	..	..	..
203¾	Bradford (Exch.) .. "	..	..	11 39	..	..	..	2S21	2S21	..	3 56	..	6 51	aft	..	..
193	67 Glossop (Central) .. arr	..	..	9V46	..	..	..	11V9	..	..	—	..	4 45	—	..	..
201	67 Guide Bridge .... arr	..	..	9 53	..	..	..	11 16	1246	..	..	..	3 33	4B10	..	..
202½	75 Ashton (Oldham Rd.) arr	..	..	..	..	..	..	11 46	..	..	..	..	3 43	..	..	..
203½	75 Stalybridge .... "	..	..	..	..	..	..	12S36	..	..	..	..	5 36	..	..	..
206½	76 Oldham (Clegg St.) . "	..	..	..	..	..	..	11 56	..	..	..	..	3 54	..	..	..
206	67 Manchester (L.Rd.) . arr	..	..	10 5	..	..	..	11 25	..	..	..	..	3 42	..	..	..
212½	67 " (Central) "	..	..	..	..	..	..	..	1 12	..	..	..	..	4 35	..	..
203½	67 Stockport (Tiv. Dale) arr	..	..	..	..	..	..	..	..	..	..	..	..	..	..	..
222½	67 Warrington (Cen.) "	..	..	11K26	..	..	..	12K53	1 53	..	..	..	4K53	..	..	..
241	67 Liverpool (Cen.) ... "	..	..	11K56	..	..	..	1K23	2 23	..	..	..	5K23	..	..	..

Miles	Station	16	17	18	19	20	21	22	23	24	25	26	27	28	29
144¼	Pilsley	..	..	..	..	..	..	..	7 8	..	..	..	..	..	..
146½	Heath	..	..	..	..	..	..	..	7 14	..	..	..	..	..	..
151½	Chesterfield (Central) arr	..	..	Reading, and Oxford (Tables 114 and 103)	aft	aft	..	..	7 26	..	..	..	..	..	..
	dep	..	..	..	4 27	5 18	..	..	..	..	..	..	7 45	..	..
153½	Sheepbridge P	..	..	..	4 31	5 22	..	..	To Sheffield arr 8 35 aft	..	..	..	7 49	..	..
155½	Staveley Works R	..	..	..	4 36	5 27	..	..	..	..	..	..	7 54	..	..
152¼	Staveley Town	..	..	..	4 41	5 32	..	..	..	..	..	..	8 1	..	..
154¾	Eckington and Renishaw	..	..	..	4 46	5 37	..	..	..	..	..	..	8 6	..	..
156½	Killamarsh	..	..	..	4 51	5 42	..	..	..	..	..	..	8 11	..	..
158½	Beighton	..	..	..	4 56	5 47	..	..	..	..	..	..	8 16	..	..
159¾	Woodhouse	..	..	..	5 1	5 52	..	..	..	..	..	..	8 22	..	..
162¾	Darnall, for Handsworth	..	..	..	5 8	5 59	..	..	..	..	..	..	8 30	..	..
164¾	Sheffield (Victoria) .... arr	..	..	4 43	5 13	6 4	..	..	..	..	8 0	..	8 35	..	..
187½	67 Retford .... arr	..	..	..	6 25	7 15	..	..	..	..	9 10	..	9Z10	..	..
208	67 Lincoln .... "	..	..	..	..	8 29	..	..	..	..	..	..	..	..	..
232½	67 Grimsby Town ..... "	..	..	..	..	9 16	..	..	..	..	..	..	..	..	..
235¾	67 Cleethorpes .... "	..	..	..	..	9 34	..	..	..	..	..	..	..	..	..
170¾	57 Rotherham T 114 .. arr	..	..	5 9	..	7 24	..	..	..	..	..	..	..	..	..
175¾	67 Doncaster (Central) arr	..	..	6 2	7r36	8 0	..	..	..	..	9r51	..	9r51	..	..
216½	98 Hull .... "	..	..	7 52	..	9 39	..	..	..	..	11k32	..	11k32	..	..
211¼	114 York 1 .... "	..	..	6 37	..	9H50	..	..	..	..	1aH2	..	1aH2	..	..
231¾	125 Harrogate 89 ...... "	..	..	8n27	..	10n20	..	..	..	..	11n58	..	11n58	..	..
253¼	109 Scarborough (Cen.) "	..	..	7 45	..	..	..	..	..	..	5 40	..	5 40	..	..
291¾	103 Newcastle .... "	..	..	8 55	..	12 18	..	..	..	..	3 0	..	3 0	..	..
416¾	103 Edinburgh (Wav.) .. "	..	..	..	..	3a58	..	..	..	..	6 10	..	6 10	..	..
463¾	103 Glasgow (Queen St. "	..	..	..	..	5R45	..	..	..	..	7R42	..	7R42	..	..
475¾	103 Dundee (Tay Bridge) "	..	..	..	..	6 11	..	..	..	..	9X22	..	9X22	..	..
546¾	103 Aberdeen .... "	..	..	..	..	8 29	..	..	..	..	11X30	..	11X30	..	..
177¾	67 Penistone .... arr	..	..	..	6 5	6 50	..	..	..	..	8 30	..	11d9	..	..
184¾	67 Barnsley U 73 ..... arr	..	..	..	6i43	..	..	..	..	..	..	..	..	..	..
191	Huddersfield ...... "	..	..	..	6 48	8 7	..	..	..	..	9 47	..	..	..	..
201¾	Halifax (Old) ...... "	..	..	..	..	8 54	..	..	..	..	10 31	..	..	..	..
203¾	Bradford (Exch.) .. "	..	..	..	7 35	9 23	..	..	..	..	10 58	..	..	..	..
193	67 Glossop (Central) .. arr	..	..	..	..	..	..	..	..	..	9V14	..	..	..	..
201	67 Guide Bridge .... arr	..	..	..	..	7 34	..	..	..	..	9 22	..	11 57	..	..
202½	75 Ashton (Oldham Rd.) arr	..	..	..	..	8‡16	..	..	..	..	9 55	..	..	..	..
203½	75 Stalybridge .... "	..	..	..	..	8E19	..	..	..	..	..	..	..	..	..
206½	76 Oldham (Clegg St.) . "	..	..	..	..	..	..	..	..	..	10 4	..	..	..	..
206	67 Manchester (L.Rd.) . arr	..	..	..	..	7z59	..	..	..	..	9 31	..	12 11	..	..
212½	67 " (Central) "	..	..	..	..	8 6	..	..	..	..	..	..	..	..	..
203½	67 Stockport (Tiv. Dale) arr	..	..	..	..	..	..	..	..	..	..	..	..	..	..
222½	67 Warrington (Cen.) "	..	..	..	..	8 41	..	..	..	..	11K25	..	..	..	..
241	67 Liverpool (Cen.) ... "	..	..	..	..	9 16	..	..	..	..	12K5	..	..	..	..

A For particulars of London Suburban Services, see Suburban Time Table
A Arr. 5 minutes *earlier*
a Morn
B Arr. 3 minutes *earlier*
D Departure time
d Arr. 9 24 aft on Saturdays
E Except Saturdays
F Change at Princes Risborough
f Arr. 1 0 aft on Saturdays
g Arr. 2 25 aft on Saturdays
H Via Doncaster
h Dep. 3 10 aft on Saturdays
i Via Chapeltown
J 10 mins. *earlier* on Sats.
K Via Manchester (Lon. Rd.) and (Central). Passengers cross town at own expense
k Via Retford and Selby
L Via Doncaster and Leeds (Cen.)
N Arr. 12 59 aft
n Via Doncaster and Holbeck
P Sheepbridge & Brimington
p Aft
R Station for Barrow Hill
R Except Sunday morns
r Via Retford
S or S Saturdays only
TC Through Carriages
T Rotherham and Masboro'
T Via Warsop
t Arr. 3 mins. later on Sats.
U Barnsley (Court House)
U Stops to set down
V Change at Dinting
V Arr. 11 34 mrn on Sats.
X Arr Dundee (T.B.) 10 3 mrn and Aberdeen 12 10 aft on Sundays
z Change at Guide Bridge. Arr. 7 54 aft on Sats.
Z Change at Woodhouse
z Arr. 12 32 aft on Fridays and Saturdays
* Via Lincoln and Market Rasen
† Via Selby
‡ Except Saturdays. Ashton (Park Parade)
‖ Via Lincoln and Louth
Ⓑ Third class only

For **OTHER TRAINS** between Leicester and Nottingham, see Table 62—Nottingham and New Basford, Table 63—Edwinstowe and Ollerton, Table 66—Woodhouse and Sheffield, Table 67.

Above and following pages: LNER — 22 May 1944 until further notice.

Table 2— *continued* LONDON, LEICESTER, NOTTINGHAM, SHEFFIELD, HUDDERSFIELD, BRADFORD, MANCHESTER, LIVERPOOL, HULL, CLEETHORPES, YORK, NEWCASTLE, and SCOTLAND

	Week Days—continued														Sundays															
	aft	aft	aft	aft	aft	aft	aft	aft	aft	aft	aft	aft	aft	aft	mrn	mrn	mrn	mrn	mrn	mrn	mrn	mrn	mrn	aft	aft	aft	aft	aft	aft	aft
	3	3	3	3			3	3			3	3						3	3				3					3	3	
LONDON (M'lebone) . dep	4 45	..	6 0	6d20	6 11	..	8 30	..	10 0	..	..	9 34	1045	..	..	..	12 45	5 23	..	..	8 20	9 50	11 20	..	3 30	..	..	5 20	..	6 9
High Wycombe ...... "	5 56	6 28	7 7	7 32	..	..	9 42	8F20	..	..	8F20	..	..	..	..	..	..	6 25	..	..	..	..	12 27	..	..	..	..	6 17	..	..
Princes Risborough.. "	6 19	6 47	7 28	8 5	..	..	10 2	8 44	..	..	8 44	..	..	..	..	..	..	6 45	8 26	..	..	..	12 46	..	..	..	..	6 38	7 2	..
Ilmer Halt	..	..	..	Zz	..	..	..	..	..	..	..	..	..	..	..	..	..	..	..	..	..	..	..	..	..	..	..	..	..	..
Haddenham (Bucks.)......	6 34	..	7 38	8 16	..	..	10 12	..	..	..	..	..	..	..	..	..	..	7 1	..	..	..	..	12 59	..	..	..	..	6 53	..	..
Wotton	6 46	..	7 50	Stop	..	..	10 24	..	..	..	..	..	..	..	..	..	..	7 13	..	..	..	..	1 11	..	..	..	..	7 5	..	..
Harrow on the Hill....	..	..	..	..	..	..	..	..	..	..	..	..	..	..	..	..	..	..	..	..	8 36	10 8	..	..	3 48	..	..	..	..	6 26
Northwood	..	..	..	..	6 37	..	..	..	..	..	..	..	..	..	..	..	..	..	..	..	8 52	..	..	..	..	..	..	..	..	6 45
Aylesbury .... "	..	7 5	..	..	7 34	..	..	9 2	11 4	..	9 2	11 9	1149	TC Except Saturdays Banbury to York	..	..	1 41	..	8 44	..	9 48	1056	..	..	4 36	..	..	..	7 20	7 58
Quainton Road........	..	..	..	..	7 44	..	..	..	..	..	..	1120	..	..	..	..	..	..	Stop	..	9 58	..	..	..	..	..	..	..	Stop	8 8
Calvert	6 58	..	..	..	7 54	..	10 36	..	Except Saturdays	..	Saturdays only	1130	..	..	..	..	..	7 25	..	..	10 7	..	1 22	..	..	..	..	7 17	..	8 18
Finmere	7 8	..	..	..	8 4	..	10 46	..	..	..	..	1140	..	..	..	..	..	7 35	..	..	1016	..	1 31	..	..	..	..	7 27	..	8 28
Brackley (Central)........	7 17	..	8 25	..	8 15	..	10 55	Except Saturdays	..	..	..	1149	..	..	..	TC Banbury to York	..	7 44	..	..	1025	..	1 40	..	5 6	..	TC Swansea to Sheffield	7 36	..	8 38
Helmdon for Sulgrave......	..	..	..	..	..	TC Swindon to Sheffield	..	..	..	..	..	..	..	..	..	..	..	..	..	..	1033	..	1 48	..	..	..	..	Stop	..	8 47
Culworth	Saturdays only.	..	..	..	Cc	..	Except Saturdays	..	..	..	..	..	..	..	..	..	..	..	..	..	1042	..	1 57	..	..	..	..	..	..	8 57
Woodford and Hinton.. arr	..	..	..	..	8 34	..	..	..	1144	..	..	Saturdays only	..	..	..	..	2 26	..	..	..	1048	1135	2 3	..	5 21	..	..	..	..	9 3
9 STRATFORD-ON-AVON arr	..	..	..	..	Stop	..	..	..	..	..	..	..	..	..	..	..	..	..	..	..	..	..	Stop	..	..	..	..	..	..	Stop
Woodford and Hinton dep	..	..	..	..	..	..	..	..	..	1148	..	..	..	..	..	..	3 20	..	..	..	..	1211	..	..	..	..	..	..	..	..
Eydon Road Halt........	..	..	Except Saturdays.	..	..	..	..	..	..	..	..	..	..	..	..	..	..	..	..	..	..	..	..	..	..	..	..	..	..	..
Chalcombe Road Halt....	..	..	..	..	..	..	..	..	..	..	..	..	..	..	..	..	..	..	..	..	..	..	..	..	..	..	..	..	..	..
Banbury .... arr	..	..	..	..	..	..	..	..	Arr. Rugby 12 12 ngt	12 6	..	..	Saturdays only	..	..	..	3 38	..	..	..	..	1229	..	..	..	..	..	..	..	..
Banbury .... dep	..	..	..	..	..	9 5	..	..	..	..	..	..	..	11 50	..	12 15	..	..	..	..	..	..	..	..	..	..	5 30	To Radcliffe-on-Trent arr. 8 39 aft (Table 63)	..	..
Chalcombe Road Halt.	..	..	..	..	..	..	..	..	..	..	..	..	..	..	..	..	..	..	..	..	..	..	..	..	..	..	..	..	..	..
Eydon Road Halt......	..	..	..	..	..	..	..	..	..	..	..	..	..	..	..	..	..	..	..	..	..	..	..	..	..	..	..	..	..	..
Woodford & Hinton arr	..	..	..	..	..	9 23	..	..	..	..	..	..	..	12 8	..	12 33	..	..	..	..	..	..	..	..	..	..	5 48	..	..	..
9 STRATFORD-ON-AVON dep	..	..	Stop	..	..	6 20	..	..	..	..	..	..	..	..	..	..	..	..	..	..	..	..	..	..	..	..	..	..	..	..
Woodford and Hinton.. dep	..	..	..	..	..	9 29	..	..	1151	..	..	..	..	12 13	..	12 38	2 28	..	..	..	1054	1137	..	..	5 23	..	5 54	..	..	..
Charwelton	..	..	..	..	..	..	..	..	..	..	..	..	..	..	..	..	..	..	..	..	..	..	..	..	..	..	..	..	..	..
Braunston and Willoughby	..	..	..	..	..	..	..	..	..	..	..	..	..	..	..	..	..	..	..	..	..	..	..	..	..	..	..	..	..	..
Rugby (Central)........	..	..	..	..	..	9c57	..	..	1219	..	..	..	..	12A39	..	1A4	3h1	..	..	..	1116	12B0	..	..	5B46	..	6J19	..	..	..
Lutterworth	..	..	..	..	..	..	..	..	..	..	..	..	..	..	..	..	..	..	..	..	1128	..	..	..	5 58	..	..	..	..	..
Ashby Magna	..	..	..	..	..	..	..	..	..	..	..	..	..	..	..	..	..	..	..	..	..	..	..	..	..	..	..	..	..	..
Whetstone	..	..	..	..	..	..	..	..	..	..	..	..	..	..	..	..	..	..	..	..	..	..	..	..	..	..	..	..	..	..
Leicester (Central) .. arr	..	..	..	..	aft	10 23	..	..	1246	..	..	..	1a11	1 6	..	1 31	3 34	..	mrn	..	1151	1228	..	..	6 18	..	6 46	..	..	..
Leicester (Central) .. dep	..	..	..	..	8E55	10 36	..	..	1258	..	..	..	1 16	1 16	1 16	1 41	3 45	..	6 56	..	1155	1231	..	..	6 23	6 33	6 54	..	..	..
Belgrave and Birstall......	..	..	..	..	9E0	..	..	..	..	..	..	..	..	..	..	..	..	..	7 1	..	..	..	..	..	..	6 38	..	..	..	..
Rothley	..	..	..	..	9E6	..	..	..	..	..	..	..	..	..	..	..	..	..	7 7	..	12 4	..	..	..	..	6 44	..	..	..	..
Quorn and Woodhouse......	..	..	..	..	9E12	..	..	..	..	..	..	..	..	..	..	..	..	..	7 13	..	1210	..	..	..	..	6 50	..	..	..	..
Loughborough (Central)...	..	..	aft	..	9E19	10A56	..	..	1*18	..	..	..	..	1A36	..	2A1	..	..	7 19	..	1216	1247	..	..	6 39	6 55	7J13	aft	..	..
East Leake	..	..	9 0	..	..	..	..	..	..	..	..	..	..	..	..	..	..	..	7 27	8 0	1224	..	..	..	..	7 3	..	8 0	..	..
Rushcliffe Halt..........	..	..	9 3	..	..	..	..	..	..	..	..	..	..	..	..	..	..	..	..	..	1227	..	..	..	..	7 6	..	8 3	..	..
Ruddington	..	..	..	..	..	..	..	..	..	..	..	..	..	..	..	..	..	..	7 37	8 9	1234	..	..	..	..	7 13	..	..	..	..
Arkwright Street..........	..	..	..	..	..	..	..	..	..	..	..	..	..	..	..	..	..	..	7 44	..	..	..	..	..	..	7 20	..	..	..	..
Nottingham (Victoria) arr	..	..	9 19	aft	9E40	11 17	..	..	1 38	..	..	..	1 50	1 57	1 50	2 22	4 19	..	7 47	8 18	1244	1 7	aft	..	6 59	7 23	7 34	8 17	aft	aft
Nottingham (Victoria) dep	..	..	..	9 20	..	11 31	..	..	1 53	..	..	..	1 54	2 12	1 54	2 37	4 24	..	..	..	..	1 12	2 15	2 30	7 4	..	7 41	..	9 43	9 55
New Basford..........	..	..	..	9 25	..	..	..	..	..	..	..	..	..	..	..	..	..	..	..	To Radcliffe-on-Trent arr 8 39 mrn (Table 63)	..	TC Marylebone to Manchester (Lon. Rd.)	..	..	TC Marylebone to Manchester (Lon. Rd.)	..	..	..	..	..
Bulwell Common..........	..	..	..	9 30	..	..	..	..	..	..	..	..	..	..	..	..	..	..	..	..	..	..	..	..	..	..	..	..	..	..
Hucknall Central..........	..	..	..	9 36	..	11f47	..	..	..	..	..	..	..	..	..	..	..	..	..	..	..	..	2 27	2 42	..	..	..	..	9 55	10 7
Kirkby-in-Ashfield (Cen.)	..	..	..	..	..	..	..	..	..	..	..	..	..	..	..	..	..	..	..	..	..	..	..	2 55	..	..	..	..	..	1020
Sutton-in-Ashfield (Cen.)	..	..	..	..	..	..	..	..	..	..	..	..	..	..	..	..	..	..	..	..	..	..	..	3 0	..	..	..	..	..	1025
Mansfield (L.N.E.R.) arr	..	..	..	..	..	..	..	..	..	..	..	..	..	..	..	..	..	..	..	..	..	..	..	3 5	..	..	..	..	..	1030
Mansfield (L.N.E.R.) dep	..	..	..	..	..	..	..	..	..	..	..	..	..	..	..	..	..	..	..	..	..	..	..	Stop	..	..	..	..	..	..
Edwinstowe..........	..	..	..	..	..	..	..	..	..	..	..	..	..	..	..	..	..	..	..	..	..	..	..	..	..	..	..	..	..	..
Ollerton.......... arr	..	..	..	..	..	..	..	..	..	..	..	..	..	..	..	..	..	..	..	..	..	..	..	..	..	..	..	..	..	..
66 LINCOLN .... arr	..	..	..	..	..	..	..	..	..	..	..	..	..	..	..	..	..	..	..	..	..	..	..	..	..	..	..	..	..	..
Kirkby Bentinck..........	..	..	..	9 54	..	..	..	..	..	..	..	..	..	..	..	..	..	..	..	..	..	..	2 43	..	..	..	..	..	10 8	..
Tibshelf Town..........	..	..	..	10 4	..	..	..	..	..	..	..	..	..	..	..	..	..	..	..	..	..	..	2 52	..	..	..	..	..	1018	..
	1	2	3	4	5	6	7	8	9	10	11	12	13	14	15	16	17	18	19	20	21	22	23	24	25	26	27	28	29	30

	1	2	3	4	5	6	7	8	9	10	11	12	13	14	15	16	17	18	19	20	21	22	23	24	25	26	27	28	29	30
Pilsley..........	..	..	..	10 9	..	..	..	..	..	..	..	..	..	..	..	..	..	..	..	..	..	..	2 56	..	..	..	..	..	1023	..
Heath	..	..	..	1015	..	..	..	..	..	..	..	..	..	..	..	..	..	..	..	..	..	..	3 2	..	..	..	..	..	1029	..
Chesterfield (Central) arr	..	..	..	1028	..	..	..	..	..	..	..	..	..	..	..	..	..	..	..	..	..	..	3 14	aft	..	..	..	..	1042	..
Chesterfield (Central) dep	..	..	..	..	..	..	..	..	..	..	..	..	..	..	..	..	..	..	..	..	..	..	3 17	7 15	..	..	..	..	1046	..
Sheepbridge P..........	..	..	..	..	..	..	..	..	..	..	..	..	..	..	..	..	..	..	..	..	..	..	3 21	..	..	..	..	..	1050	..
Staveley Works R..........	..	..	..	..	..	..	..	..	..	..	..	..	..	..	..	..	..	..	..	..	..	..	3 26	7 23	..	..	..	..	1055	..
Staveley Town	..	..	..	..	..	..	..	..	..	..	..	..	..	..	..	..	..	..	..	..	..	..	3 31	7 27	7 48	..	..	..	11 1	..
Eckington and Renishaw..	..	..	..	..	..	..	..	..	Except Sunday mornings	..	..	..	Sunday mornings only	Except Sunday mornings	..	..	..	..	..	..	..	..	3 36	..	..	..	..	..	11 6	..
Killamarsh	..	..	..	..	..	..	..	..	..	..	..	..	..	..	..	..	..	..	..	..	..	..	3 41	..	..	..	..	..	1111	..
Beighton	..	..	..	..	..	..	..	..	..	..	..	..	..	..	..	..	..	..	..	..	..	..	3 46	..	..	..	..	..	1116	..
Woodhouse	..	..	..	..	..	..	..	..	..	..	..	..	..	..	..	..	..	..	..	..	..	..	3 51	..	..	..	..	..	1121	..
Darnall, for Handsworth..	..	..	..	..	..	..	..	..	..	..	..	..	..	..	..	..	..	..	..	..	..	..	3 58	..	..	..	..	..	1128	..
Sheffield (Victoria).... arr	..	..	..	..	..	12P34	..	..	3 2	..	..	..	2 56	3 15	2 56	3 40	5 26	..	..	..	..	2 14	4 3	..	8 10	..	8 43	..	1133	..
67 RETFORD .... arr	..	..	..	..	..	..	..	..	..	..	..	..	4 12	..	4 12	..	10 27	..	..	..	..	..	6 35	..	..	..	..	..	..	..
67 LINCOLN .... "	..	..	..	..	..	..	..	..	..	..	..	..	..	..	..	..	11 32	..	..	..	..	..	9 42	..	..	..	..	..	..	..
67 GRIMSBY TOWN...... "	..	..	..	..	..	..	..	..	..	..	..	..	6 5	..	6 5	..	11H16	..	..	..	..	..	10 24	..	..	..	..	..	..	..
67 CLEETHORPES........ "	..	..	..	..	..	..	..	..	..	..	..	..	6 38	..	6 38	..	11H37	..	..	..	..	..	10 39	..	..	..	..	..	..	..
67 ROTHERHAM T 114.. arr	..	..	..	..	..	..	..	..	..	..	..	..	..	4 32	..	..	8 19	..	..	..	..	2 57	5 42	..	..	..	..	..	..	..
67 DONCASTER (Central) arr	..	..	..	..	..	..	..	..	..	..	..	..	4 13	5 3	4 18	..	8 56	..	..	..	..	..	6 19	..	..	..	..	..	..	..
98 HULL .... "	..	..	..	..	..	..	..	..	..	..	..	..	7 15	7 33	7 15	..	10 28	..	..	..	..	..	7 54	..	..	..	..	..	..	..
114 YORK 1.......... "	..	..	..	..	..	..	..	..	..	..	..	..	..	5 20	..	5 45	..	..	..	..	..	4 13	10H48	..	..	..	..	..	..	..
125 HARROGATE 89.......... "	..	..	..	..	..	..	..	..	..	..	..	..	..	8 9	..	..	..	..	..	..	..	..	8n45	..	..	..	..	..	..	..
109 SCARBOROUGH (Cen.) "	..	..	..	..	..	..	..	..	..	..	..	..	..	..	..	10 27	..	..	..	..	..	6 5	5a40	..	..	..	..	..	..	..
103 NEWCASTLE.......... "	..	..	..	..	..	..	..	..	..	..	..	..	..	9 24	..	10 22	..	..	..	..	..	8 40	12 58	..	..	..	..	..	..	..
103 EDINBURGH (Wav.).. "	..	..	..	..	..	..	..	..	..	..	..	..	..	1 49	..	8p25	..	..	..	..	..	..	4 18	..	..	..	..	..	..	..
103 GLASGOW (Queen St.) "	..	..	..	..	..	..	..	..	..	..	..	..	..	3 20	..	10L56	..	..	..	..	..	..	5 45	..	..	..	..	..	..	..
103 DUNDEE (Tay Bridge) "	..	..	..	..	..	..	..	..	..	..	..	..	..	3 35	..	10p41	..	..	..	..	..	..	6 11	..	..	..	..	..	..	..
103 ABERDEEN .... "	..	..	..	..	..	..	..	..	..	..	..	..	..	5 37	..	..	..	..	..	..	..	..	8 29	..	..	..	..	..	..	..
67 Penistone.......... arr	..	..	..	..	..	..	..	..	..	..	..	..	..	6 36	..	..	7 13	..	..	..	..	2 45	6 59	..	8 41	..	10 20	..	..	..
67 BARNSLEY U 73..... arr	..	..	..	..	..	..	..	..	..	..	..	..	..	7 38	..	..	7 55	..	..	..	..	7 5	..	..	..	..	..	..	..	..
HUDDERSFIELD...... "	..	..	..	..	..	..	..	..	..	..	..	..	..	7 21	..	..	11 24	..	..	..	..	6 19	..	..	..	..	..	..	..	..
HALIFAX (Old)...... "	..	..	..	..	..	..	..	..	..	..	..	..	..	8 12	..	..	12 11	..	..	..	..	8 48	..	..	..	..	..	..	..	..
BRADFORD (Exch.).. "	..	..	..	..	..	..	..	..	..	..	..	..	..	8 8	..	..	1 17	..	..	..	..	7 28	..	..	..	..	..	..	..	..
67 GLOSSOP (Central) . arr	..	..	..	..	..	..	..	..	6N1	..	..	..	..	..	..	..	7 57	..	..	..	..	..	8 54	..	..	..	..	..	..	..
67 Guide Bridge....... arr	..	..	..	..	..	..	..	..	4 33	..	..	..	4 16	..	4 16	..	8 27	..	..	..	..	3 26	7 41	..	9 27	..	11 7	..	..	..
75 ASHTON (Oldham Rd.) arr	..	..	..	..	..	..	..	..	5 23	..	..	..	..	..	..	..	..	..	..	..	..	..	..	..	..	..	..	..	..	..
75 STALYBRIDGE........ "	..	..	..	..	..	..	..	..	6 37	..	..	..	..	..	..	..	..	..	..	..	..	..	..	..	..	..	..	..	..	..
76 OLDHAM (Clegg St.). "	..	..	..	..	..	..	..	..	5 34	..	..	..	..	..	..	..	..	..	..	..	..	..	..	..	..	..	..	..	..	..
67 Manchester (L.Rd.). arr	..	..	..	..	..	..	..	..	4 49	..	..	..	4 31	..	4 31	..	8 47	..	..	..	..	3 40	8z2	..	9 36	..	11 19	..	..	..
67 " (Central) "	..	..	..	..	..	..	..	..	..	..	..	..	..	..	..	..	..	..	..	..	..	..	8 1	..	..	..	..	..	..	..
67 STOCKPORT (Tiv. Dale) arr	..	..	..	..	..	..	..	..	4 52	..	..	..	4 37	..	4 37	..	..	..	..	..	..	..	..	..	..	..	..	..	..	..
67 WARRINGTON (Cen.) "	..	..	..	..	..	..	..	..	5 40	..	..	..	5 16	..	5 16	..	11K43	..	..	..	..	5K14	9 2	..	10K51	..	..	..	..	..
67 LIVERPOOL (Cen.)... "	..	..	..	..	..	..	..	..	6 25	..	..	..	5 50	..	5 50	..	12K26	..	..	..	..	..	9 58	..	11K55	..	..	..	..	..

A For particulars of London Suburban Services, see Suburban Time Table
A Arr. 5 minutes *earlier*
a Morn
B Arr. 3 minutes *earlier*
Cc Stops when required to set down from Marylebone on notice to the Guard at Marylebone
c Arr. 8 minutes *earlier*
d Dep. 5 30 aft on Saturdays
E Except Saturdays
F Change at Princes Risborough
f Fridays and Saturdays
H Via Doncaster
h Arr. 2 48 mrn
i Via Chapeltown
J Arr. 4 minutes *earlier*
K Via Manchester (Lon. Rd.) and (Central). Passengers cross the town at own expense
L Arr. 10 36 aft during July and August
N Via Godley Junction
n Via Doncaster and Holbeck
P Sheepbridge & Brimington
P Arr. 12 39 night on Fridays and Saturdays
p Aft
R Station for Barrow Hill
S or S Saturdays only
T Rotherham and Masboro'
TC Through Carriages
U Barnsley (Court House)
Zz Calls to set down on notice to Guard at Princes Risborough
z Change at Guide Bridge
* Arr. 1 12 mrn
3 Third class only

B

Table 2—*continued*

SCOTLAND, NEWCASTLE, YORK, CLEETHORPES, HULL, LIVERPOOL, MANCHESTER, BRADFORD, HUDDERSFIELD, SHEFFIELD, NOTTINGHAM, LEICESTER, and LONDON

Week Days

Miles from London Rd.	Station	1	2	3	4	5	6	7	8	9	10	11	12	13	14	15	16	17	18	19	20	21	22	23	24	25	26	27	28	29	30
		mrn	mrn	mrn	mrn	mrn	mrn	mrn	mrn	mrn	aft	mrn	mrn	mrn	mrn	mrn	aft	mrn	aft	aft	mrn	aft	mrn	aft	aft	aft	aft	aft	aft	aft	aft
—	67 Liverpool (Central) dep										10‖30			5 35	7K17	7K17					9 30		10K30				2 30				4 15
—	67 Warrington (Cen.) "										11‖25			6 18	8K44	8K44					10 0		11K0				3 0				4 46
—	67 Stockport (Tiv. Dale) "																														
—	67 Manchester (Cen.) dep										mrn			7r36							1040						3r30				5 27
—	67 " (London Rd.) "										1 35			8 20	9 45	9 45					10r35		12c25				3 50				5R27
—	76 Oldham (Clegg St.) dep													8 6	9 17	9 17							12 7				1S56				4 30
—	75 Stalybridge "													7 52	8 32	8 32															5X45
—	75 Ashton (Oldham Rd.) "													8 15	9 26	9 26							12 16				2S6				5‡48
5	67 Guide Bridge dep													8 32	9 56	9 56					11 7		12c37				4 1				5 57
—	67 Glossop (Central) dep													8V10	9V25	9V25							12EV46								
—	Bradford (Exch.) dep													7 8	8 38	8 38							10S43								4 9
—	Halifax (Old) "													7 45	8 28	8 28							10S20								4 5
—	Huddersfield "											5 47		8 16	9 55	9 55							12S14								5 0
—	67 Barnsley U 73 "											6i10		8 10												1S20	4 10				6 11
28½	67 Penistone dep										2 34	6 50		9 24	1041	1041					1153		1F27			2S5	4 46				6 43
—	103 Aberdeen dep										3Z30	6P0																			5a45
—	103 Dundee (Tay Bridge) "										5Ü34	8P9																			7 53
—	103 Glasgow (Queen St.) "										6Ü0	7z55																			8 25
—	103 Edinburgh (Wav.) "										7Z50	10Z30																			1015
—	103 Newcastle "										10Z51	1a35									8 15										1p10
—	109 Scarborough (Cen.) "										8w0										8 10		10 40								1250
—	125 Harrogate 89 "										8Nn38										8t25		9n10			12C5					3n20
—	114 York 1 "										1N7	3y41									1030		12p10								3H15
—	98 Hull "													6 10							9 15		9v45			11c43					4 0
—	67 Doncaster (Cen.) "										2 49	6 45		8 32							1042		11vk30			2 5					5 30
—	67 Rotherham T 114 dep										3 14	7 30		9 13							1152		1 27			2 44					6 5
—	67 Cleethorpes dep													5H50							8 30		10a45								3H0
—	67 Grimsby Town "													6H12							8 48		11 5								3H24
—	67 Lincoln "													7 28							9 25		11 50			2 28					
—	67 Retford "											6 30		8 15							1027		12B55			3B15					4 55
—	Sheffield (Victoria) dep										6 10	7 55		9 55	11 5	11 5					1232		2 0			4 4	5 10			5 40	7 9
43½	Darnall, for Handsworth										6 17	8 1		10 1												4 11				5 46	7 15
46½	Woodhouse										6*26	8 8		10 8									2 10			4 18				5 53	7 22
47½	Beighton										6 31	8 12		1013									2S15			4 23				5 58	7 27
49½	Killamarsh										6 37	8 17		1018									2S20			4 28				6 3	7 32
51½	Eckington and Renishaw										6*44	8 22		1023					12 5				2S25			4 33				6 8	7 37
53½	Staveley Town				6 10						6 52	8 27		1029	1128	1128		1140	1211				2†23	2 40		4 39				6 14	7*46
54½	Staveley Works R				6 15						6 57	8 32		1034				1145	1216					2 45		4 44				6 19	7 51
56½	Sheepbridge P				6 20						7 2	8 37		1039				1150	1221					2 50		4 49				6 24	7 56
58½	Chesterfield (Central) arr				6 24						7 6	8 41		1043				1154	1225				2†33	2 54		4 53				6 28	8 0
	Chesterfield (Central) dep				Stop						7 11	Stop		1044				Stop	Stop				2†35	Stop		4 58				6 31	Stop
59	Heath										7 24			1058												5 11				6 45	
61½	Pilsley										7 32			11 4												5 17				6 51	
63	Tibshelf Town										7 38			11 8									2†55			5 22				6 56	
67½	Kirkby Bentinck										7 49			1117									3†4			5 31				7 6	
—	66 Lincoln dep																											12T45			
—	Mls Ollerton dep											mrn																1T35			
—	1¼ Edwinstowe											7 47																1T40			
—	8¼ Mansfield (L.N.E.R.) arr											8 1																2T11			
	Mansfield (L.N.E.R.) dep									7 14		8 5										1 48						5 48	6 42		
—	11½ Sutton-in-Ashfield (C.)									7 22		8 13										1 56						5 56	6 50		
—	13 Kirkby-in-Ashfield (C.)									7 28		8 19										2 2						6 2	6 56		
73½	Hucknall (Central)									7 40	8 3	8 33		1132								2 14	3†18			5 46		6 18	7 10	7 20	
76½	Bulwell Common									7 46	8 10	8 39		1138								2 20	3†24			5 52		6 24	7 16	7 28	
73	New Basford									7 51	8 15	8 44										2 25						6 29	7 21		
	Notes														Except Saturdays; TC Manchester (L.Rd.) to Marylebone	Saturdays only; TC Manchester (L.Rd.) to Marylebone		Except Saturdays	Saturdays only		TC Newcastle to Ashford (Kent) arr 8 32 aft. via Oxford, Reading & Guildford (Tables 103 & 114)						TC Manchester (Lon. Road) to Marylebone				

Miles	Station	1	2	3	4	5	6	7	8	9	10	11	12	13	14	15	16	17	18	19	20	21	22	23	24	25	26	27	28	29	30
79½	Nottingham (Victoria) arr									7 55	8 19	8 48		1146	1212	1212					1 33	2 29	3†32			6 0	6 11	6 33	7 25	7 35	
	Nottingham (Victoria) dep								6 25	8 0	Stop		9 25	Stop	1217	1217				1250	1 39	Stop	3b40		5J45		6 16	Stop	Stop		
80½	Arkwright Street								6 28	8 3			9 28							1253	1j45				5J48						
84	Ruddington								6 35	8 10			9 35							1 0					5J56						
87½	Rushcliffe Halt												9 46							1 6					6J2						
88½	East Leake								6 44	8 19			9 51							1 11					6J7						
93	Loughborough (Central)								6 54	8 29			10 1		1238	1238				1L26	2*6		4b2		6J18		6 36				
95½	Quorn and Woodhouse								6 59	8 34			10 6							1 31					6J23						
98	Rothley								7 5	8 40			1012							1 37					6J29						
100¾	Belgrave and Birstall								7 11	8 46			1018							1 43					6J35						
103	Leicester (Central) arr								7 15	8 50			1022	mrn	1254	1254				1 47	2 22		4b18	aft	6J39		6 50	aft			
	Leicester (Central) dep	6 20							7 27	Stop			Stop	1155	1259	1259				1 56	2 32			5 22	Stop		6 55	7 10			
107¾	Whetstone	6 29							7 36					12 4						2 5				5 32				7 19			
112½	Ashby Magna	6 39							7 46					1214						2 15				5 43				7 29			
116	Lutterworth	6 48			mrn				7 56					1223		1 21				2 25				5 53				7 39			
122¾	Rugby (Central)	6 58			7 3				8 8					1235	1 29	1 33				2*38	3j3			6 5			7*26	7 50			
127¾	Braunston and Willoughby	Stop							8 17					1244						2 47				6 14							
134¾	Charwelton								8 30					1257						3 0				6 27							
137	Woodford and Hinton arr				7 23				8 35					1 2	1 49	1 53				3 5	3 23			6 32			7 46				
161½	9 Stratford-on-Avon arr				Stop																	aft					9 27				
—	Woodford and Hinton dep								8 59												3 25	5 32									
141	Eydon Road Halt								9 1													5 41									
144¾	Chalcombe Road Halt								9 8													5 49									
148	Banbury arr								9 17		mrn		aft								3 42	5 59									aft
—	Mls Banbury dep										10 10		1 27									Stop					6 21				9 5
—	3½ Chalcombe Road Halt										10 18																6 32				
—	7 Eydon Road Halt										10 26																6 40				
—	11 Woodford & Hinton arr										10 34		1 46														6 49				9 23
—	9 Stratford-on-Avon dep				mrn																						6 20				
—	Woodford and Hinton dep				7 38				8 57						1 52	1 56				3 11							7 49				
140	Culworth	mrn			7 45				9 4										aft	3 18									aft		
143½	Helmdon, for Sulgrave	③			7 53				9 12										③	3 26									③		
146½	Brackley (Central)	6 45			8 1				9 20							2 12			2 45	3 34							8*7		8 40		
151½	Finmere	6 54			8 10				9 30										2 54	3 44									8 50		
157½	Calvert	7 4			8 20				9 41	mrn								aft	3 4	3 55		aft							9 1		
162	Quainton Road	7 12	③		8 28			③	9 49	③								③	3 13	4 3		③									
168¼	Aylesbury	7 21	7 45		8 37			8 55	9 59	1040					2 31	2 40		3 20	3 23	4 13		4 50					8 36				
192½	Northwood	8 22							1134										4 28	5h41											
196½	Harrow on the Hill	8 34				③			1150						3 18	3 30			4 34	5h55					aft		9 25				
163½	Wotton					8 26	③										③								③				9 12		
169	Haddenham (Bucks.)					8 36	8 53										3 12								7 17				9 22		
171½	Ilmer Halt			③		8 42	8 58										3 18								7 22						
174½	Princes Risborough arr		8 2	8q14		8 48	9 5	9 15		11 1							3 25	3 37				5 8			7 28				9 34		
182½	High Wycombe "		8 22	8 28		9 11	9 21	9§54		1118								4§2				5 28			8 13				9 55		
206	LONDON (M'lebone) "	8 50		9 14	9 49	10 6			12 8						3 35	3 47			4 59	6h12					1023		9 42		11 8		
	Notes			Except Saturdays										Saturdays only	Except Saturdays	Saturdays only			Saturdays only												

A For particulars of London Suburban Services, see Suburban Time Table
a Morn
B Change at Woodhouse
b 7 mins. later on Saturdays
C Via Church Fenton, Knottingley, and Doncaster
c 5 mins. later on Saturdays
E Except Saturdays
F 4 mins. later on Saturdays
H Via Doncaster
h 5 mins. *earlier* on Sats.
i Via Chapeltown
J 28 mins. *earlier* on Sats.
j Arr. 4 minutes *earlier*

K Via Manchester (Cen.) and (London Rd.). Passengers cross town at own expense
k Dep. Doncaster 12 15 aft on Saturdays
L Arr. 7 minutes *earlier*
N Except Saturday nights. Dep. 9 48 aft on Sundays via Leeds (City) and York
n Via Holbeck and Doncaster
P Sheepbridge & Brimington
P Except Saturday nights Dep. Aberdeen 5 40 and Dundee (T. B.) 8 0 aft on Sundays

p Aft
q Departure time
R Station for Barrow Hill
R Change at Guide Bridge. Dep. 5 20 aft on Saturdays
r Change at Guide Bridge
S Saturdays only
T Rotherham and Masboro'
T Via Warsop
t Dep. 9 0 mrn on Saturdays
TC Through Carriages
U Barnsley (Court House)

Ü Except Saturday nights. Depart Dundee 5 37 and Glasgow (Q. St.) 6 10 aft on Sundays
u Via Leeds (City) and York
V Change at Dinting
v Via Retford except on Sats.
w Dep. 7 45 aft on Sundays
X 5 mins. *earlier* on Sats.
z Except Saturday nights. Departs 8 5 aft on Sundays
y Via Retford
Z Except Saturday nights, but applies on Sunday nights

* Arr. 3 minutes *earlier*
† 8 mins. later on Saturdays
‡ Ashton (Park Parade). Dep 5 43 aft on Saturdays
§ Change at Princes Risborough
‖ Via Manchester (Central) and (Lon. Rd.). Passengers cross the town at own expense. Dep. Liverpool 9 55 and Warrington 10 45 aft on Sundays
③ Third class only

Table 2—continued

SCOTLAND, NEWCASTLE, YORK, CLEETHORPES, HULL, LIVERPOOL, MANCHESTER, BRADFORD, HUDDERSFIELD, SHEFFIELD, NOTTINGHAM, LEICESTER, and LONDON

Station	1	2	3	4	5	6	7	8	9	10	11	12	13	14	15	16	17	18	19	20	21	22	23	24	25	26	27	28	29	30
	Week Days—continued								Sundays																					
	aft	aft	aft	aft	aft	ngt	aft	aft	mrn	mrn	mrn	mrn	mrn	mrn	aft	mrn	mrn		mrn	aft	aft	aft	mrn	aft	aft	aft	aft	aft	aft	
67 Liverpool (Central) dep	..	..	..	..	4 15	..	..	8 30	..	..	..	..	..	..	..	..	..	..	..	..	..	..	10K30	..	..	..	..	..	..	..
67 Warrington (Cen.) "	..	..	..	..	4 46	..	4K57	9 0	..	..	..	..	..	..	..	..	..	..	6K30	..	..	..	11K21	..	..	..	..	..	..	..
67 Stockport (Tiv. Dale) "	..	..	..	..	..	..	..	..	..	..	..	..	..	..	..	..	..	..	..	..	..	..	..	..	..	..	..	..	..	..
67 Manchester (Cen.) dep	..	..	..	..	5 27	..	..	10 35	..	..	..	..	..	..	..	..	..	..	..	..	..	..	..	..	..	..	..	..	..	..
67 " (London Rd.) "	..	..	..	..	5R27	..	6 35	..	..	..	..	..	..	..	..	..	..	..	10 0	..	..	..	3 50	..	..	..	..	..	..	..
76 Oldham (Clegg St.) dep	..	..	..	..	4 30	..	6w9	10 15	..	..	..	..	..	..	..	..	..	..	..	..	..	..	..	..	..	..	..	..	..	..
75 Stalybridge "	..	..	..	..	5X15	..	6E37	8E25	..	..	..	..	..	..	..	..	..	..	..	..	..	..	..	..	..	..	..	..	..	..
75 Ashton (Oldham Rd.) "	..	..	..	..	5‡48	..	6z40	10 24	..	..	..	..	..	..	..	..	..	..	..	..	..	..	..	..	..	..	..	..	..	..
67 Guide Bridge dep	..	..	..	..	5 57	..	6 52	11 3	..	..	..	..	..	..	..	..	..	..	1011	..	..	..	4 1	..	..	..	..	..	..	..
67 Glossop (Central) dep	..	..	..	..	..	..	7V4	..	..	..	..	..	..	..	..	..	..	..	9 48	..	..	..	..	..	..	..	..	..	..	..
Bradford (Exch.) dep	..	..	..	..	4S40	..	6 23	..	..	..	..	..	..	..	..	..	..	..	7 45	..	..	..	..	..	..	..	..	..	..	..
Halifax (Old) "	..	..	..	..	5S21	..	6 50	..	..	..	..	..	..	..	..	..	..	..	8 12	..	..	..	..	..	..	..	..	..	..	..
Huddersfield "	..	..	..	..	6S4	..	7 19	..	..	..	..	..	..	..	..	..	..	..	10 0	..	..	..	..	..	..	..	..	..	..	..
67 Barnsley U 73 "	..	..	..	..	6 11	..	..	9 50	..	..	..	..	..	..	..	..	..	..	10 8	..	..	..	..	..	..	..	..	..	..	..
67 Penistone dep	..	..	..	..	6h43	..	9u20	11 49	..	..	..	..	..	..	..	..	..	..	1056	..	..	..	4 46	..	..	..	..	..	..	..
103 Aberdeen dep	..	..	..	..	8a50	..	8a50	..	..	..	..	..	..	..	6L0	..	..	..	..	..	..	..	..	..	..	..	..	..	..	..
103 Dundee (Tay Bridge) "	..	..	..	..	10a4	..	10a54	..	..	..	..	..	..	..	8L9	..	..	..	..	..	..	..	..	..	..	..	..	..	..	..
103 Glasgow (Queen St.) "	..	..	..	..	11a20	..	11a20	..	..	..	..	..	..	..	7L55	..	..	..	..	..	..	..	..	..	..	..	..	..	..	..
103 Edinburgh (Wav.) "	..	..	..	..	1p10	..	1p40	..	..	..	..	..	..	..	10L30	..	..	..	..	..	..	..	..	..	..	..	..	..	..	..
103 Newcastle "	..	..	..	..	4 1	..	6 50	..	..	..	..	..	..	..	1a35	..	..	..	..	..	..	..	10a35	..	..	..	..	..	..	..
103 Scarborough (Cen.) "	..	..	..	..	4 30	..	8 0	..	..	..	..	..	..	..	..	..	..	..	..	..	..	..	10a50	..	..	..	..	..	..	..
125 Harrogate 89 "	..	..	..	..	4 59	..	8 0	..	..	..	..	..	..	..	..	..	..	..	..	..	..	..	12n31	..	..	..	..	..	..	..
114 York 1 "	..	..	..	..	6H10	..	10 0	..	..	..	..	..	..	..	3qy41	..	..	..	..	..	..	..	12y36	..	..	..	..	..	..	..
98 Hull "	..	..	..	..	5 10	..	8J40	..	..	..	..	..	..	..	..	..	..	..	..	..	..	..	12y25	..	..	..	..	..	..	..
67 Doncaster (Cen.) "	..	..	..	..	7 [illegible]	..	..	..	..	..	..	..	..	..	8a15	..	..	..	..	..	..	..	2y22	..	..	..	..	..	..	..
67 Rotherham T 114 dep	..	..	..	..	7 35	..	..	..	..	..	..	..	..	..	8 51	..	..	..	..	..	..	..	..	..	..	..	..	..	..	..
67 Cleethorpes dep	..	..	..	..	3H0	..	6 35	..	..	..	..	..	..	..	5H35	..	..	..	..	..	..	..	9a16	..	..	..	..	..	..	..
67 Grimsby Town "	..	..	..	..	3H24	..	7 0	..	..	..	..	..	..	..	5H57	..	..	..	..	..	..	..	9 35	..	..	..	..	..	..	..
67 Lincoln "	..	..	..	..	..	..	6 50	..	..	..	..	..	..	..	..	..	..	..	..	..	..	..	1p59	..	..	..	..	..	..	..
67 Retford "	..	..	..	..	..	..	9 40	..	..	..	..	..	..	..	6 30	..	..	..	..	..	..	..	3 0	..	..	..	..	..	..	..
Sheffield (Victoria) dep	..	..	..	..	8 10	..	1158	12 29	..	..	1229	..	..	..	9 20	10 5	..	..	1120	..	..	..	5 10	..	..	..	5 40	..	..	..
Darnall, for Handsworth	..	..	..	..	IC York to Swindon	..	IC York to Swindon	Except Monday mornings	..	..	..	..	..	..	IC Sheffield to Swansea	10 11	..	..	..	..	..	..	..	..	..	..	5 46	..	..	..
Woodhouse	..	..	..	..		..			..	..	..	..	..	..		10 18	..	..	..	..	..	..	..	..	..	..	5 53	..	..	..
Beighton	..	..	..	..		..			..	..	..	..	..	..		10 23	..	..	..	..	..	..	..	..	..	..	5 58	..	..	..
Killamarsh	..	..	..	..		..			..	..	..	..	..	..		10 28	..	..	..	..	..	..	..	..	..	..	6 3	..	..	..
Eckington and Renishaw	..	..	..	..		..			..	..	..	..	..	..		10 33	..	..	..	..	..	..	..	..	..	..	6 8	..	..	..
Staveley Town	..	..	..	..		..			..	..	..	..	..	..		10 39	..	..	..	..	..	..	..	..	..	..	6 14	..	7 55	..
Staveley Works R	..	..	..	..		..			..	..	..	..	..	..		10 44	..	..	IC Manchester (L. Rd.) to Marylebone	..	..	..	IC Manchester (L. Rd.) to Marylebone	..	..	..	6 19	..	8 1	..
Sheepbridge P	..	..	..	..		..			..	..	..	From Radcliffe-on-Trent, dep. 7 8 mrn (Table 63)	..	..		10 49	..	..		..	..	..		..	..	From Radcliffe-on-Trent, dep. 7 5 aft (Table 63)	6 24	..	..	..
Chesterfield (Central) arr	..	..	..	..		..			..	..	..		..	..		10 53	..	..		..	..	..		..	..		6 28	..	8 9	..
Chesterfield (Central) dep	..	..	..	..		..			..	..	..		..	..		10 54	..	..		..	..	..		..	..		6 30	..	..	..
Heath	..	..	..	..	..	..	..	..	..	..	..		..	..	..	11 8	..	..		..	..	..		..	..		6 44	..	..	..
Pilsley	..	..	..	..	..	..	..	..	..	..	..		..	..	..	11 14	..	..		..	..	..		..	..		6 50	..	..	..
Tibshelf Town	..	..	..	..	..	..	..	..	..	IC York to Swindon	..		..	..	..	11 18	..	..		..	..	..		..	..		6 55	..	..	..
Kirkby Bentinck	..	..	..	..	..	..	..	..	..		..		..	..	..	11 27	..	..		..	..	..		..	..		7 5	..	..	..
66 Lincoln dep	..	..	..	6 25	..	..	..	..	..		..		..	..	..	..	..	..		..	..	..		..	..		..	..	..	..
Ollerton dep	..	..	..	..	..	..	..	..	..		..		..	..	..	..	..	..		..	..	..		..	..		..	..	..	..
Edwinstowe	..	..	..	7 52	..	..	..	..	..		..		..	..	..	..	..	..		..	..	..		..	..		..	..	..	..
Mansfield (L.N.E.R.) arr	..	..	..	8 6	..	..	..	..	..		..		..	..	..	..	..	..		..	..	..		..	..		..	..	..	..
Mansfield (L.N.E.R.) dep	..	..	..	8 10	..	..	..	..	..		..		..	..	..	..	1130	..		..	..	..		6 37	..		..	..	..	..
Sutton-in-Ashfield (Cen.)	..	..	..	8 18	..	..	..	..	..		..		..	..	..	..	1138	..		..	..	..		6 45	..		..	..	..	..
Kirkby-in-Ashfield (Cen.)	..	..	..	8 24	..	..	..	..	..		..		..	..	..	..	1144	..		..	..	..		6 51	..		..	..	..	..
Hucknall Central	..	..	..	8 40	..	..	..	..	..	..	..	..	..	..	..	11 42	1156	..		..	..	..		7 6	..	..	7 17	..	..	..
Bulwell Common	..	..	..	8 46	..	..	..	..	..	..	..	..	..	..	..	..	..	..		..	..	..		..	..	..	..	..	..	..
New Basford	..	..	..	8 51	..	..	..	..	..	..	..	..	..	..	..	..	..	..		..	..	..		..	..	..	..	..	..	..

Station	1	2	3	4	5	6	7	8	9	10	11	12	13	14	15	16	17	18	19	20	21	22	23	24	25	26	27	28	29	30
Nottingham (Victoria) arr	..	..	..	8 55	9 11	..	1259	1 30	..	..	1 30	..	..	..	10 21	11 57	12 7	..	1221	..	..	..	6 11	7 17	..	..	7 28	..	..	..
Nottingham (Victoria) dep	7 45	8 15	8 30	Stop	9 35	..	1 15	1 48	..	1 15	1 48	7 30	..	..	10 26	Stop	..	..	1226	..	1255	4 45	6 16	..	..	7 30	..	7 45	..	..
Arkwright Street	7 49	8 19	..	..	..	..	..	Except Monday morns	..	..	..	..	..	..	..	..	..	..	..	..	..	..	..	..	..	..	..	7 48	..	..
Ruddington	..	8 27	8 39	..	..	..	..		..	..	..	7 39	..	..	10 35	..	..	..	..	..	1 4	4 55	..	..	..	..	..	7 55	..	..
Rushcliffe Halt	..	8 33	..	..	..	..	..		..	..	..	..	..	..	..	..	..	..	..	..	1 10	5 1	..	..	..	..	..	..	..	..
East Leake	8 2	8 39	8 47	..	..	..	..		..	..	..	7 48	..	..	..	..	..	..	..	..	1 15	5 6	..	..	..	7 46	..	8 6	..	..
Loughborough (Central)	8 12	8*50	..	..	9m59	..	1v41		..	1v41	..	..	..	..	10 51	..	..	..	1247	..	1 24	5 16	6 37	..	..	..	..	8 16	..	..
Quorn and Woodhouse	..	8 55	..	..	..	..	..		..	..	..	..	..	..	..	..	..	..	..	..	..	5 21	..	..	..	..	..	8 21	..	..
Rothley	..	9 2	..	..	..	..	..		..	..	..	..	..	..	..	..	..	..	..	..	1 35	5 28	..	..	..	..	..	8 27	..	..
Belgrave and Birstall	8*26	9 8	..	..	..	..	..		..	..	..	..	..	..	..	..	..	..	..	..	..	..	..	..	..	..	..	8 33	..	..
Leicester (Central) arr	8 30	9 12	..	..	10 15	..	1 58	2 22	..	1 58	2 22	..	..	..	11 7	..	..	..	1 3	..	1 44	5 36	6 53	..	..	..	..	8 37	..	..
Leicester (Central) dep	Except Saturdays	9 18	..	Except Saturdays	10 23	Sunday morns. only	2 14	2 40	..	2 14	2 40	..	..	..	11 15	..	..	..	1 8	..	Stop	5 45	6 58	..	..	..	..	8 45	..	..
Whetstone		9 27	..		..		..	..	..	..	..	..	..	..	..	..	..	..	..	..	..	..	..	..	..	..	..	8 54	..	..
Ashby Magna		9 37	..		..		..	..	..	..	..	..	..	..	..	..	..	..	..	..	..	..	..	..	..	..	..	9 4	..	..
Lutterworth		9 47	..		10*57		..	..	..	..	..	..	..	..	..	..	..	..	..	..	..	6 10	7 23	..	..	..	..	9 14	..	..
Rugby (Central)		10*0	..		11t18		2Y53	..	..	2Y53	..	..	..	..	11*46	..	..	..	1*39	..	..	6 22	7 35	..	..	..	..	9 24	..	..
Braunston and Willoughby		10 9	..		..		..	..	..	..	..	..	..	..	..	..	..	..	..	..	..	..	..	..	..	..	..	..	..	..
Charwelton		10 22	..		..		..	..	..	..	..	..	..	..	..	..	..	..	..	..	..	..	..	..	..	..	..	..	..	..
Woodford and Hinton arr		10 27	..		11 38		3 14	3 27	..	3 14	3 27	..	..	..	12 6	..	..	..	1 59	..	..	6 42	7 55	..	..	..	..	..	..	..
9 Stratford-on-Avon arr	..	..	..		..		..	..	..	..	..	..	..	..	..	..	..	..	..	..	..	..	..	..	..	..	..	..	..	..
Woodford and Hinton dep	..	..	..		11 48		3 20	..	..	3 20	..	..	..	..	12 11	..	..	..	..	..	..	..	..	..	..	..	..	..	..	..
Eydon Road Halt	..	..	..		..		..	..	..	..	..	..	..	..	..	..	..	..	..	..	..	..	..	..	..	..	..	..	..	..
Chalcombe Road Halt	..	..	..		..		..	..	..	..	..	..	..	..	..	..	..	..	..	..	..	..	..	..	..	..	..	..	..	..
Banbury arr	..	..	..	aft	12 6		3 38	..	..	3 38	..	..	..	..	12 29	..	..	..	..	..	..	..	..	..	..	..	..	..	..	..
Banbury dep	..	..	..	1150	..	1215	..	..	1215	..	..	..	..	..	..	..	..	..	..	..	..	5 30	..	..	..	..	..	..	..	..
Chalcombe Road Halt	..	..	..	..	..	..	..	..	..	..	..	..	..	..	..	..	..	..	..	..	..	..	..	..	..	..	..	..	..	..
Eydon Road Halt	..	..	..	..	..	..	..	..	..	..	..	..	..	..	..	..	..	..	..	..	..	..	..	..	..	..	..	..	..	..
Woodford & Hinton arr	..	..	..	12 8	..	1233	..	..	1233	..	..	..	..	..	..	..	..	..	..	..	..	5 48	..	..	..	..	..	..	..	..
9 Stratford-on-Avon dep	..	..	..	..	..	..	..	..	..	..	..	..	..	..	..	..	..	..	..	B	..	..	..	..	..	..	..	..	..	..
Woodford and Hinton dep	..	..	..	..	..	..	..	3 37	..	..	3 37	..	..	9 0	..	..	..	..	2 2	3 5	..	6 46	7 58	..	..	..	..	..	..	..
Culworth	..	..	..	..	..	..	..	..	..	..	..	..	..	9 7	..	..	..	..	..	3 12	..	..	..	..	..	..	..	..	..	..
Helmdon, for Sulgrave	..	..	..	..	..	..	..	..	..	..	..	..	B	9 14	..	..	..	..	..	3 19	..	..	..	..	B	..	..	..	..	..
Brackley (Central)	..	..	..	..	..	..	..	..	..	..	..	..	8 5	9 22	..	..	..	..	..	3 27	..	7 5	8 14	..	8 23	..	..	..	..	..
Finmere	..	..	..	..	..	..	..	..	..	..	..	..	8 14	9 32	..	..	..	..	..	3 37	..	..	..	..	8 32	..	..	..	..	..
Calvert	..	..	..	..	..	..	..	Via Aylesbury	..	..	Via Aylesbury	..	8 24	9 42	..	mrn	..	..	..	3 47	aft	..	..	..	8 42	..	..	..	..	..
Quainton Road	..	..	..	..	..	..	..		..	..		..	..	9 51	..	B	..	..	..	3 56	B	..	..	..	..	..	..	..	..	..
Aylesbury	..	..	..	..	..	..	..		..	..		..	..	10 1	..	10 55	..	..	2 41	4 6	5 20	..	8 42	..	..	..	..	..	..	..
Northwood	..	..	..	..	..	..	..		..	..		..	..	1112	..	..	..	..	..	5 15	..	..	..	..	..	..	..	..	..	..
Harrow on the Hill	..	..	..	..	..	..	..		..	..		..	..	1128	..	..	..	..	3 28	5 31	..	..	9 29	..	..	..	..	..	..	..
Wotton	..	..	..	..	..	..	..		..	..		..	8 35	..	..	..	..	..	..	..	..	..	..	..	8 52	..	..	..	..	..
Haddenham (Bucks.)	..	..	..	..	..	..	..		..	..		..	8 45	..	..	..	..	..	..	..	..	..	..	..	9 2	..	..	..	..	..
Ilmer Halt	..	..	..	..	..	..	..	..	..	..	..	..	..	..	..	..	..	..	..	..	..	..	..	..	..	..	..	..	..	..
Princes Risborough arr	..	..	..	..	..	..	..	..	..	..	..	..	8 57	..	..	11 13	..	..	..	..	5 38	..	..	..	9 13	..	..	..	..	..
High Wycombe "	..	..	..	..	..	..	..	..	..	..	..	..	9 24	..	..	12§48	..	..	..	..	7§17	7 58	..	..	9 38	..	..	..	..	..
LONDON (M'lebone) "	..	..	..	..	..	..	..	5 10	..	..	5 10	..	1034	1145	..	..	..	..	3 45	5 48	..	8 45	9 46	..	10 50	..	..	..	..	..

A For particulars of London Suburban Service, see Suburban Time Table
a Morn
: Except Saturdays
H Via Doncaster
h Dep. 7 30 aft on Saturdays
J Via Selby and Pontefract

K Via Manchester (Central) and (London Rd.). Passengers cross the town at own expense
k Via Selby
L Saturday nights
m Arr. 9 54 aft
n Via Holbeck and Doncaster
P Sheepbridge & Brimington

p Aft
R Station for Barrow Hill
R Change at Guide Bridge. Dep. 5 20 aft on Saturdays
S Saturdays only
T Rotherham and Masboro'
t Arr. 11 8 aft
IC Through Carriages
U Barnsley (Court House)

u Dep. 9 40 aft on Saturdays
V Change at Dinting
v Arr. 1 35 mrn
w Dep. 6 19 aft on Saturdays
X 5 mins. *earlier* on Saturdays
Y Arr. 2 48 mrn
y Via Retford
z Ashton (Park Parade). Dep. Oldham Road 5 32 aft Sats.

* Arr. 3 minutes *earlier*
‡ Ashton (Park Parade) Dep 5 43 aft on Saturdays
§ Change at Princes Risborough

B Third class only

For OTHER TRAINS between Sheffield and Woodhouse, see Table 67—Ollerton and Edwinstowe, Table 66—New Basford and Nottingham, Table 63—Nottingham and Leicester, Table 62

British Railways — Eastern Region

The Eastern Region of British Railways continued very much where the LNER services had left off and still ran very much the same pattern of cross-country passenger services. But two years after Nationalisation, surprisingly, the Bournemouth to York and Swansea to York trains were reduced from daily services to Fridays and Saturdays only as through trains (although through portions did continue on other days). The Bournemouth train ran from Newcastle in the summer, with an additional Saturdays only service that ran from Sheffield to Bournemouth and which returned from Poole. A Nottingham to Ramsgate service that ran overnight, was introduced as well as a daily Newcastle to Swansea and an overnight York to Swindon service. The Swansea service also ran on a Sunday from Sheffield Victoria.

Above:
In early Eastern Region days, 'B1' class 4-6-0 No 61181 heads the York to Swindon service off Bulwell Viaduct and on towards Bulwell Common and Nottingham Victoria on 23 July 1949. The locomotive still carries 'British Railways' on the tender. It would take the train as far as Leicester where either a Western locomotive or another 'B1' would take over, to head the train to Swindon. *John Henton*

Right:
The overnight 9.35pm from Swindon to York leaves Rugby Central with No 5922 *Caxton Hall* in charge on 4 August 1951. The locomotive would be replaced at Leicester. This long-standing GC service ran right until the end of through services, steam locomotives being replaced by 'Hymek' diesels before the end of its period of operation. *Rev. A. W. V. Mace*

THROUGH EXPRESS TRAIN SERVICES

NEWCASTLE, YORK, SHEFFIELD, NOTTINGHAM, LEICESTER, OXFORD, SWINDON, NEWPORT, CARDIFF AND SWANSEA

Via Banbury

	WEEK DAYS			SUNDAYS	
	R				
	a.m.	p.m.	p.m.	p.m.	a.m.
Newcastle ... ...dep	10S10	...	...	...	...
Darlington... ... ... ,,	11S13	...	...	...	...
York ... ... ,,	12 20	6 30	10 20	10§20	...
Selby ... ... ,,	...	6 54	...	...	...
Doncaster (Central) ... ,,	...	7 28	...	...	...
Church Fenton... ... ... ,,	...	...	10 37	10§37	...
Pontefract (Baghill)... ... ,,	12 56	...	11 1	11 § 1	...
Rotherham & Masboro' ... ,,	...	7 53	...	...	...
			a.m.	a.m.	...
Sheffield (Victoria) ... ... ,,	1 52	8 30	12 4	12 4	9 20
Nottingham (Victoria) ... ,,	2 56	9 50	1M18	1 18	10 26
Ruddington ... ... ,,	...	...	...	...	10 35
Loughborough (Central)... ,,	3 18	10 15	1M43	1 43	10 52
Leicester (Central) ... ... ,,	3 37	10 48	2M17	2 17	11 15
Lutterworth ... ... ,,	...	11 12	...	...	11 40
Rugby (Central) ... ... ,,	4 5	11 33	2M54	2 54	11 53
		a.m.			p.m.
Woodford Halse ... ... ,,	...	12 3	3M20	3 20	12 18
Banbury ... ... arr	4 39	12M21	3M38	3 38	12 54
Banbury ... ... dep	4 44	12M35	3M40	3 40	12 58
Oxford ... ...arr	5 15	1M10	4M24	4 24	1 28
Swindon ... ... ,,	6 0	2M23	5M45	5 45	2 16
Newport ... ... ,,	7 25	...	...	...	3 37
Cardiff (General) ... ... ,,	7 45	...	...	...	4 0
Bridgend ... ... ,,	8 23	...	...	...	...
Port Talbot (General) ... ,,	8 44	...	...	...	...
Neath (General) ... ... ,,	8 54	...	...	...	...
Swansea (High Street) ... ,,	9 8	...	...	...	5 15

M Mondays excepted. **R** Restaurant Car. **S** Saturdays only.
§ Saturday night.

Passengers travelling from York by the 12 20 p.m. (except Saturdays), 6 30 p.m. and 10 20 p.m. trains, and from Newcastle by the 10 10 a.m. (Saturdays only) train can reserve seats in advance on payment of a fee of 1s. 0d. per seat.

THROUGH EXPRESS TRAIN SERVICES

SWANSEA, CARDIFF, NEWPORT, SWINDON, OXFORD, LEICESTER, NOTTINGHAM, SHEFFIELD AND YORK

Via Banbury

	WEEK DAYS				SUNDAYS
	R		E	S	
	a.m.	p.m.	p.m.	p.m.	a.m.
Swansea (High Street) ...dep	8 20	...	...	...	10 35
Neath (General) ... ... ,,	8 36	...	...	...	10 53
Briton Ferry ... ... ,,	...	...	...	...	10 59
Port Talbot (General) ... ,,	8 46	...	...	...	11 8
Bridgend ... ... ,,	9 5	...	...	...	11 32
Llantrisant... ... ... ,,	...	....	...	...	11 50
Cardiff (General) ... ... ,,	9 40	...	...	...	12 25
Newport ... ... ,,	10 0	...	...	...	12 48
Swindon ... ... ,,	11 20	7 15	9 35	9 55	3 35
Oxford ... ... ,,	12 20	8 24	11 0	11 20	4 40
Banbury .... arr	12 50	8 55	11 35	11 55	5 12
Banbury .... dep	12 58	9 6	11 50	12 15	5 30
Woodford Halse ... ...arr	...	9 24	12 8	12 38	5 48
Rugby (Central) ... ... ,,	...	9 50	12 34	1 3	6 15
Leicester (Central) ... ,,	1 51	10 24	1 6	1 34	6 46
Loughborough (Central)... ,,	...	10 52	1 31	1 59	7 9
Nottingham (Victoria) ... ,,	2 24	11 17	1 57	2 24	7 34
Hucknall (Central) ... ... ,,	...	11 47	...	...	...
Sheffield (Victoria) ... ... ,,	3 27	12 40	3 15	3 40	8 43
Pontefract (Baghill)... ... ,,	4 27	...	...	...	...
York ... ... ,,	5 6	...	5 20	5 45	...
Newcastle... ... ... ,,	7F48	...	...	...	...

E Saturdays excepted. **F** Fridays only. **R** Restaurant Car.
S Saturdays only.

Passengers travelling from Swansea (High Street) by the 8 20 a.m. and from Swindon by the 7 15, 9E35, and 9S55 p.m. trains can reserve seats in advance on payment of a fee of 1s. 0d. per seat.

THROUGH EXPRESS TRAIN SERVICES

NEWCASTLE, DARLINGTON, YORK, SHEFFIELD, NOTTINGHAM, LEICESTER, SOUTHAMPTON AND BOURNEMOUTH

Via Banbury and Basingstoke

WEEK DAYS

	S	R
	a.m.	a.m.
Newcastle ... ...dep	...	8 32
Durham ... ... „	...	9 0
Darlington ... ... „	...	9 34
York ... ... „	...	10 26
Pontefract (Baghill) ... „	...	11 1
Rotherham & Masboro' „	...	11 40
		p.m.
Sheffield (Victoria) ... „	10 50	12 2
Nottingham (Vic.) ... „	11 57	1 6
	p.m.	
Loughborough (Cen.) „	12 20	...
Leicester (Central) ... „	12 39	1 41
Rugby (Central) ... „	1 8	2 9
Woodford Halse ... „	1 31	...
Banbury ... ... arr	1 48	2 43
Banbury ... ... dep	1 53	2 43
Oxford ... ...arr	2 24	3 18
Reading (West) ... „	3 26	4 0
Basingstoke ... ... „	4 0	4 35
Winchester (City) ... „	4 34	5 12
Eastleigh ... ... „	4 45	5 25
Southampton (Cen.) .. „	5 10	5 39
Brockenhurst ... ... „	5 37	6 6
Sway ... ... „	...	6 16
New Milton ... ... „	5 53	6 24
Hinton Admiral ... „	...	6 31
Christchurch ... ... „	...	6 39
Pokesdown ... ... „	...	6 45
Boscombe ... ... „	...	6 48
Bournemouth (Cen.) .. „	6 9	6 52
Bournemouth (West) „	...	7 4

	S	R
	a.m.	a.m.
Poole ... ...dep	10 26	...
Bournemouth (West) „	...	11 16
Bournemouth (Cen.) .. „	10 40	11 26
Boscombe ... ... „	10 45	11 31
Pokesdown ... ... „	10 48	11 35
Christchurch ... ... „	10 53	11 41
New Milton ... ... „	11 4	11 52
		p.m.
Brockenhurst ... ... „	11 16	12 3
Southampton (Cen.) .. „	11 40	12 27
Eastleigh ... ... „	11 54	12 40
	p.m.	
Winchester (City) ... „	12 8	12 53
Basingstoke ... ... „	12 45	1 24
Reading (West)... ... „	1 16	1 56
Oxford ... ... „	2 3	2 38
Banbury ... ... arr	2 33	3 8
Banbury ... ... dep	2 40	3 18
Woodford Halse ...arr	2 58	...
Rugby (Central) ... „	3 21	3 52
Leicester (Central) ... „	3 47	4 17
Loughborough (Cen.). „	4 5	4 37
Nottingham (Vic.) ... „	4 27	4 56
Sheffield (Victoria) ... „	5 35	6 0
Rotherham & Masboro' „	...	6 23
Pontefract (Baghill) ... „	...	7 4
York ... ... „	...	7 39
Darlington ... ... „	...	8 35
Durham ... ... „	...	9 7
Newcastle ... ... „	...	9 34

R Restaurant Car. **S** Saturdays only.

Passengers travelling from Newcastle, Poole, Bournemouth (West) and Bournemouth (Central) by these trains can reserve seats in advance on payment of a fee of 1s. 0d. per seat.

NEW THROUGH EXPRESS

Buffet Car Train Service

NOTTINGHAM, LEICESTER, ETC. AND THE KENT COAST

Saturdays Only. June 24th to September 9th inclusive

	a.m.
Nottingham (Victoria) ...dep	12 45
Loughborough (Central) ... „	1 8
Leicester (Central) ... ... „	1 30
Lutterworth ... ... „	1 54
Rugby (Central) ... ... „	2 8
Woodford Halse ... ... „	2 31
Whitstable & Tankerton ...arr	6 0
Herne Bay ... ... „	6 10
Birchington-on-Sea ... ... „	6 25
Westgate-on-Sea ... ... „	6 31
Margate ... ... „	6 37
Broadstairs ... ... „	6 47
Dumpton Park (for East Ramsgate) ... „	6 52
Ramsgate ... ...arr	6 56

	p.m.
Ramsgate ... ...dep	12 10
Dumpton Park (for East Ramsgate) „	12 14
Broadstairs ... ... „	12 19
Margate ... ... „	12 28
Westgate-on-Sea ... ... „	12 34
Birchington-on-Sea ... ... „	12 40
Herne Bay... ... ... „	12 55
Whitstable & Tankerton... „	1 4
Woodford Halse ... ...arr	4 34
Rugby (Central) ... ... „	4 57
Lutterworth ... ... „	5 11
Leicester (Central)... ... „	5 34
Loughborough (Central).. „	5 52
Nottingham (Victoria) ... „	6 17

Passengers travelling by this service from Nottingham (Victoria) can reserve seats in advance on payment of a fee of 1s. 0d. per seat. Similar facilities are also available for passengers returning from Ramsgate and Stations Broadstairs to Whitstable and Tankerton inclusive.

Above:
BR Eastern Region — cross-country services 5 June to 24 September 1950.

Left:
Western Region locomotives were always sent back to Banbury on a revenue-earning service, thus saving a path and an expensive light engine movement with no income. One train that was almost always worked by a Western locomotive was the 3.20pm Leicester to Woodford 'Ord'. On 15 August 1960, No 4993 *Dalton Hall* passes Leicester goods yard and approaches Leicester South Goods box with this service as it returns home to the Western and its depot at Reading. *Horace Gamble*

Right:
The 'Bournemouth' was diesel-hauled from the autumn of 1962 in the shape of an English Electric Type 3 from Sheffield Darnall depot, which worked the train out and back to Banbury where it picked up the northbound working. Here, a Type 3 with headcode 1042 for the southbound working passes the closed Carrington station in Nottingham and prepares to stop at the 'Vic'. The train is formed of green Southern stock. *Tom Boustead*

British Railways — London Midland Region

On 1 February 1958 the London Midland Region absorbed the GC. Almost at once, by the winter time table of 1959, the York to Bournemouth service was cut back to and from Banbury only and amazingly, was worked out and back by a DMU set which left York at 10.19am, arriving Banbury at 2.31pm. The train 'turned round' and left Banbury at 3.11pm with an arrival back at York at 9.42pm. (Did anyone ever photograph that train?) The experiment was short-lived and the main train returned, having been extended to Newcastle. This train continued until the end of the GC as a through route and was usually hauled by a Western engine through to Leicester which then returned on a local service to Banbury via Woodford, but after the local services were withdrawn in 1963 ran back on a Swindon fish train. The Bournemouth was usually diesel hauled (see John Betjeman's marvellous poem, 'Great Central Railway Sheffield Victoria to Banbury') from the end of 1962 when the outward portion from Sheffield was worked by an English Electric Type 3 Co-Co to Banbury where it took over the northbound train from a Western engine. After the demise of steam on the Western, Southern light Pacifics were the normal power. The two overnight services from York to Swindon and return continued as well with diesels making an impact on these services in the form of the new Beyer Peacock 'Hymeks'. The 'Bournemouth' and the two overnight services came to an end on the night of 3/4 September 1966 when the London Extension was closed as a through route. However, even in LMR days, the summer saw additional Friday night and early Saturday trains.

Below:

BR London Midland Region — cross-country services 7 September 1964 to 13 June 1965.

THROUGH TRAIN SERVICES

YORK, SHEFFIELD, NOTTINGHAM, LEICESTER, BANBURY, OXFORD and SWINDON

with connecting services to South Wales

	WEEKDAYS						
	Except Saturdays		Saturdays only		Except Saturday nights/Sunday mornings	Saturday nights/Sunday mornings only. Through Train York to Bristol (Temple Meads) (arr 7 45 am)	
	pm		pm		pm	pm	
York .. ..dep	6 40	..	6 46	..	10 22	10 22	..
Selby .. .. „	7 2	..	7 8	..	..	..	..
Doncaster .. .. .. „	7 50	..	7 50	..	..	..	..
Pontefract (Baghill) .. .. „	..	..	..	..	10 57	10 57	..
Mexborough .. .. .. „	8 6	..	8 6	..	..	..	..
Rotherham (Central) .. „	8 22	..	8 22	..	..	..	..
Sheffield (Victoria) .. .. „	8 55	..	8 55	..	am 12 9	am 12 9	..
Nottingham (Victoria) ..arr	10 6	..	10 6	..	1 17	1 17	..
Loughborough (Central) .. „	10 38	..	10 38	..	1 49	1 49	..
Leicester (Central) .. .. „	10 53	..	10 53	..	2 3	2 3	..
Lutterworth .. .. .. „	11 27	..	11 27	..	..	..	..
Rugby (Central) .. .. „	11 36	..	11 36	..	2 43	2 43	..
Woodford Halse .. .. „	am 12 5	..	am 12 5	..	3 10	3 10	..
Banbury .. .. „	12 28	..	12 28	..	3 34	3 34	..
Oxford .. .. „	1 5	..	1 5	..	4 24	4 24	..
Swindon .. .. „	2 18	..	2 17	..	5 45	5 45	..
Newport (Mon.) .. ..arr	5A17	..	5A56	..	9B30	10C26	..
Cardiff (General) .. .. „	5A39	..	6A21	..	9B50	10C46	..
Bridgend.. .. .. .. „	6A22	..	7A14	..	10B29	11C27	..
Port Talbot (General) .. „	6A53	..	7A38	..	10B47	11C47	..
Neath (General) .. .. „	7A11	..	7A55	..	10B57	11C58	..
Swansea (High Street) .. „	7A35	..	8A17	..	11B20	pm 12C18	..

A—Change at Swindon

B—Change at Swindon and Bristol.

C—Change at Bristol. On Sundays 1st November to 13th December and from 3rd January to 7th February arrive Newport 11 12 am, Cardiff 11 33 am, Bridgend 12 23 pm, (change at Cardiff), Port Talbot 12 41 pm (change at Cardiff), Neath 12 53 pm (change at Cardiff) and Swansea 1 13 pm (change at Cardiff)

THROUGH TRAIN SERVICES

SWINDON, OXFORD, BANBURY, LEICESTER, NOTTINGHAM, SHEFFIELD and YORK

with connecting services from South Wales

	WEEKDAYS				
	Saturdays only	Except Saturdays		Except Saturdays	Saturdays only
	pm	pm		pm	pm
Swansea (High Street) ..dep	2A20	2A20	..	5A45	5A45
Neath (General) .. .. „	2A35	2A35	..	6 A 2	6A 2
Port Talbot (General) .. „	2A45	2A45	..	6A12	6A12
Bridgend .. .. „	3A 0	3A 0	..	6A30	6A30
Cardiff (General) .. .. „	3A30	3A30	..	7 A 0	7 A 0
Newport (Mon.) .. .. „	3A45	3A45	..	7A16	7A15
Swindon . .. .dep	7 15	7 15	..	9 50	10 25
Oxford .. .. „	8 20	8 26	..	11 0	11 35
Banbury.. .. .. „	9 10	9 16	..	11 50	am 12 20
Woodford Halse .. .. .. „	9 37	9 41	...	am 12 17	12 47
Rugby (Central) .. .. .. „	10 5	10 9	..	12 42	1 13
Lutterworth.. .. .. .. „	10 18	10F22	..	..	..
Leicester (Central) .. .. „	10 40	10 48	..	1 15	1 45
Loughborough (Central) .. „	10 56	11 4	..	1 31	2 2
Nottingham (Victoria) .. „	11 25	11 35	...	2 3	2 35
Sheffield (Victoria) .. ..arr	am 12 37	am 12 47	...	3 15	3 48
York .. .. „	..	..	..	5 2	5 24

A—Change at Swindon

F—Fridays only

Holiday and Excursion Traffic

Holiday and excursion traffic supplemented the timetabled cross-country services. In 1905, one of the longest excursions from Manchester to Plymouth was run on 20 April. It was packed and took a GC locomotive, Atlantic No 265, to Plymouth. This train carried a restaurant car, and passengers were allowed to stay up to 15 days before returning by scheduled services. The train ran back empty, but was considered to have been so successful that another was run the following year on 12 April 1906. It was strengthened at Leicester and Nottingham and was exchanged at Bristol, where it took the Temple Meads avoiding line and was worked by a Great Western locomotive. Instead of running back empty it formed an excursion to Sheffield which ran the next day.

In addition, excursions were run to and from Midlands cities and towns, especially during the various 'fortnights' when local firms closed for two weeks and their employees took holidays. Some firms even chartered their own special trains for company excursions to places such as Margate and Windsor. Other 'Mystery Trips' were run daily during the 'fortnights' which allowed passengers to go somewhere every day and return home in the evening.

The LNER introduced the 'Orient Line Specials' which ran in the summer and took passengers from Marylebone and Manchester to Immingham for cruises. The other service begun in 1937 was the forerunner of the 'Starlight Specials' that ran in the 1950s from Marylebone to Glasgow offering cheap overnight travel. The LNER ran this service, primarily to relieve the GN main line, from Marylebone to Newcastle. These summer holiday and excursion trains continued through the LNER and into the British Railways' era, but the motor car age was just beginning. Within another ten years this demand had all but been satisfied by the private car as families could not only travel as and when they pleased, but also take much more luggage and go door-to-door. The 'Starlight Specials' ran again, only this time actually branded as such, and were cheaply priced with a guaranteed seat. They operated on Fridays between 1953 and 1962 linking Marylebone and Edinburgh. The trains were regularly worked by a Neasden 'A3' as far as Leicester, where a Leicester engine would take over for the run to York. There were buffet cars on the trains but they often ran in duplicate and a shortage of buffet cars meant that food was provided en route 'Indian style' on tables on the platform at Leicester Central and other stations. These additional trains in summer 1950 (which all had return workings) were:

7.20am	(SO) Leicester to Cleethorpes;
7.45am	(SO) Leicester to Bridlington, Filey and Scarborough (on certain days this train left at 8.25am and missed out stops via Mansfield);
12.10am	(SO) Ramsgate to Nottingham.

Below:
Companies even hired complete trains for their staff to have a day out. How lucky those employees were to have 'D11/1' 'Large Director' 4-4-0 No 62666 *Zeebrugge* on the front of their train which ran from Retford to Windsor via High Wycombe, on 6 June 1953, complete with 'Northern Rubber Special' headboard. Does anyone know what happened to the headboard? The lengthy train is seen heading out of Nottingham past Queen's Walk Sidings on its run south. *John Henton*

Left:
'West Country' light Pacific No 34002 *Salisbury* ran a tour for the RCTS on 13 August 1966 in the month before closure. The train is seen passing Rugby Central heading north to Nottingham Victoria. *Brian Alexander*

Left:
The last day drew only one special train, this time for the LCGB, again headed by Southern power and starting from Waterloo using Southern green stock. 'Merchant Navy' class No 35030 *Elder-Dempster Lines* slows for the Rickmansworth curve with the down train on 3 September 1966. The 'Merchant Navy' was replaced at Nottingham Victoria by two 'B1s', Nos 61131 and 61173, which took the train on to Sheffield Victoria. No 35030 then worked the train back from Nottingham to Marylebone — the last ever excursion to run on the GC. *Bill Piggott*

Left:
Rumour that the GC was to be closed as a through route brought special workings to the line during the last years of operation. As well as locomotives such as No 46251 *City of Nottingham* and the Midland Compound No 1000, 'Schools' class No 30925 *Cheltenham* and Midland '2P' 4-4-0 No 40 worked a special train on 12 May 1962. Here, the pair prepare to leave Nottingham Victoria on the down journey to Darlington. *Tom Boustead*

Wembley

It was during Fay's time that the marketing and running of excursion traffic really began to make an impact on the London Extension. Wembley Stadium and its proximity to the GW/GC joint line at Wembley Hill also brought many specials to the GC which have been well recorded. These were advertised by the GC's own Publicity Department set up by Sam Fay in 1902 and headed by W. J. Stuart. They produced one of the most amazing railway posters ever, which accurately foretold the result and the scorer of the winning goal in the 1904 Cup Final between Manchester City and Bolton Wanderers. It pictured Billy Meredith of Manchester City scoring the winner. 'Billy Meredith Secures the Cup. He wants you to See the Match and Travel in Comfort by The Great Central Railway.' In the event, on the day, that is exactly what happened. Every year, the London Extension carried large numbers of passengers to Wembley, but another special worth mentioning is a service that ran on 22 March 1909 from Marylebone for the Manchester Championship Dog Show, which conveyed vans for the dogs and coaches for the passengers. The dogs were even fed on the journey, it costing 4s (20p) to send one from London.

The LNER benefited from Wembley as had the Great Central. The other end of the line was close to Sheffield Wednesday's Hillsborough ground and a special station was built at Manchester United's ground at Old Trafford.

In the 1950s, Wembley Stadium staged many tournament matches namely schoolboy soccer internationals and women's hockey matches. The Rugby League Cup Final and the FA Cup Final were also staged there and brought considerable business in the form of many special trains that ran in what was roughly a five-week period. Trains tended to travel via the joint line to Wembley Hill and then stable their stock in the sidings at Neasden. The locomotives would then make their way to Neasden depot for servicing. Other services would gain access to the Wembley Stadium loop line and disgorge their passengers directly at the stadium. It was not uncommon to see an array of varied motive power on display as locomotives from different regions brought in trains. But as with other traffic, the number of people travelling by train to Wembley was in decline due to increased road competition. The Wembley loop was closed and services tended to be operated on a shuttle basis from Marylebone as far as Wembly Hill. Eventually it was left to passengers to make their way on scheduled services — as was the case with virtually all trains. The days of the speculative excursion were at an end and the decline of this traffic was yet another reason that the GC became 'surplus to requirements' in 1966.

Right:
LNER motive power in the shape of 'B17' No 2849 *Sheffield United* of Leicester shed is seen near Ruddington on a Wembley excursion on 6 August 1938. The 'B17s' first appeared in 1936 and were sent to Gorton, Leicester and Neasden for GC main line services and later in the year a new batch of 'B17s' named after football clubs, and known as 'Footballers', were introduced especially for the London Extension.
T. G. Hepburn/Rail Archive Stephenson

Right:
Another Wembley excursion heads up the joint line at Harefield, this time with 'B1' No 61152 in charge on 12 May 1951. The locomotive is still waiting for the new British Railways 'Rampant lion' to be applied to its tender. *E. R. Wethersett*

Left:
By 1963, motive power from the London Midland Region was starting to dominate train services. Another Wembley service, this time from Leicester for the FA Cup Final, storms through Ashby Magna with 'Black 5' No 45335 making light work of a lengthy train. *Barry Hilton*

Below:
Once an excursion had arrived at Wembley and disgorged its passengers, the stock was stabled in sidings at Neasden while the locomotive went to Neasden shed for servicing. Brush Type 2s Nos D5847 and D5858 reverse their train into the sidings at Neasden South Junction having pulled forward off the joint line that runs in from the left. Just behind the leading locomotive are the points of Neasden South Junction, the GC line via Aylesbury running off into the distance. London Transport's Neasden depot is just to the right of the photograph. *Brian Stephenson*

5. London Suburban, 'Ords' and Locals

London Suburban

The growth of the Metropolitan Railway had led to the development of what had become known as 'Metroland', the spread of a suburban area along the railway line. The Great Central had originally let the Metropolitan run the suburban service, as it did already out as far as Aylesbury, Quainton Road and Verney Junction via Rickmansworth. At Rickmansworth, the Met electric locomotives were replaced by steam, usually one of the 'H' class 4-4-4 Jones, some of which ended their days working suburban trains out of Nottingham, having been displaced by more modern GC/LNE types. To cope with the rather 'classy' area that was being created, together with the Met the GC tried to encourage people to move to Metroland and then commute, with posters such as 'Live in the Country' and 'The Great Central is the Line of Health'. Two main routes were served from Marylebone: the Aylesbury, Quainton Road and Verney Junction route worked in partnership with the Met, and the High Wycombe line with the GW. Express trains also used these lines and the Met/GC Joint line soon became congested, which lead to the building of the High Wycombe route with the Great Western, the latter opening to passengers on 1 March 1906. The first service was a steam rail motor which ran from South Harrow, calling at Sudbury & Harrow Road and Wembley Hill to Marylebone, before services were extended to Northolt Junction on 2 April 1906. All the GC locomotives were based at Neasden with a sub shed at Aylesbury and were originally 'C13' and 'C14' 4-4-2 tank locomotives.

The rolling stock for the line was some of the most luxurious ever built for suburban trains and by 1911 a new tank locomotive, the 4-6-2 'A5' class, LNER Nos 9800-9829, were all allocated to Neasden. In addition to the normal suburban service the development of Wembley Stadium also saw additional trains from Marylebone as well as the excursions mentioned elsewhere. A loop line for the new station was added in time for the British Empire Exhibition in 1923 and it was used for all the major sporting events that followed, in addition to many long distance services that terminated at Wembley Hill. After

Below:
A classic photograph of a Great Central suburban service for Aylesbury via High Wycombe leaving Marylebone in 1913. All the 'A5s' were based at Neasden for suburban services. Not only did they work the joint line trains but they also took over Met line services at Rickmansworth for the run to Aylesbury, as well as other GC local services from Marylebone. Part of Marylebone's carriage shed and milk dock can be seen on the left together with horseboxes, and some vintage taxis can be seen on the platform behind the train. These would have run down the cab road that can be seen above the second carriage. All the carriages for the GC suburban service were based at Marylebone and most lasted well into LNER days before being replaced by Gresley designs.
A. L. P. Reavil/Rail Archive Stephenson

Left:
'L3' tank No 69061 in rather grubby postwar condition is seen turning onto the Wembley Stadium loop with a train from Marylebone in 1949. Note the indicator board on the smokebox door that showed this was a Wembley service. The 'L3s' were normally employed on freight duties around Neasden yard. *C. R. L. Coles/Rail Archive Stephenson*

Below:
The GC services were fitted into the Metropolitan main line service to Aylesbury and Verney Junction. To haul its own trains out to Buckinghamshire from Rickmansworth, the Met had its own steam locomotives. One of these, a Charles Jones design, was Metropolitan Class H 4-4-4 tank No 104 which is seen climbing the Chilterns towards Dutchlands summit in 1933. The curved approach to Rickmansworth station, always a frustrating speed restriction for GC expresses, can be seen beyond the train. *F. R. Hebron/Rail Archive Stephenson*

World War 1, the Watford branch opened and some services terminated at Marylebone. However, these only lasted from 1925 to 1927. It was around this period that GC line services were disrupted by the 1921 Miners' Strike and a potential lack of coal led to experimentation with oil burning. This proved successful, with several 'A5s' converted, but was more expensive to operate than coal, so the equipment was removed once the strike was over but stored as a precaution. Oil burning was reintroduced during the 1926 General Strike but was not continued on a long-term basis, the equipment again being removed once the strike had ended.

Services continued to grow with the population of the area. The 'A5' tanks remained almost exclusively in charge until the arrival of the newer LNER 'L1' 2-6-4 tanks after World War 2. The 'L1s' operated roughly the same service pattern as the prewar trains; indeed, GC suburban services remained virtually unchanged until the arrival of the Stanier and Fairburn tanks under 'London Midlandisation' from 1958, these locomotives residing at Neasden until the depot closed in 1962. The Met's electric service was extended out to Amersham in 1965 which saw the end of locomotive changing at Rickmansworth. By this time the steam suburban service had also gone — from 1962 — and the service was in the hands of new four-car non-gangway DMU sets that were to last for over 30 years. They connected with the Met service by stopping at Amersham, Rickmansworth and Moor Park on the now four-track line that had been laid in from Rickmansworth to Harrow to ease congestion. The GC suburban service, has been further enhanced in the 1990s by one of the most progressive of the newly privatised train operating companies, Chiltern Railways, and survives today even serving as far north as Birmingham Snow Hill with a redoubled line through to Bicester due to growth in traffic. If the GC's entire route had survived one wonders if there would now be a Chiltern service to Brackley and Rugby!

Right:
A Met electric service for Baker Street, that would have changed locomotives at Rickmansworth, is seen between Northwood Hills and Pinner in April 1956. This photograph was taken before the line was widened to four tracks. *G. C. Farnell*

Right:
An 'A5' tank, No 5158, now in LNER black livery (which, compared with the magnificent GC livery earlier, was certainly a retrograde step) is seen passing over newly re-laid track at Northwick Park with the 3.25pm train for Aylesbury via Rickmansworth on 22 February 1934.
E. R. Wethersett/Real Photographs

From LONDON by METROPOLITAN RAILWAY.

WEEK DAYS

DOWN	mrn	mrn	mrn	mrn	mrn	mrn	mrn	mrn	mrn	mrn	mrn	mrn	mrn	aft	aft	aft	aft	aft	aft	aft	aft	aft	aft	aft	aft
BAKER STREET ....dep	6 9	6 39	6 49	7 24	7 58	8 15	8 58	9 5	9 29	9 59	1027	1059	1129	1149	1217	1229	1259	1 27	1 29	1 37	1 50	1 58	2 18	2 27	2 37
St. John's Wood Road .. "	6 12	6 42	6 52	7 27	7 55	8 18	9 1	9 8	9 23	10 2	1020	11 2	1132	1152	1210	1232	1 2	1 30	1 32	1 12	1 53	2 1	2 14	2†19	2 33
Marlborough Road...... "	6 15	6 45	6 55	7 30	7 58	8 21	9 4	9 11	9 26	10 5	1023	11 5	1135	1155	1213	1235	1 5	1 33	1 35	1 15	1 56	2 4	2 17	2†22	2 36
Swiss Cottage........... "	6 17	6 47	6 57	7 32	8 0	8 23	9 6	9 13	9 28	10 7	1025	11 7	1137	1157	1215	1237	1 7	1 35	1 37	1 17	1 58	2 6	2 19	2†24	2 38
Finchley Road .... "	6 19	6 49	6 59	7 34	8 6	8 25	9 8	9 15	9 37	10 9	1027	11 9	1139	1159	1217	1239	1 9	1 37	1 39	1 26	2 0	2 8	2 25	2†26	2 40
West Hampstead........ "	6 21	6 51	7 1	7 36	8 4	8 27	9 10	9 17	9 32	1011	1029	1111	1141	12 1	1219	1241	1 11	1 39	1 41	1 28	2 2	2 10	2 27	2†28	2 42
Kilburn-Brondesbury .. "	6 23	6 53	7 3	7 39	8 6	8 29	9 12	9 19	9 34	1013	1031	1113	1143	12 3	1221	1243	1 13	1 41	1 43	1 30	2 4	2 12	2 29	2†30	2 44
Willesden Green ¶ .. "	6 26	6 56	7 6	7 42	8 13	8 32	9 15	9 22	9 44	1016	1040	1116	1146	12 6	1230	1246	1 16	1 44	1 46	1 33	2 7	2 15	2 32	2†40	2 50
Kingsbury-Neasden .... "	6 37	6 59	7 9	7 45	8 8	...	9 18	9 25	9 25	1019	1019	1119	1149	12 9	12 9	1249	1 19	1 47	1 49	1 36	2 10	2 18	2 24	2†18	2 53
Wembley Park........ "	6 32	7 2	7 12	7 48	8 11	...	9 21	9 28	9 49	1022	1022	1122	1152	1212	1212	1252	1 22	1 50	1 52	1 39	2 13	2 21	2 27	2†31	2 56
Harrow-on-the-Hill...... "	6 45	7 8	7 18	7 55	8 23	8 42	9 26	9 33	9 55	1028	1050	1128	1158	1218	1240	1258	1 28	1 58	1 58	2 0	2 19	2 27	2 42	2 51	3 1
Pinner .... "	6 50	7 13		...	8 28	8 47		9 38	10 0		1056		12 3		1245			2 3	2 3	2 6	2 24		2 47	2 56	3 6
Northwood .... "	6 55	7 18	...	...	8 33	8 52	...	9 43	10 5	...	11 2	...	12 8	...	1250	...	...	2 8	2 8	2 12	2 29	...	2 53	3 1	3 11
Rickmansworth .... "	7 2	7 30	...	8 9	8 40	8 58	...	9 50	1012	...	1110	...	1215	...	1257	...	...	2 14	2 15	2 19	2 36	...	2 58	3 8	3 18
Chorley Wood .... "	7 8	7 35	...	8 14	8 46	9 2	...		1017	...	1116	...		...	1 3	...	...		2 21	2 26		...		3 14	
Chalfont Road .... "	7 15	7 40	...	8 20	8 52	9 7	...	...	1022	...	1123	...	...	...	1 11	...	...	...		2 33	...	...	...	3 22	...
Chesham ....dep	6 40	...	...	...	8 37	...	...	...	...	...	11 6	...	...	...	1256	...	...	...	...	2 4	...	...	...	2 56	...
Amersham ....dep	7 21	...	...	...	8 57	...	...	...	1037	...	1128	...	...	...	1 18	...	...			2 40				3 26	
Great Missenden .... "	7 30	...	...	...	9 7	...	...	...	1046	...	1139	...	...	...	1 29	...	...			2 50				3 35	
Wendover .... "	7 39	...	...	...	9 15	...	...	...	1054	...	1147	...	...	...	1 38	...	...			2 59				3 44	
Stoke Mandeville........ "	7 44	...	...	...	9 20	...	...	...	...	...	1153	...	...	...	1 43	...	...			3 4				3 49	
Aylesbury .... arr	7 49	...	...	...	9 25	...	...	...	11 2	...	1159	...	...	...	1 49	...	...	Saturdays only.	Saturdays excepted.	3 10	Saturdays only.	Saturdays excepted.	Saturdays only.	3 54	Saturdays only.
Aylesbury .... dep	7 51	...	...	...	9 26	...	...	...		...	12 1	...	...	...	1 52	...	...			Saturdays only.				3 57	
Waddesdon Manor...... "	8 0	...	...	...	9 34	...	...	...	...	...	1210	...	...	...	2 1	...	...							4 6	
Quainton Road .... "	8 4	...	...	...	9 38	...	...	...	...	...	1214	...	...	...	2 5	...	...							4 11	
Grandborough Road .... "	8 13	...	...	...	9 47	...	...	...	...	...	1223	...	...	...	2 14	...	...							4 21	
Winslow Road .... "	8 17	...	...	...	9 52	...	...	...	...	...	1228	...	...	...	2 18	...	...							4 25	
VERNEY JUNCTION arr	8 21	...	...	...	9 57	...	...	...	...	...	1233	...	...	...	2 21	...	...							4 29	

WEEK DAYS—Continued

DOWN	aft	aft	aft	aft	aft	aft	aft	aft	aft	aft	aft	aft	aft	** aft	aft	‡ aft	aft	aft	aft	aft	aft	aft	aft	aft	aft
BAKER STREET ....dep	2 49	2 59	3 17	3 29	3 59	4 27	4 30	4 49	5 8	5 87	5 37	5 59	6 18	6 37	6 59	7 24	7 40	7 40	7 59	8 27	9 0	9 29	1017	1049	1159
St. John's Wood Road .. "	2 52	3 2	3 12	3 32	4 2	4 21	4 33	4 52	5 11	5 11	5 31	5 55	6 11	6 31	7 2	7 27	7 35	7 43	8 2	8 21	9 3	9 32	1012	1052	12 2
Marlborough Road...... "	2 55	3 5	3 15	3 35	4 5	4 24	4 36	4 55	5 14	5 14	5 33	5 58	6 14	6 34	7 5	7 30	7 38	7 46	8 5	8 24	9 6	9 35	1015	1055	12 5
Swiss Cottage .... "	2 57	3 7	3 17	3 37	4 7	4 26	4 38	4 57	5 16	5 16	5 35	6 0	6 16	6 36	7 7	7 32	7 40	7 48	8 7	8 26	9 8	9 37	1017	1057	12 7
Finchley Road .... "	2 59	3 9	3 19	3 39	4 9	4 28	4 40	4 59	5 18	5 26	5 37	6 6	6 18	6 38	7 9	7 34	7 42	7 50	8 9	8 28	9 10	9 39	1019	1059	12 9
West Hampstead......... "	3 1	3 11	3 21	3 41	4 11	4 30	4 42	5 1	5 20	5 28	5 39	6 8	6 20	6 40	7 11	7 36	7 44	7 52	8 11	8 30	9 12	9 41	1021	11 1	1211
Kilburn-Brondesbury .. "	3 3	3 13	3 23	3 43	4 13	4 32	4 44	5 3	5 22	5 30	5 41	6 10	6 22	6 42	7 13	7 38	7 46	7 54	8 13	8 32	9 14	9 43	1023	11 3	1213
Willesden Green ¶.... "	3 5	3 16	3 30	3 46	4 16	4 40	4 47	5 6	5 25	5 33	5 50	6 13	6 31	6 49	7 16	7 41	7 53	7 57	8 16	8 40	9 17	9 46	1030	11 6	1216
Kingsbury-Neasden .... "	3 8	3 19	3 19	3 49	4 19	4 19	4 50	5 9	5 28	5 36	5 28	6 16	6 16	...	7 19	7 44	7 56	8 0	8 19	8 19	9 20	9 49	1033	11 9	1219
Wembley Park......... "	2*56	3 22	3 22	3 52	4 22	4 22	4 53	4 53	5 31	5 31	5 31	6 19	6 19	...	7 22	7 47	7 59	8 3	8 22	8 22	9 23	9 52	1036	1112	...
Harrow-on-the-Hill...... "	3 16	3 28	3 41	3 58	4 28	4 50	4 59	5 17	5 37	6 0	6 0	6 25	6 41	6 58	7 28	7 53	8 4	8 9	8 28	8 50	9 29	9 58	1043	1118	1227
Pinner .... "	3 21		3 46	4 3	4*33	4 55		...	5 42	5 48	6 5	6 30	6 46	7 3	7 33	7 58	8 9	8 14	8 33	8 55	9 34	10 3	1048	1123	1232
Northwood .... "	3 26	...	3 51	4 8	4*38	5 0	...	...	5 47	5 47	6 10	6 35	6 51	7 8	7 38	8 3	8 14	8 19	8 38	9 0	9 39	10 8	1053	1128	1237
Rickmansworth .... "	3 33	...	3 58	4 15	4*45	5 7	...	5 30	5 53	6 13	6 16	6 42	6 57	7 15	7 44	8 9	8 21	8 26	8 44	9 7	9 46	1014	11 0	1135	1244
Chorley Wood .... "	3*39	...	4 5			5 12	...		5 59	6 18	6 21		7 3	7 21			8·26	8 31		9 14			11 7	1141	12§50
Chalfont Road .... "	3*44	...	4 12	...	...	5 18	...	...	6 4	...	6 27	...	7 10	7 27	...	...	8 30	8 36	...	9 22	...	...	1113	1146	12§55
Chesham ....dep	...	...	4 0	...	...	4 39	...	...	...	5 40	5 40	...	6 55	...	...	...	...	...	...	9 10	...	...	11 0	...	...
Amersham ....dep	...	...	4 18	...	...	5 23	...	...	...	6 24	6 32		7 16		...				...	9 28	...	...	1120	...	...
Great Missenden .... "	...	...	4 28	...	...	5 32	...	...	...	6 32	6 41		7 26		...				...	9 38	...	...	1130	...	...
Wendover .... "	...	...	4 37	...	...	5 41	...	...	...	6 40	6 49		7 35		...				...	9 47	...	...	1139	...	...
Stoke Mandeville......... "	...	...	4 42	...	...	5 46	...	...	...	6 45	6 54		7 40		...				...	9 52	...	...	1144	...	...
Aylesbury .... arr	...	...	4 48	...	...	5 51	...	...	...	6 51	7 0	Saturdays excepted.	7 46	Saturdays excepted.	...	Saturdays excepted.	Saturdays excepted.	Saturdays only.	...	9 58	...	...	1149	...	...
Aylesbury .... dep	...	...		...	...	5 53	...	...	...	Saturdays excepted.	Saturdays only.		7 48		...				...		...	...		...	...
Waddesdon Manor...... "	...	...	...	...	...	6 2	...	...	...				7 57		...				...	...	...	...	...	...	...
Quainton Road .... "	...	...	...	...	...	6 6	...	...	...				8 1		...				...	...	...	...	...	...	...
Grandborough Road .... "	...	...	...	...	...	6 14	...	...	...				8 9		...				...	...	...	...	...	...	...
Winslow Road .... "	...	...	...	...	...	6 18	...	...	...				8 13		...				...	...	...	...	...	...	...
VERNEY JUNCTION arr	...	...	...	...	...	6 22	...	...	...				8 17		...				...	...	...	...	...	...	...

SUNDAYS

DOWN	mrn	mrn	mrn	mrn	mrn	mrn	aft	aft	aft	aft	aft	aft	aft	aft	aft	aft	aft	aft	aft	aft	aft	aft	aft	aft	aft
BAKER STREET ....dep	8 47	9 53	10 7	1033	1057	1117	1 8	1 20	1 31	1 46	2 16	2 46	3 20	4 16	4 52	5 16	5 46	6 16	7 16	7 31	8 36	9 16	9 54	1016	1046
St. John's Wood Road .. "	8 50	9 56	9 56	1036	1050	1112	1 11	1 23	1 34	1 49	2 19	2 49	3 23	4 19	4 55	5 19	5 49	6 19	7 19	7 34	8 39	9 19	9 57	1019	1049
Marlborough Road...... "	8 53	9 59	9 59	1039	1053	1115	1 14	1 26	1 37	1 52	2 22	2 52	3 26	4 22	4 58	5 22	5 52	6 22	7 22	7 37	8 42	9 22	10 0	1022	1052
Swiss Cottage .... "	8 55	10 1	10 1	1041	1055	1117	1 16	1 28	1 39	1 54	2 24	2 54	3 28	4 24	5 0	5 24	5 54	6 24	7 24	7 39	8 44	9 24	10 2	1024	1054
Finchley Road .... "	8 57	10 3	10 3	1043	1057	1119	1 18	1 30	1 41	1 56	2 26	2 56	3 31	4 26	5 2	5 26	5 56	6 26	7 26	7 41	8 46	9 26	10 4	1026	1056
West Hampstead......... "	8 59	10 5	10 5	1045	1059	1121	1 20	1 32	1 43	1 58	2 28	2 58	3 33	4 28	5 4	5 28	5 58	6 28	7 28	7 43	8 48	9 28	10 6	1028	1058
Kilburn-Brondesbury .. "	9 1	10 7	1017	1047	11 1	1123	1 22	1 34	1 45	2 0	2 30	3 0	3 35	4 30	5 6	5 30	6 0	6 30	7 30	7 45	8 50	9 30	10 8	1030	11 0
Willesden Green ¶.... "	9 3	10 9	1020	1049	1110	1125	1 25	1 37	1 48	2 3	2 33	3 3	3 38	4 33	5 9	5 33	6 3	6 33	7 33	7 48	8 53	9 33	1010	1033	11 3
Kingsbury-Neasden .... "	9 6	1012	1012	1052	1113	1133	1 28	1 40	1 51	2 6	2 36	3 6	3 41	4 36	5 12	5 36	6 6	6 36	7 36	7 52	8 56	9 36	1013	1036	11 6
Wembley Park......... "	9 9	1015	1015	1055	1116	1116	1 31	1 43	1 54	2 9	2 39	3 9	3 44	4 39	5 15	5 39	6 9	6 39	7 39	7 55	8 59	9 39	1016	1039	...
Harrow-on-the-Hill...... "	9 15	1021	1029	11 1	1122	1122	1 37	1 49	2 0	2 15	2 45	3 15	3 51	4 45	5 21	5 46	6 15	6 45	7 45	8 1	9 6	9 45	1023	1045	1114
Pinner .... "	9 20	1026	1034	11 6	1127	1127	1 42		2 5		2 50		3 56	4 50		5 51	6 20	6 50	7 50	8 6	9 11	9 50	1028		
Northwood .... "	9 25	1031	1039	1111	1132	1132	1 47	...	2 10	...	2 55	...	4 1	4 55	...	5 56	6 25	6 55	7 55	8 11	9 16	9 55	1033	...	...
Rickmansworth .... "	9 32	1038	1046	1118	1139	1155	1 54	...	2 17	...	3 2	...	4 8	5 2	...	6 3	6 32	7 2	8 2	8 18	9 23	10 2	1040	...	...
Chorley Wood .... "	9 38	1042	1052	1124		12 0	1 59	...		...		...	4 14		...	6 9	6 38	7 8	8 8	8 24	9 29			...	...
Chalfont Road .... "	9 43	1047	1059	1129	...	12 5	2 4	...	...	...	...	...	4 21	...	...	6 16		7 13	8 13	8 29	9 36	...	...	...	...
Chesham ....dep	...	...	9 59	...	...	...	...	...	...	...	...	...	2 48	...	...	5 59	...	...	...	...	8 51	...	...	...	...
Amersham ....dep	9 47	...	11 3	...	...	1210	...	...	...	...	...	...	4 28	...	...	6 21	...	...	...	...	9 41	...	...	...	...
Great Missenden .... "	9 56	...	1112	...	...	1219	...	...	...	...	...	...	4 38	...	...	6 31	...	...	...	...	9 51	...	...	...	...
Wendover .... "	10 5	...	1121	...	...	1228	...	...	...	...	...	...	4 47	...	...	6 40	...	...	...	...	10 0	...	...	...	...
Stoke Mandeville......... "	1010	...	1126	...	...	1233	...	...	...	...	...	...	4 52	...	...	6 45	...	...	...	...	10 5	...	...	...	...
Aylesbury .... arr	1016	...	1132	...	...	1238	...	...	...	...	...	...	4 57	...	...	6 50	...	...	...	...	1010	...	...	...	...
Aylesbury .... dep	...	...		...	...	...	...	...	...	...	...	...	5 1	...	...		...	...	...	...		...	...	...	...
Waddesdon Manor...... "	...	...	...	...	...	...	...	...	...	...	...	...	5 10	...	...	...	...	...	...	...	...	...	...	...	...
Quainton Road .... "	...	...	...	...	...	...	...	...	...	...	...	...	5 15	...	...	...	...	...	...	...	...	...	...	...	...
Grandborough Road .... "	...	...	...	...	...	...	...	...	...	...	...	...	5 24	...	...	...	...	...	...	...	...	...	...	...	...
Winslow Road .... "	...	...	...	...	...	...	...	...	...	...	...	...	5 29	...	...	...	...	...	...	...	...	...	...	...	...
VERNEY JUNCTION arr	...	...	...	...	...	...	...	...	...	...	...	...	5 33	...	...	...	...	...	...	...	...	...	...	...	...

* Saturdays only. † Saturdays excepted. ‡ On Saturdays runs 5 minutes earlier and to Harrow-on-the-Hill.
§ Thursdays only. ¶ Willesden Green and Cricklewood.
** On Saturdays leaves at 6-29, calls at all Stations, and running at same times from Harrow to Chalfont Road.

For Trains by Great Central Railway between Aylesbury and Rugby, Leicester, Loughboro', Nottingham, Sheffield, Manchester, &c., see pages 12 to 25.

The above Service is for July, and is subject to alteration by the Metropolitan Railway Company afterwards, for particulars of which see that Company's Time Tables.

Above and opposite: GC Timetable July-September 1903 — 'From London by Metropolitan Railway'.

To LONDON by METROPOLITAN RAILWAY.

UP — WEEK DAYS	mrn	mrn	mrn	mrn	mrn	mrn	mrn	mrn	mrn	mrn	mrn	mrn	mrn	mrn	mrn	mrn	mrn	mrn	mrn	aft	mrn	aft	aft	aft	aft
VERNEY JUNCTION dep													7 46					9 21			11 5				1 5
Winslow Road "													7 51					9 26			11 9				1 9
Grandborough Road "													7 56					9 32			1113				1 13
Quainton Road "													8 8					9 46			1122				1 22
Waddesdon Manor "													8 13					9 50			1126				1 26
Aylesbury arr													8 23					9 59			1135				1 35
Aylesbury dep									7 15				8 25					10 3			1137				1 37
Stoke Mandeville "									7 22				8 32					1010			1144				1 43
Wendover "									7 29				8 37					1017			1151				1 49
Great Missenden "									7 39				8 48					1027			12 1				1 59
Amersham "									7 51				8 57		9 20			1037			1211				2 9
Chesham arr									8 4						1039			1134			1229				2‡27
Chalfont Road dep								7 44	7 58		8 19	8 46			9 30			1044	1150		1220				2 15
Chorley Wood "								7 49	8 2		8 23	8 50	9 3		9 34			1048	1154		1224				2 19
Rickmansworth "					7 9		7 37	7 53	8 7		8 27	8 55	9 7		9 39	10 9		1053	1159		1229		1*28	1†49	2 24
Northwood "					7 16		7 44	8 0	8 14		8 34	9 2	9 46	9 18	9 46	1016		11 0	12 6		1236		1*35	1†56	2 31
Pinner "			6 34		7 21		7 49	8 5	8 19		8 39	9 7	9 51	9 23	9 51	1021		11 5	1211		1241		1*40	2†1	2 36
Harrow-on-the-Hill "	5 31	6 1	6 39	7 4	7 26	7 33	7 54	8 10	8 25	8 31	8 44	9 12	9 56	9 28	9 56	1026	1046	1111	1216	1226	1246	1 6	1 44	2 4	2 42
Wembley Park "	5 36	6 6	6 44	7 9	7 31	7 38	7 59	8 16	8 37	8 37	9 5	9 33	10 1	9 33	10 1	1031	1051	...	1221	1231	1 11	1 11	1 49	2 9	3*1
Kingsbury-Neasden "	5 40	6 10	6 48	7 13	7 35	7 42	8 3	8 20	8 33	8 40	8 52	9 37	10 5	9 37	10 5	1035	1055	...	1225	1235	1 15	1 15	1 53	2 13	3*5
Willesden Green ¶ "	5 44	6 14	6 52	7 17	7 39	7 46	8 7	8 24	8 41	8 44	8 56	9 41	9 29	9 41	10 9	1039	1059	1122	1229	1239	1257	1 19	1 57	2 17	2 52
Kilburn-Brondesbury "	5 46	6 16	6 54	7 19	7 41	7 48	8 9	8 31	8 43	8 46	8 58	9 46	9 33	9 46	1011	1041	11 1	1129	1231	1241	1 1	1 21	1 59	2 19	2 57
West Hampstead "	5 49	6 19	6 57	7 22	7 44	7 51	8 12	8 34	8 46	8 49	9 6	9 49	9 36	9 49	1014	1044	11 4	1132	1234	1244	1 4	1 24	2 2	2 22	3 0
Finchley Road "	5 51	6 21	6 59	7 24	7 46	7 53	8 14	8 36	8 48	8 51	9 8	9 51	9 38	9 51	1016	1046	11 6	1134	1236	1246	1 6	1 26	2 4	2 24	3 2
Swiss Cottage "	5 53	6 23	7 1	7 26	7 48	7 55	8 16	8 38	8 50	8 53	9 10	9 53	9 40	9 53	1018	1048	11 8	1136	1238	1248	1 8	1 28	2 6	2 26	3 4
Marlborough Road "	5 55	6 25	7 3	7 28	7 50	7 57	8 18	8 40	8 52	8 55	9 12	9 55	9 42	9 55	1020	1050	1110	1138	1240	1250	1 10	1 30	2 8	2 28	3 6
St. John's Wood Road "	5 57	6 27	7 5	7 30	7 52	7 59	8 20	8 42	8 54	8 57	9 14	9 57	9 44	9 57	1022	1052	1112	1140	1242	1252	1 12	1 32	2 10	2 30	3 8
BAKER STREET arr	6 0	6 30	7 8	7 33	7 55	8 2	8 23	8 37	8 48	9 0	9 9	9 32	9 40	9 55	1025	1055	1115	1133	1245	1255	1 8	1 35	2 13	2 33	3 3

UP — WEEK DAYS—Continued	aft	aft	aft	aft	aft	aft	aft	aft	aft	aft	aft	aft	aft	aft	aft	aft	aft	aft	aft	aft	aft	aft	aft	aft	aft
VERNEY JUNCTION dep					Saturdays only.	Saturdays only.		3 40			Saturdays only.						6 0							9 15	
Winslow Road "								3 44									6 4							9 19	
Grandborough Road "								3 48									6 9							9 23	
Quainton Road "								3 57									6 21							9 32	
Waddesdon Manor "								4 1									6 26							9 36	
Aylesbury arr								4 10									6 35							9 45	
Aylesbury dep						*3 50*		4 12				5 13					6 37			7 57				9 47	1032
Stoke Mandeville "						*3 56*		4 18				5 19					6 44			8 4				9 54	1039
Wendover "						*4 2*		4 25				5 25					6 51			8 11				10 1	1046
Great Missenden "						*4 11*		4 34				5 34					7 0			8 21				1011	1056
Amersham "						*4 22*		4 44				5 43					7 9			8 31				1021	11 6
Chesham arr						*5 36*		*5†29*				6 14					7 37			9 34					1123
Chalfont Road dep						*4 30*		4 51		*5*30*		5 50	6 30			*7†5*	7 15		8 20	8 40		9 29		1030	1111
Chorley Wood "	*2†54*					*4 34*		4 55		*5*35*		5 54	6 34			*7†9*	7 19		8 24	8 44		9 34		1034	1115
Rickmansworth "	2 59		3 39	4 19		*4 39*	*4*50*	5 0		5 40	*5 50*	5 59	6 39	6 49		*7†14*	7 24	7 49	8 29	8 49	9 9	9 39	1019	1039	1120
Northwood "	3 6		3 46	4 26		*4 46*	*4*57*	5 7		5 47	*5 57*	6 6	6 46	6 56		*7†21*	7 31	7 56	8 36	8 56	9 16	9 46	1026	1046	1127
Pinner "	3 11		3 51	4 31		*4 51*	*5*2*	5 12		5 52	*6 2*	6 11	6 51	7 1		*7†26*	7 36	8 1	8 41	9 1	9 21	9 51	1031	1051	1132
Harrow-on-the-Hill "	3 16	3 36	3 56	4 36	*4 46*	*4 56*	5 7	5 18	5 36	5 57	*6 7*	6 17	6 56	7 6	7 26	7 31	7 42	8 6	8 46	9 7	9 26	9 56	1036	1057	1137
Wembley Park "	3 21	3 41	4 1	4 41	*4 51*	*5 1*	5 12	5 41	5 41	6 2	*6 12*	6 22	7 1	7 11	7 31	7 36	8 11	8 11	8 51	9 31	9 31	10 1	1041	...	...
Kingsbury-Neasden "	3 25	3 45	4 5	4 45	*4 55*	*5 5*	5 16	5 45	5 45	6 6	*6 16*	*6*49*	7 5	7 15	7 35	7 40	8 15	8 15	8 55	9 35	9 35	10 5	1045	11 5	1145
Willesden Green ¶ "	3 29	3 49	4 9	4 49	*4 59*	*5 9*	5 20	5 28	5 49	6 10	*6 20*	6 27	7 9	7 19	7 39	7 44	7 52	8 19	8 59	9 17	9 39	10 9	1049	11 8	1149
Kilburn-Brondesbury "	3 31	3 51	4 11	4 51	*5 1*	*5 11*	5 22	5 32	5 51	6 12	*6 22*	6 32	7 11	7 21	7 41	7 46	7 59	8 21	9 1	9 22	9 41	1011	1051	1110	1151
West Hampstead "	3 34	3 54	4 14	4 54	*5 4*	*5 14*	5 25	5 36	5 54	6 15	*6 25*	6 35	7 14	7 24	7 44	7 49	8 2	8 24	9 4	9 25	9 44	1014	1054	1113	1154
Finchley Road "	3 36	3 56	4 16	4 56	*5 6*	*5 16*	5 27	5 38	5 56	6 17	*6 27*	6 37	7 16	7 26	7 46	7 51	8 4	8 26	9 6	9 27	9 46	1016	1056	1115	1156
Swiss Cottage "	3 38	3 58	4 18	4 58	*5 8*	*5 18*	5 29	5 40	5 58	6 19	*6 29*	6 39	7 18	7 28	7 48	7 53	8 6	8 28	9 8	9 29	9 48	1018	1058	1117	1158
Marlborough Road "	3 40	4 0	4 20	5 0	*5 10*	*5 20*	5 31	5 42	6 0	6 21	*6 31*	6 41	7 20	7 30	7 50	7 55	8 8	8 30	9 10	9 31	9 50	1020	11 0	1119	12 0
St. John's Wood Road "	3 42	4 2	4 22	5 2	*5 12*	*5 22*	5 33	5 44	6 2	6 23	*6 33*	6 37	7 22	7 32	7 52	7 57	8 10	8 32	9 12	9 33	9 52	1022	11 2	1121	12 2
BAKER STREET arr	3 45	4 5	4 25	5 5	*5 15*	*5 25*	5 36	5 40	6 5	6 26	*6 36*	6 40	7 25	7 35	7 55	8 0	8 13	8 35	9 15	9 28	9 55	1025	11 5	1124	12 5

UP — SUNDAYS	mrn	mrn	mrn	mrn	mrn	aft	aft	aft	aft	aft	aft	aft	aft	aft	aft	aft	aft	aft	aft	aft	aft	aft	aft	aft	aft
VERNEY JUNCTION dep		7 35																	5 51						
Winslow Road "		7 39																	5 56						
Grandborough Road "		7 44																	6 1						
Quainton Road "		7 54																	6 10						
Waddesdon Manor "		7 59																	6 15						
Aylesbury arr		8 9																	6 24						
Aylesbury dep		8 11			1119					2 23									6 26		7 46		8 28		
Stoke Mandeville "		8 17			1125					2 29									6 33		7 51		8 34		
Wendover "		8 24			1130					2 34									6 40		7 56		8 39		
Great Missenden "		8 34			1139					2 43									6 50		8 6		8 49		
Amersham "		8 44			1149					2 53									7 1		8 16		9 1		
Chesham arr		9 54			1215					4 30									7 23		8 39		9 48		
Chalfont Road dep		8 52		10 9	1155		1259	1 59		2 59				5 4					7 10	7 59	8 21	9 1	9 8		1020
Chorley Wood "		8 56		1013	1159		1 3	2 3		3 3				5 8			6 33	7 5	7 15	8 3	8 26	9 5	9 12		1024
Rickmansworth "	8 14	9 1		1018	12 4	1238	1 8	2 8	2 38	3 8	3 38	4 8	4 38	5 13	5 44		6 38	7 10	7 20	8 8	8 32	9 10	9 17	9 42	1029
Northwood "	8 21	9 8		1025	1211	1245	1 15	2 15	2 45	3 15	3 45	4 15	4 45	5 20	5 51		6 45	7 17	7 27	8 15	8 47	9 17	9 24	9 49	1036
Pinner "	8 26	9 13		1030	1216	1250	1 20	2 20	2 50	3 20	3 50	4 20	4 50	5 25	5 56		6 50	7 22	7 32	8 20	8 52	9 22	9 29	9 54	1041
Harrow-on-the-Hill "	8 31	9 18	10 5	1035	1221	1255	1 25	2 25	2 55	3 25	3 55	4 25	4 55	5 30	6 1	6 43	6 55	7 27	7 37	8 25	8 57	9 27	9 34	9 59	1046
Wembley Park "	8 36	9 23	1010	1040	1226	1 0	1 30	2 30	3 0	3 30	4 0	4 30	5 0	5 35	6 6	6 48	7 0	7 32	7 42	8 30	9 2	9 33	10 4	10 4	1051
Kingsbury-Neasden "	8 40	9 27	1014	1044	1230	1 4	1 34	2 34	3 4	3 34	4 4	4 34	5 4	5 39	6 10	6 52	7 4	7 36	7 46	8 34	8 56	9 38	9 43	10 8	1055
Willesden Green ¶ "	8 44	9 31	1018	1050	1234	1 8	1 38	2 38	3 8	3 38	4 8	4 38	5 8	5 43	6 14	6 56	7 8	7 40	7 50	8 38	9 10	9 42	9 47	1012	1059
Kilburn-Brondesbury "	8 46	9 33	1020	1052	1236	1 10	1 40	2 40	3 10	3 40	4 10	4 40	5 10	5 45	6 16	6 58	7 10	7 42	7 52	8 40	9 12	9 44	9 49	1014	11 1
West Hampstead "	8 49	9 36	1023	1055	1239	1 13	1 43	2 43	3 13	3 43	4 13	4 43	5 13	5 48	6 19	7 1	7 13	7 45	7 55	8 43	9 15	9 47	9 52	1017	11 4
Finchley Road "	8 51	9 38	1025	1057	1241	1 15	1 45	2 45	3 15	3 45	4 15	4 45	5 15	5 50	6 21	7 3	7 15	7 47	7 57	8 45	9 17	9 49	9 54	1019	11 6
Swiss Cottage "	8 53	9 40	1027	1059	1243	1 17	1 47	2 47	3 17	3 47	4 17	4 47	5 17	5 52	6 23	7 5	7 17	7 49	7 59	8 47	9 19	9 51	9 56	1021	11 8
Marlborough Road "	8 55	9 42	1029	11 1	1245	1 19	1 49	2 49	3 19	3 49	4 19	4 49	5 19	5 54	6 25	7 7	7 19	7 51	8 1	8 49	9 21	9 53	9 58	1023	1110
St. John's Wood Road "	8 57	9 44	1031	11 3	1247	1 21	1 51	2 51	3 21	3 51	4 21	4 51	5 21	5 56	6 27	7 9	7 21	7 53	8 3	8 51	9 23	9 55	10 0	1025	1112
BAKER STREET arr	9 0	9 47	1034	11 6	1250	1 24	1 54	2 54	3 24	3 54	4 24	4 54	5 24	5 59	6 30	7 12	7 24	7 56	8 6	8 54	9 12	9 58	10 3	1028	1115

* Saturdays only. † Saturdays excepted. ‡ Arrives at 2-46 aft. on Saturdays. ¶ Willesden Green and Cricklewood.

For Trains by Great Central Railway between Aylesbury and Rugby, Leicester, Loughboro', Nottingham, Sheffield, Manchester, &c., see pages 12 to 25.

The above Service is for July, and is subject to alteration by the Metropolitan Railway Company afterwards, for particulars of which see that Company's Time Tables.

67753
67753

LIVERPOOL STREET
6

Above left:
The 'L1s' replaced the 'A5s' but were eventually superseded by Stanier and Fairburn tanks under 'London Midlandisation'. No 67753 is in fine condition as it is seen on an up local from Aylesbury to Marylebone via High Wycombe at Harefield (near Denham) on 17 April 1954. *E. R. Wethersett/Real Photographs*

Left:
Met locomotive No 6 has just come off a northbound Baker Street to Aylesbury service at Rickmansworth and is running back down the up main line to the sidings at the south end of the station to wait for an up Baker Street service. One of the steam locomotives in the sidings to the left will now run on to the train and take it on to Aylesbury in this October 1957 photograph. *G. C. Farnell*

Above:
Metropolitan main line steam in the shape of 'K' class 2-6-4T No 116 on a down train at Chorley Wood on 5 June 1954. Designed by George Hally, CME of the Metropolitan, these locomotives incorporated unassembled parts of SECR 'N' class locomotives made after World War 1 at the Woolwich Arsenal. The flower gatherers would be less welcome today. *E. R. Wethersett/Real Photographs*

Above:
At Chalfont & Latimer, the Chesham branch joined the GC/Met joint line and, until they were replaced by 2-6-2 'Mickey Mouse' tanks in the late 1950s/early 1960s, the services were worked by Neasden 'N5' tanks which were outbased on the line for a week. 'N5' No 69257 approaches Chalfont and Latimer with the Chesham branch train on 19 June 1954. *L. V. Reason*

Table 13— *continued*

MARYLEBONE, PADDINGTON, WEST RUISLIP, HIGH WYCOMBE, PRINCES RISBOROUGH and AYLESBURY

Week Days—*continued*

	p.m B	p.m B	p.m (Via Harrow on the Hill. To Manchester arr. 8 55 p.m. (Table 2) Restaurant Car.)	p.m B	p.m B (From Paddington dep. 2†0 p.m. Via Maidenhead)		p.m B S (Via Harrow on the Hill. To Quainton Rd. arr. 5 33 p.m. (Table 2))	p.m B (Via Maidenhead)	p.m B	p.m B	p.m (To Bicester arr. 6 9 p.m.)	p.m B E	p.m B S (To Brackley arr. 7 12 p.m. (Table 2))	p.m (Via Harrow on the Hill. To Bradford arr 10 14 p.m. (Table 2) Restaurant Car)	p.m B	p.m (Via Harrow on the Hill. To Woodford Halse arr. 7 22 p.m. (Table 2))		p.m B E (Via Harrow on the Hill)	p.m B E	p.m B S	p.m B E	p.m B E (Via Harrow on the Hill. To Quainton Rd. arr. 7 5 p.m. (Table 2))	p.m B E		p.m B S	p.m B E	p.m B	p.m B E	p.m B	p.m E (Via Harrow on the Hill. To Woodford Halse arr. 8 31 p.m. (Table 2))
Marylebone .... dep	..	3 2	3 20	3 23		..	3 50	..	4 2	4 20	..	4 35	4 45	4 50	4 57	5 0	..	5 7	5 15	5 20	5 19	5 22	5 31	..	5 40	5 43	..	5 55	5 59	6 8
Paddington .... "	2† 0	..		..		..	..	3 33	..	..	4 35	..	..		..		..	..	..	..	..	..	..	..	..	..	..	..	..	
Wembley Hill	(Via Maidenhead. To Aylesbury arr. 4 20 pm)	3 15		..		..		..	4 15	..		4 49	4 59		5 10		..		..	..	5 32		..	..	..	..	..	..	6 12	
Sudbury and Harrow Road		3 19		..		..			4 19	..		..	5 3		5 14		..		..	..	5 36		..	..	..	..	..	..	6 16	
Sudbury Hill, Harrow		3 22		..		..			4 22	..		..	5 6		5 17		..		..	..	..		5 48	..	..	..	..	..	6 19	
Northolt Park A		3 25		..		..			4 25	..		4 56	5 9		5 20		..		..	..	5 40		..	..	..	..	..	..	6 22	
South Ruislip ¶		3 29		..		..			4 29	..		..	5 14		5 24		..		..	..	5 44		..	..	..	..	..	..	6 26	
Ruislip Gardens ¶		3 31		..		..			4 31	..		..	5 16		5 26		..		..	..	5 46		..	..	..	..	..	..	6 28	
West Ruislip fr Ickenham ¶		3 34		3 47		..			4 34	4 43		5 3	5 21		5 29		..		5 39	5 43	5 49		5 56	..	6 3	..	..	..	6 31	
Denham for Harefield		..		3 52		..			..	4 48		5 8	5 27		..		..		5 44	5 48	..		6 1	..	6 8	6 10	..	..	..	
Denham Golf Club Platf'm		..		3 55		..			..	4 51		5 11	5 30		..		..		5 47	5 51	..		..	..	6 11	6 13	..	..	..	
Gerrards Cross		..		4 0		..			..	4 56	5 3	5 16	5 35		..		..		5 52	5 56	..		6 7	..	6 16	..	..	6 26	..	
Seer Green B		..		4 6		..			..	5 2	..	5 22	5 41		..		..		5 58	6 2	..		..	..	6 22	6 22	..	..	..	
Beaconsfield for Penn		..		4 10		..		..	..	5 6	5 12	5 26	5 45		..		..		6 2	6 6	..		6 15	..	6 26	6 26	..	6 34	..	
High Wycombe ..... arr	3 35	..		4 20		..		4 50	..	5 15	5 22	5 36	5 52		..		..		6 12	6 13	..		6 22	..	6 36	6 34	..	6 43	..	
High Wycombe ..... dep	3 43	..		..		..		4 52	..	..	5 23	..	5 55		..		..		..	6 15	..		6 24	..	..	..	..	..	..	
West Wycombe	3 48	..		..		..		4 57	..	..	5 28	..	6 0		..		..		..	6 20	..		6 29	..	..	..	..	..	..	
Saunderton	3 54	..		..		..		5 3	..	..	5 34	..	6 7		..		..		..	6 26	..		6 35	..	..	..	..	..	..	
Princes Risborough	4c 3	..		..		..		5c12	..	..	5 41	..	6 12		..		..		..	6 34	..		6 43	..	..	..	6 50	..	..	
Monks Risborough C	4 7	..		..		..		5 16	..	..	..	..	..		..		..		..	..	..		..	..	..	..	6 54	..	..	
Little Kimble	4 11	..		..	4 11	..		5 20	..	..	..	..	..		..		..		..	..	..		..	..	..	..	6 58	..	..	
South Aylesbury Halt	..	..		..	..	..	..	5 27	..	..	..	..	..		..		..		..	..	..	..	..	..	..	..	7 5	..	..	
Aylesbury .... arr	..	..	4 20	..	4 20	..	5 18	5 30	..	..	..	..	..	5 48	..	6 13	..	6 37	..	..	..	6 50	..	..	..	..	7 8	..	..	7 30

Week Days—*continued*

	p.m S (Via Harrow on the Hill. To Woodford Halse arr. 8 35 p.m. (Table 2))	p.m B E (To Brackley arr. 8 25 p.m. (Table 2))	p.m B S	p.m B E (Via Harrow on the Hill)	p.m B	p.m B E	p.m B E	p.m B	p.m	p.m B (Via Maidenhead)	p.m B	p.m B E	p.m B S	p.m B S	p.m B E	p.m B E (Via Harrow on the Hill)	p.m B	p.m B E (To Brackley arr. 10 29 p.m. (Table 2))	p.m B S	p.m B (Via Maidenhead)	p.m B	p.m B	p.m B S (Via Harrow on the Hill To Brackley arr. 11 49 p.m. (Table 2))	p.m F (Via Harrow on the Hill To Liverpool arr. 5 20 a.m (Table 2))	p.m E (Via Harrow on the Hill To Manchester arr. 4 12 a.m. (Table 2))	p.m B	p.m B	p.m S (Via Harrow on the Hill. To Manchester arr. 4 25 a.m. (Table 2))	p.m B	p.m. B
Marylebone .... dep	6 8	6 22	6 22	6 26	..	6 30	6 34	6 52	..	..	7 2	7 20	7 20	..	..	7 45	8 2	8 20	8 20	..	9 2	9 20	9 32	9 40	10 0	10 2	1020	1045	11 2	11 20
Paddington .... "			..	..	..	..	..	..	7 10	6 38	..	..	..	..	..	..	..	..	..	8 25	..	..				..	..		..	..
Wembley Hill			..		..	..	6 47	..	..		7 15	..	..	..	..		8 15	..	..		9 15	..				1015	..		1115	..
Sudbury and Harrow Road			..		..	..	6 51	..	..		7 19	..	..	..	..		8 19	..	..		9 19	..				1019	..		1119	..
Sudbury Hill, Harrow			..		..	..	6 54	..	..		7 22	..	..	..	..		8 22	..	..		9 22	..				1022	..		1122	..
Northolt Park A			..		..	..	6 57	..	..		7 25	..	..	..	..		8 25	..	..		9 25	..				1025	..		1125	..
South Ruislip ¶			..		..	..	7 1	..	..		7 29	..	..	..	..		8 29	..	..		9 29	..				1029	..		1129	..
Ruislip Gardens ¶			..		..	..	7 3	..	..		7 31	..	..	..	..		8 31	..	..		9 31	..				1031	..		1131	..
West Ruislip fr Ickenham ¶			6 46		..	6 53	7 6	7 15	..		7 34	7 43	7 43	..	..		8 34	8 43	8 43		9 34	9 43				1034	1043		1134	11 43
Denham for Harefield			6 51		..	6 58	..	7 20	..		..	7 48	7 48	..	..		..	8 48	8 48		..	9 48				..	1048		..	11 48
Denham Golf Club Platf'm			6 54		..	7 1	..	..	..		..	7 51	7 51	..	..		..	8 51	8 51		..	9 51				..	1051		..	11 51
Gerrards Cross		6 54	6 59		..	7 6	..	7 26	..		..	7 56	7 56	..	..		..	8 56	8 56		..	9 56				..	1056		..	11 56
Seer Green B		..	7 5		..	7 12	..	7 32	..		..	8 2	8 2	..	..		..	9 2	9 2		..	10 2				..	11 2		..	12 2
Beaconsfield for Penn		7 2	7 9		..	7 16	..	7 36	..		..	8 6	8 6	..	..		..	9 6	9 6		..	10 6				..	11 6		..	12 6
High Wycombe ..... arr		7 9	7 19		..	7 26	..	7 43	..	8 0	..	8 13	8 16	..	..		..	9 13	9 16	9 56	..	10 13				..	1116		..	12 16
High Wycombe ..... dep		7 11	..		..	..	..	7 55	..	..	..	8 15	..	8 20	8 35		..	9 15	..	..	..	10 15				..	..		..	12U18
West Wycombe		7 16	..		..	..	..	8 0	..	..	..	8 20	..	8 25	8 39		..	9 20	..	..	..	..				..	..		..	..
Saunderton		7 22	..		..	..	..	8 6	..	..	..	8 26	..	8 31	8 45		..	9 26	..	..	..	..				..	..		..	..
Princes Risborough		7 27	..		7 45	..	..	8 14	8‡ 6	..	..	8u36	..	8c40	8c55		..	9 31	..	..	..	10d32				..	..		..	12U31
Monks Risborough C		..	..		7 49	..	..	..	..	..	..	8 40	..	8 44	8 59		..	..	..	..	..	..				..	..		..	..
Little Kimble		..	..		7 53	..	..	..	..	..	..	8 44	..	8 48	9 3		..	..	..	..	..	10V40				..	..		..	..
South Aylesbury Halt		..	..	..	8 0	..	..	..	..	..	..	..	..	..	..	..	..	..	..	..	..	..	..	..	..	..	..	..	..	..
Aylesbury .... arr	7 34	..	..	7 56	8 3	..	..	..	..	..	..	8 53	..	8 57	9 12	9 23	..	..	..	..	..	10 49	11 4	1044	1055	..	..	1140	..	..

Through Trains from Marylebone or Paddington except where otherwise shown.

For Notes, see page 177

Above and opposite: Marylebone to Aylesbury via High Wycombe — 5 June to 24 September 1950.

Above:
All steam was withdrawn from Neasden in 1962 with locomotives and men transferred to Cricklewood. The new DMUs were based at Marylebone diesel depot and worked all the GC suburban services as well as a return working to Nottingham Victoria. The 1.50pm Aylesbury to Marylebone DMU was a parcels working and is seen here passing Northwood in September 1962 complete with a four-wheeled van and another DMU vehicle in tow. New track on the Metropolitan four tracking scheme can be seen to the right. *E. J. S. Gadsden*

Table 13— *continued*

AYLESBURY, PRINCES RISBOROUGH, HIGH WYCOMBE, WEST RUISLIP, PADDINGTON and MARYLEBONE

Week Days

Miles		a.m B	a.m B		a.m B	a.m B	a.m B		a.m B	a.m B	a.m B E		a.m B S	a.m B	a.m B E		a.m From Woodford Halse dep. 6 20 a.m. (Table 2) Via Harrow on the Hill	a.m B E	a.m B Via Harrow on the Hill	a.m B		a.m B Via Maidenhead	a.m B E	a.m B Via Harrow on the Hill		a.m B	a.m B		a.m B E	a.m From Woodford Halse dep. 7 38 a.m. (Table 2) Via Harrow on the Hill
—	**Aylesbury** dep									7 0				7 20			7 25		7 37			7 45		7 50						8 41
¾	South Aylesbury Halt																													
4½	Little Kimble									7 9				7 29								7 54								
6	Monks Risborough C									7 13				7 33								7 58								
7¾	**Princes Risborough**									7 18				7 37	7 44							8c 5	8 16							
10½	Saunderton									7 25					7 51							8 12								
13¼	West Wycombe									7 30												8 17								
15½	**High Wycombe** arr									7 34					7 58							8 22	8 29							
	High Wycombe dep	5 55	6 25			6 48	7 15		7 25	7 36	7 44		7 44		8 0			8 8		8 16		8 25	8 31				8 40		8 55	
20¼	Beaconsfield for Penn	6 3	6 33			6 56	7 23		7 33	7 44	7 52		7 52					8 16		8 24			8 39				8 48		9 3	
21¾	Seer Green B	6 7	6 37			7 0			7 37		7 56		7 56		8 10					8 28							8 52		9 7	
24½	Gerrards Cross	6 13	6 43			7 6	7 31		7 43	7 52	8 2		8 2		8 16			8 24		8 34			8 47				8 58		9 13	
26¼	Denham Golf Club Platf'm	6 17	6 47			7 10				7 56			8 6							8 38							9 2		9 17	
27¼	Denham for Harefield	6 20	6 50			7 13	7 36		7 48	7 59			8 9		8 21												9 5		9 20	
30	West Ruislip for Ickenham ¶	6 25	6 55		7 12	7 18	7 41			8 4	8 11		8 14					8 32								8 55	9 10		9 25	
31¼	Ruislip Gardens ¶	6 28	6 58		7 16	7 21				8 7			8 17													8 58				
31¾	South Ruislip ¶	6 31	7 1		7 19	7 24			7 56		8 15		8 20													9 1				
—	Northolt Park A	6 35	7 5			7 28			8 0		8 19		8 24													9 5				
—	Sudbury Hill, Harrow	6 38	7 8			7 31	7 50		8 3		8 22		8 27													9 8				
—	Sudbury and Harrow Road	6 41	7 11			7 34			8 6		8 25		8 30													9 11				
—	Wembley Hill	6 45	7 15			7 38			8 10	8 17			8 34													9 15				
40	**Paddington** arr				7 53																	9 38								
43¼	**Marylebone** "	7 0	7 30			7 53	8 9		8 22	8 30	8 39		8 46		8 46		8 50	8 54	8 58	9 4			9 14	9 18		9 30	9 34		9 47	9 51

Week Days—*continued*

	a.m B From Wotton dep. 8 25 a.m. (Table 2)	a.m B	a.m B From Banbury dep. 7 45 a.m.	a.m B	a.m From Birmingham dep. 7 20 a.m.	a.m. B Via Maidenhead	a.m From Nottingham dep. 6 20 a.m. (Table 2) Via Harrow on the Hill	a.m B	a.m B	a.m B	a.m. B Via Maidenhead	a.m B	a.m B E Via Harrow on the Hill	a.m B S Via Harrow on the Hill	a.m B	a.m B		p.m B	p.m B	p.m B S	p.m B	p.m B From Oxford dep. 11 24 a.m.	p.m From Manchester dep. 8 25 a.m. (Table 2) Via Harrow on the Hill Restaurant Car		p.m B	p.m B	p.m B S	p.m B
Aylesbury dep				8 54			9 44						1040	1050		1050					12 5		1 5					1 25
South Aylesbury Halt				8 56												1052												1 27
Little Kimble				9 4												11 0					1214							1 35
Monks Risborough C				9 8												11 4					1218							1 39
Princes Risborough	8 51		9 2	9 12	9 17			9 35	9 51			1051				11 8					1222	1230			1251			1 43
Saunderton	8 58								9 58			1058													1258			
West Wycombe	9 3							9 46	10 3			11 3													1 3			
High Wycombe arr	9 7		9 18					9 51	10 7			11 7										1245			1 7			
High Wycombe dep	9 10					9 35			1010		10 16	1110						1210		1230		1247			1 10		1 30	
Beaconsfield for Penn	9 18								1018			1118						1218		1238					1 18		1 38	
Seer Green B	9 22								1022			1122						1222		1242					1 22		1 42	
Gerrards Cross	9 28								1028			1128						1228		1248					1 28		1 48	
Denham Golf Club Platf'm	9 32								1032			1132						1232		1252					1 32		1 52	
Denham for Harefield	9 35								1035			1135						1235		1255					1 35		1 55	
West Ruislip for Ickenham ¶	9 40	9 50							1040	10 50		1140			1150			1240	1250	1 0		1 8			1 40	1 50	2 0	
Ruislip Gardens ¶		9 53								10 53					1153				1253	1 3						1 53	2 3	
South Ruislip ¶		9 56								10 56					1156				1256	1 6						1 56	2 6	
Northolt Park A		10 0								11 0					12 0				1 0	1 10						2 0	2 10	
Sudbury Hill, Harrow		10 3								11 3					12 3				1 3	1 13						2 3	2 13	
Sudbury and Harrow Road		10 6								11 6					12 6				1 6	1 16						2 6	2 16	
Wembley Hill		1010								11 10					1210				1 10	1 20						2 10	2 20	
Paddington arr					10 5	11 11					11 25											1 35						
Marylebone "	10 3	1025					1050		11 3	11 25		12 3	12 8	1218	1225			1 3	1 25	1 35			1 58		2 3	2 25	2 35	

Through Trains to Paddington or Marylebone except where otherwise shown.

For Notes, see page 180

'Ords' and Locals

An 'Ord' was a GC long distance stopping train which was a standard feature of all of the London Extension timetables until the introduction of the semi-fasts, which really were 'Ords', and often carried a slow train single lamp even though they were technically a semi-fast! An 'Ord' could be made up of any rolling stock that was available with a variety of motive power. They tended to be services that ran in the following pattern:

Marylebone to Woodford
Woodford to Leicester
Leicester to Sheffield

The 'Ords' were smartly timed and connected with the express services. They were also based on getting locomotives out and home from the three main depots of Neasden, Woodford and Sheffield Darnall, Annesley being primarily a freight depot. They were supplemented with stoppers which were grouped into service patterns as follows:

Aylesbury to Calvert, calling at Waddesdon and Quainton Road
Aylesbury to Princes Risborough, High Wycombe and Maidenhead
High Wycombe to Banbury
Banbury to Woodford, calling at Chacombe Road and Eydon Road halts
Rugby to Leicester, all stations
Leicester to Nottingham, all stations
Nottingham-Chesterfield-Sheffield all stations

An examination of the timetable will enlighten the reader further to the service pattern, which was aimed at serving the needs of the local communities for travel to and from work and for shopping — most services having Saturdays only services aimed at shoppers. The majority of local stations survived until 3 March 1963 — but some had closed earlier — when they were shut *en masse*.

Below:
'B1' No 61368 passes Chalfont and Latimer on Sunday, 3 February 1952 with the 9am Woodford Halse to Marylebone 'Ord'. The Metropolitan box can be seen on the left and the Chesham train is in the bay platform on the right. The area is still guarded by Met signals which are just visible above the train and to the right of the signalbox. *Neil Sprinks*

Above:
'D10' No 5436 *Sir Berkely Sheffield* passes Preston Road on an up 'Ord' from Leicester to Marylebone on 7 July 1934.
E. R. Wethersett/Real Photographs

Below:
The 5.22pm Leicester to Woodford Halse 'Ord' is seen getting under way from Rugby Central on Whit Monday, 26 May 1958. A GC regular, No 61008 *Kudu* of Leicester Central, is in charge of a mixed bag of BR and LNER coaches. *Mike Mensing*

Table 2 LONDON, LEICESTER, NOTTINGHAM, SHEFFIELD, HUDDERSFIELD, BRADFORD, MANCHESTER, LIVERPOOL, HULL, CLEETHORPES, YORK, NEWCASTLE, and SCOTLAND

Week Days

Miles	Station	1	2	3	4	5	6	7	8	9	10	11	12	13	14	15	16	17	18	19	20	21	22	23	24	25	26	27
		a.m	a.m	a.m	a.m	a.m	a.m	a.m		a.m	a.m	a.m	a.m	a.m	a.m	a.m	a.m	a.m	a.m	a.m	a.m	a.m	a.m	a.m	a.m	a.m	a.m	p.m
		Except Mondays		Except Mondays		To Nottingham arr. 7 47 a.m.	Saturdays only. Runs 24th June to 9th September inclusive.	Saturdays only. Runs 24th June to 16th September inclusive. TC Kirkby-in-Ashfield to Skegness, arr. 10 23 a.m. (Tables 79 and 70)			TC Leicester to Manchester (Central)	From Woodford Halse depart 5 40 a.m.		Saturdays only. Not after 9th September. TC Leicester to Cleethorpes	TC Leicester to Manchester (London Rd.)	Runs on 10th and 17th June and 9th and 16th September. TC Leicester to Bridlington arr. 12 36 p.m. Filey			Saturdays only. Runs 24th June to 2nd September inclusive. TC Leicester to Bridlington, arr. 12 36 p.m. Filey		Saturdays only	Except Saturdays	TC Derby (Friargate) dep. 9 0 a.m. to Bridlington, arr. 2 8 p.m., Filey arr. 2 43 p.m. Saturdays only. Runs 24th June to 2nd September inclusive.					Saturdays only
	LONDON (M'lebone) . dep	..	1 45	..	..	..	..	..	..	..	..	3 45	..	..	..	..	6 10	..	..	..	..	..	..	..	..	..	7 45	..
27¾	High Wycombe ...... "	..	..	..	..	..	..	..	..	..	..	..	..	..	..	..	7 15	..	..	..	..	..	..	7§15	..	..	..	..
36	Princes Risborough . "	..	..	..	..	..	..	..	..	..	..	..	..	..	..	..	7 35	7 55	..	..	..	..	..	8 25	..	..	..	..
38¾	Ilmer Halt	..	..	..	..	..	..	..	..	..	..	..	..	..	..	..	..	8 0	..	..	..	..	..	..	..	..	..	..
41½	Haddenham (Bucks.)	..	..	..	..	..	..	..	..	..	..	..	..	..	..	..	7 46	8 6	..	..	..	..	..	..	..	..	..	..
46¾	Wotton	..	..	..	..	..	..	..	..	..	..	..	..	..	..	..	7 56	Stop	..	..	..	..	..	..	..	..	..	..
9¼	Harrow on the Hill	..	..	..	..	..	..	..	..	..	..	..	..	..	..	..	Stop	..	..	..	..	..	..	..	..	..	8 7	..
13½	Northwood	..	..	..	..	..	..	..	..	..	..	..	..	..	..	..	..	..	..	..	..	..	..	..	..	..	8 18	..
37¾	Aylesbury	..	..	..	..	..	..	..	..	..	..	5 15	..	..	..	..	..	..	..	..	..	..	..	8 44	..	..	9 25	..
44	Quainton Road	..	..	..	..	..	..	..	..	..	..	..	..	..	..	..	..	..	..	..	..	..	..	Stop	..	..	9 40	..
48¾	Calvert	..	..	..	..	..	..	..	..	..	..	..	..	..	..	..	..	..	..	..	..	..	..	..	..	..	9 50	..
54½	Finmere	..	..	..	..	..	..	..	..	..	..	5U44	..	..	..	..	..	..	..	..	..	..	..	..	..	..	10 2	..
59½	Brackley (Central)	..	..	..	..	..	..	..	..	..	..	5U53	..	..	..	..	..	..	..	..	..	..	..	..	..	..	1013	..
62½	Helmdon, for Sulgrave	..	..	..	..	..	..	..	..	..	..	..	..	..	..	..	..	..	..	..	..	..	..	..	..	..	1021	..
66	Culworth	..	..	..	..	..	..	..	..	..	..	..	..	..	..	..	..	..	..	..	..	..	..	..	..	..	1030	..
69	Woodford Halse ...... arr	..	..	..	..	..	..	..	..	..	..	6 10	..	..	..	..	..	..	..	..	..	..	..	..	..	..	1036	..
—	Woodford Halse .... dep	12 3	..	3 20	..	..	..	..	..	..	..	Stop	..	..	..	..	..	..	..	..	..	..	..	..	..	..	..	..
73	Eydon Road Halt	..	..	..	..	..	..	..	..	..	..	..	..	..	..	..	..	..	..	..	..	..	..	..	..	..	..	..
76¾	Chalcombe Road Halt	..	..	..	..	..	..	..	..	..	..	..	..	..	..	..	..	..	..	..	..	..	..	..	..	..	..	..
80	Banbury .... arr	1221	..	3 38	..	..	..	..	..	..	..	..	..	..	..	..	..	..	..	..	..	..	..	..	..	..	..	..
—	Mls Banbury .... dep	Stop	..	Stop	..	..	..	..	..	..	..	..	..	..	..	..	..	..	..	..	..	8 15	..	..	..	10 4	..	..
—	3¼ Chalcombe Road Halt.	..	..	..	..	..	..	..	..	..	..	..	..	..	..	..	..	..	..	..	..	8x26	..	..	..	1012	..	..
—	7 Eydon Road Halt	..	..	..	..	..	..	..	..	..	..	..	..	..	..	..	..	..	..	..	..	8 33	..	..	..	1020	..	..
—	11 Woodford Halse.... arr	..	..	..	..	..	..	..	..	..	..	..	..	..	..	..	a.m	..	..	..	..	8 42	..	..	..	1028	..	..
—	Woodford Halse ...... dep	..	..	..	..	5 40	..	..	..	..	..	..	..	..	..	..	6 35	..	..	..	..	Stop	..	..	10 0	Stop	1043	..
71½	Charwelton	..	..	..	..	5 46	..	..	..	..	..	..	..	..	..	..	6 41	..	..	..	..	..	..	..	10 6	..	1049	..
78½	Braunston and Willoughby	..	..	..	..	5 57	..	..	..	..	..	..	..	..	..	..	6 52	a.m	..	..	..	..	..	..	1017	..	11 0	..
83½	Rugby (Central)	..	3F43	..	..	6 7	..	..	..	..	..	..	..	..	..	..	7r10	7 35	..	..	..	..	..	..	1026	..	1110	..
90	Lutterworth	..	..	..	..	6 18	..	..	..	..	..	..	..	..	..	..	7 22	7 47	..	..	..	..	..	..	1037	..	1122	..
93¾	Ashby Magna	..	..	..	..	6 26	..	..	..	..	..	..	..	..	..	..	7 30	7 55	..	..	..	..	..	..	1045	..	1130	..
98½	Whetstone	..	..	..	..	6 35	..	..	..	..	..	..	..	..	..	..	7 39	8 4	..	..	..	..	..	..	1054	..	1139	..
103	Leicester (Central) .. arr	..	4 8	..	..	6 45	..	..	..	..	..	a.m	..	..	..	..	7 48	8 12	..	..	..	..	..	a.m	11 2	..	1147	..
	Leicester (Central) .. dep	..	4 14	..	..	..	..	..	..	..	6 48	6 54	..	7 20	7 35	7 45	8 0	..	8 25	..	..	..	..	9 30	1110	..	..	..
105½	Belgrave and Birstall	..	..	..	..	..	..	..	..	..	..	6 59	..	..	..	..	8 5	..	..	..	..	..	..	9 35	1115	..	..	..
108	Rothley	..	..	..	..	..	..	..	..	..	..	7 5	..	..	..	..	8 11	..	..	..	..	..	..	9 41	1121	..	..	..
110¾	Quorn and Woodhouse	..	..	..	..	..	..	..	..	..	7 0	7 11	..	..	..	..	8 17	..	..	..	..	..	..	9 47	1127	..	..	..
113	Loughborough (Central)	..	..	..	..	..	..	..	..	..	7 5	7 17	..	7*36	7 50	8* 1	8 22	..	8*41	..	..	..	..	9 52	1132	..	..	..
117½	East Leake	..	..	..	..	..	..	..	..	..	..	7 28	..	..	..	..	8 30	..	..	..	..	..	..	10 0	1140	..	..	12 10
118½	Rushcliffe Halt	..	..	..	..	..	..	..	..	..	..	..	..	..	..	..	8 33	..	..	..	..	..	..	..	1143	..	..	12*15
122	Ruddington	..	..	..	..	..	..	..	..	..	..	7 37	..	..	8 5	..	8 40	..	..	..	..	..	..	10 9	1150	..	..	12 22
125½	Arkwright Street	..	4†54	..	..	..	..	..	..	..	..	7 44	..	..	8 12	8 21	8 47	..	9 1	..	..	..	..	1016	1157	..	..	12 29
126½	Nottingham (Victoria) arr	..	4 57	a.m.	..	..	..	..	..	..	7 24	7 47	..	7 55	8 15	8 24	8 50	..	9 4	..	..	..	..	1019	12 0	p.m	..	12 32
	Nottingham (Victoria) dep	..	Stop	6 0	6 15	..	..	..	..	..	7 29	..	..	8 0	8 20	8 30	..	..	9 10	9 18	..	..	..	..	..	1210	..	..
128	New Basford	..	..	6 5	6 20	..	..	..	..	..	..	..	..	8 6	..	..	..	..	..	..	..	..	..	..	..	..	..	..
129¾	Bulwell Common	..	..	6 10	6 25	..	7 6	..	..	..	..	..	..	..	8 28	8 39	..	..	..	9 26	..	..	9 50	..	..	1218	..	..
132½	Hucknall (Central)	..	..	6 17	6F35	..	7 13	..	..	..	..	..	..	8 17	8 34	8 46	..	..	..	9 32	..	..	9*58	..	..	1224	..	..
138	Kirkby-in-Ashfield (Cen.)	..	..	..	6 49	..	7 27	7 50	..	..	..	..	..	8 31	..	9 1	..	..	..	9 46	..	..	1013	..	..	1238	..	..
139¾	Sutton-in-Ashfield (Cen.)	..	..	..	6*56	..	7 34	7 57	..	..	..	..	..	8 38	..	9 8	..	..	..	9 51	..	..	1020	..	..	1243	..	..
142¾	Mansfield (E.R.) ... arr	..	..	..	7 1	..	7 39	8 2	..	..	..	..	..	8 43	..	9 13	..	..	..	9 56	..	..	1025	..	..	1248	..	..
	Mansfield (E.R.) ... dep	..	..	..	7 8	..	7 44	8 6	..	..	..	..	..	8 47	..	9 17	..	..	..	9 59	..	..	1030	..	..	..	..	..
149½	Edwinstowe	..	..	..	7 24	..	8*2	8 23	..	..	..	..	..	9*5	..	9*35	..	..	..	10 15	..	..	10*48	..	..	..	..	..
151	Ollerton .... arr	..	..	..	7Y49	..	8 5	8 26	..	..	..	..	..	9 8	..	9 38	..	..	..	10Y33	..	..	1051	..	..	..	..	..
172½	79 Lincoln .... arr	..	..	..	8Y32	..	8 41	..	..	..	..	..	..	9 44	..	..	..	..	..	11Y20	..	..	..	..	..	..	..	..
138¼	Kirkby Bentinck	..	..	6 34	..	..	..	..	..	..	..	..	..	..	8 46	..	..	..	..	..	..	..	..	..	..	..	..	..
143	Tibshelf Town	..	..	6 43	..	..	..	..	..	..	..	..	..	..	8 55	..	..	..	..	..	..	..	..	..	..	..	..	..
		1	2	3	4	5	6	7	8	9	10	11	12	13	14	15	16	17	18	19	20	21	22	23	24	25	26	27

Miles	Station	1	2	3	4	5	6	7	8	9	10	11	12	13	14	15	16	17	18	19	20	21	22	23	24	25	26	27
144½	Pilsley	..	..	6 48	..	..	☞	..	..	..	..	..	..	..	..	..	..	..	..	..	..	..	..	..	..	..	..	..
146¾	Heath	..	..	6 54	..	..		..	..	..	..	..	..	..	9 8	..	..	..	..	..	..	..	..	..	..	..	..	..
151¾	**Chesterfield** (Central) arr	a.m	a.m	7 7	..	..		..	..	..	..	..	..	..	9 16	..	..	..	..	..		a.m	..	..	..	..	..	..
	dep	5 40	6 40	7 9	..	..		..	..	7 55	..	..	8 30	..	9 17	..	..	..	..	..	9 30	9 30	..	..	..	..	..	..
153¾	Sheepbridge **P**	5 44	6 44	7 13	..	..		..	..	..	..	..	8 35	..	..	..	..	..	..	..	9 34	9 34	..	..	..	..	..	..
155¾	Staveley Works **R**	5 49	6 49	7 18	..	..		..	..	..	..	..	8 41	..	..	..	..	..	..	..	9 39	9 39	..	..	..	..	..	..
152¾	**Staveley Town**	5 54	6 54	7 23	..	..	**TC** Basford and Bulwell dep. 7 0 a.m. to Sutton-on-Sea arr. 10 6 a.m. and Mablethorpe arr. 10 14 a.m. (Tables 76, 79, 65, 68 and 71)	..	..	8 4	8 13	..	8*48	..	9 27	..	..	..	..	..	9 44	9 44	..	..	..	..	..	..
154¾	Eckington and Renishaw	..	..	7 28	..	..		..	..	..	..	..	8 54	..	..	..	..	..	..	..	9 49	9 49	..	..	..	..	..	..
156½	Killamarsh	..	..	7 33	..	..		..	..	..	..	..	9 1	..	..	..	..	..	..	..	9 54	9 54	..	..	..	..	..	..
158½	Beighton	..	..	7 38	..	..		..	..	..	..	..	9 7	..	..	..	..	..	..	..	9 59	9 59	..	..	..	..	..	..
159¾	Woodhouse	..	..	7 43	..	..		..	..	..	..	..	9 14	..	9 38	..	..	..	..	..	10 4	10 4	..	..	..	..	..	..
162¾	Darnall, for Handsworth	..	..	7 50	..	..		..	..	..	..	..	9 24	..	..	..	..	..	..	..	10 11	1011	..	..	..	..	..	..
164½	**Sheffield** (Victoria) arr	..	..	7 55	..	..		..	..	..	8 34	..	9 30	..	9 48	..	..	..	..	..	10 16	1016	..	..	..	..	..	..
187½	80 RETFORD arr	..	..	9D0	..	..		..	..	..	9L40	..	**TC** Chesterfield to Blackpool (N), arr. 12 57 p.m. **Saturdays only.**	..	..	1014	..	..	..	..	11 17	1120	1120	..	..	..	..	..
208	80 LINCOLN "	..	..	9J50	..	..		..	..	..	10L29	..		..	11S32	..	..	..	..	..	12 4	12 7	12 4	..	..	..	..	..
232½	80 GRIMSBY TOWN "	..	..	..	10t18	..		..	..	..	..	..		10d55	..	..	..	..	..	..	12 56	1 23	1256	..	..	..	..	..
235¾	80 CLEETHORPES "	..	..	..	10t36	..		..	..	..	..	..		11 5	..	..	..	..	..	..	1 9	1 39	1 9	..	..	..	..	..
170½	80 ROTHERHAM **T** 104 arr	..	..	8 34	..	..		..	..	..	9L37	..			10 12	..	..	..	..	..	11N11	1221	..	..	..	..	..	..
175½	80 DONCASTER (Central) arr	..	..	10y16	..	..		..	..	..	..	..		**Saturdays only.** Not after 9th September	10h41	..	..	..	..	..	11N35	1250	1147	..	..	..	..	..
216½	103 HULL "	..	..	..	..	..		..	..	..	..	..			12f57	..	..	..	..	..	12C38	2 16	2 16	..	..	..	..	..
211¾	104 YORK 1 "	..	..	9 47	..	..		..	..	..	..	..			12H12	..	..	..	..	..	12C50	3H56	..	..	..	..	..	..
231¾	HARROGATE 97 "	..	..	10 59	..	..		..	..	..	..	..			1l18	..	..	..	..	..	1C58	3O25	..	..	..	..	..	..
253¼	SCARBOROUGH (Cen.) "	..	..	10 58	..	..		..	..	..	..	..			2k38	1b25 arr. 1 0 p.m. and Scarborough (Londesborough Road)	..	..	1b25 arr. 1 0 p.m., and Scarborough (Londesborough Road)	..	2C38	6 9	3b 5 and Scarborough (Londesborough Road) (Tables 76, 79, 1, and 103)	..	..	..	..	..
291¾	NEWCASTLE "	..	..	12p17	..	..		..	..	..	..	..			2 56	Runs on 10th and 17th June and 9th and 16th September	..	..	**Saturdays only.** Runs 24th June to 2nd September inclusive	..	2C54	6 30	**Saturdays only.** Runs 24th June to 2nd September inclusive	..	..	..	..	..
416½	EDINBURGH (Wav.) "	..	..	3 41	..	..		..	..	..	..	..			5J54		..	..		..	5C58	..		..	..	..	..	..
463½	GLASGOW (Queen St.) "	..	..	5 2	..	..		..	..	..	..	..			7 15		..	..		..	7C58	..		..	..	..	..	..
475½	DUNDEE (Tay Bridge) "	..	..	6 16	..	..		..	..	..	..	..			8 25		..	..		..	8C25	..		..	..	..	..	..
546¾	ABERDEEN "	..	..	8 25	..	..		..	..	..	..	..			10 23		..	..		..	10C23	..		..	..	..	..	..
177½	80 **Penistone** arr	..	..	8a47	..	..		..	..	..	9 3	..			10a20		..	..		..	11 24	1143		..	..	..	..	..
184¾	80 BARNSLEY **U** 87 arr	..	..	..	..	..		..	..	..	9 47	..			..		..	..		..	12 37	1227		..	..	..	..	..
191	HUDDERSFIELD "	..	..	..	..	..		..	..	..	10 14	..			..		..	..		..	**Sats. only.**	Except Sats.		..	..	..	..	..
201¾	HALIFAX (Old) "	..	..	..	..	..		..	..	..	12 53	..			..		..	..		..				..	..	..	..	..
203¾	BRADFORD (Exch.) "	..	..	..	..	..		..	..	..	11 48	..			..		..	..		..				..	..	..	..	..
193	80 GLOSSOP (Central) arr	..	..	..	..	..		..	..	..	10 23	..		..	11V4		..	..		..				..	..	..	..	..
201	80 **Guide Bridge** arr	..	..	..	..	..		..	..	..	9 46	..		..	11 8		..	..		..	12 10	1219		..	..	..	..	..
202¼	90 ASHTON (Oldham Rd.) arr	..	..	..	..	..		..	..	..	..	..		..	11S46		..	..		..	1 4	..		..	..	..	..	..
203½	89 STALYBRIDGE "	..	..	..	..	..		..	..	..	..	..		..	..		..	..		..	12 36	..		..	..	..	..	..
206¼	90 OLDHAM (Clegg St.) "	..	..	..	..	..		..	..	..	..	..		..	11S55		..	..		..	1 15	..		..	..	..	..	..
206	80 **Manchester** (L.Rd) arr	..	..	..	..	..		..	..	..	..	..	..	..	11 20		..	..		..	..	..		..	..	..	..	..
212¼	80 " (Central) "	..	..	..	..	..		..	..	..	10 14	..	..	..	..		..	..		..	12 32	1240		..	..	..	..	..
203¼	80 STOCKPORT (Tiv. Dale) arr		..	..	..	..	..	..	..	..	..	..	..	..	..		..	..		..	..	..		..	..	..	..	..
222½	80 WARRINGTON (Cen.) "		..	..	..	..	..	..	..	..	10 51	..	..	..	12K51		..	..		..	1 11	1 11		..	..	..	..	..
241	80 LIVERPOOL (Cen.) "			..	..	..	..	..	..	..	11 22	..	..	..	1K22		..	..		..	1 45	1 45		..	..	..	..	..

A For particulars of London Suburban Services, see Table 13
a a.m.
b Londesborough Road
C Via Doncaster. Runs 17th June to 2nd September inclusive
D Change at Woodhouse
d Grimsby Docks
E Except Saturdays
F Arr. 5 minutes *earlier*
f Arr. 1 1 on Wednesdays and 12 38 p.m on Saturdays
H Via Doncaster
h Arr. 3 minutes later on Saturdays
J 4 mins. later on Saturdays
K Via Manchester (Lon. Rd) and (Central). Passengers cross town at own expense
k Arr. 1 55 p.m. on Sats. until 16th September
L Saturdays only. Not after 16th September
l 5 mins. *earlier* on Sats.
N Arr. Rotherham 12 21, Doncaster 12 50, and Hull 2 16 p.m. on 10th June. On 16th and 23rd September arr. Rotherham 12 6, Doncaster 12 30, and Hull 2 16 p.m.
O Via Doncaster. Arr. 345 p.m on Mons. and Fris.
P Sheepbridge & Brimington
p p.m.
R Station for Barrow Hill
r Arr. 10 mins. *earlier*
S Saturdays only
T Rotherham and Masboro'
t Via Lincoln and Market Rasen
TC Through Carriages
U Barnsley (Court House)
U Calls to set down only
V Change at Dinting
Y Change at Edwinstowe
y Via Retford
z Arr. 4 minutes *earlier*
* Arr. 3 mins. *earlier*
† Arr. 4 42 a.m.
§ Change at Princes Risboro'
3 Third class only

Above left and top:
Extract from ER timetable 5 June to 24 September 1950 showing main line local and long-distance stoppers.

Left:
'V2' No 60879 climbs through the Chilterns up to Dutchlands summit, between Wendover and Great Missenden, with the 6.20am from Nottingham 'Ord' for Marylebone, June 1957. *G. C. Farnell*

Above:
GC 'D11' 'Large Directors' were still regular performers on the London Extension, especially on local services, in the late 1950s and early 1960s. A Sheffield to Nottingham local calls at Bulwell Common with No 62667 *Somme* at the head on 8 June 1957. An evening local from Sheffield to Leicester, that ran up until 1963, was nearly always 'Director'-hauled and known as the 'Spitfire' due to its fast turnaround in Leicester. *J. P. Wilson/Rail Archive Stephenson*

Above:
A 'B17' in BR green livery, No 61662 *Manchester United*, calls at Nottingham Arkwright Street with a local for Leicester in the mid-1950s. *T. G. Hepburn/ Rail Archive Stephenson*

Left:
A scene that can still be viewed today on the preserved line (although the train is different) as the 9.55am local from Rugby to Nottingham arrives at Rothley on 24 July 1961, hauled by 'L1' tank No 67747. *Mike Mitchell*

Above right:
A long distance 'Ord' hauled by 'D10' 'Director' No 5437 *Prince George* passes over Charwelton water troughs *circa* 1926. Charwelton station is in the background beyond the bridge. Behind the locomotive appears to be an officers' saloon, with Gresley bogies — can anyone shed further light on this vehicle? *H. Gordon Tidey/ Rail Archive Stephenson*

Right:
The 5.25pm local service for Calvert leaves Aylesbury behind Ivatt Class 4 2-6-0 No 43127 on 6 May 1953. This train would stop at Waddesdon and Quainton Road. *Neil Sprinks*

LEICESTER CENTRAL—NOTTINGHAM VICTORIA

WEEKDAYS

		MX am	MX am	am	am	am	am	am	am	am	pm	SX pm
LEICESTER CENTRAL	dep.	12 48	1 15	6 45	6 50	7 30	8 00	9 30	10 35	11 12	1 00	3 10
Belgrave & Birstall		....	....	....	6 55	....	8 5	9 35	10 40	....	1 05	....
Rothley		.	.	.	7 01	.	8 11	9 41	10 46	.	1 11	.
Quorn & Woodhouse		....	....	6 57	7 7	7 42	8 17	9 47	10 52	....	1 17	....
Loughborough Central		1 05	1 31	7 02	7 16	7 47	8 23	9 52	10 58	11 26	1 22	3 24
East Leake					7 24	7 55	8 31	10 00	11 06		1 30	
Rushcliffe Halt		.	.	7 10	7 27	.	8 34	10 03	11 09	.	1 33	.
Ruddington		....	....	....	7 34	8 04	8 41	10 10	11 16	....	1 40	....
Arkwright Street		.	.	7 22	7 41	8 11	8 48	10 17	.	.	1N46	.
NOTTINGHAM VICTORIA	arr.	1 23	1 49	7 26	7 44	8 14	8 51	10 20	11 23	11 43	1 50	3 41

		SO pm	pm	pm	SX pm	pm	pm	SO pm		pm	pm	pm
LEICESTER CENTRAL	dep.	2 58	4 4	5 15	5 45	6 15	7 11	7 15	.	8 30	10 15	10 48
Belgrave & Birstall		....	....	5 20	....	6 20	....	7 20	....	8 35	10 20	....
Rothley		.	.	5 26	.	6 26	.	7 26	.	8 41	10 26	.
Quorn & Woodhouse			....	5 32	....	6 32	....	7 32	....	8 47	...	....
Loughborough Central		3 12	4 19	5 39	6 00	6 38	7 25	7 37	.	8 52	10 35	11 04
East Leake				5 47	...	6 46	....	....	....	....	....	.
Rushcliffe Halt		.	.	5 50	.	6 49	.	.	.	.	.	....
Ruddington		....	...	5 57	...	6 56	....	....	....	....	....	....
Arkwright Street		.	.	6 04	.	7 03	.	.	.	.	.	.
NOTTINGHAM VICTORIA	arr.	3 29	4 36	6 07	6 18	7 07	7 42	7 55	...	9 10	10 53	11 22

SUNDAYS

		am	am	am	am	pm	pm	pm	pm	pm
LEICESTER CENTRAL	dep.	1 09	1 42	3 25	8 25	12 22	3 25	6 25	...	10 36
Belgrave & Birstall		....	....	....	....	....	....	....	....	....
Rothley		.	.	.	.	.	.	.	.	.
Quorn & Woodhouse		....	....	....	....	....	....	....	....	....
Loughborough Central		1 23	1 59	.	8 40	12 36	3 40	6 39	...	10 50
East Leake		....	....	....	....	....	....	....	....	....
Rushcliffe Halt		.	.	.	.	.	.	.	.	.
Ruddington		....	....	....	....	....	....	....	....	....
Arkwright Street		...	...	...	...	...	...	...	...	...
NOTTINGHAM VICTORIA	arr.	1 40	2 17	3 55	8 58	12 55	3 58	6 56	...	11 07

NOTTINGHAM VICTORIA—LEICESTER CENTRAL

WEEKDAYS

		MX am	MX am	SO am	SX am	am	am	am	am	am	am	pm	pm	pm
NOTTINGHAM VICTORIA	dep.	1 30	2 12	5 50	6 25	7 40	8 00	8 45	.	9 20	.	.	12 25	12 45
Arkwright Street		....	....	5 53	6 28	7 43	8 03	....	....	9 23	....	....	....	....
Ruddington		.	.	6 0	6 35	7 50	8 10	.	.	9 30	.	.	.	.
Rushcliffe Halt		....	....	6 6	6 41	7 56	8 16	....	....	9 36	....	....	....	....
East Leake				6 11	6 46	8 01	8 21	.	.	9 41	.	.	.	.
Loughborough Central		1 50	....	6 21	6 56	8 11	8 30	9 3	....	9 50	....	....	12 43	1 4
Quorn & Woodhouse		.	.	6 26	7 01	8 16	8 35	.	.	9 55	.	.	.	.
Rothley		....	....	6 32	7 07	8 22	8 41	....	....	10 01	....	....	....	....
Belgrave & Birstall		.	.	6 38	7 13	8 28	8 47	.	.	10 07	.	.	.	.
LEICESTER CENTRAL	arr.	2 03	2 41	6 42	7 17	8 32	8 51	9 04	....	10 11	....	....	12 54	1 15

		pm	pm	pm	pm	pm	p.m.		pm	pm	pm		pm
NOTTINGHAM VICTORIA	dep.	1 25	3 50	4 15	5 20	5 30	6 12	...	7 55	8 45	10 19	...	10 55
Arkwright Street		....	....	4 18	....	5 33	6 15	...	7 58	....	....	...	....
Ruddington		1 32	3 57	4 25	.	5 40	6 22	....	.	.	.	...	.
Rushcliffe Halt		1 38	4 03	4 31	....	5 46	6 28	....	....	....	....	....	....
East Leake		1 43	4 08	4 36		5 51	6 33	...	.	.	.	.	.
Loughborough Central		1 53	4 18	4 46	5 38	6 01	6 43	...	8 20	9 05	10 40	...	11 16
Quorn & Woodhouse		1 58	4 23	4 51	.	6 06	6 48	...	8 25	9 10	.	.	.
Rothley		2 04	4 29	4 57	....	6 12	6 54	...	....	9 16	....	....	....
Belgrave & Birstall		2 10	4 35	5 03	.	6 18	7 00	...	8 35	9 22	.	.	.
LEICESTER CENTRAL	arr.	2 14	4 39	5 07	5 49	6 22	7 04	...	8 39	9 26	10 53	...	11 29

SUNDAYS

		am	am	am	am	pm	pm	pm	pm
NOTTINGHAM VICTORIA	dep.	1 30	1 50	10 10	...	1 25	5 35	6 15	7 50
Arkwright Street		....	....	....	....	....	....	....	....
Ruddington		.	.	.	.	.	.	.	.
Rushcliffe Halt		....	...	....	....	....	....	....	....
East Leake		...	....	...	...	...	...	...	...
Loughborough Central		1 50	....	10 29	...	1 44	5 55	6 34	8 10
Quorn & Woodhouse		.	.	.	.	.	.	.	.
Rothley		....	....	....	....	....	....	....	....
Belgrave & Birstall		...	...	...	...	...	...	...	...
LEICESTER CENTRAL	arr.	2 03	2 20	10 40	....	1 55	6 08	6 45	8 23

MX—Mondays excepted. **N**—Calls to set down only. **SX**—Saturdays excepted. **SO**—Saturdays only

These services are subject to alteration.

Above and above right:
Local services — the last one — Leicester to Nottingham and fares leaflet — 10 September 1962 to 16 June 1963.

Left:
The 'Banbury Motor' has arrived at Woodford Halse in April 1961 with one of Woodford 'L1s', No 67771 at the head. This service connected with GC main line trains and gave valuable connections to the Western at Banbury. It suffered the ignominy of being replaced by a bus for the last six months of the line's existence. *G. C. Farnell*

Right:
Another local service ran to Banbury from High Wycombe via Princes Risborough. This was usually a GW auto train and in this case it is propelled by a Banbury '54XX' Pannier, No 5417 as it calls at the remote Ilmer Halt between Princes Risborough and Haddenham in August 1960.
G. C. Farnell

SPECIAL CHEAP DAY RETURN TICKETS

DAILY BY ANY TRAIN

TO AND FROM	SECOND CLASS—SUBJECT TO ALTERATION									
	Nottingham Victoria	Nottingham Arkwright Street	Ruddington	Rushcliffe Halt	East Leake	Loughborough Central	Quorn and Woodhouse	Rothley	Belgrave and Birstall	Leicester Central
	s. d.	s. d.	s. d.	s. d.	s. d.	s. d.	s. d.	s. d.	s. d.	s. d.
NOTTINGHAM VICTORIA	—	-/6	2/-	2/5	2/7	3/10	3/10	4/3	4/7	4/10
NOTTINGHAM ARKWRIGHT STREET	-/6	—	1/6	2/1	2/5	3/4	3/8	4/3	4/7	4/10
RUDDINGTON	2/-	1/6	—	1/3	1/8	3/-	3/4	3/8	4/-	4/5
RUSHCLIFFE HALT	2/5	2/1	1/3	—	-/6	1/9	2/6	3/4	3/10	4/3
EAST LEAKE	2/7	2/5	1/8	-/6	—	1/4	1/10	2/7	3/4	3/10
LOUGHBOROUGH CENTRAL	3/10	3/4	3/-	1/9	1/4	—	1/2	1/10	2/7	3/4
QUORN AND WOODHOUSE	3/10	3/8	3/4	2/6	1/10	1/2	—	1/3	1/10	2/6
ROTHLEY	4/3	4/3	3/8	3/4	2/7	1/10	1/3	—	1/3	1/9
BELGRAVE AND BIRSTALL	4/7	4/7	4/-	3/10	3/4	2/7	1/10	1/3	—	1/1
LEICESTER CENTRAL	4/10	4/10	4/5	4/3	3/10	3/4	2/6	1/9	1/1	—

First Class Fares 50 per cent. more

Tickets between Nottingham, Loughborough and Leicester are available either route

Nottingham Suburban

GC suburban services originally centred on the main line itself from Nottingham to Chesterfield and Sheffield and south to Leicester. However, the GN was the joint sponsor of Nottingham Victoria and their services continued through LNER days up to the early and mid-1960s and thus can be seen as a feature on the London Extension. The GN lines to Nottingham originally terminated at London Road station. They operated lines to Grantham, Leicester Belgrave Road, and even LNWR services from Northampton via Market Harborough terminated there. The Nottingham suburban line services via Daybrook also terminated there as did the Derby and Stafford service. From the opening of Nottingham Victoria station virtually all these services were transferred although the Northampton service lasted until 1944 when it was transferred into Victoria. London Road Low Level did stay open for excursions to the east coast into the 1950s, but the area was still served by the new London Road High Level station opened at the same time as Nottingham Victoria. To the north of Nottingham Victoria, at Bagthorpe Junction, the Derby to Grantham line was crossed by the GC main line. Here, a fly-under junction was constructed to allow access to Nottingham Victoria and the Grantham line was then accessed again via Weekday Cross Junction and London Road High Level. The GN's branch service to Pinxton was also served by this route. All these services had ended by mid-1963, being diverted through the Midland station or withdrawn altogether. Only the Nottingham to Grantham service remained until it was re-routed into Nottingham Midland in 1967.

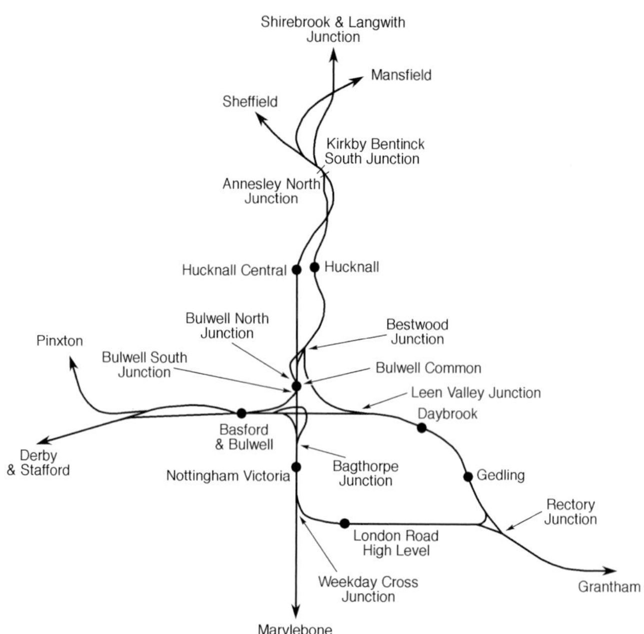

Table 210

Table 210—continued

GRANTHAM TO NOTTINGHAM AND DERBY

Miles	WEEKDAYS		a.m.	a.m.	a.m.	a.m.	a.m.	a.m.	a.m.	a.m.
0	GRANTHAM	dep.	...	5 4	...	6 34	7 20	7 42	...	9 5
7¼	Bottesford		...	5 14	...	6 45	7 31	7 53	...	9 16
10	Elton & Orston		...	...	...	6 50	7 36	7 58	...	9 20
11¾	Aslockton		...	5 21	...	6 54	7 40	8 2	...	9 24
14	Bingham		...	5 25	...	6 58	7 45	8 6	...	9 28
17¾	Radcliffe-on-Trent		...	5 31	...	7 5	7 51	8 13	...	9 34
19¾	Netherfield & Colwick		...	5 39	...	7 13	8 0	8 21	...	9 42
22¼	NOTTINGHAM London Road	arr.	...	5 45	...	7 20	8 6	8 28	...	9 48
	NOTTINGHAM High Level	dep.	...	5 46	...	7 20	8 7	8 28	...	9 48
23¼	NOTTINGHAM Victoria	arr.	...	5 49	...	7 22	8 9	8 30	...	9 51
	NOTTINGHAM Victoria	dep.	5 30	6 15	6 30	7 35	8 20	...	9 30	...
25	New Basford (A)		...	...	6 35	...	...	...	...	...
26¼	Basford North		5 38	6 23	6 41	7 43	8 28	...	9 38	...
29¼	Kimberley East	arr.	5 44	6 30	6 47	7 49	8 34	...	9 44	...
—	Kimberley East	dep.	5 45	...	6 48	...	...	...	...	...
31¾	Newthorpe		5 50	...	6 53	...	...	...	...	...
32¾	Eastwood & Langley Mill		5k58	...	6e58	...	...	...	...	...
35¾	Jacksdale		6g 8	...	7 6	...	...	...	...	...
36¼	Pye Hill & Somercotes		6 11	...	7 9	...	...	...	...	...
38	PINXTON South	arr.	6 14	...	7 12	...	...	...	...	...
—	Kimberley East	dep.	...	6 30	...	7 50	8 36	...	9 45	...
30¾	Awsworth		...	6 34	...	7 54	8 40	...	9 49	...
32¼	Ilkeston North	arr.	...	6 36	...	7 57	8 43	...	9 52	...
	Ilkeston North	dep.	...	6 38	...	7 58	8 44	...	9 53	...
35	West Hallam		...	6 43	...	8 3	8 49	...	9 58	...
41	DERBY Friargate	arr.	...	6 53	...	8 14	9 0	...	10 9	...

WEEKDAYS—continued		a.m.	a.m.	SX p.m.	SO p.m.	p.m.	a.m.	SO p.m.	SO p.m.	p.m.	p.m.	p.m.
GRANTHAM	dep.	10 0	10 35	...	...	...	11 57	...	12 36	12 58	...	1 34
Bottesford		10 12	10 46	...	...	...	12 8	...	12 47	1 9	...	1 47
Elton & Orston		10 17	10 51	...	...	...	12 13	...	...	1 14	...	1 52
Aslockton		10 21	10 55	...	...	...	12 17	...	...	1 18	...	1 56
Bingham		10 26	11 0	...	...	...	12 21	...	...	1 22	...	2 0
Radcliffe-on-Trent		10 33	11 6	...	...	...	12 28	...	...	1 29	...	2 7
Netherfield & Colwick		10 41	11e18	...	...	...	12 36	...	...	1 37	...	2 15
NOTTINGHAM London Road	arr.	10 48	11 25	...	...	...	12 43	...	1 13	1 44	...	2 22
NOTTINGHAM High Level	dep.	10 48	11 25	...	...	...	12 43	...	1 13	1 44	...	2 22
NOTTINGHAM Victoria	arr.	10 50	11 27	...	...	...	12 45	...	1 16	1 46	...	2 24
NOTTINGHAM Victoria	dep.	...	...	12 5	12 5	12 15	12 55	1 15	...	...	2 5	...
New Basford (A)		...	...	...	12 10	12 20	1 0	1 20	...	...	2 10	...
Basford North		...	...	12 13	12 15	12 25	1 5	1 25	...	...	2 15	...
Kimberley East	arr.	...	...	12 19	12 21	12 31	1 11	1 31	...	...	2 21	...
Kimberley East	dep.	...	...	...	...	12 32	...	1 32	...	...	...	...
Newthorpe		...	...	...	...	12 37	...	1 37	...	...	...	...
Eastwood & Langley Mill		...	...	...	...	12 41	...	1 40	...	...	...	...
Jacksdale		...	...	...	...	12 48	...	1 47	...	...	...	...
Pye Hill & Somercotes		...	...	...	...	12 52	...	1 50	...	...	...	...
PINXTON South	arr.	...	...	...	...	12 55	...	1 53	...	...	...	...
Kimberley East	dep.	...	...	12 20	12 22	...	1 12	...	...	...	2 22	...
Awsworth		...	...	12 24	12 26	...	1 16	...	...	...	2 26	...
Ilkeston North	arr.	...	...	12 27	12 29	...	1 19	...	...	...	2 29	...
Ilkeston North	dep.	...	...	12 28	12 30	...	1 20	...	...	...	2 30	...
West Hallam		...	...	12 33	12 35	...	1 25	...	...	...	2 35	...
DERBY Friargate	arr.	...	...	12 44	12 46	...	1 36	...	...	...	2 46	...

WEEKDAYS—continued		p.m.	p.m.	p.m.	p.m.	p.m.	p.m.	p.m.	p.m.	SX p.m.	SO p.m.
GRANTHAM	dep.	3 0	...	4 18	...	5 30	6 15	7 30	8 0	8 59	8 59
Bottesford		3 13	...	4 29	...	5 41	6 26	7 41	8 11	9 10	9 10
Elton & Orston		3 18	...	4 34	...	5 46	6 31	...	...	9 15	9 15
Aslockton		3 22	...	4 38	...	5 50	6 35	7 48	8 18	9 19	9 19
Bingham		3 26	...	4 42	5 19	5 54	6 39	7 53	8 23	9 23	9 23
Radcliffe-on-Trent		3 33	...	4 49	5 25	6 1	6 46	7 59	8 29	9 30	9 30
Netherfield & Colwick		3 41	...	4 57	5 34	6 10	6 54	8 8	8 38	9 38	9 38
NOTTINGHAM London Road	arr.	3 48	...	5 4	5 40	6 16	7 1	8 14	8 44	9 45	9 45
NOTTINGHAM High Level	dep.	3 48	...	5 4	5 41	6 17	7 1	8 15	8 45	9 45	9 45
NOTTINGHAM Victoria	arr.	3 50	...	5 6	5 43	6 20	7 3	8 17	8 47	9 47	9 47
NOTTINGHAM Victoria	dep.	4 0	4 15	5 18	5 50	6 25	...	8 23	...	10 5	10 30
New Basford (A)		4 5	4 20	5 23	5 55	6 30	...	...	...	...	...
Basford North		4 10	4 25	5 28	6 0	6 35	...	8 31	...	10 13	10 38
Kimberley East	arr.	4 16	4 31	5 34	6 6	6 41	...	8 37	...	10 19	10 44
Kimberley East	dep.	...	4 32	...	6 7	...	...	...	...	...	...
Newthorpe		...	4 37	...	6 12	...	...	...	...	...	...
Eastwood & Langley Mill		...	4 41	...	6 16	...	...	...	...	...	...
Jacksdale		...	4 49	...	6 24	...	...	...	...	...	...
Pye Hill & Somercotes		...	4k57	...	6 27	...	...	...	...	...	...
PINXTON South	arr.	...	5 0	...	6 30	...	...	...	...	...	...
Kimberley East	dep.	4 17	...	5 35	...	6 42	...	8 38	...	10 20	10 45
Awsworth		4 21	...	5 39	...	6 46	...	8 42	...	...	10 49
Ilkeston North	arr.	4 24	...	5 42	...	6 49	...	8 45	...	10 26	10 52
Ilkeston North	dep.	4 25	...	5 43	...	6 50	...	8 46	...	10 27	10 53
West Hallam		4 30	...	5 48	...	6 55	...	8 51	...	10 32	10 58
DERBY Friargate	arr.	4 41	...	5 59	...	7 6	...	9 2	...	10 43	11 9

For notes see page 471

Table 210

Table 210—continued

GRANTHAM TO NOTTINGHAM AND DERBY

		WEEKDAYS—continued p.m.	WEEKDAYS—continued p.m.	SUNDAYS a.m.	SUNDAYS a.m.	SUNDAYS a.m.	SUNDAYS p.m.	SUNDAYS p.m.	SUNDAYS p.m.
GRANTHAM	dep.	9 50	11 14	7 42	...	10 50	1 20	2 5	4 5
Bottesford		10 1	11 25	...	...	...	...	...	...
Elton & Orston		...	...	...	...	...	...	...	...
Aslockton		10 9	11 32	7 59	...	11 7	1 37	2 22	4 22
Bingham		10 14	11 37	8 3	...	11 11	1 41	2 26	4 26
Radcliffe-on-Trent		10 21	11 44	8 9	...	11 17	1 47	2 32	4 32
Netherfield & Colwick		10 30	11 53	8 17	...	11 25	1 55	2 40	4 40
NOTTINGHAM London Road	arr.	10 36	...	...	...	...	...	...	...
NOTTINGHAM High Level	dep.	10 37	...	...	...	...	...	...	...
NOTTINGHAM Victoria	arr.	10 39	12 1	8 24	...	11 32	2 2	2 47	4 47
NOTTINGHAM Victoria	dep.	...	...	...	9 15	11 35	...	2 50	...
New Basford (A)		...	...	...	...	...	...	...	...
Basford North		...	...	...	...	...	...	...	...
Kimberley East	arr.	...	...	...	9 28	11 48	...	3 3	...
Kimberley East	dep.	...	...	...	...	...	...	...	...
Newthorpe		...	...	...	...	...	...	...	...
Eastwood & Langley Mill		...	...	...	...	...	...	...	...
Jacksdale		...	...	...	...	...	...	...	...
Pye Hill & Somercotes		...	...	...	...	...	...	...	...
PINXTON South	arr.	...	...	...	...	...	...	...	...
Kimberley East	dep.	...	...	...	9 28	11 48	...	3 3	...
Awsworth		...	...	...	...	...	...	...	...
Ilkeston North	arr.	...	...	...	9 32	11 52	...	3 7	...
Ilkeston North	dep.	...	...	...	9 32	11 52	...	3 7	...
West Hallam		...	...	...	...	...	...	...	...
DERBY Friargate	arr.	...	...	...	9 45	12 5	...	3 20	...

SUNDAYS—continued		p.m.	p.m.	p.m.
GRANTHAM	dep.	6 39	8 30	9 45
Bottesford		...	...	...
Elton & Orston		...	...	...
Aslockton		6 56	8 47	10 2
Bingham		7 0	8 51	10 6
Radcliffe-on-Trent		7 6	8 57	...
Netherfield & Colwick		7 14	9 5	10 20
NOTTINGHAM London Road	arr.	...	...	...
NOTTINGHAM High Level	dep.	...	...	...
NOTTINGHAM Victoria	arr.	7 21	9 12	10 27
NOTTINGHAM Victoria	dep.	...	9 15	...
New Basford (A)		...	...	...
Basford North		...	...	...
Kimberley East	arr.	...	9 28	...
Kimberley East	dep.	...	...	...
Newthorpe		...	...	...
Eastwood & Langley Mill		...	...	...
Jacksdale		...	...	...
Pye Hill & Somercotes		...	...	...
PINXTON South	arr.	...	...	...
Kimberley East	dep.	...	9 28	...
Awsworth		...	...	...
Ilkeston North	arr.	...	9 32	...
Ilkeston North	dep.	...	9 32	...
West Hallam		...	...	...
DERBY Friargate	arr.	...	9 45	...

A—For other trains between Nottingham Victoria and New Basford see Table 183.

SO—Saturdays only.

SX—Saturdays excepted.

a—a.m.
e—Arrives 3 minutes earlier.
g—Arrives 4 minutes earlier.
k—Arrives 6 minutes earlier
p—p.m

The train service between Basford North and Nottingham London Road High Level via Daybrook and Gedling & Carlton is suspended.

RAILHEAD DISTRIBUTION SCHEME

This Scheme, available at certain selected stations, gives speedier deliveries to traders in small towns and isolated villages.

Orders are bulked to the Railhead Station, securing the advantage of truckload rates and through loading.

Empties are collected and credit notes issued, and goods unpacked by arrangement.

Left:
The Grantham service was still routed into Nottingham Victoria in 1966 despite the Derby service having been withdrawn three years before this. The 15.10 (SO) service to Grantham waits to leave on 16 July 1966. The service was now formed exclusively of the then new DMUs, this one a Derby Lightweight variant, No E56018. *William P. Power*

Right:
Nottingham Victoria saw a cross-country route — the GN's Grantham to Derby Friargate and Stafford line — cross the GC, as well as being a local point for services from around the Nottingham area. Services had now been concentrated on the Midland routes and some had gone altogether. It is only more recently that the Midland Mansfield & Worksop line has reopened passing close to the GC formation for parts of its route near Annesley. A Grantham to Derby service is seen at Nottingham Victoria on 18 August 1960 with 'K2' No 61756 at the head. *G. D. King*

Above and overleaf:
Local service — Nottingham to Derby 11 September 1961 to 17 June 1962.

Table 210

Table 210—

DERBY AND NOTTINGHAM TO GRANTHAM

	Miles	Miles	WEEKDAYS a.m.	a.m.	a.m.	a.m.	a.m.	a.m.	a.m.	a.m.
DERBY Friargate dep.	0	—		5 35				7 15		
West Hallam	6	—						7 26		
Ilkeston North arr.	8¾	—		5 51				7 31		
Ilkeston North dep.				5 52				7 32		
Awsworth	10½	—						7 35		
Kimberley East arr.	11½	—		5 59				7 38		
PINXTON South dep.	—	0					6 50		7 45	
Pye Hill & Somercotes	—	1½					6 53		7 48	
Jacksdale	—	2½					6 56		7 51	
Eastwood & Langley Mill	—	5½					7 4		7 59	
Newthorpe	—	6½					7 7		8 2	
Kimberley East arr.	—	8½					7 13		8 8	
Kimberley East dep.	—	—		6 0			7 14	7 38	8 9	
Basford North	14¾	—		6 7			7 21	7 43	8 16	
New Basford (A)	16	—		6 12			7 26	7 48	8 21	
NOTTINGHAM Victoria (A) arr.				6 16			7 31	7 53	8 25	
NOTTINGHAM Victoria dep.	17¾	—	5 30	6 20	6 55	7 30				8 50
NOTTINGHAM London Road High Level arr.	18¼	—	5 32	6 22	6 57	7 32				8 53
NOTTINGHAM London Road High Level dep.			5 33	6 25	6 59	7 32				8 53
Netherfield & Colwick	21¼	—	5 39	6 30	7 5	7 38				8 58
Radcliffe-on-Trent	23½	—	5 43	6 35	7 10	7 42				9 3
Bingham	27	—	5 50	6 42	7 17	7 49				9 9
Aslockton	29½	—	5 54	6 46	7 21					9 14
Elton & Orston	31	—		6 50	7 25					9 18
Bottesford	33½	—	6 2	6 56	7 30	7 59				9 23
GRANTHAM arr.	41	—	6 16	7 11	7 46	8 15				9 37

WEEKDAYS—*continued*	SO a.m.	SX a.m.	a.m.	a.m.	SX a.m.	SO a.m.	SO p.m.	p.m.	SO p.m.	SX p.m.	p.m.	p.m.
DERBY Friargate dep.	8 25	8 25	9 35		10 30	10 30	12 3			12 55		1 20
West Hallam	8 37	8 37	9 47		10 42	10 42	12 17			1 7		1 32
Ilkeston North arr.	8 42	8 42	9 52		10 47	10 47	12 22			1 12		1 37
Ilkeston North dep.	8 43	8 43	9 53		10 48	10 48	12 23			1 13		1 38
Awsworth	8 47	8 47	9 57		10 52	10 52	12 27			1 17		1 42
Kimberley East arr.	8 51	8 51	10 1		10 56	10 56	12 31			1 21		1 46
PINXTON South dep.											1 12	
Pye Hill & Somercotes											1 17	
Jacksdale											1 20	
Eastwood & Langley Mill											1e30	
Newthorpe											1 33	
Kimberley East arr.											1 39	
Kimberley East dep.	8 52	8 52	10 2		10 57	10 57	12 32			1 22	1 40	1 47
Basford North	8 59	8 59	10 9		11 4	11 4	12 39			1 29	1 47	1 54
New Basford (A)							12 44			1 34	1 52	1 59
NOTTINGHAM Victoria (A) arr.	9 7	9 7	10 17		11 12	11 12	12 48			1 38	1 56	2 3
NOTTINGHAM Victoria dep.	9 20	9 20		10 25	11 30	11 30		12 55	1 35			2 10
NOTTINGHAM London Road High Level arr.	9 22	9 22		10 28	11 32	11 32		12 57	1 37			2 12
NOTTINGHAM London Road High Level dep.	9 22	9 22		10 28	11 33	11 33		12 57	1 37			2 12
Netherfield & Colwick	9 28	9g32		10 33	11 38	11 38		1 3	1 43			2 18
Radcliffe-on-Trent	9 32	9 36		10 37	11 43	11 43		1 7	1 47			2 22
Bingham	9 39	9 43		10 43	11 49	11 49		1 14	1 54			2 29
Aslockton	9 43	9 47		10 47		11 53		1 18	1 58			2 33
Elton & Orston	9 47	9 51		10 51				1 22				2 37
Bottesford	9 53	9 57		10 56				1 27	2 6			2 43
GRANTHAM arr.	10 11	10 13		11 11	12 14	12 16		1 43	2 21			2 58

WEEKDAYS—*continued*	SO p.m.	p.m.	p.m.	SO p.m.	SX p.m.	p.m.	p.m.	p.m.	p.m.	p.m.	p.m.	p.m.	p.m.
DERBY Friargate dep.				4 12	4 12			5 25		6 5			
West Hallam				4 24	4 24			5 37		6 17			
Ilkeston North arr.				4 29	4 29			5 42		6 22			
Ilkeston North dep.				4 31	4 31			5 43		6 23			
Awsworth				4 35	4 35			5 47		6 27			
Kimberley East arr.				4 39	4 39			5 51		6 31			
PINXTON South dep.	2 5						5 12					6 55	
Pye Hill & Somercotes	2 8						5 16					7 0	
Jacksdale	2 11						5 19					7 3	
Eastwood & Langley Mill	2 19						5e29					7g14	
Newthorpe	2 22						5 32					7 17	
Kimberley East arr.	2 28						5 38					7 23	
Kimberley East dep.	2 29			4 41	4 41		5 39	5 52		6 32		7 25	
Basford North	2 36			4 48	4 48		5 46	5 59		6 39		7 33	
New Basford (A)	2 41			4 53	4 53		5 51	6 4		6 44		7 38	
NOTTINGHAM Victoria (A) arr.	2 45			4 57	4 57		5 55	6 8		6 48		7 42	
NOTTINGHAM Victoria dep.		4 5	4 35	5 0	5 10	5 40			6 15		7 20		8 25
NOTTINGHAM London Road High Level arr.		4 7	4 37	5 2	5 12	5 42			6 17		7 22		8 27
NOTTINGHAM London Road High Level dep.		4 7	4 38	5 3	5 13	5-43			6 17		7 22		8 27
Netherfield & Colwick		4 13	4 43	5 8	5 18	5 48			6 23		7 28		8 33
Radcliffe-on-Trent		4 17	4 48	5 13	5 23	5 53			6 27		7 32		8 37
Bingham		4 25	4 54	5 20	5 30	5 59			6 34		7 39		8 44
Aslockton		4 29		5 24	5 34	6 3			6 38		7 43		8 48
Elton & Orston		4 33		5 29	5 39	6 7			6 42		7 47		8 52
Bottesford		4 39		5 35	5 45	6 13			6 48		7 53		8 58
GRANTHAM arr.		4 55		5 50	6 0	6 28			7 3		8 8		9 13

Table 210

Table 210
continued

DERBY AND NOTTINGHAM TO GRANTHAM

	WEEKDAYS—*continued* p.m.	p.m.	SX p.m.	SO p.m.	SUNDAYS a.m.	a.m.	p.m.	p.m.	p.m.	p.m.
DERBY Friargate dep.		8 55	10 10	10 10		10 10	12 30		3 35	
West Hallam		9 7	10 22	10 22						
Ilkeston North arr.		9 12	10 27	10 27		10 24	12 44		3 49	
Ilkeston North dep.		9 13	10 28	10 28		10 24	12 44		3 49	
Awsworth		9 17		10 32						
Kimberley East arr.		9 21	10 35	10 36		10 29	12 49		3 54	
PINXTON South dep.										
Pye Hill & Somercotes										
Jacksdale										
Eastwood & Langley Mill										
Newthorpe										
Kimberley East arr.										
Kimberley East dep.		9 22	10 36	10 37		10 29	12 49		3 54	
Basford North		9 29								
New Basford (A)										
NOTTINGHAM Victoria (A) arr.		9 37	10 49	10 50		10 41	1 1		4 6	
NOTTINGHAM Victoria dep.	9 20	10 8	11 15	11 15	8 35	10 55	1 5	2 40	4 15	5 30
NOTTINGHAM London Road High Level arr.	9 22	10 10								
NOTTINGHAM London Road High Level dep.	9 22	10 10								
Netherfield & Colwick	9 28	10 16	11 21	11 21	8 41	11 1	1 11	2 46	4 21	5 36
Radcliffe-on-Trent	9 33	10 20	11 26	11 26	8 46	11 6	1 16	2 51	4 26	5 41
Bingham	9 39	10 27	11 33	11 33	8 52	11 12	1 22	2 57	4 32	5 47
Aslockton	9 43	10 31	11 38	11 38	8 56	11 16	1 26	3 1	4 36	5 51
Elton & Orston	9 47									
Bottesford	9 53	10 39	11 47	11 47						
GRANTHAM arr.	10 8	10 54	12 2	12 2	9 18	11 38	1 48	3 23	4 58	6 16

SUNDAYS—*continued*	p.m.	p.m.
DERBY Friargate dep.		10 10
West Hallam		
Ilkeston North arr.		10 24
Ilkeston North dep.		10 24
Awsworth		
Kimberley East arr.		10 29
PINXTON South dep.		
Pye Hill & Somercotes		
Jacksdale		
Eastwood & Langley Mill		
Newthorpe		
Kimberley East arr.		
Kimberley East dep.		10 29
Basford North		
New Basford (A)		
NOTTINGHAM Victoria (A) arr.		10 41
NOTTINGHAM Victoria dep.	8 30	10 55
NOTTINGHAM London Road High Level arr.		
NOTTINGHAM London Road High Level dep.		
Netherfield & Colwick	8 36	11 1
Radcliffe-on-Trent	8 41	
Bingham	8 47	11 12
Aslockton	8 51	11 16
Elton & Orston		
Bottesford		
GRANTHAM arr.	9 13	11 38

A—For other trains between New Basford and Nottingham Victoria see Table 183.

SO—Saturdays only.
SX—Saturdays excepted
a—a.m.
e—Arrives 3 minutes earlier.
g—Arrives 4 minutes earlier.
p—p.m.

The train service between Nottingham London Road High Level and Basford North via Gedling & Carlton and Daybrook is suspended.

RESERVATION OF SEATS

First and second class seats can be reserved on many of the principal week-day and Sunday trains at a fee of 2/- each seat. A list of the trains on which seats can be reserved will be found in the main line timetable or details may be obtained at the stations or agencies. Applications for reserved seats should be made either personally or by post (accompanied by the fee of 2/- per seat and stamped addressed envelope) to the Station Master at the station from which the train starts, or, for reservation from an intermediate station shewn on the list of reservable trains, to the Station Master at that station.

It is regretted that applications for seat reservations cannot be accepted over the telephone.

6. Goods Services

Although a not insignificant provider of passengers services, the London Extension was a prime mover of freight from the North to both the London area and the West. The line allowed the Great Central to move coal and other commodities from Yorkshire and its MS&L hinterland and Nottinghamshire to the South without the reliance on other carriers such as the Great Northern and the Midland, who in any case saw the GC as a competitor. Thus at the very northern end of the London Extension a large marshalling yard at Annesley was constructed strategically placed to receive wagons from the Nottinghamshire and South Yorkshire coalfields. It formed the focus for other traffic that was to be sent to the South and all parts of the MS&L former network sent wagons there for collection and sorting. From Annesley the vast majority of the traffic was sent to Woodford Halse in Northamptonshire, previously a sleepy village which had been transformed by large yards on the up and down sides of the main line. The key to the development of this flow was the link to the Great Western at Banbury, which opened on 1 June 1900 for goods trains. Within the first six months 60,676 wagons were exchanged with the Great Western and by 1904 it was up to as many as 91,014.

The Woodford to Banbury link surpassed itself during World War 1. In 1914, the GC and the GW exchanged 232,000 wagons, but by 1918 this had risen to 400,000 per year. In 1940 this figure was 689,605 and in 1950 it was 687,191. Services to the London area were taken on by Neasden or Woodford locomotives and were exchanged at Neasden yards with other railways. Another main commodity carried over the London Extension was fish. Dedicated fish trains ran from GC days from the ports of Grimsby (New Clee) and Immingham to London and the West, to Swindon, Plymouth and West Wales. Extra fish vans were attached to passenger trains as well as block train working. Fish traffic from Grimsby stood at 133,791 tons for the first 10 months of 1900

Below left:
'O1' No 63886 heads a 'Runner' through Northgate Street Bridge in Leicester, and into Leicester Central. The train is typical of its type, which could be a mix of general merchandise and coal, or any other combination as well as just long rakes of 16-ton mineral wagons. 'Runners' could be 'put inside' at Leicester for a quick examination, but most stormed straight through with little delay. *P. H. Wells*

Below:
The Great Central ran a service of transfer freights from Annesley to Woodford before the 'Runners' started and one of these trains is seen heading through Charwelton with 0-8-0 '8A' class tender locomotive No 212 providing the power in 1922. These became LNER Class Q4 and consisted of 89 locomotives built between 1902 and 1911. No 212 was built at Gorton in 1909. Withdrawals began in 1934, but by 1942, when 48 remained, Thompson rebuilt 26 of them as 0-8-0 tanks for shunting. *Real Photographs/Ian Allan Library*

BANBURY TO NOTTINGHAM

DOWN — WEEKDAYS

No.			268	3524	666‡	4		3526	112	116	790		3052		22	
Description			OP	Ety	Ety	EP			EP	EP					EP	
Class				A*	A*			D			A*		B			
Departs from						Marylebone 3.45 a.m.										
Previous Times on Page						15										
									SO				MX		SO	
			am	am	am	am		am	am	am	am		am		am	
Banbury	1															
Banbury Junction	2												5 50			
Chalcombe Road Halt	3								SUSPENDED						SUSPENDED	
Eydon Road Halt	4															
Culworth Junction	5					6 7							6 19			
Byfield Ironstone Sidings	6															
Byfield (L.M.R.)	7															
Woodford West Junction	8															
Woodford Halse	9					6 10							6 25			
Woodford Halse	10		5 40	5 50	6 5			6 15			6 20					
Charwelton	11		5 46					7 45								
Braunston and Willoughby	12		5 57					8 30								
Rugby Central	13		6 5					9 10								
Rugby Central	14		6 7	6 20	6 35			9 58			6 50					
Lutterworth	15		6 18					10 48								
Ashby Magna	16							11 0								
Ashby Magna	17		6 26	6 42	6 57			11 40			7 12					
Whetstone	18		6 35					12 26								
Leicester Goods	19							12 40								
Leicester Goods	20			6 58	7 13			2 1			7B33					
LEICESTER CENTRAL	21		6 43													
LEICESTER CENTRAL	22		6 54	7 1	7 15			2 6	7 20	7 35	7 38				7 45	
Belgrave and Birstall	23		6 59													
Rothley	24		7 5													
Swithland Sidings	25															
Swithland Sidings	26															
Quorn and Woodhouse	27		7 11													
Loughborough Central	28		7 16	7W24	7W38			2W30	7 33	7 48	8W1				7 58	
Loughborough Central	29		7 20	7 31	7 55			2 41	7 36	7 50	8 8				8 1	
East Leake	30		7 28					3 25								
Rushcliffe Halt	31															
Hotchley Hill Sidings	32															
Gotham Junction	33							3 35								
Gotham Junction	34							4 0								
Ruddington	35							4 11								
Ruddington	36		7 37					4 31		8 5						
Nottingham Queen's Walk	37							4 42								
Nottingham Queen's Walk	38			7 59	8B35			5 58			8 40					
Arkwright Street	39		7 43							8 11					8 19	
Arkwright Street	40		7 44							8 12					8 21	
Weekday Cross Junction	41		7 46						7 53	8 14					8 23	
NOTTINGHAM VIC.	42		7 47						7 54	8 15					8 24	
NOTTINGHAM VIC.	43			8 3	8 41			6 8	8 0	8 20	8 46				8 30	
Arrives at				Annesley Colly. 8.57 a.m.	Grimsby 4.10 p.m.			Annesley 7.30 p.m.	Cleethorpes 11.10 a.m.	Manchester L. Rd. 11.20 a.m.	Gascoigne Wood 3.29 p.m.				Scarboro' L. Rd. 1.25 p.m.	
Forward Times on Page				56	56			66	56	56	57				57	

22.—(7.45 a.m. ex Leicester)—Runs th to th June then rd to th September **(SUSPENDED).**
112,—Runs th June to th September inclusive **(SUSPENDED).**
268.—Advertised Loughboro' dep. 7.17 a.m.
3526.—Woodford New Yard arr. 6:20 a.m. dep. 6.58 a.m. Charwelton arr. 7.8 a.m. Braunston & W. arr. 8.2 a.m. Barby Sidings arr. 8.40 a.m. dep. 8.58 a.m. Lutterworth arr. 10.20 a.m. Whetstone arr. 11.53 a.m. East Leake arr. 2.56 p.m.

BANBURY TO NOTTINGHAM

WEEKDAYS — DOWN

–		564‡	276		3054		278	22	124	124	3440	664	564‡	3396		676	3502	282	3508	3060
		Ety	OP		Ety		OP	EP	E Pcls	E Pcls		Ety	Ety			Ety	LE	OP	Ety	Ety
		A*			C				No. 1	No. 1	A	A*	A*	D		A*			A*	C
		Neasden 3.50 a.m.											Neasden 4.50 a.m.				Swindon 5.35 a.m.			
		15											16							
		MX						SO	MX	SO			MO				MX			
		am	am		am		am	am	am	am	am	am	am	am		am	am	am	am	am
1									6 50	6 50							7 10			
2					6 25				6 54	6 54							7 13			7 45
3																				
4																				
5		6 30			6 54				7 7	7 7			7 34				7B39			8 14
6																				
7																				
8																				
9		6 35			7 0				7 11	7 11			7 39				7 45			8 20
10			6 35						7 20	7 20		7 30				7 50	8 5		8 5	
11			6 41																	
12			6 52																	
13			7 0						7 42	7 42										
14			7 10				7 35		7 50	7 50		8 0				8 20	8 35		8 35	
15			7 22				7 47													
16																				
17			7 30				7 55					8 22				8 42	8 57		8 57	
18			7 39				8 4													
19																	9 15		9 15	
20												8B43		8 48		8 58			9 31	
21			7 47				8 12		8 20	8 24										
22			8 0					8 20	8 38	8 42		8 47		8 53		9 0		9 30	9 36	
23			8 5															9 35		
24			8 11															9 41		
25																				
26																				
27			8 17															9 47		
28			8 21					8 33				9W10				9W23		9 51		
29			8 22					8 36				9 18				9 30		9 52	9 59	
30			8 30															10 0		
31			8 33					SUSPENDED		SUSPENDED										
32																				
33																				
34																				
35																				
36			8 40															10 9		
37																				
38											8 15	9 46				10B2			10 24	
39			8 46					8 54										10 15		
40			8 47					8 56										10 16		
41			8 49					8 58	9 14	9 18								10 18		
42			8 50					8 59	9 15	9 19	8U24							10 19		
43								9 5	9 38	9 46	8 58	9 50							10 28	
								Scarboro' L. Rd. 1.25 p.m.	Sheffield 12.15 p.m.	Sheffield 12.15 p.m.	Annesley 11.45 a.m.	Warsop Jcn. 12.37 p.m.		Abbey Lane Sidings 8.58 a.m.		Stairfoot 2.22 p.m.			Pilsley 12.7 p.m.	
								57	58	58	57	59				59			60	

22.—(8.20 a.m. ex Leicester)—Runs th June to th August inclusive. **(SUSPENDED).**
124.—(SO)—Runs th June to th August inclusive. **(SUSPENDED).**
3502.—Coupled to 3508.

and was still increasing. This necessitated the construction of bogie fish vans in 1902. The GC also supplied coal in the opposite direction for the trawlers! Milk was also carried to Marylebone and livestock pens were provided at nearly all intermediate stations, with horse boxes being attached to some passenger trains. Virtually all the smaller stations had small goods yards for general merchandise traffic and coal, and were served by pick-up goods services. The LNER diverted the London fish services to the GN main line soon after the Grouping, but the trains that ran down through the Midlands survived to be some of the last fish train services in the British Isles, and were worked to very fast timings on the GC. As with most freight services on the London Extension, crews worked trains between Annesley and Woodford and vice versa. Clive Boardman was based at Woodford shed in the 1950s, having applied for a job there which had come up on the BR vacancy list at his own shed on Merseyside. His account of working one of these trains follows at the end of this chapter. Through freights were also introduced for general merchandise and perishable workings, running from Dringhouse's yard at York to Cardiff, Bristol and Woodford. The famous GC newspaper train that left Marylebone at 1.45am was the fastest 'goods' service, with other parcels services being linked to perishable traffic. The LNER take-over in 1923 saw freight traffic increase even further as the new owner saw the GC as an important 'penetrating route' into other railways' territory. The rise in steel production in Yorkshire and the North East and the need for the semi-finished product to travel to other plants for 'finishing' resulted in this traffic being sent via the GC on bolster trains that left the main line at Woodford to travel over the S&MJ line to the West via Broom Junction. There was also a Class C Guinness train which ran with Eastern Region power as far as Woodford from Skelton Sidings near York to Park Royal, London with Western power. But the most important innovation that the LNER introduced was the Annesley to Woodford service of fast freights from 1947. This meant that locomotives and crews would run from Annesley to Woodford and back on an out-and-home basis. This involved some crews signing on at Bulwell Common, thus saving a trip on the Annesley 'DIDO' to get to Annesley to take over a train and thereby reducing the hours worked. Trains were allowed approximately 3hr (see the Working Timetables) and initially 31 trains a day ran in both directions. By 1957, Annesley had an allocation of 45 '9F' class 2-10-0s that took over from the Robinson and 'Austerity' types that had previously run the service. The '9Fs' were much faster and cut journey times to 2hr 40min. They were also stronger and trains were increased in length. Crews no longer had to sign on at Bulwell Common and the transfer of wagons at Woodford increased to 675,000 per year. The trains travelled at speeds well into the 50s and earned them the nicknames of Annesley 'Runners' and 'Windcutters'. The 'Runners' dominated the freight service into BR days and well into 'London Midlandisation'. The express fitted freight trains and the fish services continued but in March 1965 all were diverted to the Midland route via Derby. The 'Runners' lasted until 14 June when Woodford yards were closed. No other act as great as the re-routing of the GC freight service away to other lines was to have as great a significance. For without its express freight traffic the GC would never have sufficient receipts from passenger workings alone to keep it open. Of course, that was part of the plan and Britain's only main line route capable of carrying Continental gauge traffic was left to linger on for just one more year.

NOTTINGHAM TO BANBURY

UP — WEEKDAYS

No.		355	3565	3569	267	1113	3149	3573	3089	1115	61	3093
Description		LE	Min	Min	LE	C				Gds. & Ety	EP	
Class			C	C			A*	D	A*	A*		A*
Departs from							Bulwell 6.15 p.m.		Annesley 6.15 p.m.		Bradford 4.50 p.m.	Annesley 6.45 p.m.
Previous Times on Page							89		89		91	90
		PM	PM	PM	PM	PM	PM	PM	PM	PM	PM	PM
NOTTINGHAM VIC.	1										7 12	
NOTTINGHAM VIC.	2						6 32		6 52		7 16	7 25
Weekday Cross Junction	3										7 17	
Arkwright Street	4											
Arkwright Street	5											
Nottingham Queen's Walk	6											
Nottingham Queen's Walk	7						6 36		6 56			7 29
Ruddington	8											
Ruddington	9											
Gotham Junction	10											
Gotham Junction	11											
Hotchley Hill Sidings	12											
Rushcliffe Halt	13										SUSPENDED	
East Leake	14											
Loughborough Central	15						7w6		7W26			
Loughborough Central	16						7 13		7 33			7 57
Quorn and Woodhouse	17											
Swithland Sidings	18											
Swithland Sidings	19											
Rothley	20											
Belgrave and Birstall	21											
LEICESTER CENTRAL	22										7 43	
LEICESTER CENTRAL	23						7 37		7 57		7 48	8 18
Leicester Goods	24											
Leicester Goods	25						7 40		8 0			8 21
Whetstone	26											
Ashby Magna	27											
Ashby Magna	28						8 4		8 24			8 45
Lutterworth	29											
Rugby Central	30										8 12	9w11
Rugby Central	31						8 28		8 48		8 14	9 18
Braunston and Willoughby	32											
Charwelton	33											
Woodford Halse	34						9 5		9 25			9 58
Woodford Halse	35	7 55	8 5	8 45	9 0	9 5		9 10		9 40	8 31	
Woodford West Junction	36							9 14				
Byfield (LMR)	37											
Byfield Ironstone Sidings	38											
Culworth Junction	39	8 0	8 15	8 55	9 4	9 12				9 46	8 33	
Eydon Road Halt	40											
Chalcombe Road Halt	41											
Banbury Junction	42	8 27	8 40	9 20								
Banbury	43	8 30										
Arrives at					Aylesbury 9.45 p.m.	High Wycombe 12.52 a.m.				Neasden 12.34 a.m.	Marylebone 10.3 p.m.	
Forward Times on Page					126	127				127	125	

3565.—Conveys block load of South Wales traffic. Terminates ER Sidings.

NOTTINGHAM TO BANBURY

WEEKDAYS — UP

No.	385	3571	3313‡	1469‡	399	3095	1117	3091	3099	79	401	3101	1276	3315‡	3151	3107	587
Description	OP	Min		EF	OP		Gds& Min			EP	OP		Fish				Fish
Class		C	A	No. 3		A*	A	A*	A*			A*	No. 1	A*	A*	A*	No. 1
Departs from	•			Mansfield 7.0 p.m.		Annesley 7.30 p.m.		Annesley 8.10 p.m.	Annesley 8.40 p.m.	York 6.25 p.m.		Annesley 9.45 p.m.	Grimsby 6.25 p.m.		Bulwell 10.45 p.m.	Annesley 10.35 p.m.	Hull 6.45 p.m.
Previous Times on Page				90		90		91	91	91		92	92		92	92	92
			SX	SX			SX										
	PM	PM	PM	PM	PM	PM	PM	PM	PM	PM	PM	PM	PM	PM	PM	PM	PM
1										9 26			10 0				10 42
2	7 45			8 7	8 15	8 30		8 47	9 17	9 50	10 15	10 22	10 45		11 2	11 14	11 30
3	7 46				8 16					9 51	10 16						
4																	
5	7 49				8 19												
6				8 13													
7				9 13		8 34		8 51	9 21			10 26	10 51		11 6	11 18	11 36
8																	
9					8 27						10 24						
10																	
11																	
12																	
13					8 33												
14	8 2				8 39						10 33						
15	8 10				8 47	9w4				10 9	10 41					11w48	
16	8 12				8 48	9 11		9 23	9 49	10 14	10 42	10 54			11 34	12 2	
17					8 53						10 47						
18																	
19																	
20					9 0												
21	8 26				9 6												
22	8 30				9 10				10w12	10 30	10 59		11 25		11w57		12 10
23				9 52	9 18	9 35		9 44	10 19	10 48		11 15	11 45		12 10	12 26	1 3
24				9 56													
25			9 30	10 15		9 38		9 47	10 25			11 18	11 51	11 55	12 15	12 29	1 9
26					9 27												
27																	
28			9 53		9 37	10 2		10 14	10 49			11 42		12 22	12 39	12 53	
29					9n 47					11q12							
30					9 57			10w40		11 23		12w8					
31			10 13		9 59	10 26		11 0	11 3	11 33		12 24		12 46	1 3	1 17	
32					10 8												
33					10 21												
34			10 46	11 21	10 26	11 3		11 40	12 11	11 53		1 4		1 23	1 40	1 54	
35		10 10		12 8			11 35			12 3			12 41				2 1
36																	
37																	
38																	
39		10 20		12 15			11 41			12 7			12 43				2 3
40																	
41																	
42		10 45		12 33						12 18			12 58				2 B 25
43										12 21			1 0				2 28
Arrives at							Neasden 2.25 a.m.			Swindon 2.23 a.m.							
Forward Times on Page							127										

1469.—Runs class "A", Woodford to Banbury.
3099.—Staverton Rd., arr. 11.32 p.m. dep. 11.48 p.m.
3151.—Stops Leicester Cent. to detach ale traffic.

Above left and above:
Working Timetable of goods services, Nottingham to Banbury and Banbury to Nottingham, 26 September 1949 until further notice.

Right:
Trains ran south from Woodford Halse to the London area and were dominated by GC types and 'Austerities', the Annesley '9Fs' not venturing this far south on a regular basis. Woodford 'Austerity' No 90046 takes the up 'burrowing' line at Northolt South Junction with an empty coal train from Neasden yards to Woodford. The down line can be seen in the background on the embankment and the GW line to Paddington is behind the photographer. This train would then take the joint line to Ashendon and Grendon Underwood Junction. The date is 19 April 1952. *C. R. L. Coles/Rail Archive Stephenson*

Above:
The '9Fs' never had a total monopoly of the 'Runners' and Stanier '8F' 2-8-0s were also common performers. An up 'Runner' is seen approaching Brackley Central at 16.42 on 9 May 1964 with No 48517 at the head. It is passing milepost 145 — 145 miles from Manchester. *Mike Mensing*

Below:
At East Leake a '9F', No 92067, races through the station with an up 'Runner' for Woodford at 17.17 on 6 July 1964. The small goods yard, which has now been built on, is seen on the right together with the smart signal cabin opposite. The down siding has been lifted by this time. It is good to know that with the preserved Great Central's northern extension coming to fruition this scene will be recreated one day. *Tom Boustead*

Above:
Access to other regions at Neasden was via the West London line and wagons were transferred from there to all over the system. At Neasden South, an 'H15' Southern 4-6-0, No 30523, arrives with a train of insulated vans for transhipment north on 19 June 1954. The main line to Marylebone runs under the bridge to the left and the two lines in the foreground are the access to the locomotive depot. *Neil Sprinks*

Below:
As a major cross-country route, the GC also saw a good deal of express freights from the North East to the South West via Banbury. These fitted freights were generally worked in by 'foreign' locomotives as far as Woodford, from where they were serviced and sent back on a balancing working. These trains got progressively shorter as traffic was transferred to other routes, but on 8 June 1963 'B1' No 61275 passes through New Basford and still has a good load on a York to Woodford service. *Tom Boustead*

F60 WEEKDAYS — ANNESLEY TO WOODFORD AND BANBURY

UP		H	H	J	K	H	H	C§	H	G		C	C	K	H
		To Neasden				To Old Oak Common	To Woodford	5.30 a.m. Dringhouses to Cardiff	8.35 a.m. from Annesley	L.E.		5.55 a.m. Dringhouses to Bristol	5.55 a.m. Dringhouses to Bristol		
		1049	3029	3543	3001	1059	3031	777	3031	3383		789	789	3383	3145
			SX			SX						SX	SO		MX
			am	am	am	am	am	am	am	am		am	am	am	am
Annesley North Jn.	1							8 51				9 8	9 8		
ANNESLEY YARD arr	2											9L10	9L10		
dep	3		7 28				8 35					9L35	9L35	Gotham Works arr. 11.30 a.m., dep. 12.20 p.m. Shepherds Sidings arr. 12.25 p.m., dep. 12.45 p.m. Gotham Jn. arr. 12.55 p.m.	9 45
Annesley South Jn. arr	4							8▽54							
dep	5		7 31				8 40	8▽57				9 38	9 38		9 48
Hucknall Central	6														
Bulwell Common arr	7														
dep	8		7 41				8 51	9 7				9 46	9 46		10 0
Basford North	9														
Bagthorpe Jn.	10		7 44				8 54	9 9				9 48	9 48		10 3
New Basford	11							B							
Nottingham Victoria arr	12														
dep	13		7 52				9 2	9 18		9‖21		9 53	9 53		10 11
NOTTINGHAM arr	14		7*58							9‖25					10D20
QUEEN'S WALK dep	15		8* 9				9 6	9 21		To work 10.10 a.m. to Gotham Jn.		9 56	9 56	10 10	11*20
Ruddington arr	16													10 22	
dep	17													10 48	
Gotham Jn. arr	18													10 58	
dep	19													11 20	
Gotham arr	20							† F from Woodford							
Hotchley Hill Sidings arr	21														
dep	22														
East Leake arr	23														
dep	24														
LOUGHBOROUGH arr	25							9W39							
CENTRAL dep	26		8 39				9 32	9W46				10 13	10 13		11 53
Quorn and W. arr	27	SUSPENDED SO		SUSPENDED SO			SUSPENDED SO	SUSPENDED SO	SUSPENDED SO						
dep	28														
Swithland Sidings arr	29														
dep	30														
Rothley arr	31														
dep	32														
Belgrave and B. arr	33												B		
dep	34														
Abbey Lane Sidings	35				9 35										
Leicester Central	36		9 2		9R40		9 56	10 3	←			10 27	10 36		12 18
LEICESTER GOODS arr	37		9 7		9 45		10* 0		10* 0						12 23
dep	38		9 25				10 * 8	10 4	10* 8			10 28	10 37		
Whetstone arr	39						→					B			
dep	40												[6]		
Ashby Magna arr	41														
dep	42		9 48					10 16	10 34			10 45	10 55		
Lutterworth arr	43														
dep	44														
RUGBY CENTRAL arr	45											B			
dep	46		10 12					10 34	10 58			11 10	11 15		
Braunston and W. arr	47														
dep	48											[10]	[5]		
Charwelton arr	49														
dep	50														
WOODFORD YARD arr	51		10 46					10 57	11 32			11L43	11L43		
dep	52	10 38		10 50		11 5		11 50				12L12	12L15		
Woodford West Jn.	53														
Byfield	54														
Byfield Ironstone Siding	55														
Culworth Jn.	56	10 45		11 0		11 12		12 0				12 17	12 20		
Banbury Jn.	57			11 25				12 26				12 35	12 35		
BANBURY GENERAL arr	58														
dep	59														

ANNESLEY TO WOODFORD AND BANBURY — WEEKDAYS F61

	H	H	H	H	H	J	J	G	H		H	K	G	K	K	J	H	K	K
	To North Acton	5.30 a.m. Barnetby to Dudley		To Colwick		10.50 a.m. from Butlers Hill	To Stanton Works	L.E.					L.E.					To Quainton Road	To Quainton Road
	1065	1505	3037	3079	3039	3257	3071	3385	3041		3043	3385	3385	3549	3309	3555	3045	1099	1099
	SX	SX						SO	SX			SO	SX		SX		Q	SO	SX
	PM	am	am	am	am	am	am	am	am		am	PM	am	PM	PM	PM	noon	PM	PM
1		9 13																	
2		9L16																	
3		10E 0	10 25	10 35	10 47		10 55	11‖10	11 10		11 23		11‖45				12 0		
4																			
5		10 3	10 28	10 38	10 50		10 59	11 15	11 13		11 26		11 50				12 3		
6																			
7						11 6													
8		10 15	10 38	10 50	11 0		11 14	11 25	11 24		11 37		12 0				12 14		
9		10 20					11 19												
10			10 41	10 53	11 3			11 28	11 27		11 40		12 3				12 17		
11																			
12																			
13			10 49	11 2	11 11			11 36	11 35		11 48		12 8				12 25		
14								11‖40					12‖12				12*31		
15			10 53		11 15				11 39		11 52	12 8					12*41		
16								To work 12.8 p.m. to Hotchley Hill Sidings				12 20	To work 12.48 p.m. to Hotchley Hill Sidings						
17												1 42							
18																			
19																			
20																			
21																			
22												1 57							
23																			
24																			
25					B												1*12		
26			11 19		11 43				12 5		12 18						1*24		
27					SUSPENDED SO						SUSPENDED SO					SUSPENDED SO	SUSPENDED		
28																			
29																			
30																			
31																			
32																			
33																			
34																			
35															1 15				
36			11 42		12 9				12 28		12 41				1 20		1 50		
37															1 25				
38			11 45		12 12			J	12 31		12 44						1 53		
39																			
40																			
41																	B		
42			12 5		12 32				12 51		1 4						2 17		
43																			
44																			
45																			
46			12 29		12 56				1 15		1 28						2 41		
47																			
48																			
49								3553											
50																			
51			1 3		1 30				1 49		2 2						3 15		
52	12 55							1 35						2 15		3 5		3 25	3 35
53																			
54														2 20					
55																			
56	1 2							1 44								3 15		3 33	3 43
57								2 9								3 40			
58																			
59																			

F18 WEEKDAYS — BANBURY AND WOODFORD TO ANNESLEY

DOWN		E UB	J	E UB	G	C	G	E UB	K	C	G	H	J	E UB§
		Empties	Ironstone	Empties to Newstead Colly. Empties Sidings	L.E. to Colwick	6.15 p.m. Burton to York	L.E. to Colwick	Empties		12.42 p.m. Fruit and Veg. from Southampton Docks	E.B.V.	3.10 p.m. from Neasden		Empties to Aldwarke Main
		3532	3138	3534	3444	618	618	3536	3430	3066	660	588	3084	660
		Q	SX					Q		MSX Q	Q			Q
		PM	PM	PM	PM	PM	PM	PM	PM	PM	PM	PM	PM	PM
BANBURY GENERAL dep	1									5 1				
Banbury Jn.	2									5 4			5 12	
Culworth Jn.	3									5 20		5 33	5 42	
Byfield Ironstone Sidings	4		4 15											
Byfield	5		4 20											
Woodford West Jn.	6		4 27											
WOODFORD YARD arr	7		4 32							5 25		5 40	5 50	
dep	8	4 35	4‖43	5 5				5 20			5 40			
Charwelton arr	9		4‖52								5 44			
dep	10													6 1
Braunston and W. arr	11													
dep	12													
Barby Sidings arr	13													
dep	14													
RUGBY CENTRAL arr	15						After working 6.15 p.m. Burton to York				To work 6.1 p.m. to Aldwarke Main			
dep	16	4 59		5 29				5 44						6 20
Lutterworth arr	17													
dep	18													
Ashby Magna arr	19													
dep	20	5 17		5 47				6 2						6 38
Whetstone arr	21													
dep	22													
LEICESTER GOODS arr	23													
dep	24	5 30		6 0				6B20						6 51
Leicester Central	25	5 32		6 2				6 23						6 53
Abbey Lane Sidings	26													
Belgrave & B. arr	27													
dep	28													
Rothley arr	29													
dep	30	SUSPENDED		SUSPENDED SO				SUSPENDED SO			SUSPENDED SO	SUSPENDED SO	SUSPENDED SO	‡ H from Annesley
Swithland Sidings arr	31													
dep	32													
Quorn and W. arr	33													
dep	34													
LOUGHBOROUGH arr	35	5*50												7*10
CENTRAL dep	36	6* 7		6 18				6B49						7*21
East Leake arr	37													
dep	38													
Hotchley Hill Sidings arr	39													
dep	40													
Gotham	41													SUSPENDED SO
Gotham Jn. arr	42													
dep	43													
Ruddington arr	44													
dep	45													
NOTTINGHAM arr	46													
QUEEN'S WALK dep	47	6 33		6 37	6‖43			7B10						7 42
Nottingham Victoria arr	48				6 47									
dep	49	6B40		6 40	6 50			7 13						7 45
New Basford arr	50													
dep	51								7 25					
Bagthorpe Jn.	52	6 50		6 48				7 20	7 31					7 52
Basford North	53					7 15								
Bulwell Common arr	54					7L18		7*25	7 37					
dep	55	6 54		6 52		7L30	7‖35	7*46						7 55
Hucknall Central arr	56													
dep	57													
Annesley South Jn. arr	58													
dep	59	7 6				7 43		8 1						8 10
ANNESLEY YARD arr	60	7 9				7*47		8 4						8L13
dep	61					7*55								10E50
Annesley North Jn.	62					7 58								10 55

BANBURY AND WOODFORD TO ANNESLEY — WEEKDAYS F19

	E UB§	E UB	E UB§	J	K	C	C	J	C	J	G	D	E Bkd.	E Bkd.	E UB	J	C§	C§	J
	Empties to Wath		To Ardsley	2.12 p.m. Waltham-on-the-Wold to Staveley Works	2.10 p.m. Gotham Sdgs. to Colwick	Fruit and Veg. to Dringhouses	Fruit and Veg. to Dringhouses	8.44 p.m. Eastwood to Annesley	3.50 p.m. Park Royal to Newcastle		E.B.V.	To Dringhouses	To Sheffield Bernard Road	To Sheffield Bernard Road	Empties		9.40 a.m. Tavistock Jn. to Hull	9.40 a.m. Tavistock Jn. to Doncaster Belmont	
	660	3548	692	3376	3368	814	814	3309	846	3086	3558	812	714	714	3542	3088	696	696	3513
		SX	SO		SO	FSX	FO		TFO		SO	SX	SX	SO			SX	SO	
	PM	PM	PM	PM	PM	PM	PM	PM	PM	PM	PM	PM	PM	PM	PM	PM	PM	PM	PM
1																	7z31	7z31	
2										6 35						8 5	8 25	8 25	
3									5 50	7 4						8 34	8 43	8 43	
4																			
5																			
6																			
7									5L55	7 12						8 42	8 47	8 47	
8	5 56	6 22	6 22			6 37	6 37		7E20		7 55	7 55			8 22		11 55	11 45	
9																	→	→	
10																			
11																			
12																SUSPENDED SO			
13																			
14																			
15																			
16	6 20	6 49	6 49			7 1	7 1		7 41		8 17	8 19			8 49		Banbury South arr. 7▽2 p.m. Banbury Jn. arr. 7.35 p.m. Z—Banbury South	Banbury South arr. 7▽2 p.m. Banbury Jn. arr. 7.35 p.m. Z—Banbury South	
17																			
18																			
19																			
20	6 38	7 7	7 7			7 18	7 18		7 56		8 33	8 34			9 7				
21																			
22																			
23						7 33	7 33												
24	6 51	7B25	7B25			7 55	7 55		8 6		8 43	8 46	9 10	9 20	9 20				
25	6 53	7 27	7 27			8 0	8 0		8 8		8 44	8 47	9 15	9 25	9 22				
26																			
27																			
28																			
29																			
30	‡ H from Annesley Does not run when 660 Q runs		‡ E Bkd. from Annesley								After working 3.10 p.m. from Dringhouses. To be kept clear of 46A when running in SOQ path				SUSPENDED SO		§ D from Woodford	‡ D from Woodford	
31																			
32																			
33																			
34																			
35	7*10											9W1							
36	7*21	7B52	7B52			8 13	8 13		8 22		9 0	9W8	9 31	9 41	9 40				
37																			
38																			
39																			
40																			
41	SUSPENDED SO																		
42													On FO Nottingham Q.W. dep. 10.54 p.m.			K			
43																			
44																			
45					←						B								
46					4 6	8 33	8 33						9 52	10 2					
47	7 42	8B14	8B14		8 25	9 2	8 52		8 41		9 21	9 30	10 48	10 48	10 0				
48					8 36								→	→			SUSPENDED FO	SUSPENDED	
49	7 45	8 17	8 17	7 55	8 53	9 8	8 58		8 44		9 26	9 34			10 3				
50																			
51											B								
52	7 52	8 24	8 24	8 6		9 13	9 3		8 50		9 36	9 40			10 10	3472			
53								9 19											10 48
54							9* 7												10 55
55	7 55	8 27	8 27	8 10		9 16	9*18	9 24	8 53		9 40	9 43			10 13	10 20			
56																10 30			
57																11 18			
58								via Bestwood	9▽4			9▽55							
59	8 10	8 39	8 39	8 29		9 26	9 31		9▽7		9 53	9▽58			10 27	11 33			
60	8L13	8 42	8L42								9 56				10 30	11 39			
61	10E50		10 L 5																
62	10 55		10 15	8 34		9 29	9 34		9 12			10 3							

Above left and above:
Annesley to Woodford Halse and Banbury, and Banbury and Woodford Halse to Annesley, 9 June to 14 September 1958.

Left:
The common power for the York trains were 'B1s', 'V2s' and 'B16s' (or 'bloodspitters' as they were known by the crews). A northbound 'fitted' from Woodford is just getting into its stride at Charwelton behind 'B16' No 61475 of York shed on 27 May 1961. Note the sidings for the ironstone branch on the right of the photograph and the signalman's motorcycle. *Mike Mitchell*

Below:
The link to the S&MJ. A rather grimy 'Modified Hall', No 7927 *Willington Hall*, runs round to the junction with the GC main line at Woodford No 4 cabin on the spur that linked the two lines together, on 25 May 1963. The line carried great tonnages of freight in the late 1950s and early 1960s and was even strengthened to take heavy bolster steel trains from the North East to South Wales for finishing. Some of those wagons can be seen returning on this train as it draws up to the signals that control access to the station and Woodford yards. *Ivo Peters*

Above:
The main line freights were supplemented with the inevitable pick-up services, but most of these finished when goods services were withdrawn from most local stations in 1963. 'L1' No 67789 is seen at Woodford West Junction on the 'Round the World' pick-up from Woodford to local stations in the area. The connection to Woodford No 4 is on the left, followed by the single line to Towcester. The lines the 'L1' is shunting are the former connections to Woodford South Junction, the junction having been removed in the 1920s, not having been used since 1900. However, the lines were kept as storage sidings. *Neville Stead*

Left:
Fast parcels services ran overnight, usually attached to passenger services, but dedicated trains were also run. 'C4' Atlantic No 6085 is seen at Willesden Green with the down express van train from Marylebone on 18 April 1936. *E. R. Wethersett/Real Photographs*

Above:
A rarely photographed train was the 6.50am from Banbury to York perishables and parcels, known as the 'Rabbits', because of the large numbers of such animals carried for consumption in the North. The train races through East Leake on the morning of 7 March 1963 with 'B1' No 61158 at the head. *David Holmes*

Below:
The other main parcels service was the return of the newspaper vans to London that had been worked down earlier that morning. These left Nottingham at 10.10am, later retimed to 11.15am, and worked right up until closure. Here, 'Royal Scot' No 46125, named after a famous cavalry regiment as *3rd Carabinier*, dashes through the deep cutting south of East Leake with the return vans on 9 April 1964.
T. G. Hepburn/Rail Archive Stephenson

Working the 'Fish' — an out-and-back freight diagram from Woodford

In BR days the fish trains ran from Hull to Plymouth, Grimsby to Whitland and New Clee to Banbury. All of them dropped off wagons en route which were then positioned as empties for the return workings the next day. Woodford's rural location meant that it did not have an inexhaustible pool of labour available so it appeared on almost every vacancy list. Woodford fireman, Clive Boardman, describes a fireman's eye-view of a trip down the GC on a 'K3'-hauled Class C night freight, for this embodies all the ingredients which combined to produce footplate exhilaration of the highest order, namely three cylinders, darkness and speed. The return journey is made on a 'B16' hauling a Class C train from York to Woodford.

'The job is fairly typical in the life of Woodford Halse and is the 'Fish Tubs', a No 3 Link diagram returning fish empties to the Grimsby area under the official nomenclature of the 1.40am Woodford-New Clee. I leave the Barracks (as Woodford's train crew accommodation was known) at about midnight and walk up the cinder path from the village to the shed, arriving some five minutes before the booking on time of 12.20am and seek out my driver, Bill Howes, who, if not in the messroom, will like as not be already at the engine. A visit to the engine board bolted to the shed wall elicits the information that the motive power is one of our own 'K3s', No 61838 (it might just as easily have been an Immingham engine) and that it is on Road 3. I make my way carefully round to No 3, ever alert for moving locomotives, to find our work-stained steed on the shed front and climb aboard to stow my bag and coat in the tender locker. First off I instinctively check the state of the fire, steam pressure and water level, an average set of conditions being, fire confined to just under the door, 100lb of steam per square inch and three-quarters of a glass of water.

'So far, so good. By this time Bill is busy oiling the outside motion, giving the engine a quick examination as he goes, and my next job is to draw the 'essentials'. Repairing to the stores I give the engine number to the storeman and in return am issued with a firing shovel, coal hammer, two headlamps and a bucket. The latter contains two double-ended spanners, a gauge lamp, a handbrush and a canister containing12 detonators and a red flag. I fill and trim the headlamps with paraffin and the gauge lamp with gauge lamp oil (neat paraffin cannot be used on the gauge lamps as it tends to go on fire when exposed to the heat of the boiler).

'The 'K3s' are allowed one hour preparation time and by now ten minutes have elapsed. I return to the engine, stow the tools and check that we have a full complement of fire irons, comprising pricker, dart and short paddle. Any deficiencies I make good by purloining the

requisite items from another engine or, if such is not available, from the ashpit. Now I run the dart through the fire to liven it up, spreading it over the grate, and spray about eight shovelfuls of coal around the box. The blower is on just sufficiently to prevent the flames from coming back onto the footplate and the LNER firedoor flap is left wide open. Steam pressure begins to creep up. I shut off the water gauges in turn and remove the gauge glass protectors for cleaning, wiping all faces and the glass itself with a cloth. Protectors refitted, the bottom drain cock is left open and the steam and water cocks are opened slowly to warm the glasses thoroughly before they are put under pressure. Next the gauge lamp itself is lit and hung on the gauge glass top nut and the water level will now be plainly visible all the way to Grimsby. Bill has completed oiling the outside and I relieve him of the oil can and vanish underneath to complete the operation, Gresley's derived motion saving me a lot of work in that I only have big and small ends to do. If the engine is positioned correctly these can be reached from the outside framing, but tonight it isn't and I have to do things the hard way. They are fitted with spring loaded press studs as opposed to corks and require body contortions worthy of a circus act to squirm up behind the big end and ensure that the oil is going where it is intended. All the time I listen intently for any sounds portending danger, such as an engine approaching or the brakes being blown off, in which case I drop like lightning into the pit. I know of four instances (none of them at Woodford) where men were between the frames of a locomotive with inside motion when it moved: two survived, two did not, and I do not intend under any circumstances to become such a statistic. I return to the footplate to find that steam pressure has risen to about 125lb/sq in and try both injectors while Bill tests the vacuum brake and, all being well, another round is added to the fire, building up the back corners in the process, no big deal on a narrow firebox engine. Now the footplate is swept with the handbrush and swilled down with the hose. It is just turned 1am and an air of pleasurable anticipation is beginning to creep in. Two operations remain: I clean, light and place the headlamps, red on the tender, white at the centre bottom front, and put the bag in to top up the tank. Finally, I make a brew in the messroom and place it on the tray above the firehole door, making sure it is not directly below the gauge lamp. I can confirm from experience that as a beverage tea containing gauge lamp oil has no addictive properties.

'At about 1.15am, with a blast on the whistle and a quick glance round to make sure that nobody is in any danger, Bill opens the regulator and we drift off towards the shed exit signal tender first with the cylinder taps open to clear out any accumulation of water. I drop from the loco and phone the bobby at No 2 box with the message, '1838, 1.40 Grimsby'. The reply is, 'OK, Old Down', telling me in which of Woodford's two down yards our train is standing, the points come over, the peg comes off and we back slowly across the Byfield Road bridge into the Old Up yard, coming to a stand behind the signals protecting the main line. The engine is reversed and the cylinder taps closed as we wait while a path is set for us across the main line. This accomplished, we are signalled to proceed and chuff across to come to a stand on the loop outside No 2 box. Bill reverses again and we back gently towards our train, guided by a shunter whose lamp calls us steadily. All is hustle and bustle as I add another round to the fire, brown smoke rises vertically from the chimney top and the injector is on with the boiler pressure just below blowing off point. While the shunter is coupling up I remove the headlamp from the tender, twist the red shaded to its out-of-use position and place it at the front so that we now have two clear white lights in the middle and right configuration, indicating in our case, a freight train with vacuum brake operational throughout and scheduled to run at speeds up to 55mph.

''Blow up,' comes the cry from behind the engine and Bill opens the large ejector, drawing air out of the train pipe. The needle creeps up to 21 on the vacuum gauge and the guard has appeared to tell us that we have '41 on', ie. 41 empty fish vans. Our Mogul will not be taxed. On the footplate the fire is built up to just under the door and all goes quiet as shunters and guard fade away to cabin and brake van respectively, leaving only the solitary figure of the yard foreman who will watch the train out, and as we wait for the road the only sounds are the singing of the injector, the muted roar of the fire and the inevitable hiss of escaping steam. The reverser is wound into full forward gear, admitting steam to the cylinders for 65 per cent of the piston stroke, the road is set out onto the main line, the signal comes off and smack on 1.40am we are away. With a blast on the whistle the regulator is pulled gently forward. As this is the time of maximum effort the firedoor flap is closed and the injector is shut off, for we want neither cold air striking the tubeplate nor cold water entering the boiler. In both cases the term 'cold' is relative. A muffled exhaust beat is typical of the class and is followed by another, stronger, and then another as the three cylinders begin to get the 5ft 8in wheels on the move and the engine noses left, right, left as it negotiates the yard exit and crossovers onto the main line. In accordance with the requirements of Rule 142(d) of the British Railways Rule Book, 1950, I look back to ensure that the train is following in an orderly manner and acknowledge the guard's green headlamp waving slowly from side to side to say that all is well

Left:
Fish was a long-standing commodity that travelled on the GC, although the London trains that had originally run on the GC were transferred to the GN main line by the LNER. However cross-country services still ran from Grimsby and Hull to Whitland and Plymouth, with portions being detached en route. After the displacement of GC types, GN 'K3s' made these fish services their own until the advent of 'Britannias' from Immingham. No 61838 gets away from Leicester in typical GC style with a southbound fish on 11 April 1959. The train is passing under the Midland line from Knighton to Burton-upon-Trent. *Barry Hilton*

with the train. We are now out onto the main line which climbs as straight as a die to No 1 box and I look forward to see two lights, one above the other as Woodford No 2's starter and Woodford No 1's distant signal. Both are green, meaning right away Charwelton at least. The regulator, still in the first valve, is opened a bit more and the reverser is wound back to about 50%. The exhaust beat hardens slightly and the rhythm changes, the beats beginning to merge as the speed increases, although it will not exceed 15mph until the guard's van is also out on the main line. I listen in rapt fascination, for there is no sound like the exhaust beat of a three-cylinder expansion steam locomotive.

'By now the water level is back to three-quarters of a glass and the fire requires attention. I spray eight shovelfuls quickly round the box, drop the flap and put the injector on. Speed is about 20mph approaching No 1 box and passing into near total darkness as we leave the yard lights behind and level out onto Charwelton water troughs, which we do not need to use tonight. Bill cracks second valve of the regulator on the downward grade to Catesby Tunnel, entering the southern portal at about 30mph and 1838, enveloped in swirling smoke and steam, continues to 'get hold of them' as the tunnel walls flash past. Emerging into cool clear air we pass Staverton Road box touching 40 with regulator by now wide open and cut-off at about 20%. The fire is looking good, with the steam gauge needle glued to the red line, three-quarters of a glass of water and a healthy glow from the ashpan reflecting from the permanent way. Sitting down is not possible, firing every 2min or so renders the seats of one's overalls too hot to bear contact with the skin and by the time it has cooled sufficiently the fire requires more coal. In normal main line running, firing must be carried out with speed and precision, since it is prudent to keep the access of cold air above the fire to an absolute minimum and the delivery of eight shovelfuls to the fire should ideally occupy not more than 60sec. No 1838 rattles on through Rugby, crosses the West Coast main line and soars up Shawell untroubled by the gradient at 50mph-plus, cut-off somewhere between 15 and 20%, fire incandescent, driving wheels spinning comfortably just over four times a second until, approaching Leicester down the bank from Ashby, the regulator is closed after Whetstone and the train is allowed to coast.

'The boiler starts to fill and I have time to brush and swill the footplate and take tea as speed falls to about 20mph by the time we pass through the station under a procession of clear signals. At the platform end the regulator is opened fully and I shut off the injector as the bark from the chimney top echoes from the surrounding buildings which crowd in on the line hereabouts. Time to get busy with the shovel again. With 34 miles behind us, engine and axleboxes are hot, rolling resistance in the train is at its lowest, speed begins to increase rapidly and by Rothley we are back on song. Green lights meet us all the way to Nottingham and, with the injector back on, I continue the text book little-and-often firing which produces such good results, four sprayed down each side of the box, make sure the back corners are looked after, then partially close the flap; after 60 seconds the fire is absolutely white hot again and the procedure is repeated. From Ruddington onwards the regulator is eased so that we are able to cross the River Trent and coast round the curves at Arkwright Street without braking. Approaching the city Bill rises from his seat and checks the tank gauge. He decides that we have enough to get us to Annesley and we rumble through the cathedral-like edifice that is Victoria station and hit the foot of the bank at the north end at about 10mph. The 'K3's' breathing becomes more laboured as we climb through Mansfield Road and Sherwood Rise Tunnels, past Bulwell and Hucknall to grind to a halt at the wooden train relief platforms opposite Annesley shed where two shadowy figures emerge from the darkness and climb aboard. 'You've got 41 on,' says Bill, 'how did you get on last night?' referring obliquely to the previous night's 'K3' which had been heavy on water and prone to injector trouble to boot. 'Oh, OK,' came the reply, 'she has as many as she wanted up Duckmanton.' Railway engines are always accorded the feminine gender. They take water and go chattering away into the darkness, the exhaust plainly audible in the still morning air after the train has vanished from view, while we cross to the up side platform to partake of a brew and sandwiches as we await our return working, another Class C, although now general merchandise, through to Woodford which appears with clockwork precision some 20min later in the hands of one of York's 'B16s', No 61467. This class is a 4-6-0 but identical to the 'K3' in many respects, such as cylinder size, boiler pressure, driving wheel diameter, etc., and was even introduced in the same year (1920). However, being a North Eastern Railway design by Sir Vincent Raven, it differs markedly in appearance, having all connecting rods driving on the front axle, and a long boiler. In combination with the rather conspicuous safety valves this latter feature leads to them being sometimes called 'skittle alleys'. The footplate layout also is completely different, sometimes with right-hand drive, throw over regulator, spartan seating and, if we are unlucky, a steam reverser, surely one of the most perversely awkward contraptions to control on a main line steam locomotive. The lengthy firebox has a hearty appetite for coal at the front end, a feature which does nothing to endear the class to the more indolent members of the firing fraternity. From Annesley the regulator is opened for perhaps 100yd only, sufficient to get the train on the move, and then closed. From this point into the heart of Nottingham gravity will do all the work and I sit in quiet repose as 1467 rolls for the next nine miles under clear signals with only a slight brake application here and there to prevent it from getting too adventurous. We get the all-clear at Carrington and drift cautiously out of the tunnel mouth and into the station at no more than 10mph, seemingly according the lofty vaults the respect their dimensions warrant, then halfway along the platform the regulator is just opened and a barely audible exhaust beat ensues as we are channelled into Parliament Street Tunnel at the south end of the station and emerge at the curiously named Weekday Cross Junction where the line to Colwick curves away to the left.

'We have perhaps half-a-mile of restrained running across the Midland station and round the check-railed curves at Arkwright Street before we hit straight track over the Trent bridge and commence the climb towards Loughborough. The 'B16s' have an exhaust beat more clearly defined than that of the 'K3s' but, never regarded as front line motive power by their LNER masters, tend not to have worn so well down the years and there is a perceptible lurch forward in response to the opening of the regulator. They are also prone to fire throwing in certain conditions but we have no such problems tonight as I fire steadily as she gets into her stride at about 35mph up the hill, exhaust beat chopping off loud and clear in the crisp morning air, fire dancing on the grate at the front end. In the summer months we would now be in daylight but there is no sign of the dawn yet as we pass a silent Loughborough and clatter on down towards Leicester where, as a general merchandise train, we are turned into the Goods for a train examination, water and to put off and pick up. With typical GC enterprise we are away again within 20min and, firing as with the 'K3', hammer away up the 1 in 176 towards Whetstone and Ashby Magna, as yet unsullied by the presence of a formidable adversary, the M1 motorway, still some years in the future. Rugby Midland shed sports its usual crop of Stanier taper boilers as we approach the Birdcage and enter the last lap. Not long now.

'Rugby Central station displays no sign of life as we sprint through the cutting with driving wheels drumming on the rails, firing to the front end in readiness for the climb to Catesby and Charwelton. The odd cinder begins to appear at the chimney top as the cut-off is lengthened and speed drops as we clamber past Staverton Road. I run the dart through the fire before we enter the tunnel and hope that that will be it to Woodford. It is and we drift into the New Up reception road with a low fire,170lb/sq in on the clock and three-quarters of a glass of water. The disposal crew have no grounds for complaint. Again, depending on grate area, one hour is allowed for the disposal of a large main line locomotive but a National Agreement states that engine crews who have covered 140 miles or more shall not be called upon to perform this chore, ie. clean the fire, rake out the ashpan and shovel the char from the smokebox, irrespective of the amount of time remaining on their shift. Woodford to Annesley and return is 138 miles and it is therefore conceivable, just, that one might prepare one's engine in the manner described earlier, work to Annesley and back and dispose of the locomotive. In practice, this never happened. Deliberately or otherwise, the last hour has always been encroached upon by the time the engine gets to the shed and it is merely a case of dropping the kit off at the stores and calling it a day or, in our case, night.'

7. London Extension Motive Power Depots and Locomotive Allocations 1947 to 1966

Annesley

Annesley depot provided the locomotives for the freight workings at the northern end of the London Extension, the Woodford 'Runner' freight service and some local passenger turns. By 1962, Annesley men were also working some of the semi-fast services as far as Leicester and Rugby as well as summer Saturday relief trains. The famous 'DIDO' service acted as a pick-up for railwaymen from the local area. The depot was closed in 1966 with the withdrawal of through GC line workings, its 'Runners' having been re-routed a year before.

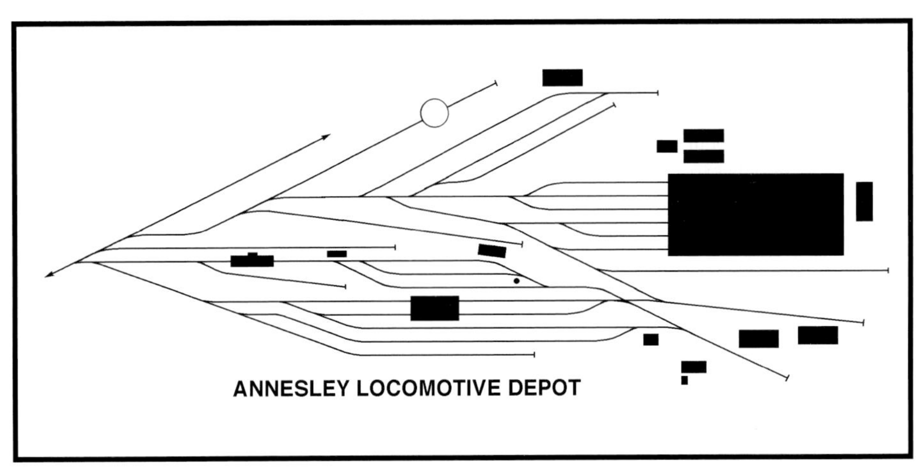

Annesley 1947, LNER

'K3'	'O1/O4'	'O1/O4'	'O1/O4'	'O1/O4'	'O1/O4'
1895	3571	3633	3700	3743	3801
1974	3575	3635	3706	3748	3804
1975	3580	3638	3716	3756	3805
1976	3582	3662	3720	3759	3809
1977	3589	3674	3722	3761	3829
1980	3596	3681	3723	3762	3841
	3614	3685	3735	3767	3851
	3618	3694	3739	3794	3853
	3631	3699	3742	3799	3859
	'O1/O4'	**'O1/O4'**	**'J11'**	**'F2'**	**'J50'**
	3862	4375	4292	7105	8927
	3873	4386	4294	7107	8929
	3876	4409	4300	8935	
	3893	4431	4318	8972	
	3894		4354	8975	
	3899		4365	8976	
	3912		4370		

Annesley 1950 — Shed Code 38B, BR Eastern Region

'B1'	'O1/O4'	'O1/O4'	'O1/O4'	'O1/O4'	'O1/O4'
61063	63571	63646	63723	63803	63873
61066	63578	63662	63739	63806	63879
61209	63579	63674	63742	63808	63893
	63580	63681	63743	63827	63901
'K3'	63589	63687	63746	63838	63912
61943	63594	63689	63748	63841	
61974	63596	63699	63752	63853	
61975	63610	63700	63767	63858	
61976	63614	63706	63792	63863	
61977	63618	63716	63795	63867	
61979	63635	63721	63798	63868	
61980	63639	63722	63799	63869	

Annesley 1950 — Shed Code 38B, BR Eastern Region *continued*

'J11'	'J11'	'J5'	'J50'
64292	64361	65494	68927
64300	64370	**'C12'**	68929
64318	64431	67363	68975
64354		67387	68976

Annesley 1959 — Shed Code 16D, BR LMR

'4MT'	'3F'	'O1/O4'	'O1/O4'	'J39'
42333	47429	63578	63789	63865
42339	47458	63579	63792	63867
42361	47638	63591	63796	63869
		63610	63806	63886
'Crab'	**'K3'**	63676	63808	63901
42769	61856	63689	63817	64739
42784	61975	63711		64747
42847	61980	63838		64798
42872	63740	63854		64955
42897	63752	63777		

'9F'	'9F'	'9F'	'9F'	'9F'	'J11'
92010	92067	92072	92081	92091	64359
92011	92068	92073	92087	92092	64375
92012	92069	92074	92088	92093	64420
92013	92070	92075	92089	92095	64439
92014	92071	92076	92090	92096	

Annesley 1965 — Shed Code 16B, BR LMR

'5MT'	'5MT'	'5MT'	'8F'	'8F'
44665	44984	45342	48166	48141
44717	45215	45346	48168	48378
44835	45234	45406	48142	48293
44846	45301	45416	48661	48304
44847	45333	45450	48037	48324
44848	45334		48057	48363
44932	45335		48079	

'9F'	'9F'	'9F'	'9F'	'9F'	'9F'
92011	92032	92069	92075	92091	92096
92013	92033	92071	92083	92092	92113
92014	92043	92072	92087	92093	92132
92030	92067	92073	92088	92094	92154
92031	92068	92074	92090	92095	

Left:
'Britannia' No 70028 *Royal Star* and 'Black 5' No 45416 stand outside Annesley shed at 19.05 on 27 June 1965. *Tom Boustead*

Above right:
Another view on the same day looking back at the shed illustrates well the general desolate scene at Annesley. The depot was starting to be run down by this time as the Woodford freight service had just ended and the '9Fs' were already transferred away to other LMR sheds. *Tom Boustead*

Leicester Central

Leicester provided express passenger locomotives that relieved expresses at the station in both directions. It was the home of some of the GC's fastest drivers as anyone reading Colin Walker's *Main Line Lament* or Frank Stratford's *Great Central From The Footplate* will know. It was once the home of GC passenger locomotives such as the 'C4' and 'C5' Atlantics and a stud of 'A3s' that included *Flying Scotsman* at one time. The decline of the GC passenger services led to its demise as jobs were transferred to other depots. It was closed in July 1964.

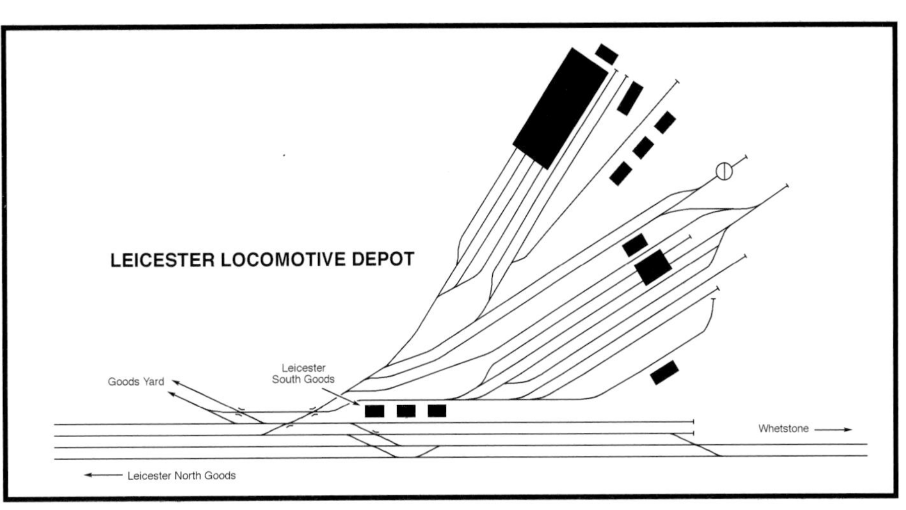

Leicester 1947, LNER

'B1'	'B1'	'B1'	'J11'	'J67'
1086	1128	1187	4361	8491
1110	1130	1188		
1111	1185	1192		
1112	1186	1225		

Leicester 1959 — Shed Code 38C

'A3'	'A3'	'B1'	'B1'	'B1'	'J2'
60048	60102	61088	61141	61188	65015
60049	60103	61092	61185	61298	65021
60052	60104	61106	61186	61299	
60054	60107	61108	61187		

'J50'	'J5'
68981	65495

Leicester 1959 — Shed Code 15E, BR Eastern Region

'3MT'	'V2'	'B1'	'B1'	'B1'
40165	60831	61008	61137	61376
40167	60842	61028	61201	61380
40182	60863	61063	61269	61381
	60879	61085	61298	
'3F'	60911	61106	61369	**'J6'**
47203				64256

Leicester 1964 — Shed Code 15D, BR LMR

'B1'	'5MT'	'Jubilee'	'4MT'	'9F'	Diesel shunter
61002	44665	45739	42161	92073	D3785
	44847				
	44848				
	44984				
	45334				
	45342				

Above:
'Black 5' No 44982 is turned on the table at Leicester shed in the late 1950s. The locomotive shed can be seen on the right, together with 'B17' No 61664 *Liverpool*.
Alec Ford

Left:
'B1' Nos 61299 and 61381 stand outside Leicester shed as they are prepared for duty in 1952. The main line runs alongside the houses in the background, London to the left, and behind the main line are the terraced houses of Western Road.
David Basset

Woodford Halse

Woodford Halse was unique amongst all railway communities in Britain. Its rural location, placed for the convenience of the link to Banbury, put rows of GC terraced houses into a country village. The crews and locomotives based there worked primarily freight turns and serviced the locomotives for the 'Runners'. Further reading on Woodford can be found in *The Last Years of The Great Central*, Chapter 5; Clive Boardman's article, 'Woodford Memories' in the October 1992 issue of *Steam Days*; and 'The Art and Practice of Rostering Enginemen'; an article in the April 1993 issue of *Steam World* by Richard Hardy.

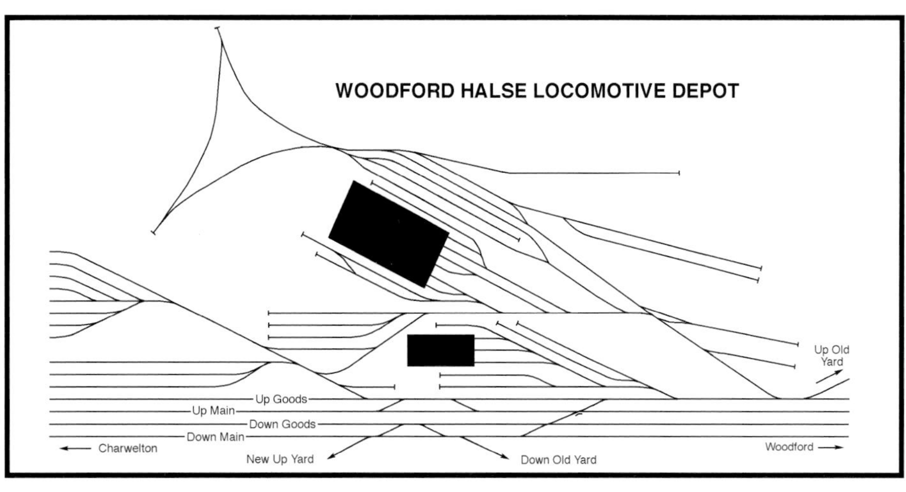

Woodford Halse 1947, LNER

'B1'	'K3'	'O7'		'J11'	'J5'
1063	1829	3033	3116	4324	5486
1066	1839	3039	3127	4327	5487
1078	1870	3040	3165	4330	5488
1088	1908	3043	3183	4363	5489
1108	1913	3046	3186	4369	
1131	1943	3056	3188	4388	
1141	1956	3065	3195	4390	
		3080	3199	4408	
		3095		4438	

'J50'	'L3'	'N5'
8891	9050	9269
8894	9069	9310
8920		

Woodford Halse locomotive allocations 1950 — Shed Code 38E, BR Eastern Region

'V2'	'B17'	'J11'	'J39'	'N2'
60815	61650	64324	64798	69560
60817	61651	64327	64838	
60818	61664	64330		**'N5'**
60820	61667	64364		69263
60826		64369	**'L3'**	69269
60830		64375	69050	69286
60831		64388	69069	69310
60832		64390		69360
60845		64408		
60853		64438		

'WD'	'WD'	'WD'	'WD'	'WD'
90033	90051	90137	90365	90509
90039	90065	90185	90486	90516
90040	90080	90218	90504	90520
90046	90095	90263	90507	90638

Woodford Halse locomotive allocations 1959 — Shed Code 2F, BR LMR

'4MT'	'3F'	'V2'	'B1'	'K3'	'J10'
43063	43330	60815	61078	61804	65158
43106	43389	60890	61186	61809	
	43394	60915	61192	61824	**'L1'**
			61271	61838	67740
			61386	61841	67771
				61842	67789
				61843	
				61853	

'WD'	'WD'	'WD'	'WD'	'WD'
90033	90095	90365	90504	90672
90040	90137	90403	90507	90697
90046	90218	90433	90516	
90065	90237	90448	90520	
90066	90299	90474	90574	
90080	90346	90486	90638	

Woodford Halse locomotive allocations 31 May 1964 — Shed Code 1G, BR LMR

'5MT'	'8F'	'9F'	'4MT'	'6P5F'	'4MT'
73032	48002	92032	42082	42951	76036
73071	48027	92092	42250		
73073	48061	92132	42251		**Diesel shunter**
73157	48081	92209	42282	**'2884'**	D3066
73159	48088			3836	D3067
	48121	**'Royal Scot'**	**'J39'**	3838	D3068
	48385	46165	64747	3863	D3069
	48527				
	48611	**'Hall'**			
	48654	6950			

Woodford Halse locomotive allocations 1965 — Shed Code 1G BR, LMR

'4MT'	'5MT'	'8F'	'8F'	'8F'
42082	44762	48002	48081	48517
42103	44763	48005	48088	48527
	44764	48010	48121	
	44814	48011	48336	
		48061	48385	

Above:
A general view of Woodford shed on 11 May 1963. The two 'J39s' in the foreground are stored out of use and are Nos 64875 and 64727. In the shed roads are some of Woodford's famous 'Austerities', a Western Region 'Hall', a '9F' from Annesley and an '8F'. Also present is 'Jubilee' No 45565 *Victoria. B. J. Ashworth*

Below:
Woodford shed originally had a turntable but that was later replaced by a triangle, as at Grantham. This allowed more locomotives to be turned at once, and a 'V2' carries out the procedure on 11 May 1963.
B. J. Ashworth

Neasden

Neasden provided motive power for all the London suburban services. It also housed the locomotives for express services starting at the London end of the line. Locomotives from all regions that brought specials in from Wembley were also serviced there, as was the Chesham branch locomotive and those goods engines that shunted Neasden sidings. It closed in 1962 with the advent of the DMU services from Marylebone.

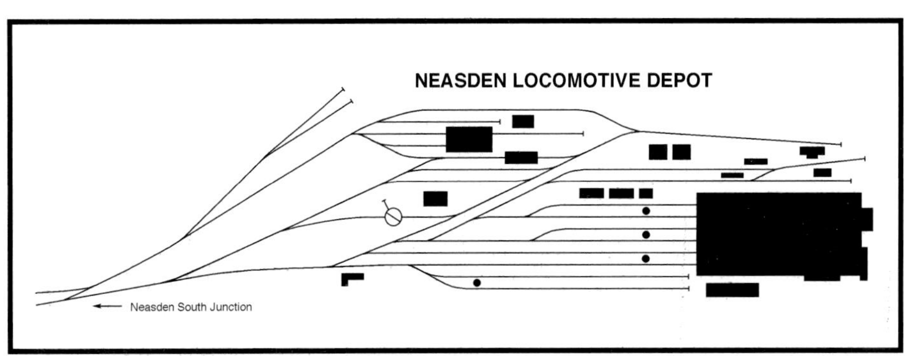

Neasden 1947, LNER

'B1'	**'J11'**	**'C13'**	**'Y3'**	**'L1'**	**'N5'**
1028	4313	7418	8172	9070	9257
1077	4329	7420		9071	9259
1083	4394	7438	**'L3'**		9273
1085			9053	**'M2'**	9283
1109	**'N2'**		9054	9076	9300
1140	9519		9055	9077	9302
1163	9461		9056		9313
1164	9567		9060		9315
1169			9061		9318
			9067		9341
			9068		9350
					9354
'A5'	**'A5'**	**'A5'**	**'A5'**	**'A5'**	9358
9800	9806	9812	9818	9824	9369
9801	9807	9813	9819	9825	
9802	9808	9814	9820	9826	
9803	9809	9815	9821	9827	
9804	9810	9816	9822	9828	
9805	9811	9817	9823	9829	

Neasden 1950 — Shed Code 34E, BR Eastern Region

'1400'	**'J11'**	**'L1'**	**'L1'**	**'L1'**	**'N5'**
1426	64313	67707	67767	67786	69350
6100	64329	67714	67768		69358
6129	64394	67715	67769	**'A5'**	69369
6166		67717	67770	69805	
	'C13'	67718	67771	69822	**'N7'**
'A3'	67418	67720	67772	69827	69690
60050	67420	67747	67773	69828	69692
60051		67748	67774	69829	69689
60111	**'Y3'**	67749	67775		69694
	68172	67751	67776	**'N5'**	69698
'B1'		67752	67778	69257	
61028	**'L3'**	67753	67779	69259	
61077	69055	67756	67780	69283	
61083	69056	67757	67781	69300	
61140	69060	67758	67782	69302	
61163	69061	67760	67783	69315	
61164	69065	67761	67784	69318	
	69067	67762	67785	69341	

Neasden 1959 — Shed Code 14D, BR LMR

'1400'	**'4MT'**	**'4MT'**	**'4MT'**	**'4MT'**	**'5MT'**
1473	42157	42250	42283	42588	44691
'5400'	42222	42251	42284	42595	44819
5409	42225	42252	42291	42618	44830

Neasden 1959 — Shed Code 14D, BR LMR *continued*

'2MT'	'4MT'	'4MT'	'4MT'	'4MT'	'5MT'
41270	42230	42253	42437	42629	44847
41272	42231	42256	42450		45006
41284	42232	42279	42453		45215
41329	42248	42281	42556		45260
	42249	42282	42568		45416
'B1'	**'N5'**	**'4MT'**	**'4MT'**	**'4MT'**	**'4MT'**
61077	69257	76035	76040	80059	80141
61116	69319	76036	76041	80083	80142
61136	69341	76037	76042	80137	80143
61187		76038	76043	80138	80144
61206		76039	76044	80140	

Left:
One of the Great Central's most trusty workhorses was the Robinson 'J11' freight locomotive, used not only on freight services but also for local passenger work if needed. No 6048 stands outside the running shed at Neasden on 1 June 1932. GC types still dominated the scene at this date before the new LNER or GN interlopers had made too much impact.
E. R. Wethersett/Real Photographs

Below:
Neasden was truly a cosmopolitan depot when special events were being held at Wembley. Standing outside Neasden shed on 29 April 1961 are 'Schools' class No 30923 *Bradfield* (formerly *Uppingham*), 'B1' No 61266 and two 'Black 5s', the right-hand one being No 45217. It was not uncommon to see locomotives from four regions together on shed at Neasden.
Frank Hornby